1914

VOICES from the BATTLEFIELDS

by
Matthew Richardson

Foreword by
Peter Liddle

Pen & Sword
MILITARY

First published in Great Britain in 2013 by
Pen & Sword Military
an imprint of
Pen & Sword Books Ltd
47 Church Street
Barnsley
South Yorkshire
S70 2AS

Copyright © Matthew Richardson 2013

ISBN 978-1-84884-777-4

Typeset in 10/12 Ehrhardt by Concept, Huddersfield, West Yorkshire
Printed and bound in India by Replika Press Pvt. Ltd.

Pen & Sword Books Ltd incorporates the imprints of Pen & Sword Archaeology,
Atlas, Aviation, Battleground, Discovery, Family History, History, Maritime,
Military, Naval, Politics, Railways, Select, Social History, Transport, True Crime,
and Claymore Press, Frontline Books, Leo Cooper, Praetorian Press, Remember
When, Seaforth Publishing and Wharncliffe.

For a complete list of Pen & Sword titles please contact
PEN & SWORD BOOKS LIMITED
47 Church Street, Barnsley, South Yorkshire, S70 2AS, England
E-mail: enquiries@pen-and-sword.co.uk
Website: www.pen-and-sword.co.uk

Contents

Dedicated to the memory of
Pat Gariepy
A true friend

Foreword

This a book for which many have been waiting and all who read will relish. It is almost four decades since several authors made attempts to draw in evidence convincingly to recreate the nature and actuality of the successive fighting dramas of British and German units engaged in action in Belgium and then France at the commencement of what was to become the 'Great War'. In such books it was understandable that the experience of the infantry predominated. This was not always the case as there were volumes where cavalry clashes or horse artillerymen in imminent peril had their story told too, but this time we have sappers and then dispatch riders (a terrific section here), men in supply units attempting to maintain their essential work in constantly changing circumstances, even airmen searching for information on enemy movement and thus vital advantage. Men using the sabre or the carbine; serving the light field gun with its limbers and team of horses; the use of the spade or the explosive charge, men employing horse, mule or motor vehicle transport, they are all here. What vision, overall comprehension and thoroughness are displayed in this book.

It is however something else which distinguishes this book most significantly from its predecessors. It answers the questions so consistently ignored hitherto: where were the Germans, what were they doing, feeling, thinking, what was it like to be among them? Previously when they have appeared it was from a small number of familiar sources as if lip service were being paid to a quite reasonable adaptation of the tango truism 'If it takes two to dance, then it certainly takes two to make a fight, and so I've got to say something about the other side'. Matthew Richardson says far more than just 'something' about the other side. We have on occasion after occasion, men from both sides, reporting in diaries and letters, or later recalling, facing each other in desperate encounters on the same day and in the same place. This is an exceptionally skilled retelling of the story of the British Expeditionary Force's encounters with its enemy, from Mons to Ypres in 1914, and with the justifiable addition of the extraordinary events of the Christmas Truce.

The author conveys superbly the sense of time, place, movement, change in circumstance and fortune. We are thus made excitingly aware from graphic evidence that the individual diarist may or may not have known that his words capture an epic moment in the sway of battle, but in every instance they illustrate how the previous hours had been imprinted on his conscience.

Mindful of the limited vision of the man in the ranks and his immediate commanding officer, it is never the less remarkable to see glimpses of overall fortune being recorded by men in the forefront of battle in these especially distinctive months. The months were distinctive because the nature of the war was being transformed as the best endeavours of the men fighting it were being frustrated. They were trying to wrest swift decisive victory from the inexorable reality of equally matched great industrial powers locked into a clinch, shorn, even bereft, of the hope of surprise.

Many years ago I had the pleasure of meeting some of the men who appear in this book. This was through work to rescue personal experience evidence from those who lived through the years of the First World War. The impression they made was such that even today I can clearly see some of their faces, hear their voices, and remember their handwriting. Perhaps this made me note with understanding a striking absence of any substantial evidence in this fine book of men in the ranks displaying apprehension, fear, anxiety, what we today gather together under the words 'combat stress'. This made me mindful of my inexperienced questioning of an Old Contemptible named Dick Chant. Dismissively he dealt with my expectation of hearing from him about such sensitivities. His answer can be summarised in an almost impatient: 'Don't you realise we were pre-war regulars?'

The war was drawing into its mangle a wider range of human fabric than solely that of the pre-war regular soldier, and accordingly it would wring out a richer kaleidoscope of reactions from that recorded by Chant. However, to say the very least, the soldiering experience of 1914, like that from August 1918 to the end of the war, somehow gets subsumed into a general perception of the stagnation of the Western Front. This book makes a splendid contribution towards eradicating any such false assumptions about the opening months of the conflict in Northern France and Belgium. The author's understanding of the war ensures that a fascinating, incompletely told story is handled with comprehensive expertise – this is a book from which to learn, a book to savour and certainly a book to keep.

Dr Peter H. Liddle F.R.Hist.S.
Founder and formerly Keeper
Liddle Collection of First World War Archive Materials
Brotherton Library
University of Leeds
2013

Acknowledgements

No book of this nature would be possible without the assistance of a great number of people, all of whom either share my interests or who are experts in their own particular field. I would especially like to thank Richard Davies of the University of Leeds, who helped me to source material within the Liddle Collection at the Brotherton Library, my dear friend the late Patrick Gariepy, who so generously shared photographs from his own collection, Jean Prendergast who assisted with Irish sources, and Walter Lyneel of Belgium who also willingly offered copies from his photographic collection. Ralph Whitehead, a highly respected authority on German sources, was a tremendous help in that area, and Kathleen Smith who provided a great deal of material (both photographic and anecdotal) about her father's wartime experiences. Mike Wood of Leeds, Barney Mattingly, Andy Horton, Alan Clare, Andrew Marsh, Neil Thornton, Gary Bentley, Robert Cull, Emily Ford and Bill Snelling all offered valuable information. Jori Wiegmans and Andrew Macdonald captured original photographs for the book, and I am enormously indebted to both for their invaluable assistance. My thanks in regard to the colour plates also extend to Sarah Stevenson at the Fusiliers Museum, Bury, together with Mike Hesp, Philip French, Peter Weedon, Scott Marchand, Paul Biddle and Jack Alexander. (Unless otherwise stated, all photographs within the book are from the author's collection.)

I would like to thank the BBC for access to the remarkable recording of Private Sidney Godley, and to my friend Andy Wint for assisting with this. I wish to acknowledge the help of the Royal Engineers Institute in providing copies of a fascinating paper on the demolition of the bridges at Mons. Teesside Archives kindly supplied extracts from the diary of Lieutenant J.B.W. Pennyman, for which I thank them.

I am indebted to the Dorchester Military Museum, Cheshire Military Museum, Ruth Hayen at Bremen State Archives, Leona Bowman at the London Transport Museum, Clive Morris and the Queens Dragoon Guards Heritage Trust, Dr Wolfgang Mährle at Stuttgart archives, and Andreas Kortstock at Prenzlau archives, all of whom provided important information. Martin Teller was most helpful in connection with the diary of Gustav Ostendorf. Menno Wielinga in the Netherlands offered help with material relating to the Antwerp operation. Simon Begent allowed me to quote from his grandfather's diary. Jeremy Burton and Colin Crabbe assisted me with photographs of Sir John (Jock) Crabbe. At this point I wish also to acknowledge the service provided to historians by a number of online archives which hold digitised collections. The foremost is probably Hathi Trust Digital Library (www.hathitrust.org). Through this website I have spent many engrossing hours discovering obscure and almost forgotten texts, and I salute the creators of this marvellous resource.

Mrs Margaret Holmes once again allowed me to quote from her father's superb memoir *Old Soldiers Never Die*, for which I am profoundly grateful. Lord Montgomery kindly allowed me to quote from the memoirs of his father Field Marshal Montgomery, which has added significant weight to this book. Jo Edkins granted permission for me to use material from the diary of her grandfather Edward Packe. Guy Brocklebank gave permission for me to use material from the papers of Major Richard Archer-Houblon, Mrs J.A. Laing similarly for use of material relating to Kenneth Godsell, Jill Hooper for use of that relating to Kenneth Hooper, Simon Baynham regarding material from C.T. Baynham, Dorothy Riordan in connection with the memoirs of Thomas Riordan, Andrew Floyer-Acland in relation to Lieutenant General Sir Arthur Floyer-Acland, Mrs M. Shovelin in connection with Fred Luke VC, and Anthony Roupell regarding the recollections of G.R.P. Roupell VC. To all of these people I offer my sincere thanks. Other holders of copyright in relation to unpublished material proved impossible to locate, in spite of my efforts in this direction.

Mr D.P. Brindley, owner of the diaries of Captain James Brindley, could not be traced but acknowledgement is made and my thanks extended to Winston Ramsey, for permission to quote extracts of the diaries as published in *The Western Front Then and Now* by After the Battle. The family of Arthur Beaumont could not now be found, but acknowledgement is made to him as author of *Old Contemptible*. Likewise, the family of John Lucy, author of the gripping memoir *There's a Devil in the Drum* could not be traced. Much of the remaining material quoted in this book is understood to be outside of copyright, but if you believe that you are a copyright holder and have not been acknowledged as such, please contact the publishers.

Once again I thank my family, Natalia, Lucie and Katie for their forbearance; my parents once again helped me to locate obscure publications, for which I am tremendously grateful. Rupert Harding at Pen & Sword again had faith in my project, and I acknowledge his support.

Lastly and most profoundly, I offer my thanks to Dr Peter Liddle, not just for the foreword (though to have this seal of approval means an enormous amount to me), but also for his vision in preserving so much first-hand material from those who served in the First World War, in the form of the Liddle Collection at the University of Leeds. Future generations will, I have no doubt, come to regard him as having a unique place in the historiography of that conflict. At a personal level I owe him a great deal, both for inspiring me with his schoolboy enthusiasm for this subject, but at the same time instilling in me a rigorous academic approach to its treatment. Much of what he taught me remains the yardstick by which I measure my professional work.

Matthew Richardson
Douglas, Isle of Man
2013

Introduction

It is not within the scope of this book to discuss in detail the reasons why the armies of two great imperial powers, Britain and Germany, came to find themselves at war in the summer of 1914. It suffices to say that it was the final explosion of years of simmering tension, resulting from the growing rivalry between the world's two most industrialised nations. The assassination of Archduke Franz Ferdinand in Sarajevo was but a catalyst; Britain's 1830 guarantee of neutrality to Belgium a mere fig leaf. German expansionism ran headlong into long-standing British foreign policy, which advocated preserving a delicate balance of power in Europe, and which decreed that a continent dominated by a triumphant Germany would be at the very least to Britain's disadvantage; at worst, a disaster. It is also beyond the scope of this book to discuss the dramatic clashes that were to take place in the East in 1914, between the armies of Imperial Russia and those of Germany and Austria-Hungary; likewise the battles that raged between the French and German armies at the same time do not form part of this narrative, epic though those engagements were.

Instead we shall follow the British Expeditionary Force (BEF), as it crossed the Channel in August 1914 to take its place alongside the far larger army of Britain's ally France in a conflict that, though long anticipated, many predicted wrongly would be over by Christmas. In the late summer and autumn of 1914, the soldiers of the regular British army and of the regular German army clashed in a series of epic encounters, which by the winter had ground into a stalemate that would last four years. These battles were very different in character from those that would follow in the years of attrition, after trench warfare had driven the protagonists to earth. They were also fought by two very different armies, raised on diametrically opposed ideals. Great Britain was predominantly a naval power, and her small army was intended mainly as an imperial police force. Thus at this early stage of the war, before the BEF grew to become a mass army comprised largely of civilians in uniform, it was still a closely knit, dedicated professional force, made up of volunteers and based on a long-service principle. There were distinctions in dress, notably those of Scottish troops, as against those of regiments raised in England, Wales, and Ireland, but the British army was still very much a homogenous force.

Although Territorial and Indian troops would join them on the battlefield before the end of 1914, and the sailors and marines of the Royal Naval Division were in action at Antwerp, it was British regular soldiers who shouldered most of the burden of the fighting that year. Career soldiers, these men had signed on for a minimum of twelve years' service. They were highly trained, excellent marksmen and possessed of a high

Men of the BEF in France, marching to their concentration area, August 1914.

degree of individual initiative. The soldier of the BEF was often from the lowest stratum of society, but the army none the less encouraged pride and self worth among its men. It was said that the army tamed lions, such was the raw material it had to work with, but the sharp lessons of the Boer War of 1899–1902 (in which the training and shooting skills of the average British Tommy had been shown to be woefully inadequate) had led to improvements in field craft, tactics and above all marksmanship. The British private soldier was armed with the Short Magazine Lee–Enfield (SMLE) rifle. A single-shot, bolt-action weapon, it none the less had a fifteen-round magazine. Tommies were taught to fire all fifteen rounds accurately in less than 60 seconds. In training it was called the 'Mad Minute', but the men took it seriously. Every year a man had to re-qualify as a First Class Shot, and his extra proficiency pay depended upon it. These individual skills in musketry to some extent compensated for the pre-war dearth of machine-guns, for each British infantry battalion had only two Maxims at this time.

Many of the men of the BEF were reservists – they had signed up for a 'five and seven'. That is to say, seven years of service with the Colours, often spent overseas, and five on the reserve. Some men even opted for a further period of service, in the Section 'D' army reserve. Clad in tough khaki serge, with a cloth cap on the head, and the latest Mills cotton-webbing equipment in which to carry ammunition and other essentials, these men were well prepared. They had practised 'fire and movement' tactics, in which sections of men supported one another as they advanced or retreated, on their great training ground – the plains of India, where most regulars had served at some point.

Edward Packe was educated at Haileybury public school, but chose to enlist in the ranks of the Somerset Light Infantry, before receiving a commission. He thus had intimate knowledge of life both as a private soldier and as an officer in the British army. He wrote:

> Discipline was exceedingly strict but there existed tremendous pride of unit amongst the men, not only for the Regiment but also for their own Platoon. Food was plentiful but unappetising.
>
> The soldier carried, in Field Service Marching Order, rifle and bayonet, 120 rounds of ammunition, pack and haversack, entrenching tool, water bottle. Carried in the pack was a greatcoat, spare shirt, socks, canteen, canvas shoes, holdall, housewife. Emergency rations were carried in the haversack, plus any private possessions and the so-called Cap Comforter and cardigan. This considerable weight was carried at all times including into battle. Later on in the war, packs were stacked and not carried in battle.

Private Edward Packe, of the Somerset Light Infantry. (Jo Edkins)

The men had the greatest respect for their officers ... I can only think of one criticism and that is that the men were never told anything, but this may have been that the officers themselves were not told until too late to pass the information on ... The Pre-war soldier had little to learn. He had to be fit and keep himself and his kit immaculate. He had to know his Drill and be able to use his Rifle and Bayonet and he had to do what he was told instantly.

In battle when he left his trench to charge across No Man's Land, he had a comrade on either side of him and was preceded by his officer. An officer was expected to be an example to his men at all times and in all things, sharing not only their hardships but their amusements. He must see his men have their food before he himself eats and he must not wear a coat when his men do not. He must win their confidence and listen to any problems that may beset them.

He does not carry so much equipment as the soldier, but he has to see to the comfort of the men when they get into billets and to return and inspect their feet and rifles after a long march. In short, the soldier has only himself to think of, the officer has to do the best he can for his men before he begins to think of himself. In battle the Officer has to lead his men and can only hope that they are following him across that stretch of No Man's Land for he has no one on either side of him, but if he has inspired their confidence in the time preceding the charge, he will have no grounds for fear on that score.[1]

By contrast the Germans in the late nineteenth century had favoured a large conscript army, in which all eligible males had to serve upon reaching the age of 20. The system was based upon regular service for a two-year period (three years in the cavalry). There were also some 'one-year volunteers', and after their active service the men passed on to the strength of a reserve regiment. In 1914 the German army raised some new regiments, akin to the British Kitchener's Army battalions, but often based them on a cadre of seasoned men from a regular or reserve formation. Under war conditions the German army operated as a single entity commanded by the Kaiser, but it was actually made up of the armies of the separate kingdoms of Prussia, Bavaria, Württemberg and Saxony. The ranks of the German army, unlike those of the British, also contained the unwilling members of subject peoples; the French from Alsace, Danes from Schleswig-Holstein, and Poles from eastern Prussia, who spoke an entirely different language from their officers.

Although the British had abandoned them, the German soldier was still using leather-made ammunition pouches and shoulder straps, which were apt to chafe, particularly when wet. On his head the German soldier sported a *pickelhaube* of polished leather with brass fittings; it was such an obvious target that on active service it was necessary to hide it under a cloth cover, but it still provided little in the way of protection from bullets and shrapnel. He was armed with the Mauser Gewehr rifle, again an efficient single-shot, bolt-action weapon, but the German army placed less emphasis on individual marksmanship, or individual initiative among its men. Although each regiment awarded a lanyard for good shooting, it was said that this usually went to the senior NCO as a matter of course. The Germans were however unquestionably better equipped in terms of numbers of machine-guns and, as the war began to bog

Die Welt starrt in Waffen im Eisenkleid,
Es klirret und rasselt und gährt weit und breit.
Da's sein muß, so zieh'n wir begeistert in's Feld,
Wir fürchten Gott nur, sonst nichts auf der Welt.

German infantry board trains bound for the West, and the coming confrontation with the men of the BEF.

down, their arsenal of grenades and mortars would give them distinct local superiority over the BEF; in 1914, the British army possessed only 200 grenades, and not a single trench mortar.

Captain Thomas Burke was in the almost unique position of being an English officer who had also served in the German army. This gave him an unrivalled insight into the German military machine, and the differences from its British counterpart. In particular he remarked upon the brutality of the German system, and its lack of imaginative training. He wrote:

> Recruiting takes place in October of each year ... One-third of every squadron is sent on reserve, and recruits are called in to fill the vacancies ... The habits of the non-coms [NCOs], soon begin to show themselves now. There is no excess of friendliness anywhere. The men who are in their second and third year make no effort to assist their new comrades, or help them to feel that they are among good fellows; and there are many cases on record of gross ill-treatment of new-comers by other troopers: a survival ... of schoolboy bullying.
>
> ... one of the most notable differences between the Armies of Germany and Great Britain is the lack of good-fellowship between officers of high and low rank, and between non-coms, and men. One may explain this by the fact that the German officer has simply no time to devote to those sports and pastimes which bring men and officers [together] in the British regiments. The long days in India are pleasantly whiled away by regimental football, cricket matches, and the evenings by dramatic performances, sing-songs, etc. The only occasion, in the German Army, that brings men and officers together is the Emperor's birthday ...

Another reason for the lack of camaraderie is that the men are not, like the British Tommy, professional soldiers, but are birds of passage, serving only two or three years, and longing to be free. You will even find, on stable doors and elsewhere in the barracks, chalked inscriptions stating the number of days between soldiering and freedom . . .

The German officer is not, as are the British and French officers, the confidants of their men. As I have explained, the men are but birds of passage, and it may be that they hardly have the chance to get acquainted with one another. Certainly, the officers in my experience gave the men no encouragement in this direction; and this, I think, is bad policy. The soldier likes to feel that he has someone who takes an interest in him, someone who will advise him where others cannot, and to whom he can take his troubles. There is, of course, the chaplain, but few soldiers of any nationality put much faith in these ready-to-wear confidants. They would much rather go to the sergeant, or the subaltern, in the case of difficulty about sweethearts, wives, money, and so forth.

The English non-com is often a father to his regiment; but there is nothing of the father about his German cousin, except that he calls his men 'my children' and thrashes them . . . when the young citizen joins for his service, he is treated as though he were a thing of the least account in the country. He is simply a Something which must be turned and knocked into shape and polished ready to fit into his corner of the machine. The English private often considers that he has grievances, but they are as nothing to those of his German cousin.

The German is not assumed to have any personality or any feelings of dignity. All his life he is overborne; and the sporting spirit which is perhaps the most outstanding feature of the British ranks has never yet entered into his military life . . .[2]

The two differing approaches to military service in the opposing countries would colour the outcome, and shape, of the battles that were to take place in 1914. This book examines the nature of the fighting that ensued, through the words of the men who were actually involved, both British and German. It offers opinions and perspectives based on first-hand eyewitness accounts from the two sides, much of which has not previously appeared in English. It analyses the attitudes and responses of the common soldier or junior officer to this new and unfamiliar form of warfare, and above all, it offers an insight into what it was actually like to participate in the opening battles of the world's first global conflict.

Chapter 1

The First Song of the Bullet

On 21 August 1914 the BEF's two army corps and its cavalry division moved off from their assembly positions around Maubeuge, across the Franco-Belgian border to the small industrial town of Mons, in order to meet the right wing of the German army sweeping in strength through Belgium and Luxemburg. The BEF formed the extreme left wing of a Franco-British force now moving eastwards to counter the German advance. By the later standards of the First World War, the Battle of Mons was not a major action. There were only about 4,000 British casualties, and the fighting there lasted just two days. However, it has largely overshadowed the much greater battle fought afterwards at Le Cateau, for the real importance of the Battle of Mons was psychological. Here in the Belgian coalfields the first shots were fired in anger by the BEF, and the first British blood spilled in Europe since the Battle of Waterloo almost a century earlier. For this reason, the battle still looms large in the British consciousness. Even those with a scanty knowledge of military history will probably have heard of the Retreat from Mons, even if they are not entirely sure when, where and why it took place.

Several roads and railways diverged from Mons, heading north-east and north-west. The bridges by which these traversed the major water obstacle of the Mons–Condé canal would be the focal points of the coming battle. The ground was not by any stretch of the imagination ideal country in which to fight a defensive battle. The *Official History* states that:

> West of Mons the line of the Canal is straight, and the actual borders are clear; the ground on both sides of it is cut up by a network of artificial water-courses, chequered by osier-beds, for a breadth of a mile or more. But the opening up of the coal measures has turned much of the country immediately south of this watery land into the hideous confusion of a mining district. The space occupied by the II Corps in particular, within the quadrangle Mons-Frameries-Dour-Boussu, is practically one huge unsightly village, traversed by a vast number of devious cobbled roads which lead from no particular starting point to no particular destination, and broken by pit-heads and colossal slag-heaps, often over a hundred feet high. It is in fact a close and blind country, such as no army had yet been called upon to fight in against a civilised enemy in a great campaign.[1]

On 22 August Trooper Ernest Thomas, of C Squadron of the 4th Royal Irish Dragoon Guards, fired the first shot from a British soldier in the First World War. The unit was reconnoitring along the Mons–Charleroi road, near the Château de Ghislain, when an enemy patrol of Uhlans (or lancers) was first sighted. One troop of the Royal

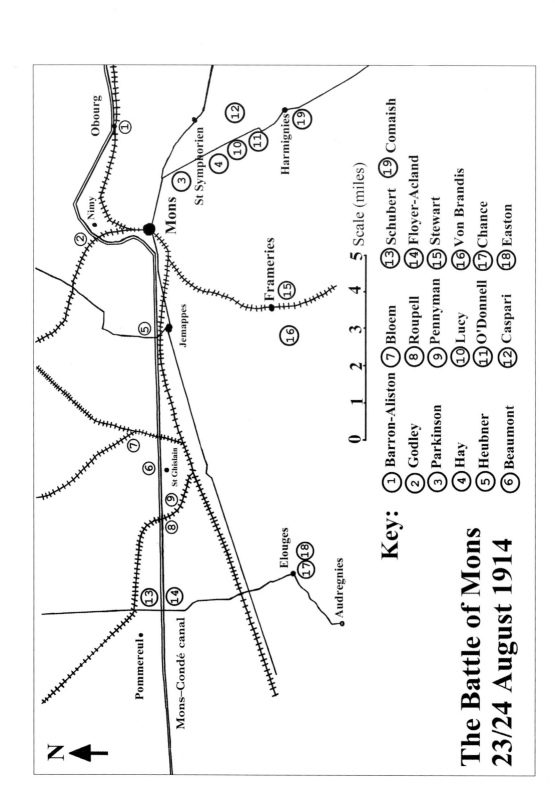

The Battle of Mons
23/24 August 1914

N

Obourg

① Obourg

Nimy

② Mons

St Symphorien

③

④ ⑩ ⑪ ⑫

Harmignies

⑲

Frameries

⑮

⑯

Jemappes

⑤

St Ghislain

⑥ ⑦ ⑨ ⑧

Pommereul

Mons–Condé canal

⑬ ⑭

Elouges

⑰⑱

Audregnies

Scale (miles)

0 1 2 3 4 5

Key:

① Barron-Aliston
② Godley
③ Parkinson
④ Hay
⑤ Heubner
⑥ Beaumont

⑦ Bloem
⑧ Roupell
⑨ Pennyman
⑩ Lucy
⑪ O'Donnell
⑫ Caspari

⑬ Schubert
⑭ Floyer-Acland
⑮ Stewart
⑯ Von Brandis
⑰ Chance
⑱ Easton

⑲ Comaish

Irish was ordered to dismount and prepare their rifles, while another troop stood ready to charge with the sabre. Thomas takes up the story:

> I saw a troop of Uhlans coming leisurely down the road, the officer in front smoking a cigar. We were anxiously watching their movements when [suddenly] they halted, as if they had smelt a rat. They had seen us! They turned quickly back. Captain Hornby got permission to follow on with the sabre troop, and down the road they galloped.
>
> My troop was ordered to follow on in support, and we galloped on through the little village of Casteau. Then it was we could see the 1st troop using their swords and scattering the Uhlans left and right. We caught them up. Captain Hornby gave the order '4th Troop, dismounted action!' We found cover for our horses by the side of the château wall. Bullets were flying past us and all round us and possibly because I was rather noted for my quick movements and athletic ability in those days I was first in action. I could see a German cavalry officer some four hundred yards away standing mounted in full view of me, gesticulating to the left and to the right as he disposed of his dismounted men and ordered them to take up their firing positions to engage us. Immediately I saw him I took aim, pulled the trigger and automatically, almost instantaneously, he fell to the ground, obviously wounded ... at the time it seemed to me more like rifle practice on the plains of Salisbury. In one respect, however, and within a second or two, it was mighty different. From every direction, as it seemed, the air above us was thick with rifle and machine-gun bullets ...[2]

With five prisoners taken, the objective of the patrol was achieved and they withdrew, not having lost a single man killed or wounded. Later that same morning, a German patrol clashed with two squadrons of the Royal Scots Greys guarding the bridges at Binche and Peronnes. The Germans opened fire from a distance, and D and E batteries of the Royal Horse Artillery returned fire in support of the Greys. A troop of the 16th Lancers, which had been sent to assist, also encountered a German patrol which it charged straight through. Nevertheless, these first encounters notwithstanding, a force of Germans far larger and far more powerful than the BEF was approaching at alarming speed. Both the French and British High

Trooper Ernest Thomas of the 4th Dragoon Guards, who fired the first British rifle shot of the war, in August 1914.

Commands had massively underestimated the strength of the German right wing, consisting mainly of General von Kluck's First Army. Field Marshal Sir John French, commanding the BEF, told General Sir Horace Smith-Dorrien of II Corps that he believed only one or at most two enemy corps would be encountered. In fact seven corps were on their way. By early afternoon of the following day two German corps were actually engaged, with a third entering the fray and a fourth about to do so. Indeed, a feature of the battle was to be the piecemeal way in which the German units involved came in to action; this to some extent negated the overall superiority in numbers enjoyed by the Germans, for the British were thus able to deal with each attack as it developed, before turning to the next.

The morning of Sunday 23 August opened in mist and rain, which by 10am had given way to clear, fine weather. The occupants of the town of Mons were astir early,

No. 4 Gun, of E Battery Royal Horse Artillery, which fired the first British artillery round of the First World War, at Binche on 22 August 1914.

heading to church in their finest clothes, as yet oblivious to the events that were about
to unfold and which would make their unprepossessing industrial town famous within
the annals of the British army. One of the British soldiers in a reserve position behind
Mons, in the suburb of Guesmes, was Private William Wildgoose of the 1st Battalion
Lincolnshire Regiment, who remembered:

> [On] the 23rd August ... my company were moved to a monastery to keep under
> cover from the German 'taubes' – reconnaissance planes. It was a lovely day and
> the nuns with the Sister Superior began to return to the monastery from mass
> which had been held in the village church. They all passed through our ranks, and
> they [like other civilians] were looking for souvenirs. I had not parted with any
> of my buttons or cap badge and [shoulder] titles, as I felt so proud of them. All
> the troops had given theirs away. The Sister Superior saw my cap badge, and she
> pleaded with me to give it to her. I was very reluctant to do so [but] the troops
> around me began to persuade me ... I took off my cap, removed the pin from the
> badge, and gave it to her. She then kissed me, and took an ebony rosary from off
> her neck and placed it over my head, and tucked the rosary inside my jacket. I felt
> so embarrassed (I was then 24 years of age).[3]

Also astir were the opposing troops; the British who were strung out along the
canal network, forming a salient to the east of Mons, sending forth scouting parties,
while German cavalry patrols began probing westwards. Each side was tentatively
feeling for the other. Opinion differs upon exactly where the first contact was made,
but around 6am the 4th Battalion Royal Fusiliers had fired upon *Husaren-Regiment
von Zieten (Brandenburgisches) Nr. 3*, the German 3rd Hussars, and captured two of
their number.[4] By 9am the weight of the wheeling German army under von Kluck
began to fall against the BEF. First to be
heavily engaged were the most northerly
British unit, the 4th Battalion Middlesex
Regiment at Obourg, who were strongly
attacked by *Infanterie-Regiment Großherzog
Friedrich Franz II von Mecklenburg-Schwerin
(4. Brandenburgisches) Nr. 24*. Reinforced by
the machine-gun section of the neighbouring 2nd Battalion Royal Irish Regiment,
the Middlesex fought for every inch of
ground, fully living up to their nickname
of 'Diehards', earned for their fighting
qualities during the Napoleonic Wars. It
was here in an orchard behind the front
line that they lost Major W.H. Abell, the
first British officer to be killed in the First

*Major W.H. Abell, of the 4th Battalion Middlesex
Regiment, killed in action at Obourg, 23 August
1914.*

World War, as he brought up reserves. A fellow officer who was with him at the time of his death wrote later to his parents:

> I had the opportunity, when I was taken prisoner, of seeing all our people who were wounded or died in hospital. I think you may be quite certain that he was buried on the ground that he defended and gave his life for. The men of his company told me many tales of his bravery, but that is only what one would have expected.[5]

The Middlesex defence centred on the station at Obourg, which stood directly on the canal bank, and many eyewitnesses testify to a soldier of the regiment who positioned himself on the roof of that building. He accounted for many Germans before he himself was shot down. One Middlesex soldier, Corporal William Bratby from Hampstead in London, was serving here alongside his brother Jack:

> The days in the beginning were swelteringly hot; but the 'Die-Hards', being typical Cockneys, made the best of them ... We began operations with trench digging, one particular trench, the machine-gun trench, being allotted to B Company. I helped to superintend the construction of the trenches, and I was proud of the work when I saw what was done from them when the Germans showed themselves ...[6]

Bratby and his brother parted company before the battle began:

> The last words I heard him say were, 'Well, Bill, I'm going right into the firing line', and I remember laughing and saying, 'Yes, Jack, but you're not the only one who's going to do that.' Jack laughed too and said, 'All right, Bill, I'll see you in the firing line,' and with that he went and I saw no more of him. Our machine-

Obourg, looking east. The 4th Battalion Middlesex Regiment held the lock in the foreground.

gun caused enormous havoc amongst the German ranks, and I am sure that my brother did his part in settling a lot of them, for he was keen on his work and full of go. The Royal Irish at this stage were doing splendidly they were not more than 350 yards from the enemy, separated from them by a railway and they were lucky enough to fetch one gun out of action again, but the enormously superior numbers of the Germans told . . . The machine-gunners had suffered very heavily and it was hard to learn anything definite about the position in the trenches.

Officers and men were falling everywhere on both sides, and I saw a reconnoitring patrol of Uhlans bowled over in trying to avoid some of the 4th Royal Fusiliers. An officer and seven men of the Uhlans were killed in that little affair without getting in a shot in return . . .

D Company [4th Middlesex] came out a shattered remnant only thirty-six men, and no officers. When what was left of us marched away, other regiments were shouting, 'Three cheers for the Die-Hards!' And three rousing cheers they gave; but I had no heart for them, because I had left my younger brother Jack, a 'Die-Hard' like myself. They told me that he had been killed by a bursting shell while doing his duty with the machine-gun section. I did not say much. I asked the adjutant if any of the machine-gun section had returned, and he answered sadly, 'No, they've all gone.' . . . I really felt as if something had gone snap in my head and that all I cared for was to get my revenge from the Germans.[7]

In fact, official records show that Lance Corporal John Bratby (sometimes recorded as Bradby) was actually a prisoner of war in German hands, though his older brother cannot have known this in 1915 at the time he was writing.

All morning the defenders held the enemy at bay, but by afternoon sheer weight of German numbers, and heavy shelling, were beginning to tell. One of the six Middlesex officers captured at Mons testified in a letter written afterwards to his mother from a Belgian hospital that, as was common practice for British officers at this time, he had taken his sword into action:

We held the Germans all day, killing hundreds, when about five p.m. the order to retire was eventually given. It never reached us, and we were left all alone. The Germans therefore got right up to the canal on our right, hidden by the railway embankment, and crossed the railway. Our people had blown up the bridge before their departure. We found ourselves between two fires, and I realized we had about 2,000 Germans and a canal between myself and my friends.

We decided to sell our lives dearly; I ordered my men to fix bayonets and charge, which the gallant fellows did splendidly, but we got shot down like ninepins. As I was loading my revolver after giving the order to fix bayonets I was hit in the right wrist. I dropped my revolver, my hand was too weak to draw my sword. This afterwards saved my life. I had not got far when I got a bullet through the calf of my right leg and another in my right knee, which brought me down . . . when I lay upon the ground I found my coat sleeve full of blood, and my wrist spurting blood, so I knew an artery of some sort must have been cut. The Germans had a shot at me when I was on the ground to finish me off; that shot hit my sword, which I wore on my side, and broke in half just below the hilt;

this turned the bullet off and saved my life. I afterwards found that two shots had gone through my field glasses, which I wore on my belt, and another had gone through my coat pocket, breaking my pipe and putting a hole through a small collapsible tin cup, which must have turned the bullet off me. We lay out there all night for twenty-four hours.

I had fainted away from loss of blood, and when I lost my senses I thought I should never see anything again. Luckily I had fallen on my wounded arm, and the arm being slightly twisted I think the weight of my body stopped the flow of blood and saved me. At any rate, the next day civilians picked up ten of us who were still alive, and took us to a Franciscan convent, where we have been splendidly looked after.[8]

The chaotic nature of the withdrawl of the remainder of the Middlesex from Obourg was described in a repatriation report made by another officer who was captured that day, Captain A. Barron-Allistone. He wrote:

The order to retire was given by Captain Glass of D Company, 4th Middlesex Regiment. I was the last to leave the station at Obourg. Running through the centre of our position was a main road on which a machine-gun was playing and causing great loss.

Immediately behind our position was a dense wood which the Germans were shelling, but thinking that our chances of escape were greater in the wood than on the road, I endeavoured to get the men I had with me, eight in number, through it. On the way I lost two of them, which owing to the density of the undergrowth, I did not discover till we were captured.

When halfway through the wood I came upon a road running parallel to our original position and connecting with the road which cut our position at right angles. I then found that bullets, apparently rifle bullets, were coming in from the rear of our original position, and thinking that they were our own, I endeavoured to come in on the right flank of the party I concluded to be firing ... After a few minutes walking along the road parallel to our original position, I saw though the undergrowth some figures moving on the other side. I was unable to distinguish who they were, but did not consider that in that place they might have been Germans. I therefore again went into the wood towards them, calling out the name of my regiment in order that they might not take us for Germans and fire on us. When I broke cover I found a line of Germans, numbering about 25–30, waiting with their rifles levelled at us. I considered the position hopeless and surrendered at discretion.[9]

In contrast with others who were captured by the Germans in the early stages of the war, and who suffered various forms of brutal treatment, Allistone and his men were well treated by their captors.

Nearby, holding positions around Nimy, were the 4th Battalion Royal Fusiliers, another proud regiment with a long tradition. They were under the command of Lieutenant Colonel Norman McMahon, who prior to the battle had addressed his men thus: 'A Royal Fusilier does not fear death. He is not afraid of wounds. He only fears

Officers of the 4th Battalion Royal Fusiliers, including front row centre Lieutenant Colonel Norman McMahon, and back row right Lieutenant Maurice Dease.

disgrace; and I look to you not to disgrace the name of the regiment.'[10] They did not let their colonel down. The Fusiliers held on valiantly all morning in the face of heavy enemy attacks. Only at 2pm did the forward troops begin to withdraw from their advanced positions at Nimy. Two valuable accounts survive from soldiers of the 4th Royal Fusiliers who were in action here on this day. Sergeant William Wallace of Regent's Park in London, stated:

> [I received] Two bullet wounds in the left leg – one through the groin, the other through the thigh. At 3pm before I was wounded, I saw the Germans force about 30 civilians of both sexes in front of the firing line, pushing them forward with their bayonets. They were about 350 yards away from us. This happened at the village of Nemy [*sic*] about half a mile beyond Mons. Captain Ashburner, in charge of the company, told us to be very careful not to shoot the civilians. The Germans who captured me were in the 26th Regiment. They were responsible for the above related infraction of the laws of war.[11]

Private Charles Duder meanwhile paints a scene of dramatic bravery as the Fusiliers, massively outnumbered, held on to their positions in spite of the odds:

> We were lining a canal with half a platoon of my battalion under Lieutenant Smith. We were under very heavy fire. A full sergeant Fitz (or Fritz), reserve sergeant of the 4th Battalion, a corporal (I don't know his name) and several others were killed. I saw the sergeant killed. Just as it was getting dusk our ammunition gave out. We were being attacked from all sides. There were only about 14 of us left and Lieutenant Smith gave the order to retire alternately to a

wood about 200 yards to the rear. We did not fix bayonets. During the retirement I saw Lieutenant Smith fall, and Lance-corporal Bowie, 4th Royal Fusiliers … told me he was dead. I also saw Lance-corporal Bradshaw, 4th Royal Fusiliers, fall. I can't say whether he was killed. Private Hackett also fell. Eventually about five or six of us got to the edge of the wood, and here we were surrounded and captured. One or two of us were wounded but we got no attention. One of our men (Private Desmond, 4th Royal Fusiliers) just after we were captured staggered up to us. He was shot through the chest, and his shoulder blade was sticking out. I saw a German smash him across the head with his rifle (he had no. 77 on his cap) and kill him. We were abused, and ill-treated even more by the German officers and under-officers than by the men … when we were captured the Germans stripped us of all our valuables, even to postcards and letters, and we never saw them again.[12]

Lieutenant Maurice Dease and Private Sidney Godley of the 4th Royal Fusiliers were to be awarded the Victoria Cross for their heroism on 23 August in defending the Nimy Bridge, holding it with a single Maxim machine-gun, and thus allowing their comrades a breathing space in which to escape. The two men came from very different worlds, and each was representative of his strata of the army at this time. Dease was of Anglo-Irish aristocracy. Born at Gaulestown, Coole, County Westmeath, Ireland on

28 September 1889, he was the son of Edmund FitzLawrance Dease JP and grandson of James Arthur Dease JP DL, Vice Lieutenant of County Cavan. He was educated at Frognal Park, Hampstead and Stoneyhurst College before attending the Army College Wimbledon, and the Royal Military College, Sandhurst from where he was commissioned in 1910. Godley came from more humble stock. He was born in 1889 in East Grinstead, Sussex and educated at the National School, Sidcup before enlisting in the Royal Fusiliers in 1909.

Dease was to make the supreme sacrifice that day and his award was a posthumous one. Godley however survived, and a remarkable recording of his voice, complete with gruff working-class accent, exists within the archives of the BBC. Originally broadcast on 4 August 1954 to mark the fortieth anniversary of the

Captain W.A.C. Bowden-Smith, of the 4th Battalion Royal Fusiliers. He was bringing up reinforcements to the firing line at Mons when he was hit and severely wounded. When the battalion withdrew, he was left in the hands of the Germans, and died of his wounds five days later.

The Nimy railway bridge, held by Godley and Dease on 23 August 1914.

outbreak of the Great War, it adds priceless detail to the bare bones of his citation and reveals that Godley was asked to remain behind. In the recording he states:

> During the time I was on the bridge before the actual action started a little boy and girl came upon the bridge and brought me some rolls and coffee. I was fairly enjoying the rolls and coffee and talking to the children the best I could, and the Germans started shelling so I said to this little boy and girl you better sling your hooks now otherwise you might get hit and they packed their basket up and left.
>
> The Germans came over in mass formation and we opened fire. The British troops, this great volume of fire, this 15 rounds rapid fire what we'd been highly trained in was very effective which halted the German's advance and we held them during the whole of the day.
>
> During the action we lost Lieutenant Maurice Dease who also received the VC on that day and I came under the command of Lieutenant Steele who then gave orders to me as to the fire. Small bursts of fire whenever he required it and we carried on towards evening. When the orders were given for the line to retire I was then asked by Lieutenant Steele to remain and hold the post while the retirement was to take place which I did though I was very badly wounded several times but I managed to carry on

Private Sidney Godley, 4th Battalion Royal Fusiliers, awarded the Victoria Cross for the action at Nimy.

then I was on my own at the latter end of the action. Of course, Lieutenant Dease lay dead at the side of me and Lieutenant Steele retired with his platoon. I remained on the bridge and held the position but when it was time for me to get away I smashed the machine-gun up, turned it in the canal and then crawled back along the main road where I was picked up by two Belgian civilians and was then taken to the hospital in Mons.

I realised then that Mons had practically been taken and the Germans were occupying the best part of the town. I was being attended to by the doctors in the hospital, having my wounds dressed when the Germans came in and took the hospital. I was asked a good many questions – what regiment did I belong to, who was my commanding officer? But I knew nothing.[13]

Both the 4th Battalion Royal Fusiliers at Nimy, and the 2nd Battalion Royal Irish Regiment holding positions nearby, were attacked by *Infanterie-Regiment von Manstein (1. Schleswigsches) Nr. 84*. The defenders fought valiantly here, but the weight of German fire soon made itself felt. The book *Die Schlacht Bei Mons* was written shortly after the battle by two German staff officers who were present, Raimund von Gleichen-Ruszwurm and Ernst Zurborn. In it they state:

Infanterie Regiment Nr. 84 encountered heavy resistance after leaving its bivouac site and passing through the woods north of Maisiers towards the canal on the northern edge of Nimy, as the III battalion clashed with the enemy and pursued him back towards the village. Here the III battalion was unable to make any further progress due to the weight of enemy fire. In number 11 company heavy casualties were sustained, whilst number 10 company had its commander, Hauptmann Stubenrauch, two platoon commanders and a great number of NCOs and men lost. Only when the commander of the regiment, Oberst von Amelungren, called forward the 2nd Battery of the *Feldartillerie Regiment Nr. 9* to support them, did the soldiers of the III and II battalions gain a foothold in the northern districts. Leutnant Herling and his platoon especially distinguished themselves here. However the enemy held firm in his entrenchments immediately on the canal bank. It was almost 2.30 in the afternoon before the enemy, under the weight of our artillery fire, gave up the canal bank. Patrols following soon after found the railway bridge west of Nimy blown up, and the swing bridge to the northwest had been opened by the local inhabitants on the south bank. Unflinchingly, Musketier Niemeyer, from the patrol of Sergeant Rower of number 8 company jumped into the water, swam across the canal and brought a barge back, over which the patrol crossed despite heavy fire. Whilst Sergeant Rower and his men drew the fire of the enemy, Niemeyer managed to close the bridge once again, so that the following soldiers could cross. In performing this brave act, Niemeyer died a hero's death.

Oberst von Amelgrun now placed himself at the spearhead of his regiment, which streamed over the bridge and penetrated deep into Nimy south of the canal. Here a fierce battle developed as all three battalions cleared the occupied houses and the barricades thrown across the streets. In spite of fierce resistance from the English, the attackers pressed on, and it took only half an hour for them to reach the southern edge of the burning town. There the mixed up detachments were reorganised, communications within the brigade restored, and preparations made for further action. A search of the abandoned enemy positions showed us that the English had suffered heavy losses in dead and wounded.[14]

As well as blowing up the railway bridge north west of Nimy, the engineers of the BEF had made extensive efforts to destroy all or most of the bridges across the Mons–Condé canal as soon as it became apparent that a retirement was imminent. The

British soldiers defending a railway bridge at Mons, 23 August 1914.

bridges on the left-hand portion of the BEF's front were in fact prepared on the night of 22/23 August, in anticipation of such a retirement, but others had to be tackled in a more ad hoc fashion. Lieutenant Pennycuick and Serjeant J. Buckle of 59th Field Company Royal Engineers prepared the plate-girder railway bridge on the front held by the East Surreys west of Lock 4, and a smaller drop bridge about a mile further west still. Both were successfully blown up, Corporal Dorey receiving the French Medaille Militaire for his work on the destruction of the railway bridge under enemy fire. A Royal Engineers officer, writing to the Corps newsletter after the war, sums up the attitude of the officers responsible for these demolitions:

> One point I think should be emphasized about hasty demolitions in the face of the enemy. Beware of calculations. I gave an order to my people not to fuss over calculations but to cover the girders with all the stuff they could tie on, and let it go. The result was we never failed through lack of power but we burnt a hell of a lot of powder! My view was that my first job was to demolish and do it thoroughly and quickly and certainly. Replacement of explosives I am afraid I did not look upon as my funeral.[15]

Tremendous heroism was shown at other points along the canal, as the Royal Engineers worked frantically in the face of heavy German shelling and small arms to demolish as many crossing points as possible. At the Nimy railway bridge Lieutenant Day arrived as the Germans were attacking. He was wounded and taken prisoner before he could destroy it, leaving Godley and Dease to do their utmost with their machine-gun. At Lock 2, Lance Corporal Jarvis and Sapper Neary worked from a small boat to attach charges to a bridge while heavy firing went on over their heads. However, when it was learned that a general withdrawal was to take place, Captain Theodore Wright, the commanding officer, realised that 57th Field Company had the problem of blowing up five bridges on a front of 3 miles with only one exploder! The decision was taken by Wright to concentrate on Mariette bridge, which stood on a main road, and where longer electrical leads run back from the explosive charges meant there was more chance of connecting the exploder. However Captain Wright and Sergeant Smith had first to cross a subsidiary canal under fire to reach them. Wright swung hand over hand under the girder bridge here in an attempt to reach the leads, but without success. After several attempts, each met with heavy fire, he dropped exhausted into the canal. He was subsequently awarded the Victoria Cross. A sapper officer of 56th Field Company, who was to gain the same distinction later in the war, was Second Lieutenant C.G. Martin, commander of Number 3 section. He recalled many years later:

> We were on the Mons canal with the central line of the Middlesex Regiment and the first job I had was to blow up a bridge on the . . . canal, but I didn't succeed in that. It was a solid concrete bridge, which held us up a bit! We had to go across the canal to get at it . . . we were under shellfire at the time, but nothing very heavy . . . we were all scattered about [but] we didn't lose anybody. Our company went further down the canal, but [the] men on the next bridge were captured by the Germans . . . the demolition work was given up, and we were told to retire.[16]

In fact, of all RE companies engaged in demolition work on the canal that day, 56th Field Company had been allotted one of the hardest stretches of all to deal with, and of the three of its sections that tried to blow up bridges near Obourg, none succeeded.

To the right of the Middlesex at Obourg, holding the line of the Mons–Harmignies road, stood the 1st Battalion Gordon Highlanders. A soldier of this battalion, a Private Smiley, remembered afterwards that the Gordons had made themselves busy in the hours prior to the commencement of the battle not only digging trenches but also clearing the ground in front of them of willows, beans, wheat and anything else that might have provided cover for an advancing enemy, for a distance of some 2,000yd. Another Gordon Highlander, Private J. Parkinson, published his account of the attack on the Highlanders and the Middlesex shortly after the events occurred. Parkinson was apparently under the impression that the troops that attacked his positions were of the Prussian Guard, which was not the case. They in fact belonged to the *Infanterie-Regiment Hamburg (2. Hanseatisches) Nr. 76*, a Hanseatic line infantry regiment. None the less Parkinson's account is valuable. He wrote:

> The Germans came out of their trenches in big heaps in close formation, because their game was to rush us by sheer weight of numbers; but we just shot them down. Yet as soon as we shot them down others came out, literally like bees … the British officer always leads shows the way [*sic*]; but the German officer seems to follow his men, and to shove and shoot them along.
>
> It was marvellous to watch the Germans come on in their legions, and melt away under our artillery and rifle fire. We simply took deliberate aim at the masses of figures, grey clad, with their helmets covered with grey cloth; but it seemed as if not even our absolutely destructive fire would stop them. On they came, still on, the living actually sheltering behind the dead. But it was no use. We kept them off, and they kept themselves off, too, for it was perfectly clear that they had a horror of the bayonet, and would not come near it. The nearest the Germans got

German soldiers charge forward in dense masses in August 1914. For the well-trained soldiers of the BEF they were impossible to miss.

to us, as far as I can tell that is, to the Gordons was about 300 yards; but that was near enough, seeing that they outnumbered us by four to one, and were amongst the finest troops of Germany. Some of the enemy's cavalry I suppose the much-talked-of Uhlans came into the sunken road in front of us, hoping to do business; but our machine-guns got on them, and we had a go at them with our rifles, with the result that the Uhlans made a cut for it and most of them got away. Even so, there were plenty of riderless horses galloping madly about.[17]

The sunken lane ahead of the Gordons, which the Germans used for cover, was in fact the Mons–St Symphorien road. Smiley remembered the Germans here advancing in lines five deep, and the Maxims of his battalion as well as its rifles caused terrible destruction in the German ranks, their first waves were stopped at 700yd range, and only by using their dead comrades as cover could the later German assaults get much nearer. Smiley himself was wounded while breaking cover with a party sent to assist the Royal Irish Regiment, which was hard pressed on the left of the Gordons. Another valuable account of the part played by the Gordon Highlanders here comes from Second Lieutenant Malcolm Hay, who wrote:

I was on the point of laying down my glasses, having made a final sweep of the ground [ahead] … when something caught my attention in the plantation, and at that same moment a body of troops in extended order dashed out of the woods and doubled across the open meadow. The sight of these men … was so entirely unexpected that, although their uniforms even at the long range seemed unfamiliar, I did not realise they were Germans. A volley from No. 14 Trench put an end to uncertainty. The line broke, each man running for safety at headlong speed; here and there a man, dropping backwards, lay still on the grass.

In the centre of the line the officer, keeping rather behind the rest, stumbled and fell. The two men nearest him stopped, bent down to assist him, looking for a moment anxiously into his face as he lay back on the grass, then quickly turned and ran for cover. A very few seconds more and the remaining racing figures dodged between trees on the main road and found safety. When the rifle fire ceased, two or three of the grey bodies dotted about the field were seen to move; one or two rose up, staggered a few paces, only to fall at once and lie motionless; another two or three wriggled and crawled away; and one rose up apparently unhurt, running in zigzag fashion, dodging from side to side with sudden cunning, though no further shot was fired.

The German attack now began to press on both flanks – on the left perhaps with less vigour, but on the right an ever-increasing intensity of rifle fire seemed to come almost from behind our trenches; but on neither left nor right could anything be seen of the fighting. The ceaseless tapping of our two machine-guns was anxious hearing during that long afternoon, and in the confusion of bursting shells the sound of busy rifles seemed to be echoing on all sides.

Three German officers stepped out from the edge of the wood behind the white house; they stood out in the open, holding a map and discussing together the plan of attack. The little group seemed amazingly near in the mirror of my field-glass, but afforded too hopelessly small a target for rifle fire at a 1,000 yards' range. The conference was, however, cut short by a shell from our faithful battery behind the wood of Hyon. A few minutes later, the officers having skipped back into cover, a long line of the now familiar grey coats advanced slowly about ten yards from the wood and lay down in the beetroot field; an officer, slightly in front of his men, carrying a walking-stick and remaining standing until another shell threw him on to his face with the rest.[18]

Later in the day *Infanterie-Regiment Nr. 76* was able to push the Gordons back into the outskirts of Mons. One of the German soldiers who was wounded here wrote later of his encounter with the curiously dressed Scots:

We ran to our first firing position in a meadow about 100 meters wide, at the other end the Englishmen had dug long ditches. Barely had we lay down, than there was uproar. No words of command could be given or heard. The hostile artillery rained down on us. Shrapnel burst, but we had almost no losses from this, some men only fell when jumping up to run forward, but this did not stop us, because everybody instinctively looks forward. We got closer and closer, to 150 meters.

However, no longer could the English stand it and they began to fall back; we fired steadily, first lying, then kneeling. The Englishmen who opposed us had heavy losses. In a trench I counted 40 dead men and 25 wounded, more may have

Unteroffizier Alwin Gottschlich, present at Mons on 23 August with Infanterie Regiment Nr. 76 *from Hamburg.*

been there earlier. But soon the fighting moved further toward the town. Here the enemy occupied every house, from every window a machine-gun fired. Here it was necessary to move fast, and as you know, I am capable of this; thus I took off my backpack and ran up to a house which was not taken, from here came the sound 'Tsching-boum'; we numbered probably 20 men, and we were certainly fired down upon from all directions. Here the first prisoners were taken: Highlanders with short little skirts, however I am convinced that they still wear trousers underneath these. Meanwhile some comrades had reached the first houses, which soon burned merrily, as the shooters did not want to come out. This game recurred several times. So at about 6 o'clock I was again on my way like a greyhound. All at once someone threw a door from the second floor . . . and I went full length on to the pavement, the blood flowed from my nose like a fountain. I quickly rubbed my shinbones – there all at once a cellar window rose, and ritsch-ratsch I received two gunshots in the left ankle, it was as if someone hit me with a whip around the legs, and soon my foot came to feel heavy. I wanted to get up, but upsy daisy I was shot once more in the ankle, and I lay back again in the mud.[19]

As the morning progressed the German attack also began to spread westwards along the line of the canal. Around 11am the attack fell against the British positions in front of Jemappes, held by the 1st Battalion Royal Scots Fusiliers. German shells fell in the village itself, but in the rear of the positions held by the fusiliers along the canal. Consequently when the Germans advanced in dense lines, they were met with a withering fire emanating from rifles and machine-guns. Taking heavy casualties the Germans were obliged to pause, before approaching more cautiously using cover. This time they were halted at a range of some 200yd from their objective, the bridge at

Destruction in Jemappes following the Battle of Mons.

Lock 2, west of Jemappes. This attack was carried out by *Infanterie-Regiment Graf Tauentzien von Wittenburg (3. Brandenburgisches) Nr. 20* and a soldier who was present with this unit was frank about the stoical attitude he had towards danger in a letter to his parents:

> We passed by Brussels unhindered and then came to the battle at Jemappes and Fleury: 40,000 Englishmen faced us, who defended themselves in a terrifically determined way. In particular our infantry had heavy losses. Whole ranks were mowed down by hostile fire. It is a quite peculiar feeling, when the bullets whiz around one's head; it is strange however just how quickly one becomes deadened against it. One says to oneself, whom death should meet, it will meet ... Three times our infantry were ordered to go forward to storm the village, twice they were driven back; every house had been transformed into a fortress. But, finally, they took it and held onto it.[20]

An officer of this same unit, Heinrich Heubner, left a graphic account of the fighting at this point in the line. He wrote:

> It was nearly 7 o'clock as the violent German attack broke for the first time against the English. The heavily defended village was cleared and the fight continued beyond it. Our regiment was now no longer in the fire, but we steeled ourselves and crossed the canal, over which our brave pioneers had thrown a superb bridge. On the other side of this waterway stood the shattered and burning railway station. In a small square, like dogs against a house wall, squatted the first English prisoners we had seen so far in the war. There was an old corporal, with about eight men. In a wider semicircle around them stood some of our enlisted men, astonished by the defenceless British soldiers. I must confess that they made a very good impression upon me, almost all deeply suntanned, well-clothed people. I very much regretted that I was not fluent in English. However, a young volunteer soldier noticed my awkwardness and offered to play the part of interpreter, as he spoke perfect English. And now this young German soldier told me something remarkable. 'Herr Oberleutnant,' he said, 'the second prisoner from the left here I know very well. I recognised him as a school friend. My parents lived for twenty years in England and I have shared a school desk with this Englishman. Here we have found each other again, though in different circumstances.' Truly, the world is a small place, and never so strange things happen as do so in war!
>
> The further we advanced into this place, the more obvious became the signs of war. Large factory buildings had been holed and smashed by German shells. The musketry of the infantry had pockmarked the red brick houses, and as we rounded a street corner in our path lay the first dead Englishman. He was an old infantryman, clad from head to foot in yellow-green khaki. In a stationmaster's house lay a whole crowd of dead Englishmen, for the English colonial troops had the habit if they were able to of getting the wounded and even the dead safely inside houses.

... the surging fire of guns and rifles shook us with its power, but soon it was to slacken and finally go out towards sunset. Never will I forget ... the mood that we felt, that we had given our all. We all felt an irrepressible pleasure that the hated English adversary had felt the weight of German blows and had been shaken by them, but indeed at the same time we had to recognise that these English soldiers, who before the war many of us had looked down upon with scornfulness and disrespect, as with other soldiers like the Belgians, had in each case fought bravely and obstinately, which was proven by the losses our German soldiers had suffered here.[21]

One member of the Royal Scots Fusiliers holding the positions at Jemappes was Private J. Ferrie. While recovering later from wounds received in the battle, he wrote to the *Glasgow Herald* newspaper. In his letter he recounted the heroism of his section commander Sergeant Arthur Cropp, of Old Cumnock, Ayrshire, in this action. He described how Sergeant Cropp rescued Lieutenant Stephens, an officer of the battalion, who had been badly hit while on the German side of the canal defending a bridge. Without the intervention of Cropp the officer must surely have fallen into the hands of the enemy:

The sergeant took the wounded lieutenant on his back, but as he could not crawl across the bridge so encumbered he entered the water, swam the canal, carried the wounded man out of line of fire, and consigned him to the care of four men of his own company. Of a platoon of fifty-eight which was set to guard the bridge only twenty-six afterwards answered to the roll call.[22]

As the morning wore on, more German attacks broke against the canal like waves against rocks. Further to the west at Mariette the position was held by the Northumberland Fusiliers. In spite of the fact that the Germans brought two field

Jemappes hospital, with the Mons–Condé canal in the foreground.

guns to within half a mile of the bridge, the Fusiliers held them at bay for much of the
day. An officer of the regiment, writing after the war, stated:

> I myself was present at the bridge at Mariette when Captain Wright and Sergeant
> Smith tried to blow it up. Actually B Company 1st Northumberland Fusiliers was
> in the act of withdrawing when Wright began his forlorn hope. Although we did
> not know it, by that time we had been practically cut off by the Germans who had
> come in about Mons. Wright's gallantry made a great impression upon the men
> of B Company of my regiment. Two days later in the early morning, as they
> were leaving a very chilly bivouac at Bavai, they recognised Wright riding by and
> cheered him heartily; rather a unique demonstration from Northcountrymen.[23]

Further west still, troops of the 1st Battalion Royal West Kent Regiment were in
possession of a portion of the canal bank at St Ghislain. One soldier from this battalion
remembered that their entrenching was interrupted by a German shell which smashed
a house overlooking the canal. The West Kents loopholed the walls of the ruin, and
subsequently used it as cover from which to fire at the advancing Germans. One
company was thrown forward on the far side of the canal acting as scouts. Among them
was Private Harry Beaumont, who wrote later:

> In skeleton order we advanced over the bridge at St Ghislain, and took up a
> position in a glass factory on the opposite side of the canal. Its walls were quickly
> loopholed. Here, concealed from the enemy's view, and covered from his shellfire,
> we came into action for the first time.
>
> The country in front of our position was flat, and dotted with numerous circular
> fenced-in copses, a common feature in that part of Belgium. The Germans, moving
> between them, made easy targets, and we opened fire. Their losses that afternoon
> must have been tremendous. Further, our two battalion machine-guns created
> havoc among the enemy when they attempted to outflank our position by crossing
> the railway, which ran at right angles and to the right of it, skirted on each side by
> wooded slopes, straight ahead as far as the eye could see. For, hidden among
> abandoned locomotives at a point where it was crossed by another line, running on
> an embankment parallel with the canal at our rear, they commanded it and before
> nightfall many bodies in field grey could be seen strewn in the permanent way.[24]

Around the middle part of the day the advanced troops of the Royal West Kents
began to withdraw under fire from the *Grenadier-Regiment Prinz Karl von Preußen
(2. Brandenburgisches) Nr. 12* (the Brandenburg grenadier regiment). Another member
of this advanced party, Sergeant George Reeves, recalled afterwards:

> I arrived at St Ghislain with my regiment about 3 o'clock on the 22nd August
> 1914. We were turned out next morning (23rd August) at 6 o'clock and advanced
> about ¾ mile in front of St Ghislain to cover the retirement of British cavalry. I
> stayed there until the Germans arrived, which was about 9.30. They were engaged,
> and my platoon was ordered to retire about 12.30. I succeeded in retiring to
> within 600 or 700 yards of the British trenches, when I was struck by shrapnel.
> Notwithstanding my wounds I crawled back behind the British trenches. There

> I was picked up by stretcher bearers and carried to a temporary hospital worked by Belgians. That was about 2 o'clock.[25]

After Reeves was given an anaesthetic, he was soon asleep, and awoke the following day to find the hospital in German hands. There were other close shaves. Sergeant Edward Turner, also of the 1st Battalion West Kents, wrote afterwards to his sweetheart: 'The bullet that wounded me at Mons went into one breast pocket and came out of the other, and in its course passed through your photo.'[26]

As the advanced party of the West Kents withdrew by means of ditches and gaps in the barbed wire defences, the main body of the Brandenburgers came on in massed formation down the St Ghislain road. They were met with a shattering fire from the West Kents, who though in the process of retiring, forced the enemy to withdraw and regroup. None the less the Brandenburgers came on again, this time against the main positions of the West Kents, King's Own Yorkshire Light Infantry and some King's Own Scottish Borderers on the canal itself. Again they were roughly handled, the British from concealed positions pouring a devastating weight of fire into their ranks. Only their neighbouring formation, *Infanterie-Regiment von Alvensleben (6. Brandenburgisches) Nr. 52*, succeeded in actually reaching the canal.

The German novelist Walter Bloem served as a captain of the reserve with the Brandenburg Grenadiers, and his book about the German drive through Belgium, *Vormarsch* (translated into English as *The Advance From Mons*), has rightly become a military classic. He writes of the encounter with the West Kents:

> And so we went on, gradually working forwards by rushes of a hundred, later fifty, and then about thirty yards towards the invisible enemy. At every rush a few more fell, but one could do nothing for them. On and on, that was the only solution. Easier said than done, however, for not only was the meadow horribly swampy, filling our boots with water, but it was intersected by broad, water-logged drains and barbed wire fences that had to be cut through ... Behind us the whole meadow was dotted with little grey heaps. The hundred and sixty men that left the wood with me had shrunk to less than a hundred.[27]

After a pause for a rather incongruous drink of champagne, produced from a resourceful soldier's knapsack and consumed while British bullets whistled overhead, the advance toward the canal bank was resumed:

> From now on the English fire gradually weakened, almost ceased. No hail of bullets greeted each rush forward, and we were able to get within 150 yards of the canal bank. I said to [Leutnant] Graser: 'Now we'll do one more 30-yard rush, all together, then fix bayonets and charge the houses and canal banks.'
>
> The enemy must have been waiting for this moment to get us all together at close range, for immediately the line rose it was as if the hounds of hell had been loosed at us, yelling, barking, hammering as a mass of lead swept in among us ... From now on, matters went from bad to worse. Wherever I looked, right or left, were dead or wounded, quivering in convulsions, groaning terribly, blood oozing from fresh wounds. The worst was that the heaviest firing now began to come on us from the strip of wood that jutted out into the meadow to our right rear.[28]

Bloem believed that his own side were mistakenly firing upon them, but frantic signalling with flags by the men of his section served only to intensify the fire. In fact, it was coming from the machine-guns of a British formation, the 1st Battalion East Surrey Regiment, who again were occupying a position forward of the canal. He continued:

> I discovered too at this time that we had scarcely any ammunition left; and here we were, isolated and 120 yards from the English position. Next to me was a Grenadier hit through both cheeks and tongue, his face a mass of blood; and beyond him Pohlenz, my bugler, a bullet hole through the bugle slung on his back, the home-made cigarette in the corner of his mouth, and himself firing shot after shot ... at the garden of the white house in front.[29]

Hauptmann Walter Bloem, of Infanterie Regiment Nr. 12 *(the Brandenburg Grenadiers).*

Gradually as the darkness of the warm summer evening gathered on this part of the battlefield, the Germans withdrew to lick their wounds. The sound of singing reached the men of the West Kents: the strains of *Deutschland Uber Alles*, which was being sung by the weary enemy troops opposite, in an effort to boost their battered morale.

One of the officers present with the East Surrey Regiment that day, Second Lieutenant G.R.P. Roupell, was to win glory later in the war, with the award of the Victoria Cross, but for now his first experience of combat was to come in the fields opposite those where Bloem's regiment were taking such heavy casualties. He remembered fifty-five years later:

> When we arrived up at the Mons–Condé canal, we had time to deploy and send two companies on the far side of the canal, and two companies on the near side, [and] these four were instructed to dig in, and while they were digging in the German attack started. You could see them very vaguely because we were behind the canal, and the forward companies were about two or three hundred yards ahead, in a little wood, so you couldn't see very much ... we lay upon the [south] bank with myself in the centre [of the line] ... As you slid back behind the canal bank you were under cover. When you got up to fire you were exposing yourself ... We were lining this bank and the bullets started to come over [but] we were in a very good position to take it because we could just get down behind the bank and it wasn't until the leading company had withdrawn that we came into action

and actually got up then onto the bank and fired . . . We were lying flat on the ground. It was an almost ideal position. It was very much like a rifle range.

The leading companies were driven back. [They] had to come back and we held the canal bank and as the companies came back the Germans then came out of the wood towards us and we got the most wonderful targets, just what we wanted . . . We held the bank of the canal and as far as we were concerned we could have stayed there any length of time because there was an open space in front and the enemy couldn't cross this under our fire. It was too heavy for them. And so they simply withdrew back into the wood, and each time they tried to come out again we shot them dead, and we thought we were going to spend the whole day there.

We had had our fire orders but in the excitement of the moment most of the details of it went by the board because normally you give an aiming mark and then you say, 'lone tree', 'so many degrees right' . . . or whatever it is. In this case there was a line of men rushing out of the wood. There's no need to give any targets. You simply gave the order, 'two hundred yards – fire!' [and] they fired at the so obvious target coming straight for us . . . [the men] were all very good shots. Very good at rapid fire. That was one of our specialist trainings that we did.[30]

Close to the East Surreys, in the district of Herbieres, the 2nd Battalion King's Own Scottish Borderers (KOSB) were holding the line of the canal and the nearby railway bridge. One of the most detailed contemporary accounts of the battle comes from Lieutenant J.B.W. Pennyman, the machine-gun officer of this battalion. Pennyman lived at Ormesby Hall near Middlesbrough, and in later years, much of the land of the Pennyman estate would be leased for housing and the development of that town. In 1915, Pennyman published his diary charting his experiences at Mons for private circulation. In it, he writes:

Sunday August 23 – We were all up before sunrise, fully expecting an attack, but this did not come. As soon as it was light I started out to look for a good place to put the [machine] guns . . . There was a line of houses on the opposite side of the canal and the only place where I could get any field of fire at all was on the second (top) floor of the highest house in the place; so I decided to go there and stay there as long as I could. It was rather a doubtful place, as I knew we should have to leave on the arrival of the first shell. We put sandbags to protect the gunners in the windows and made other holes in the walls for firing to the left by which means we covered the lock and its approaches. I had a couple of miners in my section (Black and Strain), and they did the work splendidly. As soon as we had got the guns in position we retired for a little breakfast.[31]

Around 11am rumours began to circulate that the cavalry in front had been heavily attacked, and firing was heard. Pennyman continued:

We could see the Germans debouching in extended order across a road 900 yards straight to our front. I did not open fire as the target did not seem to warrant the exposure of my position. Unfortunately a large number of them (I have no idea how many) were able to approach into a wood behind the houses in front of me,

The portion of canal bank defended by Lieutenant Pennyman and his machine-guns of the King's Own Scottish Borderers; a rare photograph taken on the morning of the battle.

without coming under fire. 'A' and 'C' Companies took these on. My sergeant (Gilmartin) pointed out to me two groups of Germans, each lying in the open. We thought they might be machine-gunners and decided to fire on them. I took the range accurately and we laid out all four in our first traverse. We then took on any Germans we saw in the open and did considerable damage. This was our first experience of killing people: it was rather horrible, but satisfactory. We searched a thicket the other side of the road aforesaid, where I think there were Germans massed preparatory to debouching, and saw evidence of certain success. I could see through my glasses one tall young officer who stood up against a tree in the open directing operations. He was at any rate not a coward.[32]

The situation was now threatening to turn against the KOSB soldiers beyond the canal, as the weight of German numbers began to tell. However the machine-guns proved again to be effective weapons against large bodies of infantry:

I could see 'D' Company below me on my left trying to turn the Germans out of the wood in front of them: men were being carried back wounded ... Suddenly I saw the front edge of the wood lined with Germans and surmised they were going to try and rush 'D' Company, so I concentrated all the fire of both guns on the edge of the wood and the Germans went back ... We continued to search the last mentioned wood with fire, as we knew it was full of Germans, although we couldn't see them. Whether we did any good or not I do not know, but the noise we made cheered on the others. Bullets were coming through the windows pretty frequently now. Gilmartin asked me whether our sandbags were bullet proof, and as he spoke one bullet just came through and dropped on the floor between us. It was nearly red hot. Soon the fire on us became so hot indeed that bullets started coming through the walls. They had found us out and though no one was hit it was obviously time to quit.[33]

Pennyman moved his section down on to the canal bank where the British line was still holding steady, but at 6pm they were ordered to withdraw, covered by the rifles of the King's Own Yorkshire Light Infantry.

To the right of the British line the Germans launched one of the last attacks of the day against the ditches and trenches held by the Gordon Highlanders and 2nd Battalion Royal Scots (who had been reinforced by two companies of the 2nd Battalion Royal Irish Rifles) along the Harmignies–Mons road. In failing light, they made one of their final efforts between 7pm and 8pm. Upon the appearance of the German soldiers the entire British line erupted into a torrent of small-arms fire. The effect upon the advancing Germans was disastrous and they were brought to a complete standstill, the musketry of the Royal Scots being particularly effective. According to a German source, one of the attacking regiments, *Infanterie-Regiment Bremen (1. Hanseatisches) Nr. 75*, the 1st Hanseatic Infantry or Bremen Regiment, alone lost 5 officers and 376 men

Soldiers of the 2nd Battalion Royal Scots in Plymouth, just prior to leaving for France. These men held the Harmignies–Mons road and together with the Gordon Highlanders, their fire brought the Germans of Infanterie Regiment Nr. 75 *to a complete standstill, 300yd from the British lines.*

to the deadly fire of the Royal Scots in this abortive assault. The history of the Bremen Regiment places the first contact with British troops here as being sometime after 5.30pm. Its leading element was its III Battalion, and the book states:

> The III battalion advanced and pivoted on the junction of the Harmignies–phosphate factory road with the Mons–Villers St Ghislain road, coming into action on the right hand side of the Malplaquet–Harmignies road, the roadside ditch alongside of which the English troops were holding. With two companies (9 and 10) in the lead and with one company (12) in the second line, it advanced first in a south-westerly direction before reaching and then following a narrow lane which joined the phosphate factory–Harmignies road. Whilst the forward companies advanced westwards following the narrow lane, the enemy artillery fire rained down to the south of St Symphorien, causing them to take cover. Whilst crossing the larger road the following company, number 12 received two direct hits, and numerous casualties were sustained. Four men were killed (Musketier Petzold, Reservists Scherfer, Martens and Peper) and a large number were wounded.
>
> 'We were certainly happy,' said the then commander of 12 company Hauptmann Mylius, 'to get out of the artillery fire, which was still searching for victims. In a sunken road the company collected itself, and remained behind 9 and 10 companies, which kept up a lively rate of fire westwards. The enemy bullets buzzed like mosquitoes above the sunken lane. Here I met the battalion staff, who tried to update me on the situation. They however knew very little. Even the Regimental Adjutant, Oberleutnant von Capelle, who galloped his horse down that sunken lane, was not able to enlighten me greatly. We knew nothing at all of the dispositions of the English soldiers, and so we were very much in the dark.' After some time, with the platoon of Leutnant Heyser in the vanguard, 12 company came into line with 9 and 10 companies, whilst Hauptmann Mylius extended platoons to the right and left. As the III battalion engaged the enemy, the II and I battalions were at this point in the small wood near Pannes farm.[34]

The history continues by describing the fortunes of 3 Company, in the words of its commander Major Walter Caspari:

> Orders came through to us to take companies 3 and 4 and advance further towards the front line. Where this lay, we did not know. We could probably have fired a long way over this rolling country towards the enemy, but we saw only a completely empty battlefield. With 2 and 3 platoons in the front line, and 1 platoon behind as support, number 3 company advanced in short rushes in a westerly direction; in spite of the heavy enemy fire we were under, we sustained a low level of casualties, and in good order we reached the first sunken lane to the east of St Symphorien which leads southwards towards Harmignies. We had to cross this lane ——! The lane offered protection from the fire sweeping the open ground ... but the enemy had apparently foreseen this. Bullets were now being fired at it in great quantities. It required an extraordinary effort of will to leave the safety of cover and advance into that fire; indeed the temptation to retire to safety

Major Walter Caspari, of Infanterie Regiment Nr. 75. *On 23 August he led his men on towards the Scots and Irish lining the Mons–Harmignies Road.*

was quite strong ... In the sunken lane swirled fragments of different companies mixed up with each other. I knew that despite our best efforts, the position ahead had not yet been overcome. From all sides however I was continually assailed with the cry of 'The 75th is bleeding to death in front' and 'we urgently need reinforcements ahead'.

In the lane we attempted to reorganise, but in spite of the energy expended we were only partially successful in reaching the forward positions. Eventually I was able to lead some 200 men of different companies forward toward the enemy. The sense of duty and feeling of comradeship with those of the 75th 'bleeding to death' ahead, drove us forward. Rarely has a greater charge been made. The bullets whistled around us, struck the ground and hissed past the sheaves of corn. Some good 75ers lay here in this open field, in which ripe grain stood in sheaves, either dead or wounded. Over 1,000 meters we charged, without firing a shot, into the gathering gloom. We felt that we must eventually reach the enemy front line at last! But – we discovered nothing. It is however possible, and I believe even very probable, that we did not recognise a front line in the breathless charge in the dark ... Just before the Malplaquet–Harmignies road we finally halted, about 9.00 o'clock in the evening.[35]

The Irish writer John Lucy, serving here with the 2nd Battalion Royal Irish Rifles, gives a graphic description of this incident in his book *There's a Devil in the Drum.* Lucy's writing is on a par with the outstanding work of Frank Richards, another authentic voice from the ranks. He describes the defensive positions taken up by the men of his battalion as trenches, but not such as those that would become familiar as the war progressed into stalemate in the years to come. The trenches of August 1914 were mere foxholes, or kneeling pits, intended to be occupied for a few hours only. Lucy placed the German assault at around 3.30pm, but admitted himself that in battle all sense of time is lost. He wrote that the battalion first came under heavy shrapnel fire before the infantry assault began:

Finally the shelling ceased, and we put up our heads to breathe more freely. Then we heard conch-like sounds – strange bugle calls. The German infantry, which had approached during the shelling, was in sight and about to attack us ... In answer to the German bugles or trumpets came the cheerful sound of our officers' whistles, and the riflemen, casting aside the amazement of their strange trial, sprang into action. A great roar of musketry rent the air, varying slightly in intensity from minute to minute as whole companies ceased fire and opened again. The satisfactory sharp blasts of the directing whistles showed that our machinery of defence was working like the drill book, and that the recent shelling had caused no disorganisation. The clatter of our machine-guns added to the din.

For us the battle took the form of well-ordered, rapid rifle-fire at close range, as the field-grey human targets appeared, or were struck down. The enemy infantry advanced, according to one of our men, in 'columns of masses', which withered away under the galling fire of the well-trained and coolly led Irishmen. The leading Germans fired standing, 'from the hip', as they came on, but their scattered fire was ineffective, and ignored. They crumpled up – mown down as quickly as I tell it, their reinforcing waves and sections coming on bravely and steadily to fall over as they reached the front line of slain and wounded. Behind the death line thicker converging columns were being blown about by our field guns.

Our rapid fire was appalling even to us, and the worst marksman could not miss, as he had only to fire into the 'brown' of the masses of the unfortunate

Corporal John Lucy, Royal Irish Rifles, author of There's a Devil in the Drum.

enemy, who on the fronts of two of our companies were continually and uselessly reinforced at the short range of three hundred yards. Such tactics amazed us, and after the first shock of seeing men slowly and helplessly fall down as they were hit, gave us a great sense of power and pleasure. It was all so easy. The German survivors began to go back here and there from the line. The attack had been an utter failure. Soon all that remained was the long line of the dead heaped before us, motionless except for the limb movements of some of the wounded.[36]

In the same battalion was Rifleman Thomas Christopher O'Donnell, who remembered later:

Many of us were bare but for our trousers availing ourselves to the warm sunshine to wash and dry our shirts and socks after our long tramp through France and Belgium, our bugles got orders to sound the stand to arms.

The Germans were then advancing in overwhelming numbers, soon the sharp crackle of musketry was added to the cannonading of the guns and the saber and lance of the Germans gleamed in the sun ... The Germans kept pressing very hard all afternoon, but we held our ground. Just before dusk the Uhlans made a charge on our lines as they were coming towards us, we opened a rapid fire on them. Many of them fell, but what was left of them kept on coming. As they were closing on us we got the order to charge; every man that was able got on his feet and was off towards them yelling like madmen.

When the Uhlans seen the mass of steel coming towards them, they turned their horses around and were off and we helped them along with rifle fire and the boys got no more excited than if they had been witnessing the finish of the Grand National.

We got back to our position again and soon afterwards came wave after wave of their infantry, but we managed to keep them in check until midnight, although we had many casualties.[37]

It is interesting to note that many of the German casualties were caused by British artillery batteries unlimbered and in action behind the infantry. Captain Arthur Corbett-Smith was a Special Reserve gunner officer on the right flank of the battle. While his descriptions of the infantry actions are somewhat vague, his detail about the activities of the artillery batteries, recorded in his book *The Retreat From Mons, by One Who Shared in It*, appears to be well informed by first-hand experience. He describes how the German artillery batteries sought urgently to silence their British counterparts as soon as they came into action:

A very considerable percentage of our total casualties were caused by high explosive shell, and the shooting of them was astonishingly accurate. Yes, the German guns did their work well, but they did not fully succeed in their object. Their local successes were great, especially against British guns and batteries. Here is a British battery which has made two mistakes – it is not sufficiently concealed, the battery commander is perched up on an observation limber, and the guns are not far enough back behind the crest. (The Germans always 'search' for some 800 yards behind crests of hills.) The B.C. is quickly spotted by an aeroplane observer and a perfect hell of fire is switched on by the enemy. In a moment telephone wires are cut, communications are broken, and within five minutes the gun detachments are wiped out.

The effect of a shell from the enemy heavier guns is overwhelming. The flank gun of the battery is hit, practically 'direct.' Some R.A.M.C. men double up a few minutes later to help out the wounded. *There is nothing* save a great hole, fragments of twisted steel, and a few limbs of brave men. Nothing can be done except, later, dig in the sides of the pit to cover the remains. The rest of the guns remain, but there is no one to work them. The horses, a little way to the rear, have also suffered badly. A subaltern officer staggers painfully through the tornado of fire from one gun to the next, slowly, deliberately putting them out of action, rendering them useless should the enemy come up to capture them ...[38]

Away on the extreme western flank of the battlefield, fresh German troops were also being committed as the day drew to a close. A fascinating (but sadly anonymous) German account of the battle here was published in the *Kölnische Zeitung* newspaper in 1915. The writer refers to passing the town of Pommeroeul before meeting the enemy. This and the fact that he describes a railway line to his left, before reaching the Mons–Condé canal, suggests strongly that he was approaching the advanced positions of the 1st Battalion Duke of Cornwall's Light Infantry (DCLI) which lay forward of the canal at Le Petit Crépin, on the left wing of the BEF line. The account, as well as illustrating the German perspective of the fighting at Mons, gives us another valuable glimpse into the lives of the ordinary British Tommy. The writer, who appears to have been a private soldier, stated:

In close formation the company advanced along a road. To the left of the road we came across a railway engine, by which the English soldiers had arrived there. Scarcely had we advanced 2 or 3 kilometres from this scene when shells began to burst above us, but luckily all went over our heads. We came across railway carriages, which also gave us cover. Between them we crawled, towards the canal which we had to take. However, the enemy had blown up the bridge.

The III battalion – we belonged to the first battalion – had swerved to the right. Far to the left of us was Infanterie Regiment —. We now proceeded in the vanguard. The railway line was now behind us. In front of us, behind the houses which we were approaching, lay a factory. We came under machine-gun fire, but it was aimed too high. After we had observed the explosion of some shells, the platoon went forward at the quick march, covering 50 metres of ground between the explosions. We met no enemy, but we were happy to reach the houses. Behind the houses we again came under fire. No one was wounded, but the roofs were already riddled with holes. Loud cracks could be heard. I said to the officer: 'Herr Leutnant, can those be bullets? Can you hear the cracks?' It seemed as if one explosion followed directly upon another.

In front of these houses, seen from the English side, they had dug trenches, but we had obviously surprised them, and they had left in a hurry. They had left some excellent equipment behind, and we noticed in particular their long handled shovels. Also some good pick axes fell into our hands. We found eatables,

A British .303 ammunition box, recovered by the Germans from the Mons battlefield. The original German caption to this photograph claimed that it contained dum-dum bullets.

especially Corned Beef, and backpacks containing many letters, from which we were able to determine which regiment lay before us. All the young ladies wrote that they wished to see their soldiers again soon, 'in your red coats'. In these letters there was no mention of the Germans, let alone any hatred for them.

We continued now over the canal. After we passed the trenches we were fired at only by artillery, and through the shelling we headed for the old bridge. Three of our men set to work whilst we covered them, and they threw planks over the remains of the destroyed bridge.[39]

Another equally detailed German account of the battle here comes from Gustav Schubert, a medical orderly with *Infanterie-Regiment Nr. 26*. He wrote:

A group of ten hussars come riding up and stop on the other side of the road. Suddenly with a ssssing-ssssing infantry shots whiz away over our heads. Nobody knows where they are coming from. Ssssssing – ssssing – sssing – ssssing – a few hussars have dropped to the ground; and a man with a bad leg, who was resting on the field kitchen, is shot down.

The hussars ride back into the wood to reach cover. However, we infantrymen advance bent down on the left and to the right of the road in the ditch – finally, we have come into contact with the enemy! On one side of the road there runs a railway on which a long train stands, without a locomotive. Shortly before our advance, English troops had arrived here in it and, hearing of our approach, have moved back a short distance to a canal. They have blown the bridge up behind themselves, have built barricades 400 yards back from it, and behind these have set up two machine-guns which control the road. The houses beyond the canal are provided with loopholes, and are prepared for defence.

Already shells whiz through the air, intended for our troops still lying in the wood. In the roadside ditches, creeping further forward, and partly also under the cover of the train creeping from wagon to wagon, the eleventh company reaches the canal, whose half-meter high embankment grants good cover to us. Both English machine-guns are now in action – tacktacktacktacktacktacktack – and continually plaster the street as well as the remains of the destroyed bridge. They are answered by the boom-boom, crash-crash of the German field-guns which have in the meantime, been driven up beside the train. Their first volleys of shrapnel burst behind the bridge and endanger us with their explosive debris. Both field-guns are now directed a hundred metres farther forward. Shot after shot passes over our heads. We must reach the canal in order to silence the two machine-guns, but how to get there?

A comrade from my company drags a long board over to it. Happily he succeeds in throwing this across the footings of the destroyed bridge without being wounded in the process.

Tacktacktack – boom boom – tacktacktack – crash! Already the first man is over and when on the other side of the canal finds cover against the gable wall of the house on the left. Two brave souls jump up after him, but they make only a few steps forward: they sink, shot down, before reaching the board.

From the left side of the road some more jump up, with rifle in hand, crouching down as they race cross the wobbling, narrow board, happily they reach the protection of the house, where they press themselves firmly against the wall, so as not to offer a target to the Englishmen shooting from the windows. Now a comrade falls into the water, and another, but thankfully those following make it over. In spite of the hostile fire coming from the direction of the bridge, no one hangs back, everyone presses forward. All the officers are already over there. When I have made it across, happily some sixty men probably have made the rush through the storm of bullets; some have also swum over. Behind a barn we gather to reorganise ourselves. The sergeant points across to the other side of the road at a wounded man lying there. With a Lance-corporal I jump up and run straight across the road to him. Sssss sss sss we hear the whistle of the bullets around the ears. Involuntarily we hold our head skew, as if we could somehow thereby protect ourselves. Happily we succeed in carrying the wounded man over the road, out of the line of fire without being hit.[40]

Lieutenant Flint of 59th Field Company Royal Engineers was responsible for the destruction of the bridge over the canal on the DCLI front, almost under the noses of the Germans. Having successfully demolished this bridge, he was at work setting charges on that over the River Haine directly behind it, when the Germans reached the destroyed bridge. They could clearly see what was going on, as the intervening mile of road was perfectly straight, and so ran up a field gun and attempted to drive off the demolition party. Lieutenant Flint posted a man to watch the gun, and at every flash of its discharge he shouted a warning to the others, who just had time to drop into a ditch before the arrival of the shell, and in this way the second demolition was completed.

The adjutant of the DCLI in this action was Lieutenant Arthur Nugent Floyer-Acland. His account, written a few days after the battle, provides a great deal of detail about the fighting at this point on the canal from the British perspective:

> [The Germans] arrived, as a matter of fact, in small but bold patrols at dawn that day, and at intervals during that day, and only a few of them went away again. But at 4pm they arrived in a large solid mass on the road we were holding on the far side of the canal, and proceeded to march up to a point we had carefully ranged on. We could only get a very few rifles to bear on the spot or they must have lost far more than they actually did. As it was they deployed quickly on either side of the road and came on quickly. Our advance companies had got orders to retire over the canal as soon as any strong attack was made, so they withdrew almost at once, as the Germans were ten to one of us. As soon as these companies were over ... the bridge was blown up, and we got back to a position about 800 yards back, on the far side of the stream called La Haine ...[41]

Floyer-Acland added further important detail to this description in an interview fifty-five years later, in which he remembered his own involvement in the demolition of the bridge:

> [whilst] we had two companies over the other side ... it was rather tricky knowing when to blow [the bridge] and so I went to see whether [we could use] these barges, which were on the other side of the canal, and we pulled them across so that we made a barge bridge across the canal, and then we blew the bridge. As soon as that had gone, all our troops were on our side of the canal and we cut the lashings on the barges, and they floated away. In fact we blew some of them I think, so that we didn't leave anything for the Germans to come over.[42]

In his written account he reflected at the end of the day upon the happenings of the previous 24 hours, and his first impressions of the enemy:

> So did I first hear the song of the bullet and the howl of shrapnel. I can't quite describe my feelings through this show, but I somehow don't believe it dispelled the old idea that we were on some big sort of manoeuvres, which had idiotically been with me since we started from the Curragh. The burst and hum of the shrapnel surprised me, and the bullets made me duck my head! It interested me, I think, when a bullet flicked the ground just in front of [my horse] as I was riding along a road to get more ammunition. I won't say I was not frightened, I'm sure I was, but I don't think I knew it. We got away well, and without much loss, and with a somewhat poor opinion of the German's rifle shooting.[43]

Contempt for poor German shooting would be a recurring theme throughout many British accounts of Mons and the battles that were to follow in 1914. Strangely, and by contrast, many German testimonies contain a sneaking, almost self-conscious and embarrassed admiration for their British foes. One such interesting first-hand account comes from Hauptman Paul Oskar Höcker, a famous writer in Germany prior to the outbreak of war. Upon the commencement of hostilities he had offered his services to the army and joined a *Landwehr* unit as a company commander. The *Landwehr* was the German equivalent of the British Territorial Force, and these units in the early months of the war usually guarded lines of communication. Höcker's regiment, after travelling through Belgium behind the main German formations, arrived in Mons and found the town still occupied by British prisoners. In his memoir *An der Spitze meiner Kompagnie* he wrote:

> The English are all slim, sinewy chaps ... They did not have a cigarette stub amongst them, instead they had pipes. They smoked them unlit, in order to save the tobacco. Nearly every one put their hands into their jacket pockets; almost all are bareheaded. This seems to be because

The German novelist Paul Oskar Höcker, who arrived in Mons in the aftermath of the battle.

> in the trenches the English put their hats on sticks, which they plant in the ground, in order to offer a target for the German fire which was too good to miss. But the German soldiers knew little of this. The Khaki material of the English uniform is much more robust than our Field Grey ... All positions from which the English had fled revealed arms and equipment. I must admit, that the English had in the light of their previous experience provided their soldiers with very good equipment. The leatherwork of the backpacks is excellent. We could also feel almost envious of the two outside breast pockets, which were sewn onto their tunics. Each backpack held a mess tin for breakfast and a shaving kit. The rifles are perfect. In the trouser pocket of each Englishman however is a weapon which is extremely effective in hand to hand combat. It is the folding dagger knife, with these they carved joints of meat – in addition possibly after an attack, they cut the throats of the enemy with them in an ambush. All branches of the English army were represented among the prisoners: cavalry, artillery, infantry. Also Scottish highlanders with bare knees visible beneath the diced tartan kilt. They are elite troops, but never the less ... [they are prisoners][44]

As night fell on that first day of battle, there was little doubt that overall the BEF had performed well in its initial encounter with the Germans. The most powerful military force in the world had been fought to a standstill, and overwhelming numbers had been countered by superior skills in musketry and better tactics. All had not gone

A German photograph showing British prisoners being marched to the rear, in the aftermath of the Battle of Mons.

in the Allies' favour elsewhere however, and that same day the Germans had broken the French line further east. Massively outnumbered by the approaching enemy, the BEF was in danger of being outflanked and to the bewilderment of its men, who firmly believed they had given the Germans a bloody nose, the order to retire was given.

Chapter 2

A Hail of Death

The following day, 24 August, the two corps of the BEF began their phased withdrawal from the positions around Mons. In a fighting retreat, it would not be nearly so easy to hold back the enemy. The I Corps under General Sir Douglas Haig was able to withdraw relatively unhindered by the Germans, but General Horace Smith-Dorrien's II Corps was for a time closely pressed. Several regiments formed the rear guard, including the 1st Battalion Dorsetshire Regiment, which had been in reserve the previous day at the village of Wasmes. While it had not seen any action then, it had a distinctly trying day on 24 August. A Channel Islander serving with this battalion, Private Emile Audrain, kept a detailed diary of events in which he records:

> Aug 24th Mon. Batt[alion] comes into action at 3.15am, murderous artillery fire, enemy shells on trenches and sets fire to village, collapse of our temporary hospital, wounded taken away safe, villagers' great hospitality, 12pm order received for a gen[eral] retirement to start at noon, our machine-gun's deadly work mentioned in dispatches, transport heavily shelled whilst retiring through village 1.15pm whilst battalion was having a temporary halt sudden appearance of enemy's cavalry, transport's helplessness, Lieut Margetts wounded in shoulder, Sergt. Kelly reported killed, loss of ammunition cart and supply wagon with days rations. German artillery surrounds village, Brig Gen Count Gleichen O.C. 15th Brigade leads his men away from village at 3pm safely and retires for about 5 kils and placed in an orchard to await stragglers. Whilst in above village, portion of Head Q[uarters] placed in a position at corner of street to give the alarm if sudden appearance again of enemy's cavalry. Total casualties today about 150 killed, wounded and missing.[1]

In spite of Audrain's assertion that cavalry overran the transport, the *Official History* has it that the attackers came from *Infanterie-Regiment Graf Tauentzien von Wittenburg (3. Brandenburgisches) Nr. 20*, which had caused the British so much trouble the day previously. In the same brigade as the Dorsets were the 2nd Battalion Duke of Wellington's Regiment, holding positions in support of the Dorsets near Wasmes. The order to retire did not reach two companies of the Dukes which in company with a battery of the XXVII brigade Royal Field Artillery were attacked by six battalions of the enemy from *Infanterie-regiment Nr. 66* and *Infanterie-regiment Nr. 26*, which advanced from the opposite side of the Boussu–Quiévrain road. The Germans received

Captain T.M. Ellis, Duke of Wellington's Regiment. Cut off by the advancing enemy at Mons, he none the less made his way to the Belgian coast and from there reached England.

such a volley from the rifles and machine-guns of the Dukes, together with a hail of shrapnel from the battery, that their advance was checked. The Dukes withdrew but had suffered heavily in the skirmish, sustaining some 400 casualties. Among the officers involved in this incident was Captain T.M. Ellis, of Skipton, who had served with the Dukes since the Boer War. As the tide of war swept past them that August day, Ellis and the men with him found themselves behind German lines. Fortunately they were befriended by Belgian peasants, who gave them disguises and hid them in straw in barns during daylight hours. Conducted across country at night towards the coast, Ellis eventually embarked for England, which he reached safely. He returned to France, only to be killed later in the war.

Among those captured here was a man whose case would become a cause célèbre. He was Private William Lonsdale, in civilian life a tram driver from Leeds, who was called up as a reservist at the start of the war. He recalled afterwards:

> The beginning of it all was on August 24th 1914, when I was captured five or six miles from Mons, along with forty-seven other men of the 'Dukes'. Our captors tied our hands behind us with telegraph wire and after a good deal of searching we were taken into a church.
>
> One of our companions on the march was an old man of about seventy years of age, who lived in a house just behind the lines we held. He was quite an innocent old man, but the Germans made out that he was a spy, and when they had gone about a kilometre they paraded him in front of us, and one of the sentries walked up to him, made him kneel down and blew out his brains.[2]

Lonsdale's troubles worsened later in 1914, when in a prisoner of war camp he struck a guard in self-defence. He was tried by a military court and sentenced to death. The sentence, at first commuted, was later re-imposed. The case was taken up by the Lord Mayor of Leeds and by the United States Ambassador to Germany, and questions were asked in both Houses of Parliament about his situation. Eventually his sentence was commuted again.

Another sharp rearguard action was fought amid the slag heaps of the mining town of Frameries, in which the Germans again were roughly handled, this time by the South Lancashire and Lincolnshire Regiments, supported by the guns of 109 Battery Royal Field Artillery. Like the Dorsets, these battalions had been in reserve the previous day and were relatively fresh. With just two machine-guns each, they inflicted severe damage upon the Germans who apparently expected to find little opposition. In fact two of the British machine-guns were under the command of Lieutenant

Eric Llewelyn Welchman, 1st Battalion Lincolnshire Regiment, who set them up in defensive positions in the orchard overlooking the Jemappes–Quaregon Road. Welchman, his fellow officer Lieutenant Holmes and the machine-guns fought to the last, the 2 officers being killed and about 130 other ranks becoming casualties of one sort or another. Captain Herbert Stewart of the Army Service Corps was tasked with supplying rations to the defenders while under fire here. He wrote:

At Frameries, a small mining town about five miles south of Mons, I found my brigade very hotly engaged with greatly superior numbers. The Staff were sheltering on the lee side of some houses in a street running parallel to the German front. Up the streets pointing towards the German position the bullets were flying continuously, knocking up splashes of dust in the road or chipping brick and mortar off the sides of the houses. Overhead was the incessant crack of the shrapnel, and as fast as one group of the little white clouds, caused by the burst of the shells, dissolved into the still morning air, another group appeared. Fortunately the shells were bursting high, and so were not as dangerous as they might have been, but they brought down pieces of chimney-pot, slates, tiles, bricks, and lengths of telegraph wire, which were showered into the streets and about our ears. The continuous rattle of rifle fire, the cracks of the bursting shells, and the discharges of our own artillery, made a babel of noise which I found very distracting ... The first groups of soldiers we met were waiting in support under cover of houses and walls; later we turned down towards the barricades or hastily constructed breastworks made from the pavé torn up out of the road, and met some companies on their way to reinforce the fighting line, while others were working at a fresh line of barricades to be occupied when the advanced ones could no longer be held. To each I distributed such bread as they wanted: some were glad indeed to get the hot fresh loaves, others were too occupied or too anxious to eat, while most were still in possession of the iron ration carried by every soldier in his haversack to meet such an emergency as the present, when it is impossible or very inadvisable to bring forward the Supply Train.[3]

Hauptmann Heinrich Heubner, of *Infanterie-Regiment Nr. 20*, was present at Frameries and put a brave face on the day's events, writing of the battle:

A veritable hail of bullets greeted us as we rushed over the bank. Then we advanced by short rushes; throwing ourselves flat after each short rush we worked our way into the first line. While our artillery was hurling shells into the village and into the factories on the right we climbed the height and entered the village of Frameries from behind. Just as on the previous day, however, the English had completely vanished. They must have run at an extraordinary speed. We got into the houses through the back gardens and by breaking open doors and windows, for everything was locked and bolted; the English had even put sand-bags against the cellar windows. In order to get into the street we had to break open the front doors, and I was nearly shot by my own men in the process, for they mistook me for an Englishman trying to escape.

Three of the enemy's wounded were discovered, two of whom were able to walk, but the third had had his shin-bone shattered by a bullet and lay in great pain behind a house. As we put a first dressing on the wound he screamed in agony under our clumsy, inexperienced fingers, but nevertheless he managed to stammer his 'thank you'.

Thus ended our second day in the great battle of Maubeuge [as the Germans referred to the Battle of Mons], and again we had driven the English out of their fortified positions, although we had to attack across the open.

It is true our losses had been heavy, but so had theirs. We had discovered that the British are brave and doughty opponents, but our Army had inspired in them a tremendous respect for the force of a German attack. Captured English officers said that they had not believed it possible for us to storm across such open country.

Several of our companies had suffered very severe losses through the enemy's artillery fire and the machine-guns which the English had very cleverly placed so as to catch our troops in the flank. There was desperate street and house-to-house fighting, but the same regiment which had met the English the day before succeeded in driving them out at the left side of the village and in making many prisoners.

An incident which I witnessed characterizes the feeling of our soldiers towards the English people. A number of prisoners were being escorted past us when our men shook their clenched fists and rained down curses of the foulest kind on Tommy Atkins, who marched past erect, with his head up and a smile on his face. When, later, French prisoners were brought in, I never observed any similar outbursts of a national hate which is only too well founded.[4]

Also in action here was *Infanterie-Regiment Nr. 64*. One of its officers who was present at Frameries, Hauptmann Liebenow, wrote later from a British prisoner of war camp that:

We too encountered the old BEF first on August 24, 1914 at Frameries, and made the same experiences ... our battalion lost the adjutant, every fourth man and of three companies every lieutenant ... [The old British Army] were brilliant soldiers, 'hunted', as we say, 'with all the hounds'; we used to compare them with our old 'Schutztruppler' [Colonial troops].[5]

Its sister regiment in the German *12th Brigade* was *Infanterie-Regiment Nr. 24*, and one of the officers of this formation, Hauptmann Cordt von Brandis, later described the action from the German perspective. He paints a vivid picture of his regiment advancing into battle following their standard, which had previously been used in the Franco-Prussian War, and with their buglers playing a traditional Prussian battle song:

Our artillery is to prepare the assault ... a continuous stream of gun and howitzer shells thunder out, hurtling and howling over our heads, and bursting in dust and smoke on the edge of the village. No human beings could possibly live there. At 8am the 11 and 12 companies and the first battalion advance to the attack. We remain impatiently in reserve ... if we thought that the English had been shelled enough to be softened up for the assault we were mistaken. They met us with well-aimed fire.

'9 company move off on the right! Raise the flag!' ... At the edge of the road Major von Hugo stood up straight in the midst of the fire. 'Clear all before you, ahead of you there are three lines!'

Musketier Helmuth Schreiner, a soldier of Infanterie Regiment Nr. 24, *recuperating from wounds in late 1914. He was almost certainly a participant in the action at Frameries on 24 August 1914.*

With our flag flying we stormed out on to the sun drenched field. Far before us, 800 meters or more, lay the edge of the village. Each wave struck out across fields of stubble and clover, devoid of cover.

Right and left, as far as the eye could see, reinforcements hurried forward, with flashing bayonets, wave upon wave. Everywhere sounded the bugles: 'Kartoffelsupp – Kartoffelsupp' their incomparable, rousing attack signal.

The blazing August sun burned down on this marvellous battle scene. What worry to us were the shells, the whistles and the bangs; what did it matter that some men sank with a loud groan to the hot ground. We followed our old flag of Vionville whose shaft, at that time twice shot through, was later after inspection by the king repaired with silver bands.[6]

As the company under Von Brandis reached those in the leading waves – the first line, now lying on the edge of a clover field, whom they had been sent up to reinforce – they shouted 'Vorwärts', expecting their comrades to rise up and join them, but no one got up. There were only dead and wounded: bloody bandages, wax-like faces and cries of 'Comrade, help me!' Von Brandis continued:

Tommy seemed to have waited for the moment of the assault. He had studied our training manuals well, and all at once, when we were still in the open without cover, turned his machine-guns on, 'Like the very Devil!'

Everywhere the gunners sprayed fire over us, right and left the bullets whistled and banged. In the corn stooks they rustled, as if they were mice. Wounded who had hidden behind them, huddled together. To be in this raging fire was like a blow to the forehead, and just one dark feeling controlled us: our only thought was not to remain there any longer! Hence, officers and non-commissioned officers roared: 'March March!' For only a few minutes this dangerous fire fell upon the pale fields whose hard, sun dried crust transmitted every striking bullet like a ricochet ...

... Then I reached the heavily depleted firing line. 'Sights at 500' came the shout. 'Sights at 500?' Nevertheless, no one fired; no Englishman was to be seen, and we had learned well only to shoot at targets.

Then this hammer from the machine-guns on the edge of the village broke off suddenly. Far from the left resounded a cheer from our other battalion, over there. The attack was rolling. Further, on and on. In a few minutes the formations were organized, reserves were distributed. Then it was forwards on to Frameries.

Once more shells crashed in the edge of the village, to shatter walls and roofs, bringing a gigantic factory chimney to the ground and hitting the boiler of a steam laundry.

And our enemies? Their many bush wars had taught the veteran English soldiers cunning, and at Frameries they knew brilliantly what was the right time to make off. They played their machine-guns as the last trump card to delay us, for as long as possible, whilst they themselves disappeared.

... in all haste the company gathered. It was a sad business. Too many comrades were there no more. Our battalion alone had lost three company commanders, and in addition every second officer, and almost every third man.[7]

   Among the other notable German soldiers who took part in the attack at Frameries was Leutnant Martin Gareis, machine-gun officer of *Infanterie-regiment Nr. 24*. Born in Berlin in 1891, Gareis would rise through the ranks of the German army to become one of Hitler's generals, in the Second World War commanding troops on the Eastern Front before being captured by the British army in 1945. Also present on 24 August, albeit further to the west at Audregnies, was Leutnant Heinrich Kirchheim, serving with *Magdeburgisches Jäger-Bataillon Nr. 4*, the Magdeburg Jäger Battalion. Kirchheim was badly wounded in the battle on 24 August, but recovered and later resumed his military career. He served in the army of the Weimar Republic, ultimately becoming a general in the Afrika Korps in the Second World War. Serving alongside Kirchheim in the Magdeburg Jägers on 24 August was another officer who would rise to prominence in the Third Reich: future Waffen SS General Wilhelm Bittrich, who would fight the British at Arnhem; in 1914 holding the junior officer's rank of *fahnrich* or ensign. Facing Kirchheim and Bittrich at Audregnies that day was the 1st Battalion the

*Oberst Kurt von Klufer
of* Infanterie Regiment
Nr. 24.

Cheshire Regiment; it made an epic stand there, which has entered regimental folklore. The war diary of the battalion for that day, compiled by Captain J.L. Shore, states:

At 3 a.m. 'C' & 'D' Coys rejoined 'A' & 'B' Coys

At 8 a.m. The Manchester Regt. relieved us.

At 10 a.m. The Battalion marched to Dour Station arriving there at 11.45 a.m.

11.45 a.m. The G.O.C. 5th Division gave Col Ballard, Norfolk Regt, orders to take the Cheshire Regt, Norfolk Regt and 119th Battery and take up a position N. West along the Elouges–Audregnies road and act as a flank guard to the Manchesters and the troops entrenched round Wasmes in their retirement.

1.00 p.m. In position Norfolk right on the Railway Embankment. Cheshire right on the 4th Kilo stone. 'D' Coy Cheshire left, 'D' Coy holding the village of Audregnies – Order of Coys 'B', 'A', 'C' 'D'. Masses of the enemy were seen moving out of Quievrain and their artillery and machine-guns opened a very hot fire on the Infantry and Cavalry and R.H.A. who were operating against the German Cavalry in the valley 1 ¼ miles to the S.E. of Quievrain.

2.30 p.m. I am informed Col Ballard gave orders for all troops to retire in an Easterly direction – these orders never reached the 2 front platoons of 'D' Coy under command of Capt W.S. Rich, who held on to the position he had reached in front of the line till 4 p.m. by which hour all troops had retired. Lieut W. G. R. Elliot behaved with great gallantry in returning during the retirement and carrying

away a wounded man under intensely hot fire, he being shot through ankles when within 3 yards of the sunken road to which he eventually took this man – Lt Elliot was left on the field (witness Corporal Oford, 1/Cheshire Regt).

4.45 p.m. About 100 men were collected in Athis.

1.00 a.m. At roll call in Bivouac at Les Bavay there were 6 Officers, a Warrant Officer and 199 men – The strength marching out at 7.30 a.m. on the morning of 24th inst was 27 Officers, 1 Warrant Officer and 933 men – A loss of 78% most of which was caused in the withdrawal.[8]

General Heinrich Kirchheim. On 24 August, as a young lieutenant with the 4th Magdeburg Jaeger Battalion, he was badly wounded at Audregnies; in later life he became a senior officer in the Afrika Korps.

The two platoons holding out under Captain Rich were eventually surrounded by soldiers of *4. Thüringisches Infanterie-Regiment Nr. 72.* The battalion had never the less held an entire German army corps at bay, thus enabling other elements of the BEF to begin to retreat. Having suffered almost 800 killed, wounded and missing for the time being it had effectively ceased to exist as a fighting formation, and among the Cheshire captives was a private soldier from Middlewich, named David Maddock. Like many other men in the BEF that summer, he was a reservist, recalled to the Colours upon the outbreak of war. He had enlisted in May 1904, and had served abroad at Secunderabad, India. His service record shows that he was wounded by a gunshot to the thigh on 24 August 1914, but was not made prisoner by the Germans until 2 September. Following the action at Audregnies, many of the wounded were left on the field, lying out overnight with no medical attention until local civilians came to their assistance.

Private David Maddock, of the 1st Battalion Cheshire Regiment. He was wounded in the thigh on 24 August 1914, during the epic action at Audregnies when the Cheshires sacrificed themselves.

The wounded were then taken to ad hoc hospitals, and many of the injured Cheshires found themselves at the Convent of Wiheries. It was some days before the Germans located these impromptu medical centres and placed them and their wounded occupants under guard. Maddock was probably among these men, and he was to spend the remainder of the war as a prisoner.

Nearby, at Elouges, two cavalry regiments, the 4th Royal Irish Dragoon Guards and the 9th Lancers made a heroic charge, in an attempt to halt the German advance and buy the Cheshires some time. Second Lieutenant Roger Chance was a subaltern with the 4th and recalled the exhilaration and adrenaline of the action:

> C squadron went to the left at the forward gallop to seize some cottages ... We formed Column of Troops at the gallop, drawn swords, I rode at the head of my troop with my troop sergeant (a remarkable man) beside me ... the harvest was just over, and this was open country, a field in which the corn was in stooks. We went full gallop down a dusty road into this field. I wasn't aware of it but there were artillery shells bursting on us, and a certain amount of rifle fire, but I never saw a German! There were some hidden behind the stooks no doubt. The first thing that happened when we went at full gallop was that my troop sergeant beside me had his horse shot dead from under him, he turned a full somersault and I thought that was him gone, though he turned up later on a loose horse, but we galloped on ... I can clearly remember a railway line going over a cutting, over a bridge, and I saw loose horses going at full gallop over that ... but I'd got my troop more or less intact, and the squadron then slowly withdrew.[9]

One of the members of the 9th Lancers was Trooper Harry Easton from Canterbury. He had enlisted in the regiment in 1906, and was thus like most of his fellow troopers a highly competent horseman, but he remembered many years later that one of the finest cavalry regiments in Europe was brought to a halt not by enemy fire but by the novel feature of a barbed wire fence, and that the lancers galloped up and down the length of it like rabbits, unsure of what to do next. Enemy fire was intense, and Easton's horse fell under him. Even after seventy-five years his memory of the events was vivid:

> We moved off under the late Sir David Campbell who gave the order 'Form Line of Squadrons'. B Squadron on extreme right of the Regiment. On our right was one squadron of 18th Hussars, swords drawn, and on our left was one squadron 4th Royal Irish Dragoons [sic]. I remember very distinctly seeing the whole line at a hand canter ... during this time the German artillery opened up and shrapnel was bursting overhead but they could not keep the trajectory of fire, it was always bursting overhead or behind. By this time about one or two hundred yards [on we] found ourselves confronted with a huge brick yard surrounded by a 12 foot high barbed wire fence. We were in to it very close when my horse fell and threw me – I'm not sure whether she had been hit or had stumbled although the ground I remember was flat, slightly downhill & a small bump here & there. The CO signalled 'Troops Right Wheel' but it was not possible because we were in total confusion. There was no room left in front for such a move to be made by mounted men. There was a terrible mix up of Hussars and Lancers trying to

Corporal Harry Easton, 9th Lancers, taken prisoner of war on 24 August 1914.
(Liddle Collection; reproduced with the permission of Leeds University Library)

extricate themselves. [There were] men, like myself who were dismounted, [who] had had their mounts shot from under them . . . I lay where I had fallen simply on account of heavy supporting fire from the Cheshire Regt who were covering our advance, which was abruptly brought to a halt by this barbed wire fence.[10]

A third account of this charge exists, in the form of a letter written home afterwards by a corporal of the 9th Lancers. It reads:

We rode absolutely into death, and the colonel told us that onlookers never expected a single Lancer to come back. About 400 charged and 72 rallied afterwards, but during the week 200 more turned up wounded and otherwise. You see, the infantry of ours were in a fix and no guns but four could be got round, so the General ordered two squadrons of the 9th to charge, as a sacrifice, to save the position. The order was given, but not only did A and B gallop into line, but C squadron also wheeled and came up with a roar. It was magnificent, but horrible. The regiment was swept away before 1,000 yards was covered, and at 200 yards from the guns I was practically alone – myself, three privates, and an officer of our squadron. We wheeled to a flank on the colonel's signal and rode back. I was mad with rage, a feeling I cannot describe. But we had drawn their fire; the infantry were saved.[11]

Trooper Jack Linder, 9th Lancers, killed in action on 24 August 1914 during the lancers' epic charge at Audregnies. (Robert Cull)

Meanwhile, the now rapidly advancing Germans soon picked up the unhorsed Harry Easton. He remembered:

I was made to advance in the front line with the German infantry, [my guard] firing his rifle from the right hip while having frequent nips from his water bottle in his left hand which I learned later contained wine (I was not offered any).

We had not gone very far before an odd cavalryman was picked up and a little further on we came across very many dead and a few sitting up, wounded – I recognised their cap badges as The Cheshire Regiment. Quite a lot of them were lying prone, having been shot and fallen on their rifles. Some, too, were face upwards – 'spreadeagled', not a pretty sight. We marched across country all the way till night began to fall and from what I can remember, and there were many of us too, we were ready to drop. We were fed at the same time and the same food as our captors – I was escorted by two infantrymen to a mobile cooker and was given a large bucket full of stew. I had gone a few yards with this towards a place where there were German infantry and officers and British prisoners, of cavalry and infantry, when a German soldier took my bucket of stew. Within minutes I had found [a] German officer ... and told him about the stew – he took me back and I recognised the German soldier who still had the bucket. Without any preamble the officer knocked down the German soldier, kicked him up and made him hand over the bucket of stew to me.[12]

Before the day was out, more bravery would be shown by the 9th Lancers, when a party under the command of Captain Francis Grenfell came to the assistance of 119 Battery RFA, which having gallantly kept the heads of the enemy down for most of the day, now found itself closely pressed by three German batteries and a machine-gun. One section of guns was safely recovered but four remained to be withdrawn, and Grenfell, whose exploits earlier on 24 August would result in the award of the Victoria Cross, led his men up to the guns to help extract them. He wrote afterwards:

It was our good fortune to be thrown by Providence (after a good hard fight which threw us into complete confusion) behind a railway embankment, near the 119th Battery. They were occasionally firing and then, I believe, stopped. The brave way the two officers there behaved, and the dignified way the guns, still challenging, remained there, filled me with an admiration which I know will last a lifetime. No English regiment could have stood by without saying 'Can we give you a hand?' Had the senior officer done so he would not have been an English-man. What we did was forced on us by the splendid example of the Battery, which had been set them by their two officers.[13]

On the eastern flank of the BEF line, a stand was also made at Harmignies on 24 August. One of the battalions involved was the 1st King's Liverpool Regiment. Private James Walter Comaish was another reservist, who had served in India prior to the war, and who had rejoined the Liverpools upon the outbreak of hostilities. In a newspaper interview afterwards he recalled the events of that hot August day:

We had just got nearly finished digging when just before daybreak a further retreat was ordered. We went back about another mile, where we were supplied with some biscuits and tea, and 'bully'. As we were eating the Germans commenced to shell the trenches we had left. They kept bombarding the empty trenches for six hours, while we lay out behind them in extended order. After the bombardment, the German infantry charged, and we let them get nearly up to the empty trenches, when our artillery and infantry went for them. The Germans charged in close order and we cut them up terribly and drove them back. They did not seem to care for the loss of life, and as soon as a gap was made, others filled it. The fighting continued all the Monday and we gradually retired. During the fight word came that the Germans were advancing in very strong force over a hill right in front of our position and soon after they came in swarms. When they got well into our view our artillery got at them, and we could see from where we were lying heads and legs flying in all directions. It was awful. Large gaps were torn in the German ranks, but on they came. I noticed that the German officers never lead their men like ours do, but keep at the back.[14]

By 25 August the strain of the fighting retreat was beginning to make itself felt. The sweltering heat, shortage of food and water and the effort of marching along uneven pavé roads took its toll on many British soldiers. In numerous cases these men were reservists who had been in sedentary occupations just a few weeks previously. Gunner John Trusty from Sunderland was serving with a Royal Field Artillery 4.5in howitzer battery on the Retreat. He remembered:

The roads were crowded with refugees. Old men and young people there, pushing their prams and beds ... I remember there ... we were feeling hungry and we saw a French farmer and he told us to come and help ourselves to his sheep. There were several of us there who got hold of sheep and we slaughtered them ourselves ... of course we had our iron rations, but we weren't allowed to eat them without being ordered to do so, and we mostly relied upon what we could get from the French people or what we could pick up in the fields and it did very often happen that we could get carrots, turnips and onions and we used to very often make a stew ourselves, which was a very simple thing to do but with regards to meat we saw very little of it, with the exception of bully beef, and there wasn't any bread of any description. It was all biscuits ... whilst on the road ... we saw a large number of infantrymen going in front of us without any equipment at all. The heat was so intense, they threw away their equipment and it was a pitiful sight to see these young chaps ...[15]

Corbett-Smith also paints a graphic portrait of the state of the retreating BEF on 25 August:

And now the vanguard of the retiring army begins to stream in and through – all arms, all regiments. Overhead a flight of aeroplanes circle, like homing pigeons, seeking where they may alight. It is incredible that these are the regiments which a little ten days ago swung gaily down the Aldershot roads.

... Here marches a battalion of the Guards. Two days ago it went into action perhaps 1,100 strong ... At the head there paces slowly an ammunition mule. On it, wearing a peasant's slouch hat, with breeches cut off above the knees, and with left arm held close by a rough bandage, there rides the colonel. Count the men as they march past in fours: 80, 120, 160, 180, 220. No, that is the next regiment you are counting in. Just 200! That is the tale of them.

Blackened by dust and powder, bearded, breeches cut short like those of their commanding officer, the few puttees that are left to them wrapped round their feet for boots, otherwise bits of sacking or cloth, bloody bandages round heads or arms, some with hats like the colonel's, most with none at all slowly they limp by. And, as they pass, the A.S.C. drivers silently offer such biscuits or bread as they have. God, how they wolf the food!

The colonel turns round on his 'charger', and in a hoarse shout:

'Battalion! 'Tention! Pull yourselves together lads; a French village!'

Ah, the pride of them! The glory of race and blood! This is not the Mons country, with its blood-soaked memories; 'tis the Horse Guards Parade, and we're Trooping the Colour!

The click of rifles coming to the slope runs down the ranks. The fours line by magic as the men straighten themselves; it is a new regiment, marching into action, which the French villagers see pass before them.[16]

In the evening of 25 August the town of Landrecies was to become the scene of an epic stand by the 3rd Battalion Coldstream Guards. The rearguard action here was fought largely in darkness, with the protagonists illuminated by the fires of burning houses. The main street of the town was the epicentre of this clash of arms. One of the survivors of the Coldstream, Guardsman George Gilliam, wrote afterwards:

It was about eight o'clock when some of us woke, and after a smoke were off to sleep again, but not for long, for almost immediately we heard the sound of a motor-cycle, and knew that the rider was travelling at a terrific rate.

Nearer and nearer came the sound, and the rider himself swept round the corner of the street. He never stopped nor slackened speed; he simply shouted one word as he vanished, and that was 'Germans!' Only one word, but enough. Rifles in hand, we rushed to the top of the street and lined the three cross-roads, lying down. Our officer, who was standing up behind us, said, 'Lie still, men'; and we did perfectly still, not a man moving. All at once, out of the darkness, an officer came and cried in English to our commander, 'Surrender!' 'We don't surrender here!' our officer answered. 'Take that!' and instantly shot him through the head with his revolver.

Our officer's shot had scarcely died away when crash went a German artillery gun, and a lyddite shell burst right over us. This was our first experience of lyddite, and the fumes nearly choked us. 'Lie still, boys don't move!' said our officer; and we lay low ... Shells now came upon us rapidly, wounding several of our men; but our maxim gunners had got to work, and very soon enormous numbers of Germans were put beyond the power of doing any further mischief.

An artist's impression of the bitter hand-to-hand fighting at Landrecies.

Many splendid things were done that night at Landrecies; but there was nothing finer than the work of our maxim-gunner Robson, who was on our left. Our machine-guns were by now at our end of the town, and they had a solid mass of Germans to go at. Robson was sitting on his stool, and as soon as the officer ordered 'Fire!' his maxim hailed death. It literally was a hail of fire that met the packed Germans, and swept down the head of the column, so that the street was choked in an instant with the German dead. Those who lived behind pushed on in desperation shoved on by the masses still further behind, the darkness being made light by the fire of the maxims and the enemy's rifles. Those behind, I say, pressed on, with fearful cries, but only to be mown down and shattered, so that the street became more than ever glutted with the dead and wounded. The Germans were thrown into frenzy, and if sheer weight of men could have driven the head of the column on to us not a British soldier could have lived that night at Landrecies.[17]

Private Whittaker, of this battalion, also described the action:

The Germans rushed at us like a crowd streaming from a Cup-tie at the Crystal Palace. You could not miss them. Our bullets ploughed into them, but still on they came. I was well entrenched, and my rifle got so hot I could hardly hold it. I was wondering if I should have enough bullets, when a pal shouted, 'Up Guards and at 'em.' The next second he was rolled over with a nasty knock on the shoulder. When we really did get orders to get at them we made no mistakes, I can tell you. They cringed at the bayonets. Those on the left wing tried to get round us. We yelled like demons, and racing as hard as we could for quite 500 yards we cut up nearly every man who did not run away.[18]

Reverend Benjamin O'Rorke, a padre with the Guards, ministered to the wounded aristocratic officers he found in a temporary hospital in the wake of the battle:

We at once made for the building which served as a hospital, where a mournful sight awaited us. The bodies of six or seven who had been killed were lying on stretchers, reverently covered over with blankets, in a quiet corner of the compound. Inside the building wounded men lay on beds and stretchers in every available space in the hall, the passages, and the rooms. As we entered at the gate one or two ambulances, under the direction of Major Falkner, were carrying away such of the wounded as were fit to be removed; and they were fortunate enough to get away from the town before it was occupied by the Germans. Part of the 19th Field Ambulance, with Major W. B. Fry, Major J. J. Fumess, Captain W. Beaman, and Lieut. A. B. Preston, had been in the town all night, and these medical officers were now busily engaged in dressing wounds and performing operations. I went at once in search of the Hon. Rupert Keppel ... He was in an upstairs room with five or six wounded men. He was lying on a bed with a bandage round his forehead, but made light of the wounds which he had received. After a few words and a short prayer at each bedside, I made inquiries for Lord Hawarden. I was told that he was already dead, but I found him in a little room by himself, still breathing although apparently unconscious. He had lost his left arm, and a portion of his back had been shot away ... The other poor patients were terribly knocked about. Limbs in some cases had been entirely blown off by shells. Lyddite had turned many complexions to a jaundiced yellow. And yet every man was calm and resigned, and proud to have had a share in the fight.[19]

A British medical officer, Captain Sutcliffe, remained behind with the wounded when the Germans occupied the town, and was given permission by them to search for further casualties. His vivid description of Landrecies in the aftermath of the fighting was written shortly afterwards, while the impression was clearly still strong in his mind:

We went on up the street, right to the end. The sight there I shall never forget. From the bridge all the way up we had been treading on cartridges, but here there were literally tens of thousands lying about. Ammunition boxes with the lids torn off and only a dozen cartridges taken, canvas bandoliers full, broken rifles, pieces of equipment, packs, entrenching tools, and broken bayonets – and the dead! At first these were mostly in the left hedge, but just as we got to the open country there were twenty, all in twelve yards of road. They lay in all sorts of attitudes, just as they had died, arms half-extended and fists clenched. The injuries were awful. One man had five holes through his Pay Book in his breast-pocket. They had used thousands of cartridges which were lying around them. We found twenty-four dead altogether, all Coldstream except one French peasant. I went up the road and found a good many German kits in the ditch, and about 200 yards away the bodies of several horses. The road was bordered by poplars, and up to a height of about twenty feet the stems were riddled with rifle fire. Just beyond the houses was a pile of German field-gun cartridges, and some German spades very long and narrow in the blade. The German trenches were littered with bottles; apparently the German soldier had had a couple of bottles of wine to keep up his spirits in the trench. The red brick wall about 100 yards from the top of the road had been loopholed, and they had even put in rough seats behind ... The house behind the wall was spattered with bullets, and so was the wall itself. The people of the house were indoors, looking very white and scared, and a large dog in the garden was utterly cowed. At the back we found two German graves, which accounted for thirty of them, their names being written up in indelible pencil on wooden crosses. We lowered the dead into the long grave which we had dug, and the Padre read the burial service. I made a rough cross about six feet by two feet out of some palings, and after putting it up we filled in the grave and marched back to hospital. It should be added that we found three bodies of German soldiers which had been overlooked by their friends. We gave them the same funeral rites as to our own comrades, and marked the place with a cross inscribed with their names.[20]

About 3 miles to the south-west, another smaller drama was played out on 25 August. A soldier of the Dorsetshire Regiment, the Jerseyman by the name of Audrain, recorded in his diary a curious and oddly incongruous task which he was required to perform:

> Sent at 12pm by Lt Col Bols DSO CO of Batt[alion] to Ors to fetch drums, flutes etc which had been left there on the advance and to have them conveyed as far back as Le Cateau where I was to meet the Batt[alion]. Rapid advance of enemy, arrived at Le Cateau about 3pm on Hospital Train. No signs of Batt[alion] so took drums back as far as Busigny, proceeded to Engineers Headquarters to report and advised to take drums back to St Quentin, arriving there about 10.30pm.[21]

One could easily be forgiven for questioning the idea of a battalion of infantry taking its drums and flutes into a theatre of war in the first place, let alone a commanding officer, who at this most critical time, dispatched some of his men to make sure that they did not fall into enemy hands! The drums and flutes of the Dorsets however were not the only link with the past; the following day, 26 August, was the anniversary of the Battle of Crécy in 1346. The weather that

Sergeant Emile Audrain, 1st Battalion Dorsetshire Regiment. He was sent to fetch the battalion drums as the retreat began.
(Dorchester Military Museum)

morning was hot and misty, much as it had been 850 years earlier. The similarities did not end there, for once again a small force found itself in a desperate situation, faced by a numerically superior and confident foe. The majority of the men of the BEF who had reached Le Cateau on the night of 25 August were exhausted, and although the original intention had been for them to continue to retire, in the early hours of 26 August General Smith-Dorrien's headquarters issued an order to them instead to stand their ground.

The two corps of the BEF had now lost touch with each other – only a thin cavalry screen covered the gap between them – and Smith-Dorrien's II Corps alone would fight the ensuing battle. One of the most famous memoirs of First World War service is that of Frank Richards, published in 1933 as *Old Soldiers Never Die*. Richards' battalion, the 2nd Royal Welsh Fusiliers, had been behind the front line on 23 August and had seen no action that day. Instead of continuing their advance however they had swung abruptly about and began marching for two days south-west, away from the enemy. Richards wrote:

> We reservists fetched straight out of civil life were suffering the worst on this non-stop march, which would have been exhausting enough if we had not been carrying fifty pounds weight or so of stuff on our backs. And yet these two days and nights were only the start of our troubles.
>
> We arrived in Le Cateau about midnight [25 August], dead-beat to the world. I don't believe that any one of us at this time realised that we were retiring, though it was clear that we were not going in the direction of Germany. Of course the officers knew, but they were telling us that we were drawing the enemy into a trap. Le Cateau that night presented a strange sight. Everyone was in a panic, packing up their stuff on carts and barrows to get away south in time. The Royal Welch camped on the square in the centre of the town. We were told to get as much rest as we could. The majority sank down where they were and fell straight asleep ... I slept the sleep of the just that night for about three hours, though I could have done with forty-three, but we were roused up at 4am and ordered to leave our packs and greatcoats on the square.
>
> Everyone was glad when that order was issued; the only things we had to carry now, besides rifle and ammunition, were an extra pair of socks and our iron rations which consisted of four army biscuits, a pound tin of bully beef, and a small quantity of tea and sugar. Iron rations were carried in case of emergency but were never supposed to be used unless orders came from our superior officers. Haversacks were now strapped on our shoulders and each man was issued with another fifty rounds of ammunition, which made two hundred and fifty rounds to carry.[22]

The contrast between the Mons battlefield and the countryside that was about to bear witness to the Battle of Le Cateau could not have been greater. Unlike the sprawling industrial townships of the Mons salient, the country around Le Cateau was predominantly rural; it was characterised by open rolling fields, and agricultural land which offered wide open fields of view – and of fire. Only the town itself sat in the steep

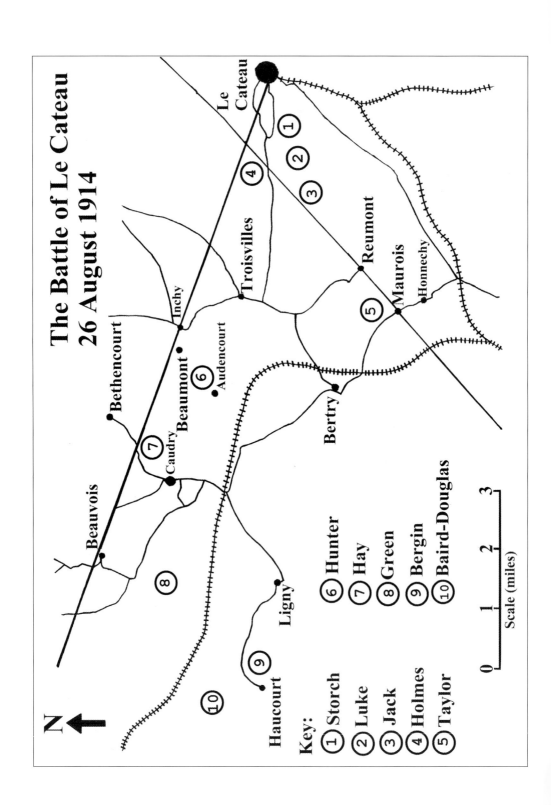

The Battle of Le Cateau
26 August 1914

N

Le Cateau

Beauvois

Bethencourt

Inchy

Caudry

Beaumont

Audencourt

Troisvilles

Reumont

Maurois

Honnechy

Bertry

Ligny

Haucourt

Key:
① Storch
② Luke
③ Jack
④ Holmes
⑤ Taylor
⑥ Hunter
⑦ Hay
⑧ Green
⑨ Bergin
⑩ Baird-Douglas

Scale (miles)

0   1   2   3

valley of the River Selle running roughly north-south. Lieutenant Cecil Brownlow served with a Brigade Ammunition Column of the Royal Field Artillery. His unit had already begun retiring early that morning, when they were abruptly halted:

> A mile or so farther on, drawn up in a field by a cross-roads, we met the Divisional Ammunition Column, and as we required ammunition we took the opportunity to replenish our wagons. While the long line of vehicles were halted along the road, and while the gunners, sweltering in the heat, stowed away round after round of shrapnel, a motor-car swung round a bend of the road and drew up with a shriek of brakes.
>
> A Staff Officer of the Division got out, and, approaching the Captain, said, 'You must return at once and at top speed. We are not retiring to-day according to the original orders. It has been decided to stand and fight.'
>
> Nosebags were whipped off the horses' heads, limber lids were shut with a clang, amid curses and imprecations the wagons were reversed on the road, and, with every vehicle bumping and rattling, we trotted as fast as we could towards the sound of the guns, which every moment grew louder and louder. Owing to the distance we had to go and to the exhaustion of the horses, it was necessary to march by alternate periods of trotting and walking, but even so the horses were soon black with sweat and flecked with foam ... When we reached the village of Clary, the Captain sent me forward to see if I could discover the whereabouts of the batteries of the Brigade, for, having left them early in the morning, we had no idea of their present positions. The noise of firing had increased until the crash of guns and the explosions of bursting shell combined to form a deep throbbing volume of sound which rolled back and forth across the battlefield and beat monotonously on the senses. Topping the crest of a rise the whole scene of the struggle was suddenly spread in panorama before me.
>
> In the foreground, tucked in a hollow, was the little village of Montigny, from whose church tower hung a Red Cross flag; beyond, the ground rose in a low ridge or swell of land on which were the villages of Beauvois, Caudry, Audencourt, Beaumont, with the tops of the houses of Troisvilles showing on the right. Just behind these villages, running clean across the landscape and shutting out all further view, was the avenue of pollarded trees which marked the Cambrai Road and which looked like a gigantic green ruler, lying athwart the countryside.
>
> The infantry were hastily entrenched along a line which connected up these villages and which was roughly parallel to and about a thousand yards from the great road. The crest of the ridge, however, hid them from my view; but, though the infantry were invisible, I could see our artillery, who presented a grand spectacle. On the southern slopes of the ridge, some fully and some partially concealed from the enemy, our batteries stretched in an irregular line from right to left. The guns and wagons and detachments stood dark and distinct, though diminished through distance to minute weapons and tiny figures. Every gun was firing, and countless flashes of light scintillated against the gold and green sweep of country. The whole of the scene was flecked with the white and yellow smoke clouds of enemy shrapnel and high explosive, the nearer of which appeared

tongued with cruel yellow flames. I could see the bursting shell smashing and crumpling the villages, sweeping the batteries with a hail of death and searching the valleys and hidden approaches.

And all the while the thunder of the guns rolled and reverberated in deep-toned waves of sound which spread and spread in ever-growing circles, striking the ear of many a distant listener and making him wonder what that sinister noise might forebode.[23]

On the right-hand portion of the II Corps line, the battle was characterised to some extent by confusion – orders to stand and fight had been issued late in the day, and had not reached the 5th Division, which was expecting to move off when the German attack upon it began at 6am. Under cover of mist and the steep sides of the Selle valley, German troops had penetrated Le Cateau and emerged from the town to attack its leading formations, which had no time to prepare positions or indeed to choose ground. Among the German soldiers of *Infanterie-Regiment Nr. 27* in action here was a reservist named Karl Storch, a book dealer in civilian life. He recalled some weeks later:

Next day, at the crack of dawn, we left our billet … my friend and I exchanged a brief and hearty handshake, and we each moved off on our way … Surrounded, we held the 'Tommies' in an iron grip; stubbornly they fought their weapons, but their trenches had become graves for them.

One always looks during such important times for some memento, by means of which in later times the events are more clearly recalled. So it was with me. There lay the paybook of an Englishman: 'Soldiers Small Book. Alfred Stratton, Corps Middlesex' was written on it. I took this with me. Maybe someone will take it carefully from my trunk in 50 or 100 years, and say, 'this was brought home from the Battle of Saint Quentin, by my dear great great uncle, what times they must have been!'

… the fighting lasted until the evening; English Lydite shells crashed and exploded violently, whilst Dum-Dum bullets whistled and sang as they flew past us, too close for comfort, and many more good German men-folk covered the ground. Finally, darkness brought the fighting to a peremptory halt, but not our legs, these fought on as they marched until midnight.[24]

Musketier Karl Storch, a German soldier with Infanterie-Regiment Nr. 27. *A book dealer in civilian life, he acknowledged the brutalising effects of war.*

German troops of *Infanterie-Regiment Nr. 66* and *Infanterie-Regiment Nr. 26* swept down upon the Roman road leading towards Beauvois, which marked the front line of the 5th division. Among those formations that bore the brunt of the attack here were the 2nd Battalion Suffolk Regiment and 2nd Battalion King's Own Yorkshire Light Infantry (KOYLI). Despite the odds being heavily against them, both battalions fought bravely. Corporal Frederick Holmes of the KOYLI was also to find glory that day. He remembered:

> There were some coal-pit hills in front of us and the Germans advanced over them in thousands. That was about eleven o'clock in the morning, and the firing began in real earnest again.
>
> The Germans by this time were full of furious hope and reckless courage, because they believed that they had got us on the run and that it was merely a question of hours before we were wiped out of their way. Their blood was properly up, and so was ours, and I think we were a great deal hotter than they were, though we were heavily outnumbered. We hadn't the same opinion of German soldiers that the Germans had, and as they rushed on towards us we opened a fire from the trenches that simply destroyed them.
>
> Some brave deeds were done and some awful sights were seen on the top of the coal-pits. A company of Germans were on one of the tops and an officer and about a dozen men of the 'Koylis' went round one side of the pit and tried to get at them. Just as they reached the back of the pit the German artillery opened fire on the lot, Germans and all, that was one of their tricks. They would rather sacrifice some of their own men themselves than let any of ours escape and they lost many in settling their account with the handful of Englishmen who had rushed behind the pit at a whole company of Germans.
>
> Hereabouts, at the pits, the machine-gun fire on both sides was particularly deadly. Lieutenant Pepys, who was in charge of the machine-gun of our section, was killed by shots from German machine-guns, and when we went away we picked him up and carried him with us on the machine-gun limber until we buried him outside a little village in a colliery district.
>
> He was a very nice gentleman and the first officer to go down. When he fell Lieutenant N. B. Dennison, the brigade machine-gun officer, took charge. He volunteered to take over the gun, and was either killed or wounded. Then Lieutenant Unett, the well-known gentleman jockey, crawled on his stomach to the first line of the trenches, with some men, dragging a machine-gun behind them. They got this gun into the very front of the line of the trenches, then opened fire on the Germans with disastrous effect. Lieutenant Unett was wounded and lay in the open all the time.
>
> This gallant deed was done between twelve noon and one o'clock, and I was one of the few men who saw it. I am glad to be able to pay my humble tribute to it.[25]

Holmes and his battalion began to retire piecemeal, but in the process he was to earn the Victoria Cross for his own remarkable feat of double gallantry. Not content with carrying a badly wounded man to the rear, he returned to the forward positions afterwards and assisted in the recovery of an abandoned field gun from under the noses of the advancing Germans. Not more than about 800yd away was another soon-to-be hero, Driver Fred Luke. He was serving with the 37th Battery Royal Field Artillery, which was equipped with 4.5in howitzers. His battery was camped just outside Le Cateau on the night of 25/26 August. They were fully expecting to continue the retreat the next day, but he recalled:

> At about 3am on 26th August we were aroused and told that we were moving on and going into action. The Battery (37th) with the rest of the brigade moved into a cornfield between 3 & 4am, 26th and took up gun positions while the Battery staff went forward to observing positions. The battery opened fire at about 4am onto the German gun positions. We were soon to come under heavy German gun fire [and this] was causing some heavy casualties among gunners and horses. This was so heavy that the drivers with their teams of horses had to move further to the rear. We did this but we were still getting severe casualties among horses. At about 3pm we had orders to bring our own guns out of position. Owing to casualties among the horses we could only get back with four guns out of the six – these four were taken to the rear at a safe distance. It was here that Captain Reynolds called for volunteers to go back to try to rescue the other two guns. Along with [Drivers] Drain and Coby and myself we volunteered to go back along with one other team. We walked the horses and limbers along the road to the guns. As we reached to within 300 yards we started to gallop to limber up. The Germans who were by this time only 100 yards away opened fire by machine-gun and rifle fire as soon as they saw what we were after. One team of horses were shot down, but our team managed to come through with only Driver Coby being killed and a few flesh wounds on some horses and bullet holes in gun wheels – we were congratulated on our effort by G.O.C. Royal artillery who had seen us going up.[26]

Waves of German infantry advance across a French cornfield, August 1914. A vision like that which confronted the British Tommies at Le Cateau.

In fact it was Driver Luke's skill in galloping his team into precisely the right position behind the gun that allowed it to be limbered up, and extracted literally from under the noses of the Germans. For his daring actions on this occasion he was awarded the Victoria Cross. Overall much heroism was shown by the gunners and drivers of the Royal Field Artillery in this part of the battlefield. The batteries were practically in the front line, and extraordinary efforts were made to save their guns from falling into enemy hands. The teams of the 11th and 6th Batteries displayed great bravery in riding forward to extract as many of their guns as possible, though several were shot down in the attempt. Driver H.J. King of the 6th Battery was awarded the Distinguished Conduct Medal for his actions here, the citation reading, 'At Audencourt, on 26th August, when the limber was upset, he helped to hook into another limber and brought a gun away under heavy fire.'[27]

Likewise those of the 122nd Battery managed to save two, whilst the 121st and 123rd Batteries lost all their guns – so exposed were they that it was all their gunners could do to remove the breech blocks before abandoning them. In all,

Corporal Frederick Holmes, King's Own Yorkshire Light Infantry, who was awarded the Victoria Cross for his heroism on 26 August 1914.

Driver Fred Luke, awarded the Victoria Cross for his bravery in saving guns at Le Cateau.
(Liddle Collection; reproduced with the permission of Leeds University Library)

twenty-five guns and one howitzer were lost on this part of the field, but given the dangers involved it is astonishing that any were saved at all.

Towards the centre of the battlefield, facing the village of Beaumont, stood the 2nd Battalion Royal Scots. Such was the desperate nature of the fighting retreat, that sometimes even senior officers who were wounded were abandoned to the mercies of the enemy. On the morning of 26 August, Colonel McMicking DSO, commanding the battalion, was hit in the shoulder while directing operations from a trench near the village of Audencourt. He was taken to a temporary hospital, and when that was shelled by the Germans, to the church. This was then set alight by the enemy's shells, and as the colonel was moved outside he was wounded again in the leg. At this point the brigade was ordered to retire, and the wounded had to be left. Colonel McMicking was not picked up by the German medical orderlies until the next day, and was wounded again as he lay helpless. Private Thomas Hunter of the Royal Scots recorded his own experiences that day:

> We held our ground at Le Cateau from an early hour in the morning till half-past four in the afternoon, a terrific fire pouring in on us all the time. The shells dropped on us like rain, many of them bursting in the trenches around. 'C' Company of The Royal Scots got the worst of it there, the shrapnel causing terrible havoc among them. The transport we had was completely destroyed. It was stationed in a farmyard – many wagons containing ammunition and provisions – and when the Germans got the range of it, it was absolutely wiped out, many of the horses being killed, and the wagons being blown into the air like matchwood ... Twelve o'clock came and no reinforcements, and five o'clock came and still no reinforcements. Half an hour later the order to retire was given. We got the order all right, but it did not reach all, unfortunately, and many held on. So we began the never-to-be-forgotten retreat, with shells and bullets flying about everywhere. We got into Audencourt. When we got between a church and a farmhouse we came across two women and a child. Pipe-Major Duff said he would stay behind and look after them. This he did, and we saw no more of them. Our Adjutant, Captain Price, who was one of the finest and most popular of the officers, said to us, 'Keep your heads, men. There are no marked men here. If the bullets are going to hit you they will hit you.' The Gordons, Royal Irish and 2nd Royal Scots were all together on the retreat, falling back steadily. On each side of the road lay wounded horses and men. Nothing could be done for them, as the ambulances could not get near them for the shell fire. When we had got back one and a half miles an artillery battery sergeant-major came running over and said to our commanding officer, 'For God's sake, give us some men to take our guns out of action, all the gunners are killed.' The Germans were reported to be coming on. Just as we were going to fire on the troops advancing, as we thought, to take the guns, we found they were some of our own men. Three of the guns were taken away out of the open, when we got the order to keep on retiring. So we kept on, and that night we slept by the side of the road. Heavy rain began to fall at four o'clock next morning, which did not make matters any more comfortable for us.[28]

Holding the line adjacent to the Royal Scots were the Gordon Highlanders, of whom Malcolm Hay was busy directing the fire of his men on to German targets:

German troops, debouching from the little wood ... now advanced across the stubble field on top of the hill, moving to their left flank across our front. My glasses showed they were extended to not more than two paces, keeping a very bad line, evidently very weary and marching in the hot sun with manifest disgust. The command, 'Five rounds rapid at the stubble field 900 yards', produced a cinematographic picture in my field-glasses. The Germans hopped into cover like rabbits. Some threw themselves flat behind the corn stocks, and when the firing ceased got up and bolted back to the wood. Two or three who had also appeared to fling themselves down, remained motionless. The enemy, having discovered that we could be dangerous even at 900 yards, then successfully crossed the stubble field in two short rushes without losing a man, and reinforced their men who were advancing through the beetroot fields on our right. Great numbers of troops now began to appear on the ridge between Bethancourt and the little wood. They advanced in three or four lines of sections of ten to fifteen men extended to two paces. Their line of advance was direct on the village of Audencourt and on the low plateau on our right, so that we were able to pour upon them an enfilade fire. They were advancing in short rushes across pasture-land which provided no cover whatever, and they offered a clearly visible target even when lying down. Although our men were nearly all first-class shots, they did not often hit the target. This was owing to the unpleasant fact that the German gunners kept up a steady stream of shrapnel, which burst just in front of our trenches and broke over the top like a wave. Shooting at the advancing enemy had to be timed by the bursting shell.

We adopted the plan of firing two rounds and then ducking down at intervals, which were determined as far as could be arranged for by the arrival of the shell. But the shooting of the battalion was good enough to delay the enemy's advance. From the 900-yard mark they took more than an hour to reach their first objective, which was the Route Nationale, 400 yards from our nearest trench. Here they were able to concentrate in great numbers, as the road runs along an embankment behind which nothing but artillery could reach them. This was the situation on our front at about three o'clock in the afternoon. I happened to look down the line and saw Captain Lumsden looking rather anxiously to the rear. I then saw that a number of our people were retiring. There was not much time to think about what this might mean as the enemy were beginning to cross the road; we had fixed bayonets, and I thought we would have little chance against the large number of Germans who had concentrated behind the embankment. For a long time, for nearly an hour, the British guns had been silent, but they had not all retired. With a white star-shaped flash two shells burst right over the road behind which the Germans were massed. Those two shells must have knocked out forty or fifty men. The enemy fled right back up the hill up to the 900 yard mark, followed by rapid fire and loud cheering from all along the line.[29]

The gun that Hay describes was probably one belonging to a sixty-pounder battery in the centre of the British line, which had inflicted fearful damage on the advancing Germans throughout the morning. As each fresh line of enemy soldiers breasted the rise ahead, its heavy shells plunged among them. Sometimes whole platoons disappeared amid the swirling fumes of each explosion. Never the less at this point in the war German numbers were effectively limitless, and for each rank swept away, reinforcements followed up. The continual firing however had depleted the ammunition reserves of the artillery. Corbett-Smith, as a gunner officer, was acutely aware of the need to maintain the supply of shells to batteries, which in some cases had been in almost continuous action since Mons. The importance of the Army Service Corps to the Royal Field Artillery was critical, and in the confusion of Le Cateau and the Retreat, Army Service Corps motor transport drivers often performed heroic deeds far beyond their calling. Corbett-Smith states that:

> The threads of communication with the ammunition supply were badly stretched to breaking-point, owing to the astonishing speed at which the British had to retire. Normally, the ammunition parks (motor transport) draw the ammunition supplies from railhead, and carry it up to the divisional ammunition columns. These, in turn, distribute to brigade columns, and the actual units draw upon the last named. Thus there are several links between railhead and the firing-line, and the motor-lorries should not come within about eight miles of the line.
>
> But on this Wednesday [26 August] and the two or three following days all this arrangement literally went to pieces. How could it be otherwise? And that is how the A.S.C. drivers came to do their bit with all the rest. Speed was vital, and the lorries could cover the distance in a third of the time taken by the horse transport. In fact, the horse transport was ignored or forgotten, although there were exceptions. One saw the divisional columns aimlessly trekking about the country, at one moment under orders to go to a certain village, only to find on arrival that the enemy were just a mile off; back they would come again as hard as the tired horses could do it.
>
> Time and again an urgent message would go back from a battery for more 18-pounder or howitzer, and the dispatch-rider would have instructions to get the stuff wherever he could lay hands on it. He generally managed to find a few lorries of a 'park', and so off the bus drivers would start with their three-ton vehicles, little dreaming that they were going under fire.[30]

In fact, the drivers often took their lorries into situations that placed them and their vehicles at great danger from German fire – these unsung heroes being at even greater risk than most as they were sitting on several tons of explosives into the bargain.

The 1st Battalion Somerset Light Infantry meanwhile held an exposed position on the western flank of the British line at Le Cateau, close to the village of Fontaine-au-Pire. Edward Packe was atypical in that he was not a regular soldier or even a reservist, but had enlisted in the Somerset Light Infantry on 6 August 1914, shortly after the British declaration of war, and found himself whisked to France with the 1st Battalion when it went overseas. He kept a meticulous diary, and recorded:

Driver Leonard Brunton, a motor mechanic in civilian life, he was also an Army Service Corps Special Reservist. In August of 1914 he was in France with 5th Ammunition Park.

British transport wagons pass through a French town.

Aug 26th. Start marching at midnight and arrive at Pierre a la Fontaine at about 4.30am and rations given out. Start advancing about 5.30 and reach a railway embankment where we stay for a bit. Told to take off packs and advance to a sunken road, certain amount of M.G. fire from the Germans. Told to fix bayonets and charge but after a hundred yards or so signalled to lie down. We were in a field of haycocks and I got behind one, a fair amount of M.G. and shell fire, top of my haycock blown off by a near one. Finally ordered to return to railway embankment where I collected my pack. A corporal (Champion) told to take four men, of whom I was one, and go back half way to the village and from a flank cover the retirement of the Regiment from the embankment to the village. We watched the retirement and the German shrapnel playing over them and when they were all back to the village, we also retired going along a sunken road and thereby escaped the German fire, assembled in the village square told by the C.O. that we had to fight to the last man etc., as the French who should have come up by 3pm. had not done so; also ordered to take off packs. Took up various positions and were eventually relieved some time after dark.[31]

Private Arthur Green from Bath served in the same battalion as Packe. He was as different from the privately educated Packe as was possible, being a regular reservist who had enlisted after the Boer War. Green's memoir was unusual in that it was published while the war was still in progress. Entitled *The Story of a Prisoner of War*, it is a striking tale. Simply educated, Green's writing is full of colloquialisms and quaint turns of phrase, which reinforce its authenticity. He writes of the fighting on 26 August:

We were just having a bit of bully and biscuit when the order came we were going into action. We soon packed away our traps and were skirmishing towards a ridge a mile away, when, bang! I thought it was my birthday. A shell burst 800 yards in front of us. I looked up and down the line, but not a man had fallen. Then there were a shower of bullets flew over our heads. They had machine-guns on us, but we were going down an incline. Well, all the fatigue and tiredness was out of us. We could see some men of the Rifle Brigade in front falling down now and then. Billy Care shouted, 'Don't you get popped over Jim, or else I shan't have any dinner,' as I was carrying two tins of bully beef and a tin of jam. Well, that's the last I seen of Billy.

Captain Watson was leading us. We rushed the first ridge. The bullets were like rain. No one seemed to take much notice of who was falling. I had a look in front. 'Nine hundred yards,' roared the captain. I passed it on, as I was next to him. Being an observer, I had to pass all messages. We could see the enemy in thousands. Well, we let them have it hot and holy for a few minutes; then the order came to retire, and just as I was getting up I got one through the hat, hitting it off. Near shave, I thought. We retired about 100 yards at a rush, seeing nothing, as we were over a bit of a ridge. We had to rush back about twenty yards. It was then that I ran to the wrong place, as me and Jonnie Ashment ran in the way of a machine-gun. I got mine in the thigh. I thought I'd been kicked by an elephant.

It hit me sickey, I can tell. I riggled [*sic*] my straps off, drank all my water, tried to get up, thinking I could run; but I found my leg would not let me go. But I managed to get 100 yards back behind a hedge. Here I seen the two captains, Captain Jones Mortimer and Captain Watson, in my company, with about thirty men of different corps. Only two Somersets were with them. Jones Mortimer said: 'Well, hard luck, Green. Buck up. Keep up courage, and lie low. Perhaps you'll get picked up later.' Just then they had to retire from under this hedge across about eighty yards of open ground; the Germans opened fire on them with rifles, and I was glad to see not a single man fell. I was feeling very uncomfortable at the time, as the Germans were firing over and through this bit of a low hedge I was under. Well, I laid low enough, I can tell you. That was the last I seen of the regiment.

I suppose I'd been there about an hour when I heard voices coming about forty yards off which I knew were foreign. Well, they came – four men. The leader says, 'Spraken German?' I says, 'No,' so as he could speak a bit of broken English, he was asking me questions, and he got some good answers to some, I can tell you. Well, one of the men, who seemed a ruffian, threatened me with the butt of a rifle, and I know I done a foolish thing at the time – I laughed at him, so he ups and takes about fifty paces off. I seen he was loading and I only prayed, and prayed out loud saying, 'Pray God he may fire straight.' Well, I thought I had it come then, when the corporal who was in charge shouted to him, and made him take off his equipment and stand aside, the corporal asked me then what I said out loud. He thought I said God strike him; but in the finish he and his squad ran round the back of the hedge. I could hear them talking all the time, but after a while they went and left me. Later I was bandaged up by two Germans. I'd lost a lot of blood by then, this was about 10am. Well, I was not interfered with then for hours; I remained as I was then very weak and faint, but never went off. I turned on my side and watched the battle all the afternoon.[32]

Later, towards nightfall German troops returned and covered Green up with three greatcoats, but left him in the open. That evening there was heavy rain, but in spite of being soaked to the skin, exhaustion and loss of blood caused him to sleep until early the next morning. French civilians, who tended his wounds, then picked him up.

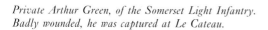

Private Arthur Green, of the Somerset Light Infantry. Badly wounded, he was captured at Le Cateau.

Equally exposed on the extreme left flank at Le Cateau were the 1st Battalion the King's Own Royal Lancaster Regiment, holding positions near Longsart, and the 2nd Battalion Royal Dublin Fusiliers, nearby at Haucourt. Captain D. Baird-Douglas of the former battalion has left an account of events as he saw them. As several regiments of German Jäger troops swept down upon them, Baird-Douglas was wounded and captured:

> I was taken prisoner on August 26th, 1914, at Le Cateau. My battalion first came into action early in the morning, at about 5 o'clock, near the village of Hautcourt [Haucourt], five miles from Ligny in Cambresis. When the Germans first opened fire on us I was ordered by my colonel to extend my platoon and to cover the retirement of the battalion, who were to form up behind a hill 400 yards to the rear and then advance again over the ground which my platoon were holding. Within half an hour or so, owing to the very heavy machine-gun and shell fire, there were only about two of my men not hit, the remainder having been killed or were incapable of moving. I was wounded within ten minutes of the start by a rifle bullet in the left leg, and then about twenty minutes later I was hit by a shrapnel in the right leg, which, owing to the loss of blood, rendered me unconscious for two or three hours. When I became conscious the rifle and machine-gun fire had then practically ceased, but the ground was still being shelled. The shelling eventually ceased about 2 o'clock in the afternoon. An hour later about 12 German infantry came up to us and disarmed us. Except in two cases, they treated us quite well; the only two cases I saw were the kicking of two wounded men lying on the ground. I cannot say what regiment these Germans belonged to, as I was too weak to notice anything or take in any details.[33]

Two soldiers of the Dublin Fusiliers (which formed the rearguard for the 10th Infantry Brigade) also provided detailed accounts of the fighting on this western edge of the battlefield to the *Kildare Observer* newspaper in the weeks that followed. Private Bergin, of Dublin, was like a number of other men serving alongside his own brother. He recalled that:

> I saw no Germans, but we knew they were in front of us. Their shells fell all round, about and amongst us, and I saw many of my comrades stretched wounded in the trenches. We got no chance of firing, as we saw nothing to fire at. Anything would have been better than lying there waiting for . . . the shell fire . . . We got accustomed to it after a while, and our fellows were in good spirits considering what we had to put up with without doing anything ourselves. About three o'clock [I saw] my brother's head blown off by a shell. He was close beside me at the time and I can't tell you how I felt. It was terrible! You get accustomed to seeing things in trenches, but when I saw my own brother killed I needn't tell you it upset me.[34]

Corporal James O'Donnell of the same battalion added:

> The German Infantry made desperate effort[s] to break through in the centre, and it was our artillery and the Warwicks that kept them back. Two shells struck the ground where the officer and I were standing and simply half buried us in

mud. A minute later two or three of our men on our right were killed and several wounded. You will think it rather strange when I tell you that toward evening with shells dropping all around and the thunder of artillery, I went to sleep in the trench I was so absolutely fatigued. I seemed to have slept for a couple of hours, and when I awoke it was still bright and the booming of the guns was worse than ever. It was terribly trying lying there not able to move and not knowing what moment a shell might drop on you. When I awoke I was surprised and rubbed my eyes for a minute before I could realise where I was or what was happening. Then some biscuits were passed along the trenches, but it was hard to get water and we suffered a lot from thirst. It was a broiling hot day. This bombardment continued until daylight failed. That night we were ordered down on to the road with fixed bayonets, expecting a cavalry attack. Our stretcher bearers and doctors went

out to collect some wounded on the left, the church in the village I told you of being used as a hospital, and I moved off to get a drink of water from a well that had almost been drunk dry. The houses in the village were all wrecked, and there was a perfect hell there for a few minutes when the German Cavalry and Infantry attacked it under the cover of darkness ... There was a tornado of fire in this village and bullets whizzed and sang all round the place for about half an hour. It was a dreadful melee. There was a regular hail of bullets and I, who in seeking a drink had got detached from my comrades, lay flat on the road. Eventually the Germans were repulsed ... When this had ended we decided on a retirement. The whole countryside was like a half moon on fire – villages and farm houses were burning and illuminating the country for miles around, and some of the house[s] at least, I know could not have been set on fire by the shells.[35]

Lance Corporal Christopher Borthwick, King's Own Scottish Borderers, who was taken prisoner on 26 August 1914 at Le Cateau.

Late in the afternoon of 26 August, a staff officer, Captain James Jack, was attempting to contact some of those units on the eastern side of the battlefield, those closest to Le Cateau, whom he had shortly before ordered forward to try to check a German advance. It was by now imperative that he try to extricate them, before they were too closely pressed by the Germans to be able to get away. In later years, Jack remarked that Le Cateau was the only battle of the Great War in which he was directly engaged with the enemy. His diary was published some years after his death and in it he records:

> Being now most anxious for the safety of the troops recently placed by me ...
> I ran forward along the outskirts of the village to warn our friends to retire.
> Presently a tremendous crash of musketry fire broke out in front. Following a
> hedge which obstructed the view I came on the Argylls just below me, manning
> the bank of a road at the south-eastern corner of Reumont. They were firing hard
> at the Germans whose advancing lines were flooding all over the ground from the
> direction of St Benin, the closest being some four to six hundred yards distant.
>
> A fusillade of bullets was skimming the road bank and a wire fence stood
> between me and the Highlanders. Expecting to be hit at any moment, I called
> to the men to tell their colonel to retire at once; then to their kindly warnings
> 'Be careful, Sir', climbed the fence, slid down the track, and hastened crouching
> along ... we divided those present into two parts ... and doubling back out of the
> enemy's view re-formed between 5.30 and 6pm.[36]

He notes that in spite of the heavy rifle and shellfire to which they were exposed as they ran back, he believed that not a single man was lost in the affair. Many years later in May 1960, word reached him from a friend that while on holiday he had met a former soldier who referred to Le Cateau, and the heroic efforts of a certain Captain Jack, who got his battalion out of a difficult situation that day. Jack would no doubt have drawn quiet satisfaction from this. More significantly, the incident disproves the popular misconception that staff officers were both universally incompetent, and despised by the rank and file.

As the II Corps began to withdraw from the battlefield, Jack's brigade, the 19th, was ordered to provide the rearguard. Two of its battalions which had not thus far been heavily committed were the 2nd Royal Welsh Fusiliers and the 1st Battalion Cameronians, which now made a stand at Maurois. Among the latter was Private H.A. Taylor who remembered:

> The battle [of Le Cateau] continued until 3.30pm, when orders came for us to
> retire ... it was from now onwards that units became confused, this unit mixing
> with that, orders issued then countermanded, it was a general mix-up. Some
> order was, however, obtained as the retirement continued. I remember entering
> the small town of Bertry and seeing Gen. Smith-Dorrien taking the salute
> from the steps of the Marie. We were halted, [and] our officers were called for a
> briefing. We were to remain and cover the retirement of our sector. My regiment
> and the Welsh Fusiliers were the last to pull out, we did so in extended order,
> so we continued through fields and orchards, with Uhlans harassing us all the
> while, the 19th Hussars were our covering screen, on and on we went ... we took

up a delaying position on a railway embankment and opened up, firing at a party of Uhlans, who were being chased by a squadron of the 19th Hussars, there were casualties on both sides, among them was a farrier of the 19th Hussars who managed to ride through our lines, he was severely wounded in the groin. I helped to bandage him, we trussed him up with his knees under his chin, to help stem the flow of blood, two of our stretcher bearers and a corporal we told to remain with him, they were all captured, as we heard later. It was a pity, for two of these stretcher bearers were twins, who had joined the regiment in India in 1908, they were both cornet players in the band, whose careers were promising, their name was Ash. I have never heard what happened to them, I hope they survived.[37]

In fact, 8447 Henry Ash and his brother 8448 Alfred Ash, from Gardent Hill in Glasgow, both survived the war, having spent time in German prison camps. Upon his repatriation Alfred Ash gave a detailed account of this incident in an interview:

On the night of 26th August at Maretz I was attached to D company of my regiment as a stretcher bearer. About 8pm we opened fire on the enemy; presently Corporal Lee came to the company and asked for stretcher bearers to bring in some wounded. I went and brought in a sergeant major of the Hussars badly wounded. Lance Corporal Ash my brother, and Smith were with one stretcher, and myself and Bandsman Austin with the other. We were told to remain with the wounded till help was sent to us; this never came, and in the morning of 27th August, having previously got the wounded into a house, I went out to see if I could see any of our men coming to help, when I saw some Uhlans riding towards us, and I was captured and taken to the village of Maretz ... On first capture I was knocked about, abused and kicked by the Germans and even by an officer – the officers were as bad as the men – belonging to an infantry regiment, I don't know which. All the prisoners I saw were treated in the same way. My brother who was captured at the same time, looking after that sergeant major we had brought in at first, told me some Germans, evidently a looting party, came to the house with fixed bayonets and tried to stab the sergeant major, and when my brother tried to stop them they started on him and threw him outside.[38]

As darkness fell on the Le Cateau battlefield that night, many British soldiers found themselves not captives, but marooned behind German lines. Some hair-raising escapes and extraordinary acts of evasion followed. Captain Alfred Trigona of the 2nd Battalion Royal Dublin Fusiliers and seventeen of his men had held the Germans at bay all day from their positions in a turnip field near Haucourt. At nightfall however they found that the Germans had pushed past them on either side and they were now cut off. Reaching a nearby village, they hid their uniforms and donned civilian clothes. They made an eight-day journey in disguise, travelling mostly at night and hiding in barns and haystacks in the daytime, to reach Boulogne, where they crossed to England. After re-fitting at the regimental depot at Naas, the men returned to France.

Similarly, on 26 August Claude Henry Bushell became separated from the British forces near the village of Escaufort, just south of Le Cateau. Bushell, from Claro,

North Yorkshire was a Lieutenant in the Queen's Bays (2nd Dragoon Guards), under normal circumstances commanding Number 2 Troop, of C Squadron. That afternoon, while acting as a galloper, Bushell had ridden forward with orders for the 11th Hussars to fall back to St Quentin. After delivering these instructions to their headquarters, he advanced further to notify their patrols. In doing so, he unwittingly passed through the lines and soon found himself surrounded by Germans. He was forced to release his horse and hide in a drain at the bottom of a railway embankment, where he remained for three days without food or water. As the Germans continued their pursuit of the BEF, their numbers thinned and, by the evening of 29 August, he was able to crawl out of his hiding place to make contact with villagers from Honnechy. They provided him with some food but, while eating, a peasant warned him that German soldiers were approaching, compelling Bushell to once again take cover among some nearby hedges.

While still in hiding, Bushell was informed by a villager that there were other concealed British soldiers. As an officer, Bushell felt it was his duty to take charge of these men. Wearing some borrowed civilian clothes over his uniform, he marched to their location and encountered Sergeant Taylor and ten men of the 11th Hussars. They remained in a plantation for the next eight days, repeatedly eluding German patrols while being greatly aided by the local inhabitants, including the Mayor of Honnechy, who hid and fed them.

Bushell decided to relocate the group to an abandoned hut on the western edge of the Forêt de Mormal where other Allied soldiers soon joined them. The forest was

large and densely wooded with heavy undergrowth, offering the soldiers an excellent hiding place. Bushell found himself in charge of thirty-five men representing several regiments, including the 11th Hussars, Royal Artillery, Manchester Regiment, Gordon Highlanders, Scots Greys, Munster Fusiliers and the King's Own Scottish Borders. There they remained for the next month, being fed by the locals while constantly under the threat of capture. Always on the move, and with autumn closing in, the party were aided at great risk by friendly Belgians. Eventually, Bushell was smuggled across the Dutch border and returned to England.

Other stragglers from the Le Cateau battle continued to fight on, and the following day, 27 August, Karl Storch was involved in mopping up British rearguards still holding

Lieutenant Claude Henry Bushell, Queen's Bays. While riding forward at Le Cateau he found himself behind enemy lines. (Museum of the Queen's Bays)

their ground. A refined and well-read man in civilian life, the war had already begun to brutalise him as he himself admitted:

> We could not for long enjoy the pleasure of slumber. As early as 4 o'clock [in the morning] the issue of food rations had started, the day before nothing could be distributed. Now here we had yesterday's ration: peas and bacon. This was splendid and tasted delicious, but we did not get to enjoy as much as we would have liked, very suddenly we were fired upon once again by the enemy, and bullets and food do not get on with each other. The thoughtless enemy, who had spoiled our well-earned pea soup, drove us into a rage. We attacked from the village, overran their firing line, and within half an hour we had captured 400 Englishmen. They all held up their hands and had suffered many dead and wounded in such a short space of time.
>
> A 'New Testament' had fallen out of an English backpack; I turned the leaves inside. There was a dedication written on the first page. I snapped the black book shut again and flung it at a wounded Englishman among the turnips, who cried and whined. I had no more compassion, at that time everything within me had turned to stone, and now when I remember it I regard myself as brutal, as I called to him, 'Look at here, old fellow, that's a praying book [*sic*].' Others may talk in such cases of mercy, but there are times in war when one is taken over by the other side of one's nature, by the hatred for these island people who have caused so much untold grief, such sadness and misery in the world.[39]

To German eyes, there was evidence of the scale of the British defeat at Le Cateau all around. Hans Stegeman was a sergeant or *Feldwebel* in *5. Hannoversches Infanterie-Regiment Nr. 165*, with its headquarters at Quedlinberg. A student of forestry before the outbreak of war, his unit was among those pressing down on the BEF as it fought its rearguard action at Le Cateau. He wrote to his parents on 28 August 1914:

> Our men, like heroes, did not yield a foot! Sergeant Struck, a good comrade, fell close to me, shot through the lungs, and died immediately. We buried him with Lieut. Lorenz in the churchyard ... I wrapped the bodies in pine branches, as no coffin was to be had. We put up a cross over the grave. My Lieut. Rogge had a bullet through his shako; it grazed the top of his head and he fell to the ground, but he was only stunned and is now quite fit and back again in the saddle with us. Corporal von Heimburg fell saying, with a smile: 'We shall win all the same!'
>
> On the day after the battle I was in the church, which has been turned into a hospital. All the men with lung wounds are getting on very well, almost better than the lightly wounded. Lungs heal quickly, and a clean shot makes only a small hole and goes right through. Their one and only question was: 'How are things going, Sergeant? Is it all right again?' 'Lads, I've come straight from the line; everything is going well, we have advanced a bit. The English haven't half caught it on the jaw!' Then they smiled and fell asleep like happy children. They are all perfectly calm and confident, and suffer uncomplainingly, but it is dreadful to see the dangerously wounded, especially those who are raving in delirium.

I rode over the battlefield yesterday. There were about ten English dead to one of ours. I will write no more about the battlefield. It is difficult to imagine how anybody came out of it unharmed. One gets quite cold-blooded and indifferent.[40]

Heinrich Heubner displayed a similar degree of satisfaction at the turn of events when he wrote:

On the following day we continued the pursuit of the English. In order to stop our advance they made another stand at Le Cateau, but, in spite of a most gallant defence, received a crushing defeat. Our regiment did not participate in this fight, but as we marched near to the battlefield, on our way southwards, we found numerous traces of the English retreat. The enemy artillery had left great heaps of their ammunition on both sides of the road, in order to save at least the guns.

For quite an hour we were marching between these remarkable monuments of German victories and English defeats, and never have we enjoyed a higher degree of malicious joy than during that day's march. The countryside teemed with small parties of English troops who had got cut off from the main body. As it was easy for them to hide in the woods, and as one was never sure of their strength, a lot of valuable time was lost in rounding them up.

One of our cavalry patrols discovered a party of them near the village W——, and our battalion, with my company in front, was detached to clear them out. Very soon we got glimpses of the well-known English caps, and here it must be admitted that in making use of cover and in offering a stubborn defence the English performed wonders. When we advanced against their first position we were received with rifle-fire, then they vanished, only to pop up in a second position. They were dismounted cavalrymen whose horses were hidden farther back, and, after decoying us to their third line, they mounted and fled.[41]

It was some days before all of the wounded could be found and brought in from the battlefield by the Germans. A graphic description of the suffering of these badly injured prisoners in a field hospital comes from a German soldier, himself wounded in the foot by shrapnel at Le Cateau:

Here in the hall, where I lie, is an Englishman who arrived yesterday [30 August]. He was badly wounded in the trenches on the 26th and was picked up only yesterday, very emaciated. His shattered leg had to be removed. I asked him beforehand what he had to say for himself. There was nothing more for the poor devil to say. If it was quite quiet for us before, now it was fair to say we had no more rest that night. After the operation the Englishman roared like a bull for about an hour. After a morphine injection he became gradually more peaceful, however, he cried at regular intervals 'O Lord, O Lord, O Lord, what shall I do!'

In the adjoining room lies another with fiery red hair, doubtless when he had his health he was a proud fellow. He spoons water from a bowl with a ladle, then almost immediately brings it back up again, and then screams loud enough to make one's ears ring. Reassuringly, amidst all these moans of pain, the sisters are quietly working away.[42]

The aftermath of the battle: German soldiers survey a mass grave of British soldiers at Le Cateau.

While Smith-Dorrien's II Corps had been fighting to extract itself from the situation at Le Cateau, Haig's I Corps had been retreating to the south of the mighty Forêt de Mormal. While not as closely pressed as their comrades to the north, the men of its two divisions none the less had their share of fighting against the pursuing Germans. On 27 August the 2nd Battalion Royal Munster Fusiliers, faced by seven battalions of German infantry, three artillery batteries, cavalry and numerous Maxim guns fought a desperately one-sided action at Etreux, and, like many battalions in this heroic campaign, sacrificed themselves so that other units might make their escape. Some 260 officers, NCOs and men surrendered at the end of the day – the only survivors of the battalion. An account of the action by one of the officers who was captured was published in *The Story of the Munsters* in 1918. The author was originally anonymous, but it was probably Captain Drake. At 2.30pm, having successfully held up the enemy for most of the day, with little loss to themselves, the Munsters began to withdraw. However, passing through Oisy they came under heavy fire and found their path blocked. The colonel now decided that attack was the best form of defence; Drake takes up the story at this point:

> In addition to the artillery and rifle fire from the East, a raking rifle fire took us in flank from the environs of Etreux, and it was this position the Commanding Officer decided to attack. Lieutenant O'Malley was sent to C Company to direct them to keep the road clear as Lieutenant Chute was to open fire with his machine-guns at the enemy advancing from North. Lieutenant O'Malley bicycled back under heavy fire, and a couple of ammunition carts came up to us at a gallop before the horses were shot, indeed a gallant feat.

B Company, with half A Company in support, shook out to attack. The enemy was located in a loopholed house on the West side of the road and also in the near fields. On the other side of the road a farmhouse had caught fire and blazed furiously. The Commanding Officer, Captain Wise, and Lieutenant Mosely succeeded in approaching to within fifty yards of this house, creeping along a ditch followed by their men. The enemy's fire was intense, and though Captain Wise succeeded in reaching the house, the whole party was put out of action. Major Charrier renewed the attack, and again later made a third attack,

with his usual determination, but was shot dead at close range in the last charge. B Company was heavily engaged from both sides of the road, and Captain Simms was killed gallantly leading the attack. C Company reinforced this position, and D Company, which was in the orchard East, converged into the open and was met by a flank attack from the enemy holding the cutting. Aided by the fire of a platoon of A Company, D Company advanced by alternate rushes to within 70 yards of the hedge, where the officer in command (Captain Jervis) ordered a charge. The men sprang up with a cheer, fixed bayonets and charged. The enemy's fire redoubled, and Lieutenant Phayre fell, shot through the heart. Man after man went down, and only Captain Jervis reached the hedge alive, subsequently falling into the enemy's hands. The remnants of the Battalion fell back to the orchard where Captain Hall was wounded. Lieutenant Gower organised a defence facing N.S.E. and West. The ammunition was exhausted and most of the gunners killed. Major Bayley wounded. The enemy had entirely surrounded the Battalion, but, encouraged by the few remaining officers, the men fought on until 9 p.m. Sounds of approaching help were listened for in vain, and the Battalion ... surrendered.[43]

Corporal James Milton, 2nd Battalion Royal Munster Fusiliers, captured in the epic Battle at Etreux, on 27 August 1914. (Jean Prendergast)

In the same vicinity, near Etreux, another drama was being played out around the same time as the Munsters made their stand, albeit on a much smaller scale. In the early days of the war the Royal Automobile Club (RAC) had supplied twenty-five volunteers and their motor cars to act as liaisons between divisional headquarters. Two of them, H.S. Wescott and Frederic Coleman (an American) subsequently wrote of their extraordinary experiences during the Retreat from Mons. With no fixed front lines it was easy for the fast-moving motorists to find themselves in difficulties, as did Westcott. His account was later published in the RAC journal the *Week*:

> Arriving at Havre we were all motored to Amiens where we were drafted to different Divisions. I got attached to the Headquarters Staff and went straight away to join the column at Etreux. The next day owing to the sudden advance of the enemy we found ourselves in Landrecies, the place in a great state of excitement owing to the fact that the Germans had suddenly entered the town. So great was the congestion of refugees, artillery baggage wagons and troops that we had to leave the car for a moment and take a rifle. For a time the Germans were apparently beaten off and we attempted to get back to Etreux to stop the column. It was pouring with rain and pitch black. The state of the roads was terrible and I took a side slip and went into a ditch, breaking up the car. Well here was a pretty kettle of fish. However I had to do the best I could. Unfortunately for me our troops did not come back on the road where I was. After waiting for some time I decided to walk in the direction of Etreux, which was about eight miles away. When I arrived at Lagrosse being very wet and exhausted I stopped and was immediately surrounded by the villagers who were in a fearful state of panic as they had heard that the Germans were on the outskirts of the village. After resting a while I proceeded to Etreux and the next day went to our Headquarters to get permission to go back to Landrecies to rescue my car not knowing that the Germans were actually in possession of the town. As I was only in khaki with no distinctive badges of any kind the officer immediately suspected me for a spy and I was placed under arrest. It was only with great difficulty that my identity was accepted.[44]

Coleman meanwhile published his memoirs as *From Mons to Ypres with French*. His was an equally exciting experience, the possession of a motor car allowing him to observe (and subsequently record) much more of the whirlwind of events than could an ordinary infantry officer, for example. He wrote:

> When I arrived most of G.H.Q. was being shifted from St. Quentin with a considerable amount of bustle. No effort was made to disguise the fact that the battle along the Cambrai–Le Cateau front was going against our 2nd Corps. There was no actual panic, but on all sides was that obvious effort to be cool which bespeaks strain. Running north in the direction of Le Cateau I found the roads becoming blocked. As I turned the car with difficulty at a point near Renancourt I realised that to remain there would be to become involved in the maelstrom of southbound transport. At that point four roads in a radius of less than a kilometre debouched from the north with but one main outlet to the south-ward ...

Just before midnight as I was turning in, Borritt, the member of the R.A.C. corps who usually transmitted orders from Major Evans of G.H.Q. Staff to the R.A.C. drivers, came to my billet and told me that a volunteer was required for a precarious piece of work. Borritt's insistence that the driver must volunteer for the job, and the general air of mystery in which he wrapped it, roused my curiosity. I could only elicit from him at first that whoever drove the car which was required for the mission in hand would be called upon to dash through one or possibly more towns that were in German hands. Pressure elicited the further information that no news had come to G.H.Q. from General Smith-Dorrien during the evening, and just how much of the Left Wing of the Army remained, and where it was, was unknown. Therefore, if a message did not come from the 2nd Corps by three o'clock in the morning a staff officer was to be sent by car to establish communication with whatever might remain of Smith-Dorrien's Command.

When I learned that Loch was the staff officer who had been chosen for this mission I was glad to volunteer to act as his driver. I had cut away the exhaust of my car and rendered it unusually noisy. As this did not appear to be an advantage in such circumstances, I woke Jimmy Radley, an R.A.C. comrade, and obtained his permission to use his Rolls-Royce car for the journey, in case I should be called upon to make it. Before retiring I spent an hour in becoming familiar with any little eccentricities of Radley's car and putting in its tank twelve precious gallons of petrol which I had conserved in the tonneau of my car against emergency.[45]

In the event, the mission was cancelled, but Coleman was to have other hair-raising moments during the Retreat. Captain Alfred Clifton-Shelton, who commanded a horse-drawn transport company attached to the 19th Infantry Brigade, gives another example of the assistance rendered to the army by civilian motor drivers. Having marched up to Mons, once the BEF began to retreat Clifton-Shelton's company had to retrace their steps amid the confusion of the retirement. He wrote:

From the time we had begun to withdraw from the Mons line we had ... been marching practically day and night, and the horses had been dropping like flies, and had to be left on the side of the road. It was, and continued to be, a very difficult thing to replace them. With the line of communication constantly shutting up like a concertina, it was pretty well hopeless to expect refitments of any kind; and I had continually to be on the search for horses, of any description, that had been left in fields by the civilian population.

With a long stream of transport, marching on unknown roads at night, it was a most difficult thing to keep one's own little command intact; the roads being blocked in many places, and wheel vehicles of other units constantly chopping into the column. To obviate this to a certain degree, I hit upon the plan of driving at the head of the column in the motor-car, which, being an old London taxi-cab, was able to go at the slow speed at which we marched; and it had, moreover, a red tail-lamp, which, being lit, acted as a most invaluable guide to the leading wagon of my column. The men knew that wherever that lamp went they had to go; and as I invariably halted at cross-roads until the leading wagon came up, they never took the wrong road, and they always knew where to go. After a few nights the men looked upon this lamp as a regular mascot, and it was extraordinary how they found the oil for it, for it never went out till we got to the Aisne.

The driver of this taxi-cab was a civilian who had left a very comfortable job to serve his country; and I must put on record his remarkable services, for he had to drive that car night and day, with only one very bad side-light, and no one to relieve him at the wheel. Instead of taking any rest that came his way, this man spent all his time looking after the engine and tyres, so that I should not get 'let down' with the car;[46]

Motor-car owners were not the only civilians to put their machines at the disposal of the army in 1914. Numbers of motorcyclists did something similar, though in many cases they were on safer ground than Wescott and others, for they were actually enlisted into the Royal Engineers. They performed a vital role in maintaining communication between scattered units during the Retreat. Among them were a number of well-known motorcycle racers, such as Bert Sproston, Harold R. Davies (founder of the HRD firm which later became Vincent-HRD) and Vernon Busby, the latter two having ridden for the Sunbeam team at the Isle of Man TT races prior to the war. Busby gave a detailed interview to a journalist describing his experiences:

I was one of 1,000 men who signed on in Birmingham for active service at the beginning of the war. On August 10th sixty of us were sent to the Engineers' headquarters at Chatham. From here we were distributed to various parts of the country, nearly all of us being sent to Signal Telegraph Companies. I was sent to the Signal Telegraph Company attached to the Second Army [Corps] ... it was about three or four o'clock on Sunday morning that the German guns started playing on Mons ... we retired from the place where we were located about nine o'clock in the morning. It was strongly entrenched, but was blown to pieces a few hours afterwards. We retreated about four miles, and

Corporal Vernon Busby, a former TT rider and in 1914 a Royal Engineers dispatch rider. (Bill Snelling)

remained there three of four hours. Then we retired to Bavay. This made up three telegraph stations that we had had in one day . . . It was on Monday night that I got wounded. I was riding from the firing line towards Bavay. There were plenty of stray bullets knocking about, and one of them caught the machine, split up, and caught me in the leg. I did not stop of course, and four minutes later I was in hospital.[47]

In a different letter, published in *Motorcycle* magazine, Busby describes how the Sunbeam machine which he rode in France was registration number MN 496, actually the same machine that he had ridden in the TT races earlier that year. Much of his work during the Retreat from Mons consisted of keeping contact between headquarters staff and stragglers, and on one occasion he was commended for locating an ammunition column that had gone astray. So close did they come to the fighting, that motorcyclists were instructed to ride with a revolver with them at all times. Busby was particularly impressed by the German use of aircraft to spot retreating British columns many miles in front of their ground troops, and this may have inspired his decision to transfer to the Royal Flying Corps. He was to be killed later in the war while serving as a pilot.

Another Royal Engineers motorcycle dispatch rider who had participated in the Isle of Man TT races was a Manxman man, Corporal Duggie Brown; Brown was competing in a race at Brooklands on the day war was declared, and he immediately volunteered to serve as a dispatch rider. He went to France in August 1914, and took part in the Retreat from Mons. He wrote to his parents in Douglas on numerous occasions and one of his letters offers an insight into which makes of machine were best suited for this type of work:

> I am very well and comfortable, considering all things, but the only thing that we do require are cigarettes and matches, especially in tins of 50. We are kept very busy riding day and night. The French roads in the country districts are good, but in the towns and villages, or rather what the Germans have left of them, are really vile. I have had to give up my Rover bicycle, and now ride a Douglas. All the riders in our company have to ride the same machine, so as to solve the 'spare part question'; and then, again, the Douglas being very light, we can carry it over potholes and other places. Of course it is slow, especially after the Rover, which I left at the base.[48]

Brown added in a further letter that his party consisted of eight riders, of whom two were former TT competitors: Davis of the Sunbeam team and Boyton who had ridden for Triumph. Corporal Eric Williams meanwhile had actually won the 1914 Junior TT race, before enlisting as a dispatch rider upon the outbreak of the war. His family in Hereford received the following letter from him:

> Our work is carrying despatches from headquarters to the trenches . . . the roads here are awful, mostly pavée and very uneven and dangerous to ride on, especially when greasy. We work all hours day and night. I think if we get shot it will be

by our own sentries, who as you might imagine, are very nervous, and seem to get excited when they hear a motorcycle coming . . . I am getting quite used to the guns blasting away all day and night. They never seem to rest and when I go along the road near them they nearly blow me off my machine. I have had some shells burst within a hundred yards of me – quite near enough.[49]

Irishman Patrick Corcoran was another of those who signed up as a dispatch rider at the start of the war, and found himself in the Retreat. He published his memoirs after the war as *The Daredevil of the Army*. In the book he describes how he and his fellow riders waited wearily in their billets for messages to carry. All were respectable young men who had volunteered for this dangerous work upon the outbreak of war. Suddenly an urgent message needs to be carried:

Hudson and Harrison are the next on the list, but Grant and I accompany them to the farmhouse door, in case the Subaltern might care to choose us for this crisis. Harrison has only arrived the day before. But it's his turn, and it seems he has to take it.

'You know what to do? That's right. Swallow it, if they get you. Remember there are stray Uhlans about, and Poole and Lawrence may have been caught. Now for directions. Go together to the cross-roads – those with the crucifix. Then take separate routes to the town. One of you may get through, if the other two don't.'

A pleasant prospect. The Subaltern looks at Harrison, as he presents it, as if expecting some protest from the new recruit. But none comes, and the youngster, their age and station but for an accident, is suddenly moved to put out a hand.

'Good luck!' He gives each a grip in turn, before they double out of the room.

'Better strap the thing on your forefinger, old chap,' advises Hudson with the wisdom gleaned in a week. He is referring to the precious tissue paper. 'Handier to your mouth that way.'

It takes them but two minutes to memorise the message and then they mount and are off on the darkening, dangerous road. Soon the crest of a hill hides them, and left alone, we lie down again. Among our new accomplishments is a facility for sleeping anywhere. But before slumber could come to soothe us, we hear voices nearby, and we listen. Some straggling Tommies are talking, and we are the subject under discussion.

'Not so bad for bloomin' civvies,' says one, apropos of our departed friends. We feel that we have accomplished much in these two weeks.[50]

However, perhaps the best personal account by a motorcyclist serving in France in 1914 comes in the form of William Henry Lowe Watson's *Adventures of a Despatch Rider*. Watson was an Oxford student upon the outbreak of war. In his excitement and eagerness to join the fighting, he purchased a motorcycle and offered it and himself as a dispatch rider to the Royal Engineers. Interestingly, he notes that numbers of his fellow recruits were, like Busby and company, experienced motorcycle racers. Watson was posted to the 5th Division Signal Company and proceeded to France on 19 August 1914. In his book he writes of the Retreat:

> An hour before dawn we wearily dressed. The others devoured cold stew, and immediately there was the faintest glimmering of light we went outside. The column was still passing, – such haggard, broken men! The others started off, but for some little time I could not get my engine to fire. Then I got going. Quarter of a mile back I came upon a little detachment of the Worcesters marching in perfect order, with a cheery subaltern at their head. He shouted a greeting in passing. It was Urwick, a friend of mine at Oxford ... I cut across country, running into some of our cavalry on the way. It was just light enough for me to see properly when my engine jibbed. I cleaned a choked petrol pipe, lit a briar – never have I tasted anything so good – and pressed on ... On the morning of the 27th we draggled into Saint Quentin. I found the others gorged with coffee and cakes provided by a kindly Staff-Officer. I imitated them and looked around. Troops of all arms were passing through very wearily. The people stood about, listless and sullen. Everywhere proclamations were posted beseeching the inhabitants to bring in all weapons they might possess. We found the Signal Company, and rode ahead of it out of the town to some fields above a village called Castres. There we unharnessed and took refuge from the gathering storm under a half-demolished haystack. The Germans didn't agree to our remaining for more than fifty minutes. Orders came for us to harness up and move on. I was left behind with the H.Q.S., which had collected itself, and was sent a few minutes later to 2nd Corps H.Q. at Ham, a ride of about fifteen miles.
>
> On the way I stopped at an inn and discovered there three or four of our motor-cyclists, who had cut across country ... Five minutes and I was on the road again. It was an easy run, something of a joy-ride until, nearing Ham, I ran into a train of motor-lorries, which of all the parasites that infest the road are the most difficult to pass. Luckily for me they were travelling in the opposite direction to mine, so I waited until they passed and then rode into Ham and delivered my message. The streets of Ham were almost blocked by a confused column retreating through it. Officers stationed at every corner and bend were doing their best to reduce it to some sort of order, but with little success. Returning I was forced into a byroad by the column, lost my way, took the wrong road out of the town, but managed in about a couple of hours to pick up the Signal Co., which by this time had reached the Chateau at Oleezy.
>
> There was little rest for us that night. Twice I had to run into Ham. The road was bad and full of miscellaneous transport. The night was dark, and a thick mist clung to the road. Returning the second time, I was so weary that I jogged on about a couple of miles beyond my turning before I woke up sufficiently to realise where I was.[51]

Watson received the Distinguished Conduct Medal for his work as a dispatch rider in 1914, and later in the war was commissioned into the Tank Corps. Motorcycles however were not the only technical innovation to begin to make an impact on the battlefield at this early juncture. Aircraft were also present, though they were fully yet to realise their potential. Numerous British diaries note the presence of a German 'Taube' overhead during the Retreat, but dismiss it as ineffective because it did not drop any bombs, little realising its role in reconnaissance. The pilot of one such German aircraft, flying over the Forêt de Mormal, was Unteroffizier Werner, who wrote of his patrol:

> I had received the order to ascertain the positions of the English and French troops after the English defeat at Mons. An officer went along as an observer. We flew first in a southern direction along the main road to Paris, leading us past a splendid wood, in which about 40,000 inhabitants from this area have sought shelter. After around a one-hour flight by which we could ascertain the fact that the Englishmen had withdrawn – we saw possibly a hundred abandoned vehicles still there, and not too far from this place, the French artillery together with the English infantry had taken up a new position – the observation officer did a sketch and we turned back.
>
> At this moment I saw about 300 meters above me a Bristol twin-decker, which pursued us. We were possibly at a height of 1,600 meters. As my monoplane had a lower speed than the Bristol, he soon caught up with us. In vain I attempted to get away from the enemy; however, I did not succeed. On the contrary, the Bristol always kept with us. My God, when would the bomb, which we expected any minute, hit us! The twin-decker descended further and further and was barely 150 meters above us.
>
> We had the same feeling that a bird must have, if a falcon is floating above him. We believed that the enemy approached nearer to have a better target for his bomb. We pulled our revolvers out and started to shoot. It had become clear to us, in the meantime, that fortunately the Englishman had no bombs or that he could not fire them in front of his aeroplane, because the engine and propeller were right at the front.
>
> It was a dreadfully exciting moment. The twin-decker had sunk even further and now the battle began on both sides. The observer and pilot of the double-decker opened fire, when we were at the same height and about 150 meters apart. Obviously they only had guns and did not dare to get closer, because they were afraid that we could throw our own bombs. Minute on minute went by. It seemed like hours to us. I had the feeling that my machine had reached its limit, and believed any minute that my end had come. This lasted half an hour. Then my observer patted me on the shoulder and pointed out to me, about 300 meters higher, a small French Bleriot, in a frantic haste in our direction to help the Bristol twin-decker.
>
> He travelled in circles around round us and the bullets whistled around our ears. But suddenly above the rattle of the engine we heard the explosions of artillery. We were above the German lines, and our side were firing on the Bristol and Bleriot.[52]

Back on the ground, the Retreat from Mons continued for day after weary day, and in the broiling August sun it was those who had neither horse nor motor vehicle beneath them who suffered the most. Frank Richards had like so many other reservists been thrust back into army life from his civilian occupation (as a timberman in a colliery) only a few weeks previously, and it was these men who found the going hardest. Writing in *Old Soldiers Never Die*, Richards remembered:

> We retired all night with fixed bayonets, many sleeping as they were marching along. If any angels were seen on the retirement, as the newspaper accounts said they were, they were seen that night. March, march, for hour after hour, with no halt: we were now breaking into the fifth day of continuous marching with practically no sleep in between. We were carrying our rifles all shapes and it was only by luck that many a man didn't receive a severe bayonet wound during the night. Stevens said: 'There's a fine castle there, see?' pointing to one side of the road. But there was nothing there. Very nearly everyone were seeing things, we were all so dead-beat.[53]

An account which closely parallels that of Richards exists in the form of *With a Reservist in France*, by Private Frederick Bolwell of the Loyal North Lancashire Regiment. Written in a similarly frank and down-to-earth manner, Bolwell recounts not only the physical hardship of the Retreat but also the frustration that it engendered among the men:

> Most of our men had thrown away all their heavy kit, such as top-coats, etc. . . . All this [retiring] was all very well, but it did not suit the men. This running away from the enemy could not be stood at any price, and the constant cry was: 'Why don't we stand and fight them? What are we afraid of? If you bring us here to fight, let's fight – otherwise put us all on a boat and dump us down in England.'
> On several occasions we passed food-supplies left on the roadside – left for the Germans: whole cheeses, tins of mustard, one of which I carried for four days, but, on getting nothing to eat with it, I threw it away. We would arrive outside a village, allotted for billets, perhaps about 7.30pm, and, after having marched the whole of the day, we were not allowed to enter the village until eleven or twelve o'clock at night to make ourselves comfy. The reason, I believe, was that it might be shelled by the enemy. No one was allowed to touch a thing – not even fruit – or he would be punished for looting; yet we knew very well that, perhaps on the morrow, the Germans would secure it all. Various bulletins were issued during

Trooper Charles King, Royal Horse Guards (The Blues), wounded and captured at Viesley in a skirmish on the retreat from Mons, 28 August 1914.

that Retirement, I suppose to cheer up the troops. One I remember contained the report of a German who had been taken prisoner, and who had upon him a diary, which – according to the bulletin – declared that the German Army was starving. Another, a very strong rumour, went the rounds, to the effect that we were doing a strategical retirement for the purpose of drawing the main body of the German Army into France, whilst the Russians came in on the East. Two days after that, a report was out that the Russians were marching on Berlin, and were within a few days' march of the capital itself. Imagine our feelings, our delight. Remember, we were absolutely cut off from all outside news. What were we to think? Most of us expected that the war would be over in a very short time. After the first five days, we were given a day's halt. The whole of the day before we had been marching until three in the morning, and were told on this day's rest that we had done so well, outpacing the enemy and outwitting them so successfully, that we should no doubt be able to rest for the next three days. On that day they paid us out, giving each man five francs, which, however, were of no earthly use to us, as we were all brigaded in a large field, and there was not a shop for miles. Our three-days' rest, however, did not materialize: we were off again next morning, with the enemy hot on our heels, having overtaken us by motors. So we had to continue our weary task sooner than we had anticipated.[54]

When some of the footsore soldiers of the II Corps arrived at St Quentin, an incident occurred that has become infamous in the annals of British military history. The remnants of two British battalions, the 1st Royal Warwickshire Regiment and the 2nd Royal Dublin Fusiliers, exhausted by many hours of marching over hard pavé roads in the blistering summer sun, without food, water or shade, had arrived in the town. Some of them had been given wine by well-meaning French civilians, but in their exhausted condition, and not having eaten for 24 hours or more, the result was in many cases drunkenness. Their respective colonels, A.E. Mainwaring and J. Elkington, both middle-aged men suffering as much if not more than their soldiers in these trying conditions, had allowed themselves to be persuaded by the Marie of St Quentin that with the Germans hard on their heels and no means of getting their weary men on the move again, that the only way to avoid a bloodbath would be to surrender. Both men signed a document to this effect, which the Marie was to convey to the Germans. Only the arrival of a group of British cavalry officers prevented the wholesale capture of over 400 men. One of the newly arrived officers was Captain A.C. Osburn who recalled:

> As far as I could understand, the official – Mayor or whoever he was – was very indignant; he kept on saying: 'You understand, m'sieur . . . it is now too late. These men have surrendered to the Germans!'
>
> 'How? The Germans are not here.'
>
> 'Their colonel and officers have signed a paper giving me the numbers of the men of each regiment and the names of the officers who are prepared to surrender, and I have sent a copy of this out under a white flag to the commander of the approaching German army.'

'But you have no business, m'sieur, as a loyal Frenchman, to assist Allied troops to surrender.'

'What else?' urged the Mayor. 'Consider, m'sieur … the alternatives. The German army is at Gricourt? Very well; I, representing the inhabitants of St. Quentin, who do not want our beautiful town unnecessarily destroyed by shell-fire because it happens to be full of English troops, have said to your colonels and your men: "Will you please go out and fight the German army *outside* St. Quentin?" But your men, they say, "No; we cannot fight! We have lost nearly all our officers, our Staff have gone away by train, we do not know where to. Also, we have no artillery, most of us have neither rifles nor ammunition, and we are all so very tired!" Then, m'sieur … I say to them, "Then, please, if you will not fight, will you please go right away, and presently the Germans will enter St. Quentin peacefully; so the inhabitants will be glad to be tranquil and not killed, and all our good shops not burnt." But they reply to me, "No, we cannot go away! We are terribly, terribly tired. We have had no proper food or rest for many days, and yesterday we fought a great battle. We have not got any maps, and we do not even know where to go to. So we will stay in St. Quentin and have a little rest." Then I say to them, "Since you will neither fight nor go away, then please you must surrender." So I send out a list of those who surrender to the German commander, and now all is properly arranged.'[55]

Osburn observed one of the colonels, who he described thus:

My recollection is that he looked very pale, entirely dazed, had no Sam Browne belt and leant heavily on his stick, apparently so exhausted with fatigue and the heat that he could scarcely have known what he was doing. Some of his men called to him encouraging words, affectionate and familiar, but not meant insolently, such as: 'Buck up, sir! Cheer up, daddy! Now we shan't be long! …' Actually I saw him saluting one of his own corporals, who did not even look surprised. What with fatigue, heat, drink and the demoralization of defeat, many hardly knew what they were doing.[56]

Another of the cavalry officers present, Major Tom Bridges, took the 'surrender document' from the Marie, and at once began the organisation of transport for those men who were unable to walk any further. Every cart or wheeled conveyance that could be found in St Quentin was requisitioned in order to get the stragglers out of the town and get them moving again. For those who were capable of walking, Bridges came up with a novel idea:

The men in the square were … so jaded it was pathetic to see them. If one only had a band, I thought. Why not? There was a toy shop handy which provided my trumpeter and myself with a tin whistle and a drum, and we marched round and round the fountain where the men were lying like the dead, playing 'The British Grenadiers' and 'Tipperary', and beating the drum like mad. They sat up and began to laugh and even cheer. I stopped playing and made them a short exhortation and told them I was going to take them back to their regiments. They began to stand up and fall in, and eventually we moved slowly off into the night to the music of our improvised band, now reinforced with a couple of mouth-organs. When well clear of the town I tried to delegate my functions to someone else, but the infantry would not let me go. 'Don't leave us, major,' they cried, 'or by God we'll not get anywhere.' So on we went, and it was early morning before I got back to my squadron.[57]

As for the two colonels, both were later court martialled and cashiered. Mainwaring was cleared of the charge of cowardice in the face of the enemy, but convicted of the lesser offence of scandalous conduct. He wrote later: 'The fact is that the men could do no more for the time being. Their limit of endurance was reached. I considered it my duty to protect these men, who so nobly had done theirs. I still consider that it was so, and my conscience is quite clear.'[58] He disappeared into obscurity but the other commanding officer, Elkington, subsequently joined the French Foreign Legion where he was badly wounded but also decorated for his bravery. In recognition of this, His Majesty King George V later reinstated him in the British army.

A curious epilogue to this incident exists in the form of the Distinguished Conduct Medal awarded to Sergeant Alfred Charman of the Royal Warwickshire Regiment. Charman's citation reads simply: 'For conspicuous good service, at a critical moment, whereby he was mainly responsible for averting the capture of many men.'[59] This citation sits oddly with many others published in the early part of the Great War which are, on the whole very detailed and often mention both places and dates at which the act for which the award was made occurred. It also took an unprecedented two full years for even this brief statement to appear in the *London Gazette*. Further light is shed on the matter by a commercial postcard which was produced later in the war showing a portrait of Sergeant Charman. The card adds: 'During the great retreat about 250 men would inevitably have been taken prisoners at St Quentin had Charman not acted promptly, and despite many dangers brought up reinforcements.'[60] There is a strong possibility that Charman was in some way involved in the 'Colonels' surrender' and perhaps the rather vague DCM citation deliberately obscures some of the detail of this embarrassing incident.

The most famous minor action of the Retreat was probably the clash at Néry on 1 September 1914, when the Germans, having initially surprised a mixed British force of artillery and cavalry at rest in its bivouac area, were eventually driven off with great loss. The artillery comprised 'L' Battery of the Royal Horse Artillery, while the cavalry included troops from the 2nd Dragoon Guards (Queen's Bays) and 5th Dragoon Guards. Captain Jack Giffard was the only officer of 'L' Battery to survive the action at Néry. His published diary contains a vivid description of the events of 1 September. That day he had risen at 4am, with orders to be ready to move off an hour later. He was examining one of the battery horses which was suspected to have gone lame, when in his own words:

Suddenly a terrific burst of shrapnel and rifle and machine-gun fire was opened onto us at a range of 600 to 800 yards. No one had the slightest idea of their being any Germans in the vicinity, and I am not sure if it was the fault of our own Cavalry or the French outposts.

HERO OF MONS RETREAT.

SGT. A. CHARMAN, D.C.M.
(ROYAL WARWICKSHIRE REGIMENT).

The official description of the act of bravery was: " For conspicuous good service at a critical moment, whereby he was mainly responsible for averting the capture of many men."

With "THREE CHEERS."

Sergeant Alfred Charman DCM, 1st Battalion Royal Warwickshire Regiment, awarded the DCM for bravery on the retreat from Mons.

The horse was killed at the first burst and I and Sgt Weedon dropped onto the road and crawled along to one side of the camp and got up close to it under cover of some stacks. We found Bradbury, John Campbell and Mundy and about a dozen men there or so, we rushed out and got 2 guns into action, myself on one with ½ dozen men and Brad, John, Mundy, the Sgt Major and Sergeant Nelson on the other. I had only fired a few rounds when the whole of my crew were wiped out, so I went on till I'd finished the ammunition and then got hit through the left leg above the knee by a splinter and peppered on the right arm and back and grazed along the hip bone by a whole shell or a very large fragment. Then a shell pitched on the gun wheel and smashed it, something getting me on the top of my head. As I could do no good there, I crawled back to the stack where some of our wounded were sheltering, they were terribly knocked about most of them. A few minutes later a shrapnel [burst] swept along our side of the stack, a fragment going clean through my right leg, missing the main artery by an eigth of an inch and I think missing the bone. 2 or 3 more pieces pierced the leg as well, several fellows were killed by it and horribly wounded. The terrific fire was kept up for some time and eventually the Household Brigade and 'I' Battery came up on the right and the Middlesex Regt on the left and drove them off. I think we did a great deal of damage and must have fired about 150 rounds.[61]

Trooper William Clarke served with the 2nd Dragoon Guards and was also present at the action at Néry. He wrote many years later of his memories of that misty morning which were still remarkably vivid, adding that the fog had delayed the Bays from saddling up, and they were having breakfast when the first shells struck. He continued:

I was one of a small party of about 15 men who were ordered forward to try to stop a German advance towards the sugar factory. The Germans had occupied some buildings alongside it. Lieutenants de Crespigny and Misa and a Sergeant Major led the attack. We managed to stem the Germans advancing for a time but due to casualties we had to withdraw. The Germans were machine-gunning us from the sugar factory and I remember that the Germans were finally shelled out of the factory and outbuildings by 'I' Battery of the Royal Horse Artillery. Our casualties were heavy, Lieutenant de Crespigny was killed, and so were 2 or 3 other men and the rest were wounded. Lieutenant Misa, myself and one other man were the only ones to come back unwounded. I was incredibly lucky. That day, and to this day, I can't remember how long we were actually engaged during our attack on the sugar factory.

Then cavalry reinforcements arrived. They had come across our horses stampeding and they opened fire on the German guns ... When the battle had ended, somewhere about 10am we helped to collect the wounded and cleared up, collecting bits and pieces of useful equipment. It was my first sight of multiple deaths in battle. Many men and horses,

Trooper William Clarke, Queen's Bays, present at the Néry action, 1 September 1914. (Liddle Collection; reproduced with the permission of Leeds University Library)

both German and British, dead and abandoned. At the count I think the Queen's Bays lost about 150 horses, at least half that amount killed, the others lost by stampeding. One officer and three or four men killed and perhaps 50 wounded. That's not counting men and horses of other regiments, such as 'L' Battery RHA, the heroes of the day. Everything seemed to happen so quickly, events were out of our control. I know that I felt frightened and excited at the same time. We were a very highly trained and efficient regiment, and we did as we were trained to do, responding quickly to a situation without question. And if you wanted to live you had to kill.[62]

Lost that day was the commanding officer of the 5th Dragoon Guards, Lieutenant Colonel George Ansell. A fellow officer, Charles Blackburne, wrote of him:

Now about poor George; we were attacked at daybreak and the Germans nearly succeeded in stampeding our horses, we turned out dismounted close to the lines and held the Germans in check. I came up and, as I happened to be there, we had a word about the position (our left flank was unprotected). George told me to go there with what men I had. I collected a few. He then galloped back, mounted two squadrons, and went off with them, wide round the left flank. He rode up to the top of one ridge, ahead of his men, to reconnoitre, and they, the Germans, were close to him. They hit him and he rode back about fifty yards. One of the last things he said to his orderly was to go up into the firing line, as he would be of more use there. He was a brave man and I feel his loss most awfully. They got a doctor to him, but nothing could be done, shot through chest and back I am told.

In my opinion the action George took in going round the flank not only saved the whole situation but established a panic among the Germans, who fled, and we captured eight of their guns.[63]

A remarkable and rare German account of the Néry action exists, in the form of a diary kept by a soldier who was present with the *Husaren-Regiment Königin Wilhelmena der Niederlande (Hannoversches) Nr. 15*, a man named Gustav Ostendorf:

From approximately at 10 o'clock in the evening, until 4am on the 1 September we were continuously on the march again, i.e., the only halts made were necessary ones to soak [the horses]. That made three days and nights [continuously advancing], fortunately in the meantime I had received an extra half loaf of bread from my Vizewachtmeister [sergeant] Hass. By this exhausting ride we had caught up with the enemy, who were occupying the village lying 2 km before us. Obviously they [the enemy soldiers] were also very tired, because for the time being everything remained calm in Néry, as the village was called. We attacked immediately, with our three cavalry brigades in an encircling movement, which meant that we came into the village from all sides at once, however we received heavy machine-gun fire from the houses, which cost us heavy casualties. In order not to be overwhelmed by the English infantry, we had to pull back and we now proceeded in skirmish line [again into the attack]. Our guns had taken up the fight with the English artillery, which at the strength of three batteries came into action before the lime sandstone factory left of the village. We took cover in the oats field as our artillery roared, this artillery fire had already destroyed seven enemy field guns. One enemy gun [pulled by horses] came out at the gallop from the village, it had hardly been touched whilst at the factory, but then this also was hit by two shell bursts together. Thus we did not have much more trouble from hostile shells, however at the same time, our guns had been reduced just to four, partly by barrels exploding. Suddenly we heard the Englishmen shouting to the left of us, they were quickly halted [by artillery], but they had already taken prisoner 10 or 15 men from the left wing.

On the following day, 2 September we set off away from the enemy, since they possessed a substantial superiority over us. We tried throughout the day to escape, but we did not find a way out. The noose pulled ever more closely around us, who were then silently with man, horse, wagon and cannon waiting in the darkness of a forest, with thick undergrowth and mountains towering

Gustav Ostendorf, of the German Husaren Regiment Nr. 15, *who provided one of the few German accounts of the Néry action.* (Martin Teller)

above. So complete was this cover, that all were protected by it. Field guns, machine-guns, flags and banners were buried. In this serious situation we spent full 2 days and nights, until by [sending out a] lone patrol we succeeded in making contact with our own troops behind us. In time we were again ready for combat, but for the moment however we required a rest, because for 3 days there was nothing to ease the growling stomach. It was all the more pleasing that we received two days of peace, which were completely spent preparing horses and riders, so that they were again freshly strengthened for the coming days.[64]

In the chaos of the Retreat, men could be temporarily made prisoners and then liberated again in a matter of days, if not hours. One remarkable case was that of Lieutenant H.M. Hill of the 5th Dragoon Guards, who was also involved in the Néry action. One of his fellow officers wrote to Hill's sister on 4 September:

Maurice was in my troop and I daresay you know three days ago we had a sharp skirmish with the Germans and my troop was heavily engaged in dismounted action against the enemy at about 300 yards. When the order came to retire we stopped to cover the retirement of another troop then retired again by sections – Maurice's section was the last to go. They lay down steadily firing while the other sections retired and when their turn came to go there was no covering fire from behind and I had to tell them to bolt for it. Of the section of 4 only one got out. Two were shot at once and Maurice wounded in the head within 10 yards of me and about 100 yards from safety. My troop sergeant returned about 2 hours later and got him into a farm where he is being well looked after.[65]

In fact, the sergeant had removed Hill's identity disc and when the farm was overrun by the Germans, Hill was made prisoner. Still unconscious from his head wound, the Germans had no idea as to his identity. Later still, the farm fell back into Allied hands, and he was taken to a hospital in Paris. He was still unable to tell the nuns who were nursing him who he was, and it was only some weeks later that his identity came to light, via a number on his handmade boots. He never however made a full recovery, and later had a metal plate fitted to his skull. Hill died shortly after the war as a result of his wounds.

Another British officer who was a temporary German prisoner for just a few hours was Aubrey Herbert MP. He was serving at the time with the 1st Battalion Irish Guards, having applied for and been granted a commission upon the outbreak of war. On 1 September 1914 the Irish and 2nd Battalion Coldstream Guards were acting as rearguard, covering the retirement of the 2nd Division, holding a line across the forest of Villers Cottérêts. A second line was formed further behind by the 3rd Battalion Coldstream Guards and 2nd Battalion Grenadier Guards. Around 10.45am the Irish Guards were heavily attacked. This was the first serious engagement of the regiment in the war, and during it, the colonel was killed. Retiring by stages, the Guards regiments, by now intermixed but still maintaining iron discipline, reached the village of Villers Cottérêts itself, having lost over 300 men in total in this action. Herbert himself was badly wounded in the incident, being hit by a ricochet in the side. After dressing his wound, medics had little choice but to leave him on a stretcher:

> I lost consciousness for a bit; then I heard my regiment charging. There were loud cries and little spurts of spasmodic shooting; then everything was quiet and a deep peace fell upon the wood. It was very dreamlike … As I lay on the stretcher a jarring thought came to me. I had in my pocket the flat-nosed bullets which the War Office had served out to us as revolver ammunition. They were not dum-dum bullets, but they would naturally not make as pleasant a wound as the sharp-nosed ones, and it occurred to me that those having them would be shot. I searched my pockets and flung mine away. I did not discover one which remained and was buried later on – but neither did the Germans. It was first hearing German voices close by that jogged my memory about these bullets, and the Germans were then so close that I felt some difficulty in throwing the bullets away. The same idea must have occurred to others, for later I heard the Germans speaking very angrily about the flat bullets they had picked up in the wood, and saying how they would deal with anyone in whose possession they were found.
>
> The glades became resonant with loud, raucous German commands and occasional cries from wounded men. After about an hour and a half, I suppose, a German with a red beard, with the sun shining on his helmet and bayonet, came up looking like an angel of death. He walked round from behind, and put his serrated bayonet on the empty stretcher by me, so close that it all but touched me.

The stretcher broke and his bayonet poked me. I enquired in broken but polite German what he proposed to do next; after reading the English papers and seeing the way he was handling his bayonet, it seemed to me that there was going to be another atrocity. He was extraordinarily kind and polite. He put something under my head; offered me wine, water, and cigarettes. He said: 'Wir sind kamaraden.' Another soldier came up and said: 'Why didn't you stay in England – you who made war upon the Boers?' I said: 'We obeyed orders, just as you do; as for the Boers, they were our enemies and are now our friends, and it is not your business to insult wounded men.' My first friend then cursed him heartily, and he moved on. The Germans passed in crowds. They seemed like steel locusts. Every now and then I would hear: 'Here is an officer who talks German,' and the crowd would swerve in like a steel eddy. Then: 'Schnell Kinder!' and they would be off. They gave a tremendous impression of lightness and iron. After some hours, when my wound was beginning to hurt, some carriers came up to take me to a collecting place for the wounded. These men were rather rough. They dropped me and my stretcher once, but were cursed by an officer. They then carried me some distance, and took me off the stretcher, leaving me on the ground.[66]

When a British counterattack drove them back, Herbert's captors abandoned him.

On 5 September the Retreat finally ended, on the outskirts of Paris. That it did so was largely due to a failure of nerve on the part of the German High Command. Their infamous 'Schlieffen Plan' had called for the northern tip of the sweeping German arc to pass down the western side of Paris, thus encircling the city. Instead, at the end of overstretched supply lines, the Germans chose to abandon the plan, and pass down the eastern side of the city. Thus while still fighting on the left flank, their right flank lay open to attack from the garrison of Paris. In the coming battle, the tables would be turned as the German First Army and Second Army were forced apart, much as the British I and II Corps had been forced apart following the Battle of Mons. The greatest opportunity that the Germans would have of capturing Paris, not just in 1914 but perhaps in the entire war, would be lost.

Chapter 3

Most Awful and Bloodthirsty

The German advance, and the pursuit of the retreating French and British armies, had by early September begun to run out of steam. Just as with the men of the BEF, the constant marching had taken its toll on the German soldier. Furthermore, as in almost every case when an apparently victorious army follows on the heels of a defeated enemy, the latter is able to fall back on supplies and reinforcements, while the advancing force finds itself at the end of ever longer and more precarious supply lines. Remembering this phase of the campaign, Hauptmann Walter Bloem wrote:

> The most depressing factor . . . was our own exhausted selves: we were all literally done in. For exactly two weeks since August 23rd, we had been in constant touch with the enemy, and lately had had minor encounters with him daily. If this was modern warfare we had not been trained, nor were we prepared for it . . . At this early period . . . our ideas of war . . . were based entirely on the 1870 campaign. A battle, according to that, would begin at 6am and end, victoriously of course, at 6pm . . . But this was something entirely different, something utterly unexpected. For a month now we had been in the enemy's country, and during that time had been on the march incessantly . . . without a single rest-day. We were astonished at our own powers of endurance.[1]

As the German First Army and Second Army swung around to face southwards, the garrison of Paris advanced to meet them. Von Kluck, commanding the First Army, peeled off to deal with the threat, in the process creating a gap between his army and that of his opposite number, Von Bulow. This precise moment gave birth to the legend of the 'Miracle of the Marne'. Winston Churchill would later identify it as the critical juncture at which the Germans came closest to winning the war, but instead let the opportunity slip through their fingers. As the BEF (which had now grown in strength to three corps) halted its retreat, and began to advance into the gap, Von Kluck realised almost too late that he had thrust his head into a giant bag which was in danger of closing. It was now the turn of the Germans to begin retreating. Lieutenant C.T. Baynham, a Royal Field Artillery subaltern, wrote in his memoirs later:

> It was on this day, 5th September, that the rumour began to circulate that the enemy's advance had been stemmed and that a general offensive was contemplated. From that moment, new life and interest was apparent in all ranks. Colour was lent to this by orders received about midnight for all troops to be prepared to 'advance at 2.00am', our destination being the village of Juivsy. The 6th September

was occupied in reconnoitring gun positions in view of the contemplated offensive referred to above. These positions were never occupied as the dramatic with-drawal of the enemy occasioned by the presence of the VI French Army on our left allowed little time for a set engagement. From this day until we reached the Aisne, the positions of the opposing forces were completely reversed. We now became the pursuers and the enemy the pursued. On the 7th September, the division followed up the enemy without, however, enjoying any serious action. I secured on this day a notebook and letters off a dead German cavalryman, shot in the streets of a small village to which I went to obtain a supply of bread.

The march on this day took us on to the outskirts of Coulommiers. It was not, however, till the following day, 8th September, that we came into serious contact with the enemy rearguard. On this day we arrived at Les Corbeilles overlooking La Ferté sous Jouarre, a most picturesque town on the Marne. Both banks of the river being extremely hilly and wooded, one could look down on the town with its bridge over the river and see on the opposing hills long columns of reteating German troops, out of range, unfortunately, of our field guns. The enemy rear-guard was still occupying the town when we arrived and endeavouring to stop us from crossing and coming within range of his retreating columns ...[2]

Walter Bloem was among those German soldiers providing the rear-guard in La Ferté sous Jouarre. He wrote a graphic description of the state of the town, and offers a vivid insight indeed into the mindset of the German soldier at this time:

The streets were now filled with a host of men, moving back across the Marne, a whole army and an army retreating. It must have been obvious now to the most dense what was happening. We knew well what a victorious advance was like and

British 60-pounder guns in action in September 1914. These were the heaviest weapons operated by the Royal Field Artillery at the time.

the spirit that animated it; we had lived with it for a month; but this was very different. We did not understand, but we could see, and that sufficed. The town reflected this fateful hour in its country's struggle for existence ... The houses were deserted and shuttered up, their doors smashed open by a succession of troops searching for a lodging; those on both banks of the river had had great holes torn in the walls and all the windows broken by the force of the explosions when the bridges were blown up, the curtains inside were hanging in shreds, and the furniture smashed to pieces. The few inhabitants left skulked about like shadows, like poverty-striken beggars.

I was so impressed by the sight that, when we halted just after crossing back over the Marne, I made my company a small speech: 'You see that, men,' I said, pointing back at the town, 'that's what they hoped to do to us, and now we've done it to them. You can understand now why we are here: so that that should take place in this foreign land and not in our own homes. That is why we have had not a minutes rest for the past four weeks, that is why you have marched the soles off your feet, that is why we have fought in a dozen engagements, and it is for that, too, so many of our friends have given their lives. Think that over, men, and be proud and thankful that it is you, you yourselves, who have spared your homes such a fate!'[3]

Even at this early stage of the war air power was beginning to show what it was capable of, and several times airmen demonstrated the potential of this new weapon. It was a reconnaissance flight by the Royal Flying Corps that had established that

the German columns had begun to retreat away from Paris, and a few days after that, a daring raid by Lieutenant Gilbert Mapplebeck of Number 4 Squadron demonstrated what else might be possible with aircraft. While on recon- naissance he came across a German transport column of thirteen wagons. He had three bombs with him, and these he used to such effect that within minutes the entire column was a smoking ruin. The wagons were laden with explosives, and the first bomb landed near the tail end. In Mapplebeck's own words: 'That began the firework diplay.'[4] The other bombs he dropped near the centre and these triggered a series of terrific explosions which enveloped the column. Not surprisingly, he was awarded a DSO in consequence of this action.

Second Lieutenant Gilbert Mapplebeck, Royal Flying Corps, awarded the DSO for his daring attack on a German convoy.

A German motorised column after destruction from the air in September 1914 – quite possibly that which was attacked by Mapplebeck.

The initial contacts on the ground during the Battle of the Marne were characterised by short, sharp cavalry actions. The Germans were attempting to screen their withdrawal by using several regiments of mounted troops strung out along the Grand Morin River. This was largely unsuccessful, as all three army corps of the BEF were across the river by nightfall on 7 September. British cavalry led the advance, and Lieutenant Jock Crabbe of the 2nd Dragoons (Royal Scots Greys) in his memoir describes a typical encounter with the Germans. A troop from the regiment had already been ambushed at Rebais, and the survivors were pinned down in houses unable to make further progress. Crabbe was hastily ordered to go to their assistance. He writes:

> I gave orders [to the men] to hand their horses over to the horse holders and got ready to attack, and while this was being done my plan had to be framed. What was I to do? There was Rebais, its roofs just visible through the trees, on a rise about 600 yards distant, and in some houses somewhere on my right front were the remainder of the [other] troop unable to get on. Obviously my task seemed to be, not so much to take Rebais independently but to do so in conjunction with them. Then what was the best way to do it?[5]

Crabbe and his men charged headlong up a stream, with the tall nettles along the side and the tree canopy above making it seem increasingly like a tunnel as it narrowed towards the end. His plan brought them out into the main square, where the horses of the Germans were corralled. He told a party of men off to try to stampede them. The excitement and adrenaline of what happened next is palpable:

> Off I and my trumpeter dashed, he with a rifle and I with a revolver, through houses and back gardens, across a street, more gardens and through another

house, until we came out in the corner of a second square just north of [that] where the horses were. I had just started to cross the square when there was a crack of a bullet past my head. I flung myself behind a front garden balustrade just as another hit it by my ear. There was I in the middle of a village for all I knew full of Germans, armed only with a revolver. I looked for the trumpeter, only to see him lying taking cover behind the corner of a house about 15 yards to my right but in such a position that he could not fire down the square. I shouted to him to fling me his rifle which he very skilfully did as it landed on the little piece of grass behind my balustrade. It is hard to say how thankful I was when I had that rifle safely in my hand as it gave me such a sense of confidence compared with that revolver. I peered slowly round the right side of my balustrade and at once spotted my friend taking cover behind a tree at the far end of the square. He had his rifle to his shoulder ready to fire when I gave him a sufficiently good target. But he just waited a fraction too long as I got in the first shot and he fell backwards into what looked like a ditch.[6]

Crabbe now decided to wait for events to take their turn:

It could not have been more than a few seconds later when, to my great relief, rapid firing broke out on my right and I hoped my troop were shooting straight and being successful. Amidst the shooting I could hear shouts and the galloping of horses. A few mounted Germans crossed me going all out; I speeded them up unsuccessfully with some parting shots … I gave the trumpeter back his rifle and left him at the northern exit of the village to keep watch, while I went back to find out what my troop had done or were doing. When I got to the main square where the German horses had been, I found the bulk of my troop either rounding up some loose horses or being hugged by the local inhabitants who at the departure of the Germans had suddenly come out of their cellars and hiding places. There were a few dead horses lying about and a couple of wounded Germans of the 8th Dragoons, but to prove that they left in a panic 47 lances were picked up.[7]

The life of an ordinary British infantryman at this time is well documented by the diary of Private William Pelling of the 2nd Battalion Royal Sussex Regiment. The German rearguard was still able to deliver a nasty punch when cornered, even though they were now the hunted and the British the hunters. Pelling's brother was serving in the same battalion, and this briefly added an extra dimension of tension to the casualties that the Royal Sussex sustained in spearheading the advance. Pelling wrote:

Woke up wet through and found ourselves as advanced guard to 1st Army Corps. Regt is main guard – BCDA [companies]. At Priez the bn attacked the German rear guard at Rassey. As the Bn got in extended order a terrific artillery & rifle fire caused our regt & N. Lancs to retire in disorder leaving many dead and wounded. The Germans were well concealed at short range and we hardly fired a round in

Soldiers of the Queen's (Royal West Surrey) Regiment fire from behind brick stacks at Meaux during the Battle of the Marne.

reply. A 'coalbox' landed under the leading ammunition wagon killing 3 and both horses including the Regtl Sergt Major. The Divnl Cyclist Section had to throw their bicycles and escape on foot. Men were cutting off each other's packs. I kept mine & jolly pleased I did after. Meanwhile our artillery had got to work & the Germans fled. The battalion collected after & the casualties estimated at 14 killed and 85 wounded. I had not seen G for several hours during the day & got rather anxious but I found him eventually alive and well. The Bn billeted at Rassey for the night. I slept in the open.[8]

There were many instances of brutality on both sides during the campaign of 1914, and often little evidence of the camadarie between opposing front-line soldiers which was supposedly a feature of the Great War. Prisoners of war fared particularly badly in many cases. However there were occasional instances of humanity between enemies. Writing to his regimental journal in 1934, Major E.D. Martin stated:

Lieut Baron von Bischoffshausen of the Jäger battalion was wounded in the advance of the 5th Dragoon Guards at Sablonnieres on the Petit Morin on the 8th September 1914. We were both wounded very near each other; perhaps he got me – I certainly did not get him as I was hit before I really saw anything. We spent that day in an ambulance together, then two days in a train to St Nazaire, and two more on the *Carisbrooke Castle* coming home to Southampton. There our ways parted. He asked me to try to get word home to his mother through the Chilean Embassy. As his brother had already been killed he knew she would be in great anxiety about himself as missing. I did my best but am afraid without success ... I feared that he might have died or lost his leg – he had a terrible wound in the thigh, which went gangrenous on the boat.[9]

That year of 1934, Martin had obtained von Bischoffshausen's address in Berlin and wrote to him. The German officer replied:

> I was more than pleased to receive your letter. Not only do I remember, but I have always to my mind the circumstances of our meeting and your comradeship and kindness in looking after me.
>
> Sablonnieres, field hospital, transport etc are as fresh to me, and I can scarcely realise that twenty years have passed ... I still have in my possession your card with the annotation '5th Dragoon Guards' ... I have saved my leg thanks to the masterly and perfect care of the Chirurge, Dr Maloney, in Netley Hospital.[10]

Of course, the fact that the two individuals involved in this incident were both officers and from a higher social caste made a great deal of difference to their circumstances; and men from Pelling's class could expect rather less understanding and compassion if they fell into enemy hands, as gunner officer Cecil Brownlow found the following day. As his battery advanced they came upon stark evidence that the tide of war was turning now in the favour of the Allies, and also of the cost paid by animals in human conflict:

> On 9th September we bivouacked at Nanteuil by the banks of the Marne, which flows serenely along a deep and winding valley, flanked by wooded heights, and at dawn on the morrow were on the march once more, crossed the river, and, after climbing a long hill, reached the rolling uplands to the north. The more we progressed the more we saw evidences of the German retreat and of the rearguard fighting. On either side of the main road two parallel tracks were beaten, showing that the enemy were in such haste that they had retired in the old Napoleonic treble column: vehicles on the road, cavalry and infantry on either flank.
>
> Along the roads were scattered empty tins, cartridges, rifles, lances, fragments of field-grey uniform and discarded packs, made of hide with the hair still on. Occasionally we came upon derelict German motor-lorries and German transport. In many places were gruesome evidences of fighting: hasty entrenchments scooped a foot or so into the soil, with a litter of empty cartridges and a corpse stiffly twisted in a self-made grave. At one spot a German battalion must have been caught in the open by our guns, for a soft stubble field showed the marks of many feet, was pitted with shell-holes, and was strewed with dead men. At another place an enemy column of transport had been caught crossing the crest of a ridge. The line of horsed vehicles with attendant drivers was still in the terrible immobility of death. The wagons were torn and shattered, white splinters of wood bristling upwards like bones. The horses, gashed and disembowelled, lay in groups, weltering in congealed ponds of blood, while on the horses and across the vehicles huddled the crumbled forms of what lately had been men. Batches of prisoners passed by under guards, who seemed filled with the importance of their task, and who showed off the points of their charges like a dog-fancier with a new purchase.[11]

Frank Richards and the 2nd Battalion Royal Welsh Fusiliers arrived in the village of La Ferté sous Jouarre on 8 September to find the Germans on the opposite bank of the Marne still resisting, and directing a heavy fire at them. Richards recalled the following morning:

> Some [of our men] were drumming up – that is, making tea – others wandering about on the scrounge, when suddenly a machine-gun opened fire from across the river, sweeping the street. Second-Lieutenant Thompson of my battalion was badly wounded; most of the men had taken cover as soon as the gun opened out. Two men named Jackson and Edwards rushed forward, in spite of the machine-gun, and carried him to safety, Jackson getting shot through the wrist ... The

Private Frank Richards, of the 2nd Battalion Royal Welsh Fusiliers, who arrived in La Ferté sous Jouarre on the Marne on 8 September. (Mrs Margaret Holmes)

> enemy were fighting a rearguard action and seven of us were told to get up in the toilet of the house and make loopholes in the walls with our entrenching tools. We found a couple of picks in a toolhouse and we soon made the loopholes. We could now see right across the river and the rising ground behind the village on the other side. There were a few more bursts of machine-gun fire from the other side of the river and then silence. We spotted some of the enemy making their way up the rising ground and opened out with rapid fire which we kept up until we could see no one to fire at. We had some excellent shooting practice for about five minutes and saw a lot of men fall.
>
> A few hours later the engineers had constructed a pontoon bridge across the river which we crossed without having a shot fired at us. There were a lot of dead Germans in the village on the other side of the river and they were soon relieved of any valuables they had on them. As fast as we retired on our retirement, the Germans were equally fast on theirs from the Marne to the Aisne.[12]

That same day, the 1st Battalion Lincolnshire Regiment took part in the dramatic capture of a German field battery in the woods west of Bezu. Captain Hoskyns of this battalion recounted the incident in a letter to a friend shortly afterwards:

> Never have I had such big gun hunting. We first started in file, not knowing if Germans were in the wood or not – we never knew when machine-guns would open on us unawares as we crossed the many side tracks in the wood. At last, after some time, we came to a broad ride and felt that here at least the Bosche must surely have someone, as the reports of his guns seemed quite close. A minute's anxiety as we pushed a few men across at intervals, and as no horrid 'phut, phut'

German field guns, captured by the Lincolnshire Regiment on 8 September, being moved by rail. The name of the regiment has been chalked on one.

came, I got my Company over and formed them into line, C Company doing the same on my right, to beat through the wood. I went ahead with my Sub, Thruston – and as we got near to the further edge we went warily and silently, followed by our men, who had thoroughly entered into the spirit of our hunt. As Thruston and I got near to the edge we distinctly saw the German artillery in line, firing at right angles to our advance on their left, and nearest gun about one hundred and fifty yards from the wood, and to our horror, we also saw a few yards off a Bosche sentry looking in our direction. We stopped dead for what seemed an age, and then to our relief, he turned away and walked slowly off. Suddenly, however, he stopped again, and we saw that he thought all was not well as he looked in our direction. I now felt that the game was up and called to Thruston, who was carrying a rifle to 'down him.' No sooner said than the Bosche was shot and our men, who were level with us, opened fire on the German gunners; these, taken entirely by surprise, tried to turn their guns round on us, but long before this was done we had shot them down.[13]

The extraordinary skill and bravery shown in this episode was however marred, when immediately afterwards in a 'friendly fire' incident gunners of 65th (Howitzer) Battery RFA fired on the battalion, mistaking them for German gunners attempting to recover abandoned guns. The Lincolns sustained casualties of four officers and thirty men killed or wounded, the latter including Captain Hoskyns. One of the guns was later presented to the regiment as a trophy, and may still be seen at the Museum of Lincolnshire Life in Lincoln. Some of the bullet holes resulting from the time of its capture are visible in the trail even today. Frederick Bolwell, of the Loyal North Lancashires, recounted a similar 'red on red' incident in his memoir:

> Our worst day – the one on which we did the most fighting – was the tenth of September. On the morning of that day we marched off particularly early, and we must have done close on ten miles, as we were halted for rest on two occasions. On breasting a hill about two miles from the last halt, we were again called to the halt, and the Artillery, brought up from behind, opened out on each side of the road and the crest of the hill. The word was then passed down the ranks that a large German convoy was expected to leave this village, and that we were to capture it. Every one was in high spirits, as food had been none too plentiful, and we were all looking forward to the capture of this convoy in the hopes of recompense.
>
> The North Lancashires were the second regiment, with the 2nd Royal Sussex leading, they and the King's Royal Rifles taking the left of the road, and the North Lancashires and Northamptons taking the right. We then commenced to advance in Artillery formation, three hundred paces distant and fifty paces interval: this we did until reaching the bottom of the hill and to the right of the village half a mile away. In this village, by name Preiz, were the Germans, and running out the other side, but up the hill, was the German convoy retiring, the village itself being in a basin. On reaching the bottom of the hill, we had to cross a stream: once on the other side we opened out in extended order, our idea being to skirt the village and come up with the Germans going over the other crest. Unfortunately it was a wet morning, and the men had taken the advantage of putting their oil-sheets round their shoulders to keep them dry, the oil-sheets when wet being of a similar colour to the German uniform. In the distance our gunners bombarded us, mistaking us for the retiring enemy; and we had no sooner come into view of our gunners than they let go. However, we plodded on, going up in short rushes by platoons … On crossing a narrow track of road near the crest of the hill we were joined by the C.O., who had come up there by the road to give us final instructions. He got hit by a piece of shell, which passed through his horse's neck and entered his stomach: he died a few minutes afterwards.[14]

The death of the colonel in this fashion must have been a bitter blow for the battalion.

Lieutenant Arnold Gyde of the 2nd Battalion South Staffordshire Regiment wrote of his experiences with the BEF in 1914 under the pseudonym 'Casualty'. His book *Contemptible* ably captures the mood and spirit of the British regular army in those first months of the war (throughout the book, Gyde refers to himself in the third person, as 'the Subaltern'). The South Staffords crossed the Marne unopposed at Charly, over a bridge that the Germans in their haste had neglected to destroy. They then proceeded through wooded country towards Coupru, acting as advanced guard. On 10 September they were again in the vanguard, and at Hautevesnes the enemy were encountered still in position. These men were actually a strong rearguard, left behind by the Germans to hold up the advance of the BEF for as long as possible. After a sharp fight, 300 prisoners were taken. Following this attack his men were eager for souvenirs, helmets especially, but Gyde also witnessed, if not exactly camaraderie with, then at least a grudging respect for the captive Germans. Referring to his own men, he says:

> When the Subaltern came up the 'show' was over. There were a great many dead Germans lying, as they had died, behind the embankment. The thought of taking something which they had worn never occurred to him. If it had been he would have dismissed it on the grounds that there was no means of sending such things home, while to add to the weight and worry of his kit by carrying a 'Pickelhaube' about, indefinitely, for the rest of the campaign, was, of course, unthinkable.
>
> Then the 'rally' sounded, and the companies that had taken part in the attack began to re-form. There was a considerable delay before two of the platoons appeared at the rallying point. The men did not come in a body but by driblets . . . A large band of prisoners had been captured by our troops that day. Small detachments had from time to time been captured ever since the turn at Chaumes, but this was different. There were long lines of them, standing bolt upright, and weaponless. The Subaltern looked at them curiously. They struck him as on the whole taller than the English, and their faces were not brown, but grey. He admired their coats, there was a martial air in the long sweep of them. And he confessed that one looked far more of a soldier in a helmet. There is a ferocity about the things, a grimness well suited to a soldier. . . . Not that clothes make the man.
>
> He sternly refused himself the pleasure of going to get a closer sight of them. He wanted very badly to see them, perhaps to talk French with them, but a feeling that it was perhaps *infra dignitatem* debarred him. The men, however, had no such scruples. They crowded round their captives, and slowly and silently surveyed them. They looked at them with the same sort of interest that one displays towards an animal in the Zoo, and the Germans paid just as much attention to their regard as Zoo animals do. Considering that only a short hour ago they had been trying to take each other's lives, there seemed to be an appalling lack of emotion in either party. Fully half an hour the Tommies inspected them thus. Then, with infinite deliberation, one man produced a packet of 'Caporal' cigarettes and offered one, with an impassive countenance, to a German. As far as the Subaltern could see, not a single word was exchanged nor a gesture made. They did not move away until it was time to fall in.[15]

After this skirmish there followed yet another friendly fire incident, in which British gunners inadvertently fired on their own infantry, again because they were wearing the bluish-grey groundsheets; the adjutant of the 1st Battalion Royal Berkshire Regiment and several other men were killed in this incident.

That day, 10 September, it dawned misty, and cavalry patrols from the Scots Greys reported large bodies of Germans near the village of Gandelu, apparently in bivouacs and unprepared to defend themselves. More than an hour was lost as in the mist conflicting reports mistakenly identified the body of men as French. Eventually an advance on the village was ordered but by then most of the Germans had left, with just a rearguard left behind and a column of wagons tantalisingly visible upon the horizon! Lieutenant Jock Crabbe takes up the story, describing another dismounted action, full of the chaos and confusion inherent in house-to-house fighting. The plan was for his troop to rush the village, before the Germans had time to react:

Off we all started together in line, and once over the top the pace increased to a mad race as it was far steeper than we expected; our legs completely ran away with us and we were over the wall and into the garden before we realised how far we had come. I believe the Germans fired at us the whole way down and also at point blank range in the garden, but though several tripped up falling head over heels, we all reached the houses in safety. As soon as we emerged into the street I quickly realised that we were being fired upon from all sides, and as there was no place to hide, I shouted to carry on through the other houses and out into the wood beyond, where I knew we would be both under cover and have the village surrounded. We got there alright, and as now we were being sniped from both the village and the woods, I ordered one section of 5 men to watch the village and prevent the defenders retiring, while with the remainder I turned about and having extended to about 10 paces between each, we beat the wood as if for rabbits. Nearly all the Germans encountered were stragglers and had little fight left. Some were, however, foolish enough to have a last despairing shot and then hold up their hands imagining they would be taken prisoner. We had some quite good shooting at extremely close range though I did not feel bloodthirsty myself enough to fire at such poor game, and cleared the wood as far as the river. On reaching it, thinking it was only a foot or so deep, I plunged in, but was completely taken in by the mud as it took me to the armpits. Just as I was clambering up the far bank, two Germans appeared from out of the undergrowth; so seizing my rifle by the muzzle I rushed at them and they threw down their rifles and fell on their knees.

[Now] we recrossed the river and went back to collect the section at Gandelu. When I reached them I noticed a white flag waved from a window, so boldly walking up to the village, Germans there began to come out of every house and fall in on the street. There were 39 in all, and when I was close to them the officer called them to attention and told them, what sounded like a few home truths in German. Then he turned to me and after saluting, drew his sword from its scabbard,

Lieutenant Jock Crabbe, of the Royal Scots Greys. (Colin Crabbe)

and holding it by the point handed it to me in the old fashioned manner. At the same time he said in excellent English, 'These men are pigs; you should never have got down that hill; but most of them hid in the cellars; but you will not find the whole German Army like them.' I felt quite embarrassed as I did not know whether I was expected to say something in return and besides I was hardly looking my best, wet and muddy all over. But I merely told him to tell his men to lay down their arms on the ground and when my men had picked them up, we all marched back up the hill together to where I had left my horses.

With the exception of that mad rush down the hill, when one had no time to be afraid, the whole fight was a picnic, as nearly all the Germans met were either so footsore that they were reconciled at being captured or they were completely lost in the woods. Again, we were lucky as we had no casualties, while in addition to the officer and 39 men captured, we had accounted for about 25 in the wood one way or another.[16]

Crabbe narrowly averted another friendly fire incident, when the gunners again mistook retiring British troops for advancing Germans, and he was able to warn them of the error. He continued:

The whole fighting for the ridge had now become very scattered and no further progress was made until the Cornwalls who had crossed the river east of Gandelu, made an attack from that quarter, and with their help the ridge was cleared. Then orders for a further advance were given ... Much as I had enjoyed watching the battle from a safe place, I was very pleased at the thought of getting back to the squadron as I could not help feeling I was missing something. So we did not waste time; however crossing over the river I took the very sound precaution of making my troop throw all the captured revolvers etc. into the river, and along with them went the presentation sword. Not only did the collection of souvenirs add weight on the horse, but it was a certainty that one of these revolvers would go off in inexperienced hands and hurt someone ... we took things peacefully only moving a further 5 miles forward to Passy-en-Valois. Now the very hot weather which we had had for the last fortnight broke, and we were deluged by a pitiless thunder storm. As I was already wet from my effort in the river it made little difference to me, but we all welcomed it as we were fed up with the dust and heat.[17]

For C.E. Green of the Scots Guards, writing in his diary for 10 September 1914, far from being welcome the wet weather was now as much of an enemy to be contended with as were the Germans:

For 12 hours we rested, and marched 11 miles, entered a wood and halted. We were wet through, raining all the time. It was most uncomfortable, no shelter being found for us. Big wood fires were lit, and we found some straw and branches to build a little cover if possible. The rain however found faults in our structures, and dawn next morning came as a welcome relief. At 9am we paraded.
12-9-14 marched to P—— 14 miles, and the rain once more came down. We halted whilst shelter was being found for us, if possible. After considerable delay, & by this time wet to the skin, our officers marched through a vegetable & fruit

garden to a brick wall, our only cover from the weather. About an hour afterwards, we decided to beg borrow or steal wood to light a fire, and surround it for the night. This was done, gates, doors, farm implements etc forming part of the 'loot' we searched for. The weather turned somewhat at daybreak ... A gale had also been blowing during the rainfall.[18]

As more German-held villages were retaken in the advance on the Marne, disturbing evidence began to come to light of Teutonic methods of dealing with the civilian population. Lieutenant C.T. Baynham takes up the story once again:

On September 11th, the pursuit was continued through La Ferte Millon, the inhabitants being overjoyed at our arrival and acclaiming us as deliverers. Men and officers alike were loaded with fruit of every description and with the red and white wine of the country. On the other hand, the roads were strewn with the debris of a retreating army, dead horses and men, broken wagons and straw litter taken to form a temporary bed from adjoining fields. Occasionally, one would see in a village the gruesome sight of a civilian who had paid the penalty with his life for some act which had displeased the enemy. In villages where similar scenes had occurred, the inhabitants were nowhere to be seen, having locked and bolted themselves into their houses with their shutters up, and suspicious even of our approach, not having seen British troops before. The village of Crouy was one such. At the entrance to the village, on a green patch, lay the lifeless body of the village Mayor, shot against the wall, because the village had not been able to produce the necessary forage and food imposed upon them by the German authority. In the village itself, the contents of the houses had been turned wholesale into

the street, cots, clothing, sewing machines, tables and chairs being in one broken and confused mass on the roadway, whilst the never ending trail of broken bottles told their own story.[19]

The leading troops of the BEF, the I Corps, now crossed the River Aisne at Bourg, and took up a covering position on the northern bank. Meanwhile, to the west, patrols from the 2nd Division reported that the bridge at Chavonne had been destroyed, and that the approaches were covered by German snipers. At Pont d'Arcy however, the demolition of the bridge by the enemy had been only

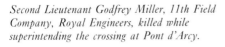

Second Lieutenant Godfrey Miller, 11th Field Company, Royal Engineers, killed while superintending the crossing at Pont d'Arcy.

The partially destroyed bridge at Pont d'Arcy on the Aisne, crossed by Lieutenant Martin of the Royal Engineers.

partially successful, and it was still possible to cross by foot. One of the RE officers who arrived to inspect the bridge was Lieutenant C.G. Martin, of 56th Field Company, who remembered:

> I was sent up to reconnoitre ... And I went up with my Commanding Officer, and we just got onto the bank when the Germans crossed to the other side, shooting at us ... My Commanding Officer wasn't killed, luckily, but he was wounded and had to go, and then after that I was sent back to reconnoitre what the Germans had left ... and they had destroyed a steel section of the bridge but had left a little tank in it, about 30 yards long on the bridge, and the men were sitting at the side ... they wanted to know if it was safe to cross. I couldn't send them across, but I went across this thing, fearful that I was going to drop into the river, and I tied it up with bits of wire and stuff, and then of course, the men could cross the river ... the next job that [I] and the rest of 56 had [was] to build a bridge over the Aisne and we did that under pretty heavy fire ... the Adjutant by the name of Wright [Theodore Wright of Mons fame], he was killed on the edge of the river. He happened to be unlucky. A shell got him [when] he was helping to build the bridge ... [it was made of] pontoons. They were carried on pontoon wagons, boats about 15 feet long, each wagon had two and each company had two wagons, so there were four of them, and [we] put them in the water. They were put in parallel and [we] had all these timbers joining them up, in order to make the bridge.[20]

Among the officers serving here with the 1st Battalion Kings Royal Rifles was His Highness Prince Maurice of Battenberg, the youngest grandson of Queen Victoria.

Although born at Balmoral in Scotland, educated at English public schools and now serving in the British army, Prince Maurice was none the less a member of one of the German royal families. The difficulties caused by this position would lead the other members of the British royal family to renounce their German titles later in the war, but Battenberg was none the less popular with his men. One of them wrote of him later:

> It was in one of the charges on a bridge which was held by the Germans, just before we got to the Aisne, that Prince Maurice distinguished himself. He was very daring and was always one of the first in the fighting, no matter where or what it was. I was not actually in the charge, being in the supports behind; but I saw the charge made, and a grand sight it was to watch our fellows rush forward with the steel and take the bridge. At another time the Prince was in action with a German rearguard and narrowly escaped death. I was in this affair, and saw a German shell burst about a yard away. It plugged into the ground and made a fine commotion and scattered earth and fragments around us; but a chum and myself laughed as we dodged it, and that was the way we got into of taking these explosions when we became used to the war. You could not help laughing, even if you were a bit nervous. During this fight Prince Maurice was shot through the cap, so that he had a shave for his life, but he made light of his escape, and was very proud of the hole in the cap, which he showed to us when he talked with us, as he often did ...[21]

Battenberg was to be killed shortly afterwards and today his body is in Ypres Town Cemetery.

On the evening of Sunday 13 September 1914, the leading elements of the British Expeditionary Force crossed the Aisne, and the men had dug themselves in well up on the farther slopes; early next morning, British engineers were busily strengthening the new bridges and repairing some of the old, which the Germans had partially destroyed, so as to enable them to bear the weight of heavy traffic. A general advance was now begun along the whole western section of the Allied front, and along the whole frontage of the BEF, 14 September was a day of general attacks designed to drive the Germans back. British divisions came on to the battlefield in a piecemeal fashion to reinforce the vanguards already holding isolated posts. They found the enemy not only in position, well dug-in and supported by heavy artillery, but in such force that he clearly had no intention of continuing his retreat and instead made every effort to throw the BEF back across the river. It was to be a day of bitter and confused fighting. On the part of the British, the main offensive was entrusted to the I Corps, under Sir Douglas Haig, which had bivouacked on the northern bank of the river between Chavonne and Moulins. Its objective was the Chemin des Dames ridge, 4 miles to the north, the possession of which would give the British command of the southern part of the Craonne Plateau from Soissons to Berry-au-Bac. The 3rd Brigade, in capturing the village of Chivy, had a particularly severe task, the enemy being in immensely superior force and very strongly posted. The 2nd Battalion Welsh Regiment, in the centre, advancing by sections, had to clear the crest of the hill behind which lay the village.

Among them was another young officer fresh from Sandhurst, and experiencing war for the first time. His name was Second Lieutenant C.A.B. Young; aged just 19 and newly commissioned, he crossed to France in August 1914 in time to join the battalion on the Retreat from Mons. The Welsh saw no further action until the Battle of the Aisne, when Young recalled:

> Our objective ... was the ridge of the Chemin des Dames. The approach to it was up about 600 yards. A grassy slope with no cover, even a hillock. Absolutely open. There was no possible chance of taking the position because it was too far and there was no cover. We had no artillery worth having ... [we advanced] in extended open order. The colonel's order: officers to the front, drawn swords. [There was] heavy fire coming from the German position ... rifle fire and some machine-gun fire ... Mark Haggard of course, was one of the famous characters of that [incident] ... he was hit and couldn't move and he kept shouting out, 'Stick it Welsh!' but he died poor chap. A fellow went out and picked him up and got a Victoria Cross for it. Brought him back. [But we] hadn't gone more than about forty yards before we all came to a halt ... We all saw that it was impossible and started to come back ... [it was] not more than a quarter of an hour, before everybody realised it was an impossible job.[22]

Captain Mark Haggard, a nephew of the author Sir Rider Haggard, was a company commander in Young's battalion. He had ordered his men to lie down, and had advanced alone to reconnoitre the German position. Having assessed the lie of the land he then turned and shouted, 'Fix bayonets, boys,' and the Welshmen, rising to their feet, had dashed forward, only to be met by a withering machine-gun and rifle fire. Calling on his men to follow him, Captain Haggard, who carried, like them, a rifle and bayonet, rushed forward. He attempted to capture a Maxim gun, which was doing the worst damage. Just before he reached it however, he was struck by several bullets and fell to the ground mortally wounded.

Seeing Haggard fall, Sergeant William Fuller ran forward under tremendous fire to reach him and carried him back about 100yd. When he reached the shelter of a ridge,

he laid him down and dressed his wounds. He then, with the assistance of a private and the machine-gun officer Lieutenant Melvin, carried Captain Haggard to a barn adjoining a farmhouse some distance to the rear, which was being used as a dressing station. Here that evening the wounded officer passed away, and was buried close to the farmhouse. Sergeant Fuller, from Swansea, received the Victoria Cross for his actions that day.

Captain Mark Haggard, 2nd Battalion the Welsh Regiment. Haggard, a nephew of the writer Sir Rider Haggard, died at the Battle of the Aisne. As he did so he shouted, 'Stick it, the Welsh!'

After bringing in Captain Haggard, Fuller attended to two other injured officers of the Welsh Regiment, Lieutenant the Honourable Wellesley Fitzroy Somerset and Lieutenant Richards, who were both lying wounded in the same barn, until the ambulance came to remove them. Somerset remembered the details of the day's fighting, and how he came to be hit:

> I could see some Germans on the hill about 400 yards away. I took my platoon on to the road, where there was some cover, and we soon mopped up the few Germans we could see about on the hill front.
>
> I then got orders from my captain to proceed to the top of the hill with my men, and the whole company followed. The German big guns were firing, and the shells flying in all directions ... some of the Germans were lying about – some 20 to 25 yards in front of us, suffering from wounds, and we were going among them making them hold up their hands because we thought that some of them were merely shamming, and that as we passed they would take the opportunity of potting us.
>
> I was just looking round further, to see if there were any more Germans about, when I got a bang in the shoulder. I am not sure whether it was a bullet or not. The doctors seemed to think from the nature of the wound that it must have been done by part of a shrapnel shell ... At any rate, I was knocked over; and the man next to me bandaged me up as well as he could with my field dressing, and later I was taken on an ambulance stretcher to a farm house close by. I had a rather worrying time as long as the particular action lasted, because there was a good deal of give and take play in the fighting, one side retreating and then other side doing the same, and so on. I was afraid the Germans would retake the hill while I was lying there helpless. But, luckily for me, they did not come down the hill again ... There was a lot of close-quarter fighting going on all about this point, but as, unfortunately, I was knocked over just in the very beginning, I did not even see what took place.[23]

Somerset was not aware at that moment that his own brother, Lieutenant the Honourable Nigel Somerset, of the Gloucestershire Regiment, was also lying wounded in another dressing station close by. The two brothers' respective battalions were part of the same brigade, though were in action some distance apart. Nigel Somerset was wounded behind the right ear by a shell splinter. He later recounted a remarkable *ruse de guerre* which occurred when he was in action, as well as his own lucky escape:

> It was on the Tuesday morning, when the Germans made an attack on our position, just at dawn. Now, as far as I can make out, and I was not alone in observing it, many of the Germans whom we saw in this action were dressed as Highlanders. We noticed that many of them were shot down by our men, and as they were being helped away, we remarked upon their dress, and we knew it was impossible for them to be Highlanders. Proof of this remarkable fact was forthcoming on the following day, when some wounded Scotsmen were brought in, and they were absolutely naked.

Well, our little band was behind a regiment which was entrenched on the brow of a hill. We were on the higher ground, and were told to fire over the heads of our entrenched comrades below. This we did for a time, but found a difficulty in continuing, and I was then ordered to try and find a position for my platoon, comprising about fifty men, from which we could direct our fire more forward in the direction of the enemy.

I went along to ascertain the position, and noticed from some of the Black Watch and other regiments whose bodies I saw, that they had been enfiladed on the previous day, and shots from the left told me that the Germans would repeat the operation if I took my men there. It was, therefore, useless to take my platoon to that spot. Then I was told to get in touch with Company B and for that purpose I extended my company of forty men through the wood, which was very thick and dense, making the extension most difficult. The other ten of my platoon had been killed or injured by this time ... I told my men to keep to cover, and just at that moment there was an explosion and I was struck at the side of the head by something, and I was knocked down. I expect it was a splinter from a shrapnel shell but I was exceedingly lucky to get off with so slight a wound, as the same shell not only killed two of my men but injured several others.

[Another] rather queer thing happened to me while I was on the field, and I did not discover it until I had been removed. A corporal looked at my haversack, which contained a variety of things, including papers, maps etc, and remarked that it had evidently been struck by a portion of a shell, but when we came to look at it, we found that the bag had been struck by a bullet, and the bullet had gone clean through the bag, the maps and papers.

I then recalled that during the fight I felt something in my side, and put my hand down, noticing there was slight heat of some kind, but I noticed nothing further. I remarked to myself, 'That's alright.' It now turns out that it must have been a bullet which struck my bag as I was lying down, but whether it was a direct shot or a stray bullet, of course I cannot say. At any rate, it was regarded as rather a remarkable occurrence.[24]

The death of Lieutenant Sir Archibald Gibson-Craig of the Highland Light Infantry, also on 14 September 1914, typifies the reckless bravery that was exhibited by these aristocratic young officers during the first three or four months of the war in general, and on the Aisne in particular. He was shot while leading his men in an attack on a German machine-gun hidden in a wood. Having located the gun, which was causing a great deal of havoc, Gibson-Craig asked his company commander if he might take a party of twenty or so men and try to capture it. The Major agreed, and the party set off, crawling up a slope overlooking the position. As they reached the top they found themselves unexpectedly face to face with a much larger body of Germans. Gibson-Craig at once stood up, drew his sword and shouted, 'Charge men! At them!' As they rushed forward he was shot and mortally wounded. The party was still able to capture the gun, but never the less the loss of such gallant young officers, who felt it was their duty to lead from the front in these situations, was reaching unsustainable proportions. In case it should be assumed that only officers were capable of displaying such initiative

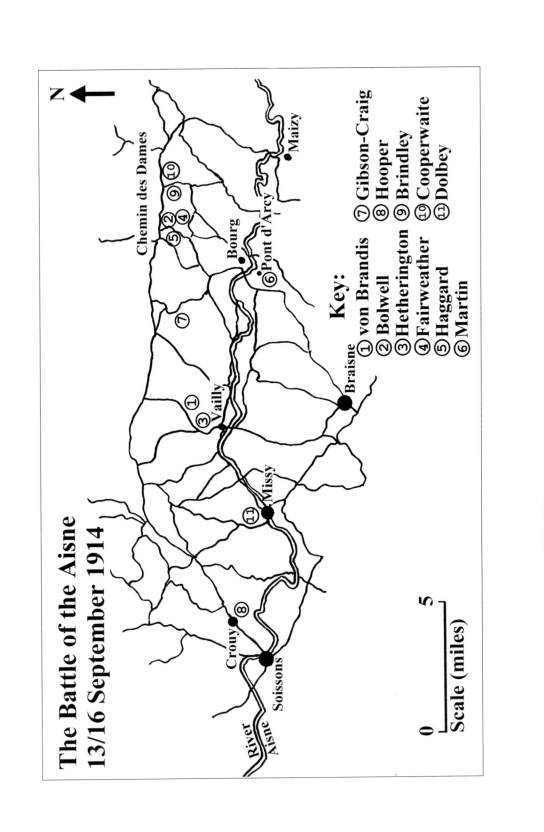

The Battle of the Aisne
13/16 September 1914

N

Chemin des Dames

Bourg

Pont d'Arcy

Maizy

Braisne

Vailly

Missy

Crouy

Soissons

River Aisne

Key:

① von Brandis ⑦ Gibson-Craig
② Bolwell ⑧ Hooper
③ Hetherington ⑨ Brindley
④ Fairweather ⑩ Cooperwaite
⑤ Haggard ⑪ Dolbey
⑥ Martin

0 5
Scale (miles)

and enthusiasm, a Private Wilson of this battalion, from Edinburgh, performed on the same day an equally valiant task. He encountered six Germans operating a machine-gun. Having shot five with his rifle he bayoneted the sixth. He then turned the enemy gun on the remaining parties of Germans opposing his battalion, until the gun jammed.

Another noble Scottish officer who lost his life in this battle was Lieutenant Colonel Sir Adrian Grant-Duff, commanding the 1st Battalion the Black Watch. Grant-Duff was the author of the War Book, a detailed plan for mobilisation in the event of war, which he had prepared while on secondment to the War Office. Among his men on the Aisne was a soldier by the name of Joe Cassells, who published his war memoir as *The Black Watch A Record in Action*. A first glance this has the appearance of a volume as rich in detail and as authentic as that either of Frank Richards or Frederick Bolwell, but sadly this is not the case. Comparison with Cassell's army service record quickly reveals that much of what he wrote was pure fantasy. One incident that may however be grounded in truth is his description of the death of Grant-Duff, for it is known from other sources that he was carrying ammunition at the time he met his death. Cassells writes:

> Our commander, Colonel Grant Duff, was in the thickest of the fighting. I saw him distributing bandoliers of ammunition along the firing line. His men tried to make him go to the rear, but we were having a tough time to keep fire superiority, and we needed every man in the line. Suddenly Colonel Duff staggered and slouched forward on his hands and knees. The bandoliers he was carrying, scattered. Several men rushed to him but he got to his feet himself and ordered them back to their posts. An ugly red stain was spreading over his tartan riding breeches and leggings, but he staggered onward with the ammunition. He had not gone a dozen steps when both his arms flew up into the air and he fell backward. This time he did not move. He had been shot straight through the heart, and another commander of the Black Watch had gone to join the long line of heroes who had so often led this regiment to victory. Many of our company commanders were picked off by the enemy because of their distinctive dress, their celluloid map cases affording excellent targets.[25]

Another Black Watch soldier who was in action here was Private Frederick Fairweather. Like Cassells, he was a Londoner, possibly attracted to a highland regiment by its romance and history (and, because of shortages of recruits, many Scottish and Irish regiments contained a share of Londoners prior to 1914). He too wrote of the difficulties that were now presenting themselves, when men had to cross large tracts of countryside fully exposed to enemy fire:

> The Guards went up first and then the Camerons, both having to retire. Although we had watched the awful slaughter in these regiments, when it was our turn we went off with a cheer across 1,500 yards of open country. The shelling was terrific and the air was full of the screams of shrapnel. Only a few of us got up to 200 yards of the Germans. Then with a yell we went at them. The air whistled with bullets, and it was then my shout of '42nd forever!' finished with a different kind of yell. Crack! I had been presented with a souvenir in my knee. I lay helpless and our

fellows retired over me. Shrapnel screamed all around, and melinite shells made the earth shake. I bore a charmed life. A bullet went through the elbow of my jacket, another through my equipment, and a piece of shrapnel found a resting place in a tin of bully beef which was on my back. I was picked up eventually during the night, nearly dead from loss of blood.[26]

Perhaps the best account of this day of bitter fighting on the Aisne comes from Frederick Bolwell, who expertly captures the mood of this rain-soaked battle, fought on wooded slopes against an often invisible enemy. Of the fighting near Troyon he says:

> We were roused next morning with kicks from the platoon commanders, and, after much struggling and putting on of wrong equipments, we marched out, but not before each man had received two ounces of Gold Flake tobacco, the first English tobacco we had seen since leaving home.
>
> It was the fourteenth day of September, and raining. Leaving the village, we marched down a road for about five hundred yards, bordered on each side by high banks. There a halt was called . . . We then doubled by platoons through an avenue of trees exposed to the enemy's fire, and gained some fields on the further side of the road, lining the hedges.
>
> From there into the valley led one road which was little more than

A silk bookmark printed in memory of Private James Clarke who died on the Aisne.

In Loving Memory of
PRIVATE
James Clarke,
(1st Lincolnshire Regiment.)
The beloved husband of
ALICE CLARKE,
Who was killed in action
in France,
September 14th, 1914,
AGED 29 YEARS.

No loved one stood beside him,
To hear his last farewell;
No word of comfort could he have,
From those who loved him well.
Little he thought his time so short,
In this world to remain,
When from his home he went away,
He thought to come again.
He is lying now in a distant land
We know not how or where;
But oh we hope God took his soul,
Into His loving care.
His Country called and he
answered.
17 James Street, Preston.

a narrow defile; then it wound away to the right front over the crest which the Germans held. Halfway up this road was a small village called Tryon [Troyon]. At the rear and facing the crest held by the enemy was another and smaller hill thickly wooded. Before taking us through the defile and into the valley, the words of the Brigadier were: 'That ridge has to be taken by nightfall otherwise we shall be annihilated.'

. . . Our particular front was facing a beet-sugar factory just off the main road, and there the fighting was very furious. By midday we had taken several of the Prussian Guard and of the Death's Head Own Hussars prisoners; also [a] report went round that we had captured twelve guns, which news cheered us greatly. One prisoner, a Prussian Guardsman, remarked on the way back: 'Never mind, boys; we shall soon be back in dear old London again!'

On one occasion early in the day, having to retire from the top of the crest down into the valley, our Company-Sergeant-Major took us via the other hill through the wood to the position at the summit of the hill which the Germans held. It was a splendid move, well carried out, and without the loss of a single man.

On gaining the summit on the first occasion one team of our machine-gunners took up position and held it the whole of the day, helping us greatly to secure the position against all enemy assaults. The men stood their ground splendidly, three of them being recommended for the Distinguished Conduct Medal . . . We continued to advance and retire the whole day through. First we gained ground and the Germans drove us off again; then we came back with redoubled energy, until towards evening we began to hold on and the Germans to retire. On the right of the road was a haystack on fire, and we were in a small trench just thrown up behind it.

The bullets were flying from that rick as if a magazine was on fire and it was very unhealthy. At one time we were in a swede field, and a large shell burst in front of us, covering us with dirt. A chum of mine, being hit very forcibly with a flying swede, up he jumped, shouting: 'I'm hit, I'm hit!' but came to the conclusion that he wasn't as bad as he had thought.

As darkness came on we all formed up in line, and the Brigadier, coming to the crest, remarked: 'The Brigade will bivouac on the ground they now hold. Dig in.' There and then we commenced a line of trenches, which are there to this day.

It had been a most awful and bloodthirsty day, with two of the finest bodies of men that ever faced each other opposed to one another. There was bound to be a good fight, and it was the cleanest and most sporting day's battle I have ever fought.[27]

The results of the widespread attacks by the BEF's I Corps on 14 September were on the whole disappointing. Bolwell's battalion had lost over 350 casualties, and it was by no means alone in this – it was a similar story in at least five other battalions. Little progress had been made in driving the Germans back. However, it is now known that Von Bulow, commanding all three German armies defending the Aisne, had intended to sweep the British back across the river and secure footholds on the south bank. Here, as on other occasions in 1914, the sheer audacity of the British in attacking the Germans with inferior numbers wrong-footed them, and made them believe that far larger reserves lay behind the impudent attacking force.

Further west, the II Corps was fighting its own battle on 14 September. Several battalions tried to force the passage of the Aisne over the hastily constructed pontoon bridge at Vailly, but were soon retreating back over it after having been roughly handled by the enemy. The 1st Battalion Northumberland Fusiliers, fighting its way uphill through thick woodland soaked by recent rain, suddenly emerged into open country in full view of the Germans. The leading company attempted to charge with the bayonet, but was thrown back. Among them was Lance Corporal Fred Hetherington, a reservist, who told a journalist later:

Lieutenant Rhys Ivor Thomas, 1st Battalion Connaught Rangers. Killed in action at Cour de Soupir, on 14 September 1914, he was later awarded a posthumous Military Cross for his bravery on this day.

> We were so near the German trenches that we got the order to charge. When they saw the steel glittering on our rifles they squealed like rats and bolted from the trenches. To escape us they had to get over other trenches behind, and some of them were not quick enough. One fellow scrambled out just in front of me. He may have had a mother living, a wife, children, a sweetheart. I cannot say; I did not stop to think of that, but while I ran blindly towards their fire, I just thought of our fellows lying dead and wounded in the trenches. As I struck, I tripped and fell right over him. By the time I had picked myself up, the charge was practically over. They opened fire on us from the trenches behind, and we had to fall back. We were about 300 yards from shelter. I think I did that 300 yards in shorter time than it would take me to do 100 at another time. They trained a couple of machine-guns on us, and then all they had to do was to move it from side to side, while it went 'br-r-r-r', just like a motorcycle with its engine racing. Every inch we ran the bullets were spitting all around us. Every step we took we were saying to ourselves, 'The next one is mine; the next one is mine; the next one – hah.' Then a man would drop, but still we ran on in the hail of bullets. Out of the 200 of us that went out in the charge, forty answered the roll! When we reached shelter and looked behind, we could see the wounded crawling, inch by inch, to our lines. Then one of them would give a spasmodic jump, and we would know that he would crawl no further. Yes, it's a bit vivid, perhaps, but it is war – real war. To live in it is to go through purgatory on earth.[28]

Nearby on 14 September, the 4th Battalion Royal Fusiliers, having crossed the Aisne relatively unopposed, took up positions in close proximity to the German lines. Several times the enemy tried to force them back. Two platoons of X Company occupied Rouge Maison Farm, about a mile north-east of Vailly, and on 15 September they were heavily attacked by the Germans who tried to wrest the farm from them. The enemy was driven off at the point of the bayonet, as Private G. Bridgeman, who was involved in this action, describes:

> We were being knocked over in dozens by the artillery and couldn't get our own back, and I can tell you we were like a lot of schoolboys at a treat when we got the order to fix bayonets, for we knew we should fix them then. We had about 200 yards to cover before we got near them, and then we let them have it in the neck. It put us in mind of tossing hay, only we had human bodies. I was separated from my neighbours and was on my own when I was attacked by three Germans. I had a lively time and was nearly done when a comrade came to my rescue. I had already made sure of two, but the third would have finished me. I already had about three inches of steel in my side when my chum finished him.[29]

Remarkably, an account of the fighting here also survives from one member of the opposing German forces, Hauptmann Cordt von Brandis of *Infanterie Regiment Nr. 24*. His account is more detailed than that of Bridgeman, and not surprisingly he chalks up the inconclusive fighting here as a German victory:

> Our first attack wave was caught by flank fire and held up, and had to seek cover in a sunken lane. Thus the attack could not advance. Into this pickle drove up behind us at the gallop two field guns. The Leutnant put shots among the poplars from which the fire came. The white shrapnel smoke drifted by as tattered crowns. Leutnant von Sichart came up with two machine-guns. 'If you go forward, I will shoot away any opposition, until you reach your objective. If these open their mouths, those over there will have their noses in the dirt!'
>
> And now finally it started. On the left roared the 'hurrahs' of the men over the pale beet fields, to the right the horns blared in the forest gorges of the village of Aizy. About us raced and crackled the machine-gun bullets of Leutnant von Sichart who served the machine-gun with the iron clutch of his sailor's fists, and the eyes of a lynx.
>
> 'Forward, at them, at the Englishmen, at these damned island pigs who are guilty of starting the war!' First we were fifty, then thirty of us as we approached their raised earth defences. There the foremost ones jumped up, with hands held high! One ran towards me, quite a young fellow, saying 'Sir Sir, don't kill me'. The second line defended itself, a wounded Briton who had been shot flung his clasp knife, blade outstretched, against the cartridge pouches of a corporal; it stuck there, shaking.
>
> It was with this great 'hurrah', this roar of courage, that our people attacked the mercenaries of 5 Company Royal Fusilier Regiment. It was a terrible eruption of the courage with which the men had borne the retreat, and revenge upon those

responsible for our strain. Across the battlefield, Khaki clad men lay crumpled, felled by spades and rifle butts, but in death still the features of their clean-shaven, tough faces looked relaxed.

They were manful opponents, the experienced colonial warriors of the first English army. The officers, the captain and the second lieutenant who also both lay dead in the firing line, proved this. As the day came to an end we entrenched, alternately shooting and digging, in view of the wide Aisne valley over which sailed grey clouds full of rain, whipped on by the winds.[30]

Von Brandis was possibly slightly confused as to the identity of his opponents; the Royal Fusiliers were reinforced by men from the Nortumberland Fusiliers, tradition-ally known by their old regimental number as the 5th Fusiliers, and it may be that he conflated the two names. The salient held by the II Corps on the northern bank of the Aisne at Vailly was smaller and more precarious than that of the I Corps further east, and several times the Germans almost succeeded in driving them back across the river. An anonymous officer of the 2nd Battalion Royal Scots here recorded in his diary:

September 16 – The Royal Scots were holding a position covering the village of Vailly and also a pontoon bridge which had been made at this point over the Aisne. The bridge (the position of which had no doubt been given away by spies) was under the constant shell fire of the Germans day and night. They were also shelling Vailly with the same gun, a 90-pounder. The village was reduced to a heap of bricks and mortar, but they never hit the bridge, luckily, as over it all rations and supplies had to be brought by night.

The Royal Scots' position was a very unpleasant one, as they were holding a salient on either side of which was rising ground held by other regiments. We were not only under heavy shell fire from the front, but stray bullets were coming over very thickly when the positions right and left were attacked.

On the afternoon of the 16th Captain C. Lempriere Price DSO, was killed, and was buried that night at Vailly, to the great sorrow of all ranks.[31]

Further details of this gallant officer's death are given by an unnamed private of the same battalion:

Here we lost Captain Price, who had saved so many men at Cambrai. He gave up his life trying to save another's. One of our NCOs was wounded and began to yell. Captain Price was in his bomb-proof dugout when he heard the shouting, and he called out to the man, 'All right, man, I will be with you in a few minutes.' Just as he got out of the trench he was hit by a bit of shell, and died a few hours afterwards. His loss was deeply regretted, because he was beloved by everybody.[32]

The last of the attempts to cross the Aisne on 13/14 September was made by the III Corps at Missy, near a wrecked bridge. The Royal West Kent Regiment and King's Own Scottish Borderers were in the vanguard and crossed the river here under cover of darkness by means of rafts and boats. Their advance on the northern bank was quickly checked by enemy fire, and the medical officer of the latter battalion, Captain

Robert Dolbey, was requested to come to the assistance of the many wounded in urgent need of treatment on the far bank. His account of his daring approach to the river and subsequent crossing of it under fire illustrates something of the dangers that medical officers deliberately placed themselves in, in their selfless efforts to tend to the men in their care:

> We were badly wanted, that I felt sure; and we could not wait very long. Still another wide open field had to be crossed before we could gain the shelter of a bank and a row of big poplars near the river edge. Another sprint, and we were under cover again behind the bank. In this spot was the Major commanding the field company of Engineers, cool and most collected, disdaining the shelter the bank gave us, and he doubted whether I could get across. The temporary pontoon bridge the Engineers had put up, further down the river, had just been blown up by a shell, and the only way for me was the canvas raft that, by chance, might still be intact. The two battalions were across, he told me; there had been very many casualties he was sure; there was no doctor across the river; and he wished me luck.
>
> Telling the stretcher bearers to keep open order and take good cover, I found a practicable ditch that led to the rushes by the river bank, and gained the friendly shelter of the reeds; outwardly calm, for one of my men had plumped down near and was watching me; but inwardly trembling. A hail across the river; a subaltern of the Engineers answered me and said that the canvas raft was sinking, and would I go to the pillars of the ruined bridge; there I might shout to the Sergeant-Major, who would ferry me across. This meant a run of 50 yards along the tow-path, and a glance showed me the danger. For, beside a long heap of white stones, there lay four of our men; and they were very still – for the snipers had got their range well against that white background. But the snipers failed this time; and, from the shelter of the twisted steel girders of the bridge, I hailed the Sergeant-Major of the Engineers. A machine-gun was posted close behind him, and it took me some time before I heard that this boat was sunk and my only hope of crossing lay in the canvas raft, if it could be persuaded to float.
>
> ... there was [again] that fifty yards of the path to be covered. How I hated those white stones! But the sniper was late again, and I was beside my stretcher bearer in the friendly rushes. Another conversation shouted above the tumult, and the Sapper officer consented to try the crossing to ferry me across. Now, this raft was constructed of green canvas, stuffed with hay, attached by a guy rope to a wire that spanned the river. But the raft had already done yeoman service in ferrying men and officers of the two battalions across, and was waterlogged. Anxiously I watched him, balancing precariously, as he worked the clumsy thing ashore. But, for this fellow, the bullets flicked the surface of the stream in vain. I looked round and, of all my sixteen stretcher bearers, only one was beside me. Gingerly we stepped upon this submerged craft and pulled ourselves across, and I was with the reserve company of my battalion.[33]

By now the strain was beginning to tell on officers and men alike. Nothing like this protracted, relentless fighting had been seen previously in modern warfare. One officer who was clearly reaching the limit of his endurance (after being in constant action for about three weeks) was Captain C. J. Paterson, of the South Wales Borderers, fighting on the I Corps front. On Wednesday 16 September, he wrote the following account, which is appended to the battalion War Diary:

I have never spent and imagine that I can never spend a more ghastly and heart-tearing 48 hours than the last. Not a moment in which to write a word in my diary. We have been fighting hard ever since 8am on the 14th and have suffered much ... We were cheered on about midday by a message from Field Marshal French to say that we of the 1st Division had saved the situation and by holding on had allowed the crossing of the river to be made. Since then we have been under fire of all sorts, rifle fire from snipers, shell from enemy, shell (bursting short) from our own guns and we have not lacked experience. I am thankful that I and my particular friends have not taken a knock yet, but there is lots more to come. However, we have done and shall continue to do, please God, what we have to do and that is all about it. The sights were ghastly. Wounded crying all night for help and no one to help them. The doctors have done all they can, but the casualties are ever heavier than they can easily cope with. We have had a good few German prisoners and many Germans wounded have come through our hands, poor fellows, absolutely done and half-starved. I am certain that given a reasonable excuse they will surrender en bloc. Our total casualties are Yeatman and Johnson killed, Richards and Vernon wounded, and of the R & F 18 killed, 76 wounded and 122 missing, of whom I trust many may be found alive and well, as one must always lose some in the dark.

Here I sit outside our headquarters trench in the sun. The rain which we have had without a break for the past two days has now stopped and the world should look glorious. The battle has stopped here for a bit although in the distance we can hear the 2nd English Army Corps guns and their battle generally. As I say all should be nice and peaceful and pretty. What it actually is is beyond description. Trenches, bits of equipment, clothing (probably blood-stained), ammunition, tools, caps, etc etc, everywhere. Poor fellows shot dead are lying in all directions. Some of ours, some of the 1st Guards Brigade who passed over this ground before us, and many Germans. All the hedges torn and trampled, all the grass trodden in the mud, holes where shells have struck, branches torn off trees by the explosion. Everywhere the same hard, grim, pitiless sign of battle and war. I have had a belly full of it. Those who were in that South Africa say that that was a picnic to this and the strain is terrific. No wonder if after a hundred shells have burst over us some of the men want to get back into the woods for rest. Ghastly, absolutely ghastly, and whoever was in the wrong in the matter which brought this war to be, is deserving of more than he can ever get in the world. Everyone very cheery and making the best of things. Men of course wonderful, as T. Atkins always is. I must try and write to mother now.[34]

Captain E.J. Needham of the 1st Battalion Northamptonshire Regiment, in the same brigade, was advancing against prepared German positions on the Chemin des Dames ridge on 17 September. Having gone forward at the charge with bayonets fixed, the men were now in an extended line across a muddy field. He remembered:

> We lay where we were for some considerable time, keeping up a steady fire at the trench ahead of us. We were being well sprinkled with shrapnel all this time, and ... owing to the rain and misty conditions, were getting no artillery support from our guns. I remember vividly a man immediately behind me letting off his rifle in my right ear and deafening me for a long time. He must have just missed blowing my head off. Now it was, and for the next hour or so, that I found how very difficult it is to command one's men under active-service conditions. To control fire with an extended firing line was absolutely impossible. I shouted until I was hoarse and just *could not* make myself heard above the firing.[35]

Very heavy fire had been received from the German trenches ahead and most of the Northamptons officers along with all of the officers of the adjacent 2nd Battalion King's Royal Rifles had become casualties. Needham and his men were pinned down and in urgent need of reinforcements. However,

> Suddenly I heard the men shouting, 'They're surrendering!' and, looking up, I saw a line of white flags (or rather white handkerchiefs or something of the kind tied to the muzzles of rifles) held up all along the German trench in front of us right away to the left. I shouted out to the men to cease fire and stop where they were. After a few minutes I saw a large number of Germans, two or three hundred of them at least, moving forward from their trench towards 'A' Company on the road, some with their rifles, but many with white flags tied to them, and many with their hands up. They got down to 'A' Company's trench and stood there for some time apparently conversing. All this time the white flags in front of us continued up and many Germans were standing with their hands up.
>
> All of a sudden a burst of heavy firing broke out down by 'A' Company's trench and we saw the Germans and our men engaged in a hand-to-hand fight. Still the white flags in front of us remained up. Just as Gordon and myself had decided to reopen fire and to chance whether we were right or wrong, I saw

Lance Corporal George Gibbs, 1st Battalion Northamptonshire Regiment. He was evacuated from France with a gunshot wound to the right arm on 20 September 1914, but would undoubtedly have been a witness to the incident described by Needham a few days previously.

Captain J.A. Savage of 'D' Company and Lieutenant J.H.S. Dimmer, of the 60th, walk through the left of 'C' Company and on up to the German trench in front of us. Apparently they could talk German. Anyway, they stayed there talking for about five minutes and then started to walk back to us, the white flags still being up.

To our horror, after they had got about half-way to us, the Germans opened fire on them, and we saw Savage pitch forward dead, shot in the back. Dimmer threw himself down and started to crawl back to us, eventually reaching our line alright ...[36]

Heavy machine-gun fire from the nearby 1st Battalion Queen's Regiment now ripped into the Germans out in the open, who tried to bolt back to their own trench; few made it. Later that afternoon a white flag again went up from the German lines but this time was ignored. Eventually the firing stopped and the enemy trench was found to contain only dead and dying Germans. Needham confessed frankly to his own personal unsteadiness in the aftermath of what had been a truly shocking afternoon:

I was feeling just about all in, being wet through to the skin, chilled to the bone and nerve-wracked after having one of my very best friends in Parker killed, in having poor young Gordon practically killed beside me, and in seeing poor old Savage butchered in that foul style; also the whole show had been such an awful muddle and I was terrified of having done the wrong thing. I shall never forget that afternoon till my dying day, nor the horror and uncertainty of it.[37]

The third British salient on the northern bank of the Aisne was that held by the III Corps at Missy, and this corps perhaps saw the least of the fighting. None the less, on 17 September Second Lieutenant Kenneth Hooper, a young officer of the 1st Battalion East Lancashire Regiment, was wounded during a counter-attack east of Crouy on this front. Hooper was a member of the Special Reserve, and had applied for a commission to fill in time whilst he waited for a university place to become available, never expecting to go to war. He remembered:

We had moved out of the village that we were in and we moved through some fields of Kale. Well the Kale was up to [thigh] height and soaked with rain. So we were soaking wet and ... then we advanced in extended order ... We were just on the reverse slope of the hill and there was a platoon in front of us, and we were I suppose 30 or 40 yards behind them just down below the brow of the hill. Well the shell fire started on front of us and there was a lot of musketry fire ... I was hit when I got a short distance up this hill [by] a shrapnel bullet. I had my Burberry on, it went through the Burberry, the jacket, and through the thickness of my sleeve ... it was a sizeable bullet ... a shrapnel ball is fairly sizeable and [this one] had just penetrated the chest. It was going straight for my heart, absolutely straight for my heart and it just felt like a sledgehammer and I was completely knocked over by it.[38]

Staggering to his feet Hooper made his way to the rear where he met the Regimental Sergeant Major, who was loading more seriously wounded cases on to a farm cart for evacuation. By an irony, the fact that he could walk meant that Hooper was directed to the dressing station in the village, rather than being evacuated, and this resulted in his capture the following day when his battalion was forced to retreat:

> Directly they [the medics] saw me they stuck me on the floor [of the dressing station] and gave me a shot of Morphia and I lay there ... I simply lay from Thursday to Sunday on the floor of this village school. I think there were six officers one of whom was Major Collins of my own regiment ... we were just lying all round the floor ... and then we all saw a German, a couple of Germans [who] just looked in at the door ... Well, we had all heard about their brutalities in Belgium and that sort of thing and I was quite prepared to be bayoneted ... I wondered whether they would come in and bayonet us but all they did was look in the door ...[39]

On this western edge of the BEF's battlefield, German NCO Sergeant Hans Stegemann of *Infanterie Regiment Nr. 165*, facing the III Corps, experienced the severity of British rifle and machine-gun fire first hand. Both he and his horse had close shaves. He wrote to his parents on 18 September, describing an incident that occurred a day or two previously:

> A cyclist comes sliding rather than riding down the steep hill on the right. Breathlessly he shouts: 'Order from Major —— Jägers out of ammunition!' I put spurs to my bay, swing him round and gallop back. I find some ammunition wagons belonging to the Jägers. 'Gallop! Right wheel! March!' Off they go at the gallop, flogging the horses! Up the hill, on and on, through the heavy guns which are blazing away over our heads. We can see the great sugar-loaves in the air, because we are straight behind them, so that our eyes can follow their flight.
>
> On we go! 'Where are the Jägers?' I shout to everybody. Shrapnel bursts. Wounded hobble and crawl back. There is a Jäger, too, with a broken arm. 'Well old chap, how goes it?' He smiled gaily all over his face. 'Jolly well; we're giving 'em beans again! Only they want cartridges, Sergeant!' 'Good-bye, good luck. Hope you'll soon be all right!' All this in passing – the last words shouted over my shoulder.
>
> Another green coat. A Corporal on his way back. 'Hallo, what's wrong?' 'Not a single cartridge left!' 'Good Lord! Here they come!' 'Thank God!' 'Hop up on the wagon. Now show us the way!' We trot a little farther and then, there they are! As they catch sight of me, they are just firing their last round. Now there are some more! I've got four thousand.
>
> But meanwhile things are beginning to look black! The man who was sitting just now on the wagon is lying beside it with a smashed leg, which has since been amputated. I am still perched up on my horse beside an ammunition column – six wagons as well as my cartridge wagon. The enemy has got the range, and now the fun begins. Ssss ... rrrr ... sch! It goes, as if a giant were beating the foliage of the oak trees with his stick. All of the horses of the fifth ammunition wagon – three on the right and three on the left – are lying struggling, with their legs in the

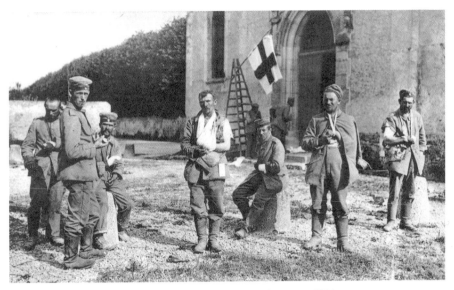

German wounded at a field dressing station on the Aisne, September 1914.

air, though those of the next are untouched. The gunners are crawling about on the ground. Many have been killed. A moment ago the column was hale and hearty: now it looks like somebody had brought an enormous fly-clapper down on it. My wagon was in the middle of it all.

The whistling continues. For the present I don't dismount. 'Who's hit, *is* hit!' my Jäger says, and he is right. My men unload as coolly as if we were doing a slow-march in the village square at Gorlitz on a Sunday: one hundred, two hundred, three hundred, four hundred, and so on, as they pile up the packages. The Jägers come and fetch the little pointed things in quite a leisurely manner: the English won't run away, and nothing upsets the composure of a Holsteiner. When a 'heavy' comes whistling over they grin, and imitate the sound with their lips. On seeing my pipe one of them says, 'By gosh, that's a good idea!' pulls out a battered cigar and begins to smoke: 'that pretty nearly got spoilt in my pocket'. They are equally self possessed. One takes off his shako, which is full of bullet-holes and looks at it: 'Well, as long as it don't let the rain in,' he says, and puts it on again.[40]

The same day, on the same part of the battlefield, near Missy, a British padre was writing home to his mother. The Right Reverend Monsignor Francis Bickerstaffe-Drew was serving as a Roman Catholic padre with the 15th Field Ambulance of the Royal Army Medical Corps. An important part of a padre's role was to offer succour to the wounded, and Bickerstaffe-Drew like most padres drew no distinction between friend and foe, when providing comfort to men who knew that they were facing their last moments on earth. He wrote to his mother:

A lot of wounded came in this morning, but we were able to send them on within an hour or two. Meanwhile I chatted to most of them, and gave Extreme Unction to a dying German prisoner. He was only twenty-one, a sad-faced, simple country lad from Prussian Poland, with no more idea why he should be killed or should kill anyone else than a sheep or a cow. He was horribly wounded by shell fire on Sunday, and had lain out in the rain ever since, till our people found him in the woods last night (this is Thursday). Isn't it horrible to picture? Starving, drenched, bleeding, so torn and shot in the buttock as to be unable to drag himself out of the woods. So his wounds had gangrened, and he must die. He could only lie on his face; he was fully conscious and joined in where he could in the responses of the office of Extreme Unction. But I know nothing more awful than the broken-hearted patience of such lads: the whole face, the dumb eyes, the agonized posture, without cry or moan; if ever anything was an appeal to Heaven from a brother's blood crying from the earth, it was one.

I dare say you do not know any more than I did what a field ambulance is or does. Well, its great function is to be mobile, able to move always with the fighting troops, and be at hand for the wounded in every action. So it can never retain the wounded it treats; if it did, it would at once become immobile (a hospital full of wounded men cannot rush about, and its troops would move on and leave it, and they would have no ambulance any more in attendance. Our wounded, there-fore, are always 'evacuated' within six hours i.e., we send them in ambulances to the 'rail-head' (the nearest place where there is a train running), where they entrain and are conveyed, first to a 'clearing hospital,' then to a general hospital, or perhaps direct to the 'base' hospital, whence they embark for England.[41]

For the 15 hours which he spent under fire on one occasion ministering to the wounded, Bickerstaffe-Drew was recommended for a Mention-in-Dispatches – as he himself noted, not a bad achievement for a man of 56 years of age. In the First World War, even those men who were not devoutly religious seem to have drawn comfort from the spiritual certainties offered by padres. Services were often well attended, and a few days later Bickerstaffe-Drew noted:

Yesterday morning we had Mass in one of the immense Gothic barns, and it was crammed. Some tell me that there were 1,000 men present, but I think there were over 600. The men were most devout and full of piety, attention, and interest. They sat on the hay while I preached for over half an hour and listened with all their eyes, ears, and mouths. An officer said afterwards: 'I wished you would go on for hours.' It was really interesting and impressive; the great dim barn, the crowd of soldiers crouched in the hay, the enemy's guns booming three miles off, and the thought that once again (after 500 years) Mass was being said in this old place of religion, built by warrior monks, by a foreign priest, belonging to a foreign army, for foreign soldiers. At the end I gave away medals, and the crushing up to get them was funny. 'Here,' I heard one young corporal expostulate, 'this ain't a dance, and you aren't a swell tryin' to get an 'am and chicken!' It was a loft barn, and all that huge crowd had to get down by a very shaky ladder! While they were slowly getting off, some officers came and talked to me ... The Protestant officers were all impressed by our Mass and our people; it struck them how cheery and chatty the men were, and how glad to get to Mass, though having to walk far in the rain and mud.[42]

After a brief lull in the fighting in mid-September, towards the end of the month the Germans renewed their efforts to break the deadlock and drive the British back along the entire Aisne front. During that month more British battalions arrived in France; the 6th Division, which had been retained on the English east coast during August because of fears of a German invasion across the North Sea, went into action for the first time on the Aisne. Among its constituents was the 18th Brigade, which relieved the hard-pressed troops on the extreme right of the British front. Regimental Quartermaster James Brindley, of the 1st Battalion East Yorkshire Regiment, a veteran of the Boer War, was here and recorded the events relating to this battalion in his diary. Again, as with Walter Bloem, one gets the sense of a veteran of an earlier conflict struggling to come to terms with the scale of the casualties from a single day of fighting in this war:

> 20th September: The enemy, north of Vendresse and on a frontage of about 15 miles, attacked us with great force at dawn. The noise of the musketry fire was terrific and shells were flying about in all directions. The Germans came right up to our trenches and things looked serious but they were charged by the regiments on our left and right; the 2nd DLI and the E. Yorks left their trenches and lost a good many men. Col. Benson, Major Campion and Major Maxwell, also Lieutenants Englefield and Mellor, were wounded and Captain Edwards died in this action. Fifty men were casualties. The 1st West Yorks also had numerous casualties. German artillery fire was fierce all day long and the enemy made several charges but were repulsed with heavy losses; very many dead and wounded lay between the lines, which were about 500 yards apart; the wounded had to be left to die where they fell and one man who had a leg off cried out but had to be left as he drew fire when attempts were made to help him. At about 10am the rattle of rifle-fire slackened off; 20 men were buried in the small churchyard, their wounds being almost too terrible to describe; the weather was very unsettled and although the troops were cheerful they were very displeased at being wet through; there is plenty of food and no-one can grumble about being hungry; a seven-mile journey has to be made, there and back, to get the rations up. The Germans attacked in force at about 12.30pm along the whole line and fierce fighting occurred; they pressed forward in masses but were met by the British with the bayonet. Losses were heavy, with the West Yorks having about 662 casualties, the East Yorks 182, Notts and Derby 250 and Durhams 200.[43]

In fact 20 September was a day of disaster for the 1st Battalion West Yorkshire Regiment, which was the right-hand flank battalion of the entire BEF. To its right lay a French Moroccan unit. Several German attacks during the course of the day forced the Moroccans back, leaving the flank of the West Yorks in the air. The commanding officer sent a company out to the east to cover the exposed flank, but the Germans, attacking through the gap in the line left by the Moroccans, enveloped

*Private John Hall,
1st Battalion East
Yorkshire Regiment,
killed in action on
20 September 1914.*
(Mike Wood)

and captured this company. Within half an hour, working down the front-line trenches of the West Yorks, they had captured the remnants of two more companies. The situation was saved only by the timely arrival of reinforcements from the British cavalry. Lieutenant Bertram Ratcliffe of the 1st Battalion West Yorks recorded later:

> On the 19th September 1914 on the heights of Craonne, we replaced the Coldstream Guards. The following morning, very early, the Germans launched an attack unsuccessfully. At 6.15am they made a second attack, and I was wounded by a rifle bullet in the right lung, and lost consciousness. The French were on our right, but they gave way, and in consequence, we were surrounded by the Germans, and I was picked up by them and taken prisoner at 2pm. I was conscious at the time.
>
> I was taken to a small village behind the lines, where I remained the night. I saw no infractions of the ordinary laws of war. A number of other officers were captured at the same time as myself, but they were taken off the first day, as they were able to walk. The Germans tried to force me to walk, but I could not. I had a

British soldier with me, a man of my own regiment, who was very badly wounded in the arm ... when a sentry noticed that I could not get along, he allowed me to get on to the tailboard of a cart in which were a number of German soldiers. The soldier with me, however, was forced to march.[44]

The testimony of another eyewitness to this incident exists, in the form of an account from a Private W.H. Cooperwaite, of the neighbouring formation, the 2nd Battalion Durham Light Infantry. Cooperwaite states:

On Sunday, the 20th [September], with the West Yorkshires on our right, we were in the very thick of heavy fighting. The artillery on both sides was firing furiously, and the rifles were constantly going. Our own fire from the trenches was doing very heavy mischief amongst the Germans, and they were losing men at such a rate that it was clear to them that they would have to take some means of stopping it, or get so badly mauled that they could not keep the fight going.

Suddenly there was a curious lull in the fighting and we saw that a perfect horde of the Germans were marching up to the West Yorkshires, carrying a huge flag of truce. It was a welcome sight, and we thought, 'Here's a bit of pie for the Tykes they must have been doing good.' They had lost heavily, but it seemed from this signal of surrender that they were to be rewarded for their losses.

A large party of the West Yorkshires went out to meet the Germans with the flag, and I watched them go up until they were within fifty yards of the enemy. I never suspected that anything wrong would happen, nor did the West Yorkshires, for the surrender appeared to be a fair and aboveboard business.

When only that short distance separated the Germans and the West Yorkshires, the leading files of the surrender party fell apart like clockwork and there were revealed to us, behind the flag of truce, stretchers with machine-guns on them, and these guns were set to work at point-blank range on the West Yorkshires, who, utterly surprised and unprepared, were simply mown down, and suffered fearfully before they could pull themselves together.

Now, this dastardly thing was done in full view of us; we could see it all, and our blood just boiled. What we would have liked best of all was a bayonet charge; but the Germans were too far off for the steel, and it seemed as if they were going to have it all their own way. They had given us a surprise, and a bad one; but we had a worse in store for them we also had machine-guns, and they were handy, and we got them to work on the dirty tricksters and fairly cut them up. The whole lot seemed to stagger as our bullets showered into them. That was one of the cowardly games the Germans often played at the beginning of the war; but it did not take the British long to get used to them, and very soon the time came when no risks were taken, and the stretcher dodge was played out.[45]

German abuses of the flag of truce seem to have been fairly commonplace in 1914, however it is somewhat surprising that Ratcliffe, who must surely have been aware of this incident, failed to mention it, particularly as he gave his testimony to an enquiry specifically concerned with German violations of the laws of war. It might have been supposed that Cooperwaite chose to embellish his own account with the addition of an

Drummer R.E.G. Cross, 1st Battalion West Yorkshire Regiment. He was captured in the debacle on 20 September 1914.

incident that he had heard about from elsewhere, but the story is given credence by Captain W.A.W. Crellin an officer of a neighbouring British unit, the 1st Battalion Nottinghamshire and Derbyshire Regiment. Crellin also stated that the Germans advanced to the West Yorks line here under a flag of truce. Whatever the truth, the collapse of the West Yorks for a time placed the flank of the Durhams in jeopardy, and Cooperwaite now describes an attack launched to recover the lost trenches:

> To carry out an attack like that was a desperate undertaking, because the Germans were six hundred yards away, and the ground was all to their advantage. It rose towards them, and they were on the skyline, so that it became doubly difficult to reach them. Well, the order was given to advance, and we got out of our trenches and covered most of the distance in good order. Bit by bit we made our way over

the rising ground towards that skyline which was a blaze of fire, and from which there came shells and bullets constantly.

There could be no such thing, of course, as a dash, however swift, towards the skyline; we had to creep and crawl and make our way so as to give them as little to hit as possible; but it was terrible too terrible.

We fell down under that deadly blast, and though I am not a particularly religious man, I'll own that I offered up a prayer, and the man on my left said something of the same sort too. Poor chap! He had scarcely got the words out of his mouth, when over he went, with a bullet in his neck, and there he lay, while those of us who were fit and well kept up and crept up.

At last we were near enough to the skyline to give the Germans rapid fire, and we rattled away as fast as we could load and shoot, till the rifles were hot with

Private Raymond Hardy, 2nd Battalion Durham Light Infantry, killed in action on 21 September 1914. (Pat Gariepy)

firing. After that rapid fire we crept up again, and it was then that I saw Major Robb lying down, facing us, and smoking a pipe at least he had a pipe in his mouth, just as cool as usual.

He sang out to my platoon officer, 'How are you feeling, Twist?' Lieutenant Twist answered, 'Oh, I'm about done for.' I looked at him and saw that he was

British soldiers in action in the densely wooded Aisne country.

wounded in the chest and arm. We had to go on, and we could not take him back just then. The lieutenant had scarcely finished speaking when I saw Major Robb himself roll over on his side. A poor lad named Armstrong, with four more of our men, crept up to attend to the major, but a piece of shrapnel struck the lad on the head and killed him and other men were falling all around me.

There was no help for it now we had to get back to our trenches, if we could; that was our only chance, as the Germans were hopelessly greater in number than we were. So we made our way back as best we could, and we took with us as many of the wounded as we could get hold of.

Time after time our men went back for the wounded; but, in spite of all we could do, some of the wounded had to be left where they had fallen. We got back, the survivors of us, to the trenches, and we had hardly done so when we heard a shout. We looked up from the trenches, and saw Major Robb on the skyline, crawling a little way. Instantly a whole lot of us volunteered to go and fetch the major in; but three were picked out Lance-Corporal Rutherford, Private Warwick, and Private Nevison.

Out from the trenches the three men went; up the rising ground they crawled and crept; then, at the very skyline, Rutherford and Nevison were shot dead, and Warwick was left alone. But he was not left for long. Private Howson went to help him, and he actually got to the ridge and joined him, and the two managed to raise the major up; but as soon as that had been done the officer was shot in a vital part, and Warwick also was hit.

More help went out, and the major and Warwick were brought in; but I grieve to say that the poor major, who was loved by all of us, died soon after he reached the trenches.[46]

Major Alexander Kirkland Robb, a veteran of the Tirah campaign on the North West Frontier in India, is buried in Vendresse British Cemetery, near Laon. The bodies of his would-be rescuers, John Nevison and Frederick Rutherford, were not recovered and they are now commemorated on the memorial to the missing of the Aisne campaign at La Ferté sous Jouarre.

On the II Corps front north of Vailly the fighting was equally severe as the Germans tried and failed to break the deadlock. Soldiers of the South Lancashire Regiment were heavily attacked by *Infanterie-Regiment Nr. 56* and *Infanterie regiment Nr. 64* and drove them back, but not without heavy loss both to defender and attacker alike. The official history of the latter German formation describes 20 September as a 'hard, blood soaked day'. It identifies on this date a change in the character of the campaign, with the beginning of trench warfare. Describing the events of that day it states:

The 1st battalion had not been able to attack at first because the 24th [*Infanterie Regiment Nr. 24*, on the flank] was not yet in position. Only at around 10.30 am could Hauptmann von Werder give the order to attack. The 1st battalion on the left (with number 6 company along side it on the right) left their ditches about midday, once again going into fierce battle across open ground without cover. It was unsupported; from the German storm trooper of 1914 there was no hesitation. Number 6 company made good progress in the more favourable area of Rouge

Maison, although it sustained considerable losses. Also the right wing of the 1st battalion, attacking with it, came under first machine-gun and infantry fire and then bombardment by artillery from La Cour de Soupir. Never the less the remnants of this faithful company assaulted the well defended enemy positions again ... Major von der Decken had, in the meantime, made the daring decision that the 1st battalion would penetrate the wood further to the south. If it succeeded in reaching the southern edge of the wood, it would be able to outflank the enemy in front of it. Around 12 noon he ordered first number 11 company to go forward towards the southern edge of the wood, in order to devise a path around the hostile positions in the wood.

As soon as the company was lined up, it was met by heavy fire from the thick undergrowth ahead. Immediately Hauptmann Friedrichs ordered his men to fix bayonets and led his courageous musketeers toward the Englishmen with the bayonet. Gradually the enemy gave way. Now Major von der Decken placed numbers 12 and 10 companies to the right and left of number 11. Leutnant Meissenburg brought his machine-guns into position and in the wonderful momentum of the attack the men of the regiment advanced inexorably forward, in spite of heavy losses, until they reached the southern edge of the wood. Here at the edge of the forest the battalion still succeeded in taking an English trench, although the German artillery was unable to observe the fight and fired only a few shells. From there, however, further progress was impossible. The isolated troops which had broken through received the strongest possible hostile fire, from three sides. They had to face all directions at once, and dig in.

The losses were heavy. However, the heaviest blow was the heroic death of the noble, courageous commander, Major von der Decken. He stood upright in the midst of the greatest fire – so recounted his loyal adjutant Leutnant Droyfen that evening – and a bullet hit him in the arm. 'Droyfen, I have one gone,' he said laughing. Shortly thereafter a shot to the hip brought him halfway to the ground. 'Droyfen, now I have number 2!' He did not give up the leadership of his musketeers, until a shot in the head ended his heroic life. An exemplary soldier, and a leader who cared for his subordinates, he met here a glorious death. A special monument to him was later placed at this point.

As the bloody day slowly drew to a close, Hauptmann von Schenckendorff with the 3rd battalion clung to the hard-won ground. The regimental commander sent him number 7 company under Hauptmann Jacobs, which had played a courageous part in the fighting, to help. It was not possible to send any more reinforcements. Thus Oberst Jancke ordered Hauptmann von Schenckendorff to withdraw the battalion to its old position, if it could no longer hold on. Ammunition began to run short, there was no water for the machine-guns, and hostile fire inflicted more and more losses. With a heavy heart, Hauptmann von Schenckendorff decided to retreat. In the evening the brave little band of heroes returned to the northern part of the wood, with twenty prisoners and carrying almost all of their wounded. The enemy did not pursue them. The three companies numbered little more than 200 rifles, of the machine-gun platoon only five men were fit for battle. The flag of the battalion, carried by Sergeant Wenndorf, had been shot through by rifle fire.[47]

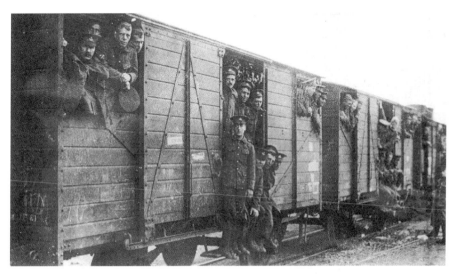

Heading north. Men of the BEF entrain in cattle trucks once more.

In spite of the at times almost suicidal bravery that had been shown by the soldiers of the BEF, the fighting on the Aisne had ground to a stalemate. The Germans were proving themselves increasingly difficult to dislodge from prepared positions; indeed many of their trenches dug here in 1914 would remain in use for the next four years. The focus of the war on the Western Front however was now shifting northwards. The conflict was entering a new phase, the so-called 'Race to the Sea', as each side sought to out manoeuvre the other by finding an open flank. In order for the BEF to be closer to its supply chain, the decision was taken to withdraw it from the Aisne, and it entrained for the north, in order to resume its position on the French left flank once more.

Chapter 4

A Splendid Adventure

As the German army swept through Belgium in the late summer and early autumn of 1914, the continued resistance of the citadel of Antwerp on the Belgian coast posed an increasing threat to its already stretched lines of communication. The Belgian army had previously sallied forth from the coast to attack them in the flank; fearing that the Antwerp garrison might well have the capacity to do so again, the German High Command dispatched General Hans von Beseler to subdue the city. The mighty River Schelde (Scheldt) formed a formidable barrier on the western side, but to the south the River Nethe presented far less of an obstacle, and on this side and to the east it was defended by an obsolete fortress system dating from 1859. As the fate of Liège and Namur had already demonstrated in this war, Antwerp would have been able to offer little in the way of resistance to the superior German heavy guns should they be brought into action against it. However, Winston Churchill, as First Lord of the Admiralty, was eager to keep the Belgian army in the game, and came up with a daring (or perhaps, as some said at the time, foolhardy) plan to attempt to bolster the resistance of Antwerp. This it was hoped would draw German forces away from the desperate fight on the Aisne – indeed Churchill, for his part, saw Antwerp as representing the extreme left-hand end of an Allied front which ran in an arc through Belgium and north-western France, the right-hand end of which rested upon the Aisne. Churchill himself spent two days at Antwerp, personally superintending the defence.

Thus it was that the British government began to send whatever resources it could spare, for the assistance of the Belgians at Antwerp. Initially this took the form of heavy guns provided by the Royal Navy. One batch of 6in naval guns was sent out under Lieutenant L.F. Robinson RN in early October. When he reached Antwerp, he discovered that a previous batch of 4.7in guns had not been installed in the Belgian forts, as originally planned, due to their inherent weakness. Instead the guns had, using the help of Belgian army engineers, been mounted in two trains, specially armoured for the purpose. Robinson was on 4 October assigned to one of these, known as HMAT *Jellicoe*. He wrote:

> The methods of laying and training the guns were most primitive, for up till lately all firings out to the southward of the Nethe had been direct. Now that the Germans had advanced and were actually assaulting the city's defences, cover was necessary, and in such flat country firing had to be indirect, or blind.
>
> A position was chosen where the map showed a straight piece of line, the line of the rails being taken as the zero for training. Bearing and ranges were taken off the

map. The guns were laid to the elevation corresponding to the range required, and a bearing arc was painted round the pedestal, the zero pointer being a plumb-line slung from beneath the mounting.

With such means success in indirect laying was a matter of luck, and it was obvious that calibration and greatly improved ideas were necessary.

As soon as the train stopped, telephone communication was always established with the Headquarters under which the train was working at the time, and so kept in touch ready to fire whenever required.

The target was a battery position to the south-east of Duffel at a range of 5,000 yards, and over this area a steady fire was placed. A hostile captive balloon was observed to ascend, so I asked ... if I could try and down it. We opened fire on it with long-range shrapnel, and after four rounds it was hurridley hauled down. However, it had time to see us, so we retreated a few hundred yards; and sure enough, after a lapse of some minutes, our previous position was subjected to a searching but weak fire from some battery ... As for myself, it was the first time I had been under fire. I heard an awful shriek overhead, so dived into a ditch alongside. It did not take very long to learn that a shrieking shell had already passed overhead and out of danger.[1]

It was now decided to mount the heavier 6in guns which Robinson had brought out on girders attached to a railway bogie, in a similar fashion to the 4.7in guns already in use. Due to the heavier recoil of these guns it was decided only to fire these in line with the truck, so as not to risk overturning it. Robinson continued:

I took my section out via Vieu Dieu and stopped at Kleine Meil, on the Brussels line, in a position which was screened by a dense wood over which we could fire.

Storming the outer defences of Antwerp in 1914 – an idealised German view.

A British armoured train mounting 6in guns, Belgium 1914.

Headquarters telephoned the position of two targets which were to be engaged – the bridge over the River Nethe east of Lierre, which village had been evacuated by the Belgians and was being occupied by the advancing German troops: Ander-Stad-Farm on the southern bank of the Nethe, more to the westward. I was informed that the Belgians had all crossed the river and were taking up positions along its western bank as far west as Willebroeck. The above farm was a little shelter from which the Germans would launch an attack to cross the river.

I opened fire on these two objectives and continued a slow bombardment at irregular intervals. In the early part of the forenoon a battery commenced searching for us, but, beyond an occasional uncomfortably close one, most of the shells did not fall close enough to look dangerous, so I held on to our screened position.[2]

[R]obinson continued to fire at German troops trying to cross the Nethe until [app]roaching darkness led him to retire once more on Antwerp: 'It was the general [rul]e that the train should not work at night, when the flashes would draw hostile [fire to th]eir surroundings and so interfere with the passage of reliefs and food etc, [...] to the front, and also stray shells were liable to cause a derailment in the

[...] the Royal Navy should have enough men to man its ships in time of [... t]wentieth century two new reserves of sailors were created: in 1900 the [...] was formed, mainly comprising ex-regular stokers who had signed [... w]ith a further period of reserve service with liability for call-up in [...] In 1903 the Royal Naval Volunteer Reserve was formed. This was an entirely different animal, consisting of young men from good homes who undertook naval training in their spare time. It was in effect a naval equivalent of the Territorial Force. The success of these two reserves meant that in August 1914 there was an excess of approximately 30,000 sailors above and beyond the capacity of the fleet.

On 16 August 1914 Winston Churchill had stated that in order to make the best possible use of the surplus naval reservists of different classes, it was proposed to constitute permanent cadres of one Marine and two naval brigades. Thus the Royal Naval Division (RND) was born, and while its four Royal Marine Light Infantry (RMLI) battalions carried the names of the main Royal Marine depots of Chatham, Deal, Plymouth and Portsmouth, the naval battalions were named after British seafaring heroes: Anson, Benbow, Collingwood, Drake, Hawke, Hood, Howe and Nelson.

Musician Stanley Billings, Royal Marines Band. At Antwerp he served with the Headquarters of the RND.

As well as the naval reservists, the division was bolstered by surplus recruits who at that time could not be accommodated by Kitchener's New Army. Many of them were tough Yorkshire miners, who had originally enlisted in the King's Own Yorkshire Light Infantry. Churchill's new naval force was now to be the physical embodiment of Britain's moral support for Antwerp – and was sent to stiffen the resistance of the Belgians.

Geoffrey Sparrow was a doctor in civilian life but in 1914 was commissioned as a naval surgeon with the RND. He has provided a good description of the outward appearance of this unusual force:

> After only thirty-six hours in depot I was appointed to the Royal Naval Camp at Walmer, and duly arrived there with three others of my professional confreres to commence duty with the then unknown RND. The Royal Naval Division had only been formed for a few weeks, and the 1st Brigade, consisting of the Collingwood, Hawke, Benbow, and Drake Battalions, was under canvas on Walmer Downs, two miles from Deal. The 2nd Brigade, composed of the Howe, Hood, Anson, and Nelson Battalions, was at Bettysanger ... The scene on the Downs ... was, to my civilian eye, full of interest. The predominant note was blue, with here and there a splash of khaki – outfitters' experiments in khaki naval uniform. The latter, as far as officers were concerned, consisted of a tunic built on the plan of the ordinary blue monkey jacket, but, as a concession to our military occupation, a Sam Brown belt was worn. Just a few compromised by wearing a blue monkey jacket with khaki breeches and pig-skin leggings. The cap adopted by most was

the ordinary naval one with a khaki cap cover. The men, as a whole, wore blue shore-going rig, though a small number were the proud possessors of a khaki uniform with black naval buttons and a khaki cap adorned with a black ribband bearing the legend 'Royal Naval Division.' These few remarks regarding our clothing are made, not because we were over proud of it, but because people who read the papers in those days seemed to get the impression that the RND was naked, or at any rate that one ambulatory organ was encased in a blue, bell-bottomed trouser leg, whilst the other rejoiced in khaki and a ragged puttee. No doubt some of us presented a somewhat variegated appearance, but this only tended to increase the interest of the local inhabitants, though it must have been a matter of some astonishment to the active service members of the Division ... Most of the men, however, before they went to Antwerp, were at least equipped with rifles, bayonets, bandoliers, and other offensive implements, and I cannot say I ever saw a bayonet tied on with string, although at the time this fact was confidently stated in the newspapers.[4]

The first troops of the division to arrive in Antwerp were the four battalions of the Royal Marine Brigade, which was already operating on the Belgian coast, and which arrived in Antwerp by train in the early hours of 4 October. That same morning, Churchill's suggestion that the two naval brigades at Walmer should also be dispatched, was approved. Jim Begent was a clerk in the London, Home Counties and Midland Bank prior to the war. He had been a member of the London Division of the Royal Naval Volunteer Reserve since 1912, and with the gathering stormclouds of war over Europe, his call up along with other naval reservists on 2 August 1914 was not wholly unexpected. He was posted to Hawke Battalion, and undertook several weeks of training at Walmer and Deal. However it was the issue of heavy marching boots and rifles, which indicated that serious work now lay ahead. On 15 October he wrote to his father in Worthing:

> On Sunday Oct. 4th our Brigade [the 1st] left Deal for Dover whence we embarked for Dunkirk. We arrived there on Monday and on that night took the train to Antwerp. We did not expect to get to Antwerp without meeting the enemy, but we arrived safely on Tuesday morning [i.e. the 6th] and were joyously received by the Belgians. Our maxim gun section was first billeted in a barn, but we had not been there very long before we had orders to move off to the trenches. That night we slept by the roadside with artillery pounding away on all sides, not much sleep you bet.[5]

Horace Laking was from Harthill on the South Yorkshire/Nottinghamshire border. A regular stoker of the Royal Naval Reserve, he served with the Collingwood Battalion. He arrived at Antwerp on 6 October 1914, and left the following account of his experiences:

> Although it was early, there were thousands of Belgians to welcome us, as they were expecting us. I shall never forget that morning as long as I live! We were all very hungry and thirsty, but not for long. They gave us coffee, and drinks and

eatables of every description. What a grand reception it was! The Belgians are the best-hearted people in the world. When we got in the streets we were surprised to see a lot of London omnibuses. Then we were billeted to different quarters, but before we had time for a sleep, and we were all very tired, we were ordered into the trenches. Although very tired, our hearts were good, and we were all eager to be doing our share. After marching some miles we heard the bad news that the shellfire was so heavy that it would be impossible to reach the trenches in daytime. All the time we were at Antwerp we could hear nothing but the booming guns, and it was surprising how the population behaved.

Ordinary Seaman Arthur Lunness, Hawke Battalion RNVR. A Yorkshire miner, he enlisted in 1914 and was drafted straight into the RND. He was later interned at Groningen in Holland.

On the 10 miles' march to Antwerp we passed ambulance after ambulance with wounded, and they told us it would be a sheer madness to try and enter the trenches in that direction. If we did, it would be no use without big guns to back us up. This was the downfall of Antwerp. It was like a dwarf fighting a giant. The fort guns could not reach the guns of the Germans, which belonged to the Austrians, and were christened 'Jack Johnsons,' and well we knew it before we had been there many hours. We lay under cover on the outskirts of the city until early on Wednesday morning, and then in the darkness we reached the trenches, which were partly ready to receive us. All day on Tuesday we were building and strengthening the trenches, and making necessary improvements, and before the day was over we had made good friends with the continual rain of shells travelling over our heads to the doomed city. A Taube came over our position, and then the fun started. I was on guard all night, in case of an attack, and a pretty sight it was watching bursting shells which could be seen coming, looking like balls of fire in the sky. Although they were dealing out death and destruction, they formed a most interesting spectacle.[6]

The Royal Marines were by now already occupying trenches north of the Lierre–Antwerp road. The naval brigades were dispatched to reinforce the Belgian forts, the 1st Naval Brigade taking up positions in the intervals between Forts No. 1 to No. 5, and the 2nd Naval Brigade between Forts No. 5 to No. 8. The trenches here were shallow and it was impossible to deepen them due to the high water table. In addition, the open ground ahead of them made them perfect artillery targets. The Reverend H. Clapham-Foster was a Temporary Naval Chaplain, attached to the 2nd Naval Brigade at Antwerp. He wrote of his experiences later:

At 2am [on Wednesday 7 October] we were awakened by a Belgian officer . . . and were told to fall in at once and leave for the front trenches. We had the most romantic march in the darkness to Fort No 7, one of the forts on the inner ring. It was a calm, still night, and the men marched along quietly, having been warned of the serious nature of the task in front of them . . . at dawn we reached our destination and for the first time saw the trenches that were to be our home for only two days. These open trenches had been cleverly constructed by the Belgians, but they would have proved utterly useless had they been subjected to a violent bombardment . . . our trenches were at the end of a large turnip field, and about 150 yards behind them there was a modern villa, surrounded by a pretty garden. It was empty and devoid of furniture, and in this house the doctor and I were installed and were told to transform it into a hospital.[7]

Sparrow formed a similar first impression of the positions that his battalion was to hold:

My own battalion occupied a position between Forts 6 and 7, and the intervals between the other forts were likewise held by other units of the division. The large numbers of Belgian troops we met on our way up to the trenches assured us that things were going well – an opinion quite in contrast with that of a Marine

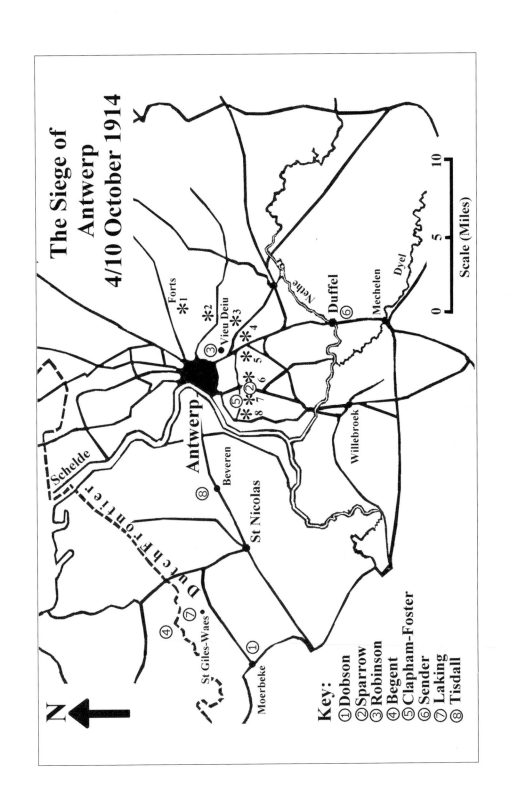

The Siege of Antwerp
4/10 October 1914

N

Schelde

Dutch Frontier

Antwerp

Forts

Vieu Deiu

Nethe

Duffel

Mechelen

Dyel

Willebroek

Beveren

St Nicolas

St Giles-Waes

Moerbeke

Scale (Miles)

0   5   10

Key:
① Dobson
② Sparrow
③ Robinson
④ Begent
⑤ Clapham-Foster
⑥ Sender
⑦ Laking
⑧ Tisdall

whose opinion was, 'it's 'ot, Sir, 'ellish 'ot!' a description which I later entirely agreed with.

My impression of these trenches, the first I had ever seen, was distinctly discouraging. They were shallow and broad, and instead of being dug in, were mainly built up. Where the fire-step should have been were primitive dug-outs which afforded neither comfort nor safety. In front of the trenches was an elaborate system of electrified barbed wire on which our searchlights played

Private J.J. Maher RMLI from Dublin, who served at Antwerp with Plymouth Battalion Royal Marines.

incessantly. Roofing over us was an artificial network of branches and foliage – a mode of camouflage, it struck me at the time, on a par with the ostrich who buries his head in the sand and hopes to pass as a palm-tree. Battalion Headquarters was a small unpretentious stone erection which might possibly have kept out a summer shower, but was totally unfitted to withstand even the lightest artillery. There was no sign of any support or reserve lines.

On arrival, the battalion at once commenced to deepen and improve generally the trenches, whilst I attempted to make arrangements for evacuation of wounded. This was somewhat complicated by the fact that my stretcher-bearers, who had merely been selected at random from the fighting personnel of the battalion, were all anxious to rejoin their comrades in the firing line.

It was extraordinarily difficult to find a suitable aid post. There were one or two buildings within a short distance of the trenches, but many were still occupied by their owners, who were quite unprepared for a sudden evacuation and could not believe that such a course was ever likely to be necessary. One building, which appeared to be of the nature of a monastic infirmary, seemed to be suitable for my purpose, and so was commandeered as a field hospital. It was truly a most affecting sight to see the good people moving their patients and household goods along the road to safety. Some were able to walk, many had been bedridden for years and had to be carried, whilst a few were conveyed in rough carts which jolted them terribly.

On returning to the trenches, I was somewhat disconcerted to find no trace of my battalion, but eventually I ran them to ground in their new position between Forts 3 and 4, where they were busily employed improving the very primitive trenches in that situation.[8]

Men of the RNVR in the trenches at Antwerp. The head cover might have provided protection against small arms fire but was wholly inadequate against artillery.

Outside the ring of forts surrounding the city, German troops were moving in, slowly tightening their grip. One of the attackers wrote:

> In the evening the storm columns went forward, about 5 o'clock. We approached to 400 meters [from the enemy line], there we were met with terrible fire. Here I lost my best companion, the Gefreiter Karl N . . . who was hit by two shells. Now we had to go forward crouching and on the belly, and at 180 meters before the fort we dug ourselves in. We lay the whole night in this ditch, partially standing in water, always bombarded by hostile mortar fire, and awaited the events which would happen there. Finally, the dreaded morning arrived; forts and positions were stormed. From first meeting the enemy we advanced further, at Duffel we came to the Nethe which is 200 meters wide here, we were ferried across in small boats, and again came into action. Nothing however could delay our advance, though often we came to several lines of trenches, until we came . . . to the internal forts.[9]

In the German military system, as with the British, in time of war musicians doubled up as stretcher-bearers. One of these men, from the German *Matrosen Division*, has left a fuller account of the fighting in front of the forts at Antwerp:

> This fort . . . is well defended. Around it there is a 15–20 meter wide water jump which is filled with mines and wire. 800 meters before the fort there is a flooded area . . . About evening the battle started. We approached up to 500 meters from the enemy, however, it seemed impossible to take the fort by storm. We lay thus till 12 o'clock. Every now and then there fell a shot. Now and again we picked up

Sailors of the Kiel Battalion of the German 1st Matrosen Division, *which fought against the British Royal Naval Division at Antwerp.*

Looking north-east from the Mons–Harmignies Road. On 23 August 1914, the line of the road was held by the 1st Battalion Gordon Highlanders. German soldiers of *Infanterie Regiment Nr.75* approached over the crest in the distance. (*Andrew Macdonald*)

The original wooden marker erected by the Germans on the grave of Major Stuart Hamilton Rickman, commanding 1st Battalion the Rifle Brigade, at Le Cateau where he was killed. (*Peter Weedon*)

The approach to the village of Néry from the south-east. It was an early morning patrol of the 11th Hussars that first made contact with the enemy near here on 1 September 1914. (*Jori Wiegmans*)

The modern bridge spanning the Marne at La Ferté sous Jouarre. It was here on 8 September 1914 that Frank Richards and his comrades crossed by pontoon bridge, after the retreating Germans had destroyed the original structure. (*Jori Wiegmans*)

A German field gun captured on
8 September 1914, by the 1st Battalion
Lincolnshire Regiment in the woods west
of Bezu, during the Battle of the Marne.
(*Courtesy of the Museum of Lincolnshire Life*)

Rouge Maison Farm on the Aisne heights. It was here on 15 September 1914 that Hauptmann Cordt von Brandis of *Infanterie Regiment Nr. 24* encountered soldiers of the 4th Battalion Royal Fusiliers.
(*Jori Wiegmans*)

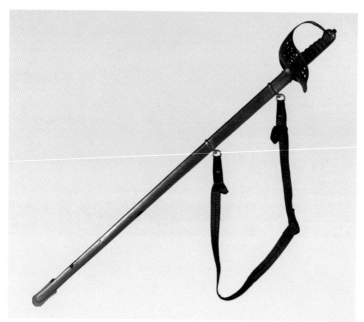

A sword, carried by a British infantry officer Lieutenant W.A.W. Crellin of the Nottinghamshire and Derbyshire Regiment in action on the Aisne, September 1914.

Crossing the River Nethe at Duffel; the village was captured by German troops on 7 October 1914 in the advance on Antwerp. (*Jori Wiegmans*)

The church at Meteren. It was from this vantage point that the future Field Marshal Bernard Montgomery, then serving with the 1st Battalion Royal Warwickshire Regiment, was shot by a sniper on 13 October 1914. (*Jori Wiegmans*)

The level crossing at La Houssoie; on 25 October 1914 it was gallantly defended against repeated German attacks by D Company of the 1st Battalion Leicestershire Regiment.

The Iron Cross and original award document presented to Musketier Staaden, of *Reserve Infanterie Regiment Nr.222*. The award was for the attack on the British positions near Rue du Bois in October 1914. (*Paul Biddle*)

Looking towards Langemarck from Korteek Kabaret. Over these fields on 24 October 1914 the German student battalions charged towards the British lines – and were annihilated. (*Jori Wiegmans*)

The funeral of Private Richard Lancaster, 2nd Battalion Lancashire Fusiliers. He was killed in action near Ypres in November 1914, but his body was not recovered until 2007.
(*Colonel Glover/Courtesy of the Fusiliers Museum, Bury*)

Some of the personal effects found with Lancaster included this badge and shoulder title. (*Mike Heap/Courtesy of the Fusiliers Museum, Bury*)

A boot brush found with the remains of Private Lancaster.
(*Mike Heap/Courtesy of the Fusiliers Museum, Bury*)

Unfired .303 Lee–Enfield rifle bullets, found in 2007 with the remains of Private Lancaster.
(*Mike Heap/Courtesy of the Fusiliers Museum, Bury*)

The remains of Private Lancaster's pipe.
(*Mike Heap/Courtesy of the Fusiliers Museum, Bury*)

The Distinguished Conduct Medal and 1914 Star trio awarded to Sapper J. Wilson, 5th Field Company Royal Engineers, for his part in the fighting on 11 November 1914 at Polygon Wood, during the First Battle of Ypres. (*Scott Marchand*)

The plate from a Prussian pickelhaube helmet. It was souvenired from a dead German soldier by Private Charles Rutherford of the 2nd Battalion Highland Light Infantry, during the fighting at Nonnen Boschen near Ypres, November 1914. (*Jack Alexander*)

(*Left*) An early type of German grenade, this *kugelgranat* was developed by the Germans prior to 1914 in response to lessons learned in the Russo-Japanese War; it was in use during the battles of Armentières and Ypres.

(*Right*) The earliest British grenade of the war, the Battye Bomb. It was developed at Bethune Ironworks by Major B.C. Battye of the Royal Engineers in December 1914.

A German Maxim machine-gun, captured by the 2nd Battalion Leicestershire Regiment at Festubert in December 1914. (*Philip French*)

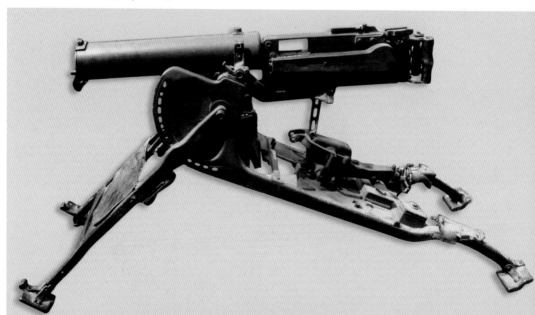

a casualty and carried him back to headquarters. One night it was stormy; clouds covered the sky and gave only brief glimpses of the moon, which then eerily lit up the paths. We lay behind a house with our stretcher, 100 meters before us was the company. About 12 o'clock two doctors ordered us forward with the stretcher, in order to fetch wounded. We ran there on a path lined by trees, to the right and left the land was flooded. When we had passed beyond the cover of the 1st company, we received rifle fire from the left. Shells made a 'pink' sound around us. We numbered, on the whole, eleven men; two doctors from the navy, two stretchers to each four men, and one corporal who would lead us to the wounded. To offer no further target to the enemy, who seemed to number only one sentry, we threw ourselves down in the ditch on the right of the road and found ourselves up to our knees in mud. Then we crept along in the ditch, and lay down flat on our bellies. After crawling forward along the ditch under continuous cover, the leader tried to peek out; as soon as one of us lifted his head, the invisible rascal shot at us, but his aim was always too high.

It is a peculiar hissing noise, which a bullet makes when whizzing by in the air. No matter, we were ordered forward! A stretcher party crept toward the front, however, the announcement came that the casualty had been already been brought safely back by another way, and we could return to our old position. At 2 o'clock began a violent barrage which lasted one hour. The hostile fire, which was aimed too high, flew over us . . . At 3 o'clock there came the order: 'Everyone fall back!' Our battalion went back about 100–200 meters. Only the extreme outposts still had contact with the enemy . . .[10]

British wounded were collected by a different method. Arthur Ruhl was an American journalist who found himself inside besieged Antwerp. Turning his hand temporarily to medical work as a volunteer hospital orderly with the Royal Naval Division, he noted:

Down through [the] mass of fugitives pushed a London motor-bus ambulance with several wounded British soldiers, one of them sitting upright, supporting with his right hand a left arm, the biceps, bound in a blood-soaked tourniquet, half torn away. They had come in from the trenches, where their comrades were now waiting, with their helpless little rifles, for an enemy, miles away, who lay back at his ease and pounded them with his big guns. I asked them how things were going, and they said not very well. They could only wait until the German aeroplanes had given the range and the trenches became too hot, then fall back, dig themselves in, and play the same game over again.

Following them was a hospital-service motor-car, driven by a Belgian soldier and in charge of a young British officer. It was his present duty to motor from trench to trench across the zone of fire, with the London bus trailing behind, and pick up wounded. It wasn't a particularly pleasant job, he said, jerking his head toward the distant firing, and frankly he wasn't keen about it. We talked for some time, every one talked to every one else in Antwerp that morning, and when he started out again I asked him to give me a lift to the edge of town.[11]

He continued:

> We turned into the avenue of trees leading up to an empty chateau, a field-hospital until a few hours before. Mattresses and bandages littered the deserted room, and an electric chandelier was still burning. The young officer pointed to some trenches in the garden. 'I had those dug to put the wounded in in case we had to hold the place,' he said. 'It was getting pretty hot.'
>
> There was nothing here now, however, and, followed by the London bus with its obedient enlisted men doing duty as ambulance orderlies, we motored a mile or so farther on to the nearest trench. It was in an orchard beside a brick farm-house with a vista in front of barbed-wire entanglement and a carefully cleaned firing field stretching out to a village and trees about half a mile away. They had looked very interesting and difficult, those barbed-wire mazes and suburbs, ruthlessly swept of trees and houses, when I had seen the Belgians preparing for the siege six weeks before, and they were to be of about as much practical use now as pictures on a wall.
>
> ... the British marines and naval-reserve men who manned these trenches could only wait there, rifle in hand, for an enemy that would not come, while a captive balloon a mile or two away to the eastward and an aeroplane sailing far overhead gave the ranges, and they waited for the shrapnel to burst. The trenches were hasty affairs, narrow and shoulder-deep, very like trenches for gas or water pipes, and reasonably safe except when a shell burst directly overhead. One had struck that morning just on the inner rim of the trench, blown out one of those crater-like holes, and discharged all its shrapnel backward across the trench and into one of the heavy timbers supporting a bomb-proof roof. A raincoat hanging to a nail in this timber was literally shot to shreds. 'That's where I was standing,' said the young lieutenant in command, pointing with a dry smile to a spot not more than a yard from where the shell had burst.
>
> Half a dozen young fellows, crouched there in the bomb-proof, looked out at us and grinned. They were brand-new soldiers, some of them, boys from the London streets who had answered the thrilling posters and signs, 'Your King and Country Need You,' and been sent on this ill-fated expedition for their first sight of war ... Yet not one of the youngest and the greenest showed the least nervousness as they waited there in that melancholy little orchard under the incessant scream of shells. That unshakable British coolness, part sheer pluck, part a sort of lack of imagination, perhaps, or at least of 'nerves', left them as calm and casual as if they were but drilling on the turf of Hyde Park. And with it persisted that almost equally unshakable sense of class, that touching confidence in one's superiors – the young clerk's or mechanic's inborn conviction that whatever that smart, clean-cut, imperturbable young officer does and says must inevitably be right – at least, that if he is cool and serene you must, if the skies fall, be cool and serene too.[12]

One of the most notable British figures to serve at Antwerp was just such an officer, the war poet Rupert Brooke, who was commissioned as a Sub-Lieutenant in the RNVR and who fought with Hood Battalion. Another RNVR officer of note was Sub-Lieutenant

Arthur Tisdall of Anson Battalion, who would later be awarded the Victoria Cross at Gallipoli. Tisdall was born in Bombay, India in 1890, and after attending Bedford School from 1900 to 1909, he studied at Trinity College, Cambridge, for whom he rowed. There he attained a double first in classics. He wrote to his brother afterwards about his Antwerp experiences, and the letter reveals a thoughtful and articulate young man. Both Tisdall and Brooke were proof of the notion that the Royal Naval Division was an elite force, in as much as the best and the brightest young men were attracted to it to serve as officers. Tisdall's letter offers one of the most vivid accounts of the fighting at Antwerp, and reads:

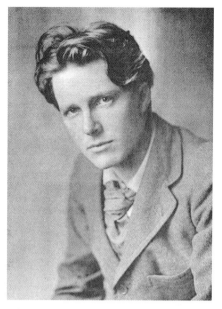

The war poet Sub Lieutenant Rupert Brooke RNVR. One of the 'best and brightest' of Edwardian society, he served with Hood Battalion at Antwerp.

> Since last writing to you I've had a very full sort of life & have changed a great deal. The old civil life in London is like a book read long ago and forgotten & I am now a serious officer with all my thoughts on making my platoon a force that I can enjoy leading in battle, & with a reckless enjoyment of any momentary pleasure that comes along. As a result I am very happy & all the old troubles are practically forgotten.
>
> You saw my letter written home from Antwerp; to pick up the story at that point we continued in the suburbs of Antwerp that Tuesday & the Wednesday & Thursday & retreated on Thursday night. It was a splendid adventure & I enjoyed it through & through, but it was one long round of hunger, thirst, want of sleep, marching & digging & all through it ran the endless roaring of big guns, & all night there was the glare of burning villages outside the lines & all day columns of smoke from the same. It was filled with bits of pure joy when we got water & bread & biscuit & beef & stole turnips & when Belgians gave us handshakes & tobacco & drinks & when we slept on straw in the sun in Ostend & got onto a clean steamer in mid channel: because I personally lost all the thinking that worries us in ordinary life; at a time when a whole population was on the run & towns were burned to the ground we lost all care for life or death or the next meal & simply thought of the moment. Also I was splendidly fit – until I got a good meal in England. The Belgians were splendid people, especially the country women, but the soldiers left in Antwerp were a mob. The main army retreated while we and the Marines held the Germans assisted by a frightened mob of Belgians, who ran as soon as shells struck their trenches, had no order or discipline, got panicky at nights & spoilt everybody's sleep by blazing away for ten minutes

together at nothing at all – a set of Englishmen stood over the crew of a Belgian gun with bayonets to keep them from running one day.

There was no real infantry fighting, all gunnery, & our guns were hopelessly inferior to the Germans. There were a few English naval guns there (4.7 & 6 inch & one 9.2) otherwise there were bad Belgian guns badly served. One Belgian battery kept dropping shrapnel on my company for a whole morning while we were making head-cover for our trench; we ducked when we heard the gun go off – it was about ½ a mile behind us & so only 7 or 8 men were hit & only two badly hurt & we were too tired to care if it hit us & so weren't afraid. The Germans didn't use their infantry much: we had one attack in the dusk of evening and killed lots of them, poor chaps; you should have seen them dropping & their places being taken at once by new men. It got too dark to see them after a bit & we fired volleys & they seem to have retreated. While advancing they fired a bit but hit no one.[13]

In spite of the undoubted bravery of the men of the division, they were sadly lacking in both training and equipment. Colonel Walter Trefusis commanding the Collingwood Battalion, kept a brief diary of events at Antwerp, part of which reads:

Wednesday 7th October: Left Bochout at 2.30am arrived at trenches between forts 3 & 4 at dawn. Worked all day at improving and deepening trenches and cutting communication trenches. In the evening the men were jumpy and started firing at nothing – control was difficult owing to lack of discipline, shortage of Officers and a mixture of Belgian soldiers. This was the first night in the trenches, the men were largely raw recruits, and many of them had never fired off a rifle before. No rest that night.

Thursday 8th October: Fairly heavy shelling all the morning, when Col. Maxwell and others were killed and wounded. Intermittent shelling all the day – further improved the trenches made splinterproof shelters etc. More unnecessary firing after dark, but this soon stopped.[14]

He submitted these remarks to the Officer Commanding 1st Naval brigade in a report in which he was scathing of the lack of suitable equipment with which his battalion was equipped, noting a shortage of haversacks, mess tins and waterbottles, entrenching tools, web equipment and rifle slings, all of which made the mens' work more difficult. He added: 'Perhaps I may be permitted to remark here, that although the sending of untrained troops to Antwerp may have been fully justified by the military situation, it does not seem easy to justify the sending of badly equipped troops.'[15]

The Germans however were closing the noose around Antwerp. Cavalry and other reinforcements were advancing northwards from the direction of Lens. More seriously, the *37th Landwehr Brigade* which had been closely investing the city, and which had thus far been held at bay by the Belgian army, succeeded under cover of fog in the early hours of 7 October in crossing the Schelde in boats at Schoonaerde, 9 miles above Termonde. At the same time, heavy guns were carried over the Nethe and severe bombardment of the inner line of forts commenced. A good account from the German perspective, contrasting the effect of war upon dumb animals with the new machinery of warfare, comes from Gerd Leberecht, a reserve officer and journalist from the *Täglichen Rundschau*:

Disapprovingly Lance Corporal Piefke shakes his head at the bad shooting of the Belgians. Also it seems that much of their ammunition is faulty, at least there are many duds, the shrapnel shells landing ineffectively; a few steps to the left of me one hissed impotently in a furrow; I will take it home as a souvenir, one that will make a beautiful heavy ashtray. The only ones which exert themselves are the sturdy horses, which almost charge up pulling ammunition wagons, with fresh rounds for the guns. Truly, our heavy horses can gallop! And then they stand with trembling flanks amid the thunder, while it crashes around them, hissing and howling. Humans know for what reason they fight, and get accustomed to the fear of death very quickly. But the animal stands speechless in this terrifying time. A cow from the nearby meadow, with udders full of milk, approaches with hesitating steps almost to the front line, probably in the hope that perhaps someone will milk it, and so free it from its pain. Whimpering and with its tail wagging roams a dog, begging for food; nobody has time for it, and its Belgian master is either somewhere under the rubble or has fled to Holland. 'Tacke, tacke, tacke, tacke!' is the sound made by the machine-guns about three kilometres before us. Piefke smiles: 'the Englishmen are being mown down up there!' To the left of us on the road rattles past a motorcycle on its frantic journey. It is unbelievable at what mad speeds it weaves and wriggles between the wagons in the column on the highway; on bends the rider lays it almost flat on its side.

Directly behind it however there comes something with a more peaceful purpose. Into the garden of a large house is driven the 'Gulaschkanone', the mobile army kitchen, and makes noodle soup with pork. The beasts were still alive a half hour ago; they got here very quickly. Unfortunately it is usually very difficult to get such freshly slaughtered meat; because naturally one cannot carry along meat for days at a time. The dessert is shaken down from a pear tree. Some eight hundred meters over us stands a large yellow caterpillar, the moored balloon in the sky, which carries out sterling work of observation. Past it, in elegant flight drifts a 'Taube', whose engine cannot be heard in the ongoing cacophony here. A smoking monster emerges from the avenue of poplars, quickly grows larger as it approaches, and is already past again: an armoured car, from which a machine-gun stares. Tonight, with its enemy dazzled by the powerful headlight, it has driven far into their territory and has also fired a few shells at the railway line. A Hamburg engineer, now just a sergeant, steers it, whilst a crew of several officers and men are carried within the steel body of this new Trojan horse. One of the crew was a man that I had seen previously in the wagon park of the division, he was downright filthy, from head to toe, with the dirt of campaigning, puffing as he dragged a heavy iron plate and then standing to attention before an NCO. Something prompted me to ask after this man. 'That is war volunteer Dr. Seeger, in civil life district magistrate in Cameroon!' Here all barriers fall. No work is too lowly, if through it one is useful to the nation.[16]

The Germans were not alone in exploiting armoured cars – fast, highly mobile and useful for causing mayhem behind enemy lines – in this campaign. Commander Charles Rumney Samson was Britain's most prominent naval pilot of the years immediately before the First World War, but he was also responsible for pioneering armoured fighting vehicles. He had arrived in Belgium in August 1914 initially with the Eastchurch Squadron of the Royal Naval Air Service. The squadron was sent to Belgium to provide the RNAS with a suitable base on the Continent from which it could attack the enemy; Samson was critically short of serviceable aircraft for this primary role, but his aggressive spirit was aroused when he used two of his squadron transport cars (commandeered civilian vehicles armed with Maxim guns) to attack from 500yd range a German staff car. Two of the enemy were wounded in the engagement and the staff car quickly turned about.

Two days later Samson set out again with four of his cars for another foray, this time into Lille, evacuated temporarily by the enemy, to capture or destroy any German transport that he might find there. This roving commission suited Samson well and his next assignment was to support the Royal Naval Division at Antwerp. To increase their protection, a pair of his cars – a Mercedes and a Rolls-Royce – were quickly given rudimentary armour in the form of a covering of ¼in-thick boiler plate, in the dock-yards of Antwerp. It was soon found however that the armour fitted was inadequate, and a heavier vehicle was required. Part of the squadron's transport consisted of com-mandeered London 'type B' buses. Two of these were adapted and became armoured lorries. The cab was covered with armour plate and the main body work was replaced with what was in reality an open-topped armoured box with sloping sides, from which a crew of Royal Marines could fire their rifles. These vehicles were intended to act as armoured personnel carriers allowing infantry to support the operations of the lighter

An armoured bus from Commander Samson's squadron, operated by men of the Royal Marines and Royal Naval Air Service.

armoured cars. Alas the weight of the boiler plate made the armoured buses too slow to keep up with the armoured cars, and as a result they were mainly used during the Antwerp operations as mobile blockhouses guarding crossroads. One of these, used by Samson's brother Felix, was further armed with a machine-gun. In the course of these operations, German light field guns were encountered for the first time, and it became apparent that an armoured vehicle mounting an artillery piece was needed to support the lighter armoured cars. One of the B type buses was fitted with a three-pounder naval gun. This proved successful at providing cover for the armoured cars, and two Mercedes Daimler lorries were also adapted to carry the same weapon.

For Jim Begent and the men of the RND, German artillery was also the problem, and they were on the receiving end of the increasingly destructive German bombardment:

> On Wednesday morning [the 7th] we took up our position in the trenches which stretched between the forts. The line of our first Brigade stretched for about 2 miles. All day the heavy guns were working while we made the trenches stronger and more shrapnel proof. All day and all night the shells screamed and burst overhead, but without damaging us very much. We were up all night watching and waiting – with loaded maxim and rifles – for an infantry attack; although we had many alarms the attack did not come off. By Heavens, it was an experience that first night under fire. In front of the trenches about 100 yds away were vicious barbed wire entanglements through which passed electricity of high power so even if the Germans had reached them I don't think they would have stood a chance of getting through.
>
> On Thursday [the 8th] we made the trenches much stronger in case they used Lyddite shells on us and because we knew that there would be a terrific artillery duel. We expected some British heavy artillery, but they never came, and all we had were the forts, the guns of which were not half as good as we had believed, and the Belgian artillery which was old and hopelessly outclassed by the Germans. That day the firing was terrific and the 'damned Germans' used those 17″ guns and bombarded the town over our heads. We could hear the low drone made by the great shells as they passed high overhead. They did terrible damage in the city, causing it to break into flames and killing many poor refugees, helpless men, women & children.
>
> This day I was as near death as I have ever been. We, the maxim section, six of us went along the line in our motor lorry in order to get some more guns and ammunition. The road we had to go along had Belgian batteries on either side of it; the Germans appeared to have got the range as every now and again a shell would come whizzing overhead. We got safely along the road as far as we had to go, & had left the lorry & were going up the lane towards the lines when there was a bang & we saw in a field just ahead of us a cloud of smoke arise, then another bang & shrapnel burst all over us, but with marvellous luck none of us were hurt. We beat a hasty retreat and safely reached our own lines. Later on we fetched the guns & that night we had three ready to let out 400 rounds a minute at the Germans, but unfortunately we never used them.[17]

On 7 October naval officer L.F. Robinson received word that the Germans had succeeded in forcing back the Belgians, and that he was now to evacuate Antwerp, taking with him as many guns as could be saved, and destroying the remainder. The railway-mounted heavy guns were withdrawn on the night of 7 October, Robinson writing:

> The night had become as red as day, as the glare of the burning houses and buildings everywhere mounted to the sky in huge streaks of light, showing where everything was being blown up, burnt, and destroyed in the endeavour to open up the area in front of the inner defences. The roads were packed with a seething mass of men, women, and children of all ages, household effects, and hundreds of soldiers, all streaming towards the city in head long retreat before the threatened advance of the Huns.
>
> It was such a picture as only an artist could give us on a canvas. No man is more tender to the helpless than the British 'blue', no one more cheerful; and not one of us but felt his heart wrung by the infinite pathos of this terror-stricken mob. As we drew up at Wilryck the station-master started waving his arms in frantic gesticulations, and told us that we could not go on via Contich, as that village was already occupied by the enemy. There was still one way left by which we could reach the Boom Bridge – the single line round by the bank of the Scheldt via Hoboken.
>
> It was now just past midnight, and our chances of getting away in the darkness seemed to be getting thinner and thinner. However, we started off on our new line, but had hardly got a mile before we were brought up all standing with a grinding of brakes. Jumping out to see what was in the way, we found about a hundred trucks and wagons barring our path, all in the various stages of unloading but quite deserted by the owners, the Naval Divisions, and not another engine in sight. Such a load was beyond the power of our own two engines, and even then we could not push all this lot out in front of us, so after a few moments' consideration we decided to abandon the train and walk to Hoboken, where if we could not get out by rail, we could cross the river and get away to the west on foot.
>
> The railway-side was strewn with all manner of articles and food-stuffs. Littlejohns borrowed a bicycle, and as soon as we met a road made off for the city. Girouard took charge and led the way along the line, all stumbling over the rails and sleepers in the darkness, but trying to keep as quiet as possible, with a very much open eye to the left for the enemy, who might pop up at any moment on our flank. Behind us the villages were burning, whilst to the south the roar and flashes of the guns showed where the battle was raging.[18]

The German advance however was not as rapid as had been feared, and the train crews the next day were able to return, clear the line and get their engines moving again towards Ostende.

The critical moment in the ill-fated defence of Antwerp came on 8 October. During the course of this day, not only was the whole of the *37th Landwehr Brigade* across the Schelde, but it was now reinforced by the *1st Bavarian Landwehr Brigade* and

A German Landwehr
*soldier in Belgium in
1914.* (Pat Gariepy)

the *9th Ersatz Brigade*. Troops of the German *Matrosen Division* were also closing in
on Antwerp. Heavy guns had moved closer and shells were now being directed at the
city itself. The enemy increased his efforts against Forts No. 1, and No. 2, for once
these had fallen to German troops, this would effectively render the continued defence
of the city untenable. From this position, the Germans could fire into the rear of the
other forts and cut off the retreat of their defenders. After only a few more hours
of resistance, these critical forts were captured by the end of the day. Among the
Germans fighting here was a soldier in a reserve regiment, named Gottfried Sender.
Writing on 9 October to a friend, describing the previous day's action, he says:

> My battalion lay in a wood of young oak trees. The sun played through the
> branches and lit up a tranquil picture, infinitely more peaceful in comparison to
> the awful places which lay behind us! The outer forts had fallen; and so our

regiment was now moved into the front line. The enemy had moved back behind the Nethe. In front of Duffel we lay in a trench, upon which a terrible artillery fire fell. A patrol received the order to find out whether the bridge over the Nethe was destroyed. I joined voluntarily. Shrapnel scattered in our path; we came to the village. There was no sign of the enemy. The officer and I crept under the shelter of the houses to the bridge. It was destroyed. However – clap, clap! – we came under infantry fire. We went back to our patrol which had stayed behind at the entrance to the village. I quickly returned on a bicycle with the news. This was relayed back, and an order came for the patrol to return. Their task was fulfilled.

Gefreiter Gottfried Sender, the German reservist who took part in the capture of Antwerp.

A hostile airman had observed our position; we came under awful artillery fire. A shrapnel shell burst in the house in which I had just taken cover. As if by a miracle I escaped the falling debris. Covered with dust, I reached some shelter. The hostile observation post must have been well sited. One could barely venture out of cover without being fired upon.[19]

The decision was taken to withdraw the Belgian field army from the city, before it was completely encircled and while there was still a possibility of escape. Late that evening the British government ordered the withdrawal of British forces across the Schelde, but General Paris in command of the RND had already anticipated this, and events on the ground forced the retirement of the division from about 5.30pm. General Paris's orders reached the Marine and 2nd Naval Brigades between 6.30 and 7pm. At that time 2nd Naval Brigade was on the right from Fort No. 7 to midway between Forts No. 4 and No. 5. 1st Naval Brigade was on the left of it up to Fort No. 2, Royal Marine Brigade in reserve behind the centre. The three brigades were ordered to withdraw by different routes and rendezvous across the Schelde, however the orders for 1st Naval Brigade to withdraw reached only Drake battalion, with the other battalions unaware of the departure of their comrades.

There were chaotic scenes as withdrawing troops – Belgian and British – became caught up in the exodus of a fleeing and terrified civilian population. Only those too old or infirm remained in their homes, and the streets and trains by which the RND were to escape were choked with refugees. Clapham-Foster recalled:

Our men loathed the idea of a retreat, but the majority realised that every minute the position was becoming more critical and that immediate retreat was our only hope of escaping capture. Almost all the Belgians had gone, except those in the forts, and in our covering fort only one Belgian gunner remained. One of our naval gun crews gallantly offered to remain and work the guns in order to cover our retreat, which they did up to the very last minute ...

In order to cross the Scheldt, we were forced to pass by the blazing petroleum tanks at Hoboken. The road was narrow, but it was the only road left. The fumes were overpowering and the intense heat proved too much for some of the men. The flames at times blew right across the road, and large German shells were falling in amongst the tanks at the rate of four a minute. Sometimes a shell would burst with a terrific report in the boiling oil, and flames shot up to the height of two hundred feet.

As we approached the blazing tanks it was like entering the infernal regions. The burning oil had flooded a field on the side of the road and dead horses and cattle were frizzling in it. 'Now, boys,' shouted an officer, 'keep your heads and run through it!' And we did – but I don't know how we did it. Once we had got past the oil tanks we were in comparative safety for a hundred yards because the road was sheltered, but for some thousand yards it was exposed again to the enemy's fire.

We were ordered to run at the double over this bit of road, and most of us were fortunate enough to reach the pontoon bridge over the river. A spy was caught by one of our battalions in the act of trying to blow up this bridge, but his designs were frustrated just in time, and a bayonet ended his career. Sentries were posted at intervals while we went across, and shouted 'Change your step!' every few yards. At last we were safely on the other side and breathed again. The relief felt

A wounded Royal Marine is helped from the line by a comrade, who escorts him to a dressing station in Antwerp.

by all ranks on getting across the river can hardly be imagined, and, although even there we were by no means out of danger, yet we knew that a most important step had been taken.[20]

Laking was also among those men now retreating as best they could away from the Germans. In this he was assisted by a bearded figure who had by now become a familiar figure among the British forces at Antwerp:

We were on the move all that night, led by civilians who knew the road through the woods, and I might say that we were in the German lines no less than seven times in our retreat. We were well on our way, when we were stopped by an armoured motor car, and a voice called out, 'Here! Where the —— are you taking these men to? You will be right in the midst of them if you keep on this way.' And that voice was that daring man's, Commander Samson. All at once he espied two men who were leading us, but am pleased to say they will not lead any more the wrong way, for they were spies, and they spent their last few minutes on earth with the First Naval Brigade, for, without giving them time to say their prayers, we bayoneted them. We turned in the right direction, and could see all the oil tanks, etc., in flames, and as we went along we passed dead and wounded women and children lying in the streets. This is where the horrors of war come in.

By and by we arrived on the bank of the River Scheldt and were taken across in two steam boats, as all pontoon bridges had been blown away. We started on our way, and came to a place called ——. Then we were given a piece of meat, and I ate mine raw. Then we travelled on, passing thousands of refugees, some in dog carts, some wheeling their aged parents in hand-carts, every age, from a week old to grandfathers. I saw one poor little mite eating a turnip, which brought the tears in my eyes and a lump in my throat, so I gave my biscuits to the child, and, God knows, I could have eaten them myself. I was saving them, for we did not know when we should get any more. It was a sight I never want to witness again. It made us think of our very own wives and children. We kept on walking until we came to a place called St. Giles Was, where we were to entrain for Ostend, to come to England, but fate was against us, for the Germans had cut the lines. So we must either fight it out or come into this country (Holland), but our Commander would not run us into a death trap. Had we reached St. Giles Was two hours earlier we could have diddled the Germans, but it was not so.

We crossed the border into Holland on the Saturday morning, and came into this town, Groningen, on Sunday, October 11th. From the time we left England we had been in three countries in a week, and I never had my boots off or any sleep until I reached here. We were all foot sore, tired, and hungry, not having had much food for a week. We walked 58 miles in 18 hours, and I carried 300 rounds of ammunition and a rifle, and I can tell you I did not want rocking to sleep when I got on my bed of straw that Sunday night. I think now the affair was mere bluff. There were two Naval Brigades and one Marine Brigade – total number 8,000 – against a German horde of 60,000.

I think I have told you all that I can remember, only I wish we were free so that we could have another go at them.[21]

Tisdall too was retreating, though fatigue and hunger were working against him and his men. He also reports an instance of attempted sabotage, though whether this was a figment of the heightened emotional state that he must have been in is not clear:

Our retreat on the Thursday was a grand experience. That afternoon we were so weak that we could hardly stand – I have never known such weakness before – but at 7 o'clock we started this awful march of 20–25 miles; we were carrying 250 rounds each and our rifles & had had no food since two. We were hopelessly mixed up, companies all among each other; Antwerp was blazing ahead of us & German shrapnel was flying about at intervals; in Antwerp the houses were deserted until we got down near the river & there the people were huddled together in great silent crowds. There were … broken glass & great holes blown in the cobbles & at intervals houses on fire, while by the river there was a huge pillar of red flame & black smoke from the burning oil tanks & shipping. None of the shrapnel hit us but it fell on the road just in front & among the houses on the side. We crossed the Scheldt by a bridge of boats – a spy was caught trying to blow it up while we crossed & marched into the country. I got a slice of bread from a Belgian & a lump of sugar – halved the bread with Clarke. We got more & more mixed. Twice we halted & men fell asleep by the road in crowds, so there were no more halts for a long time; the roads got more & more crowded with transport carts, Belgian guns, London motor buses, refugees with furniture in a cart, old women & children on top & cattle tied behind, & cavalry & infantry in retreat. Once our own battalion struggled in single file through a village – after about 18 miles we halted in the market place of a town called Beveren on the main road to Ghent & Ostend & officers went to enquire about trains; we lay down on the cobbles & slept leaving a narrow gangway down which passed an endless file of refugees and troops. After half an hour the march began again on bad roads & cart tracks – the railway was commanded by the Germans in another station called St Gilles. At about 3 or 4 miles from there the motor buses having put all their cargo in the trains started carrying men as quick as they could. I got a lift & before it, got some bread & butter & beer from a farmer who wouldn't take pay. He let me take away a big crust with me, but I had to give so much of it away that I had very little left in the end. So ended a nightmare.[22]

Sub Lieutenant Arthur Tisdall RNVR, who served at Antwerp with Anson Battalion RND.

The omnibus drivers were recruited to provide transport for the Antwerp expedition directly from the London General Omnibus Company and were drafted to Belgium still wearing their LGOC uniforms. Nominally they were part of the Corps of Royal Marines and were given temporary service numbers. Among them was Charles Lee, who in September 1914 left his bus garage in Putney and joined the crews of seventy D-type buses, which were sent via Dunkirk to Antwerp. They reverted to their civilian status after their return home from the expedition, though most chose subsequently to re-enlist in the army as drivers. Whilst the motor bus drivers were classed as enlisted men, albeit temporarily, the owners of motor cars who volunteered to go to Antwerp were on the whole given temporary officer status.

Gottfried Sender, writing on 10 October, was on two wheels rather than four. He described the final German push beyond the Nethe and on towards the city itself:

London omnibus driver Charles Lee, from Putney, who drove his bus at Antwerp. (London Transport Museum)

It was 12 o'clock. The company received its food from the recently arrived field kitchen, as usual, tasty and filling. Then the order suddenly came to move off. Each man received about 200 cartridges, as bread for the enemy. From the far distance we heard the thundering of cannons. In a forced march we approached the recently damaged bridge. I with my bicycle accompanied the major, who gave battlefield directions to the captains. With the cycle on my back I crossed the shaking bridge, jumped over ditches, and waded the swampy meadows. Everywhere there were dead and wounded Belgians; dead horses, and dead cattle revealed how frightfully our cannons raged. The company gathered, then spread out. Where are the 10th company and the machine-gun detachment? Anxious tension. A gap opened up in the firing line. A dreadful burst of mortar fire. With a crash they hit a party marching to the bridge. I had to go back, to search for the missing company. Again I crossed the bridge. Before it lay a half dead Belgian, who thirsted after water. I would have liked to help him, however, I had to go on. Hundreds of human lives depended on the message. A captain helped me in my mission. He took the message; I gave a drink to the wounded man. He pressed his hand to mine. I travelled further, through the field of fire. The company had done a detour. It crossed the bridge and spread out. In the undergrowth I lost them. The young captain who took my message fell, killed by five bullets in the heart; shrapnel tore off a comrade's head. There were shouts, and groaning all around.

I lay in the trench of the 9th company. A fine rain made our limbs grow stiff. However, mounds of sand were quickly thrown up. Those who had no shovel dug with their hands. The bullets whizzed like a whirlwind; little white clouds showed where shrapnel burst. One of the shrapnel balls hit my arm, without injuring me. Suddenly there was loud shouting, and cheers. The Belgians had collapsed. With fixed bayonets they were driven back.[23]

Other members of the RND were not as fortunate as Tisdall, and a large portion of the 1st Naval Brigade, having found its escape route cut by the now advancing Germans, turned north instead to cross into neutral Holland, where they were disarmed by Dutch troops. Jim Begent was among them and wrote home to his parents:

At 9 o'clock that night (Thursday) we were given orders to retire so we dis-mounted our guns & rushed them up to the lorry; meanwhile a party of marines arrived just to keep the fire up while our men left the trenches, & very soon afterwards Hawke Battalion started off on one of the most awful marches I should think it possible to experience. We marched right along past the Belgian batteries who were pounding away at the Germans & the shells were bursting all over the place, many of them quite near; it made me wonder how long it would be before we were struck down. That duel was the most awful thing I have ever seen; the country around was in many places in flames & and in the lurid glare we could see the gunners hard at work. Twice I saw a German shell burst right in the midst of a battery & and then all was quiet; all killed I expect. How far we marched through the country I don't know, but all night we passed burning farms, & batteries. Here and there we would meet two or three Belgians marching away from the fight, and here and there we would pass dead and dying men by the roadside. We continued until we passed some blazing oil tanks, & then we began to march beside the river.

By this time a great many were feeling the strain & marched along as if they were dazed. I nearly went to sleep while marching, & got so fed up that I did not care one bit whether I survived or not, as along the docks the shells were bursting and smashing the houses. It was pitch dark here, & we almost had to grope our way. It was owing to this darkness that D company to which I belonged dropped behind & lost their way & have not been seen or heard of since, so heaven only knows what happened to them. My friend and I crawled under some railway trucks & joined up with the rest of our battalion. We thought the others were following but evidently they were not. However, we continued more dead than alive until we came to the Pontoon Bridge [over the Scheldt] which we crossed at 5 a.m. after marching for 8 hours.

We rested for an hour at daybreak [i.e. on the 9th] & then continued our journey towards a place called St. Nicholas where we were to take the train for Ostend. We marched all day although we could hardly drag one foot before another, but just as we were nearing St. Nicholas we had to turn back as we were warned of the presence of a large body of Uhlans. We marched back about 2 miles, & were then told that we had 4 miles to march in ¾ hour or we should probably be cut off by the evening. Well, despite our feelings we marched like demons & almost reached our destination when a Belgian brought news that the Uhlans were just in front. We spread out in extended order & waited, but after a couple of shots the Uhlans, five in number, scooted when they saw how many of us there were, & we arrived safely at St. Gillis where we were going to take the train. Our commander heard however that the Germans were cutting off the line so he would not let us get on. It was lucky for us that we did not as that train was blown up with all the refugees on it. With no other course open we marched a further 4 or 5 miles into Holland where we had to lay down our arms. We settled comfortably into an engine shed for the night but were awakened about 10.30 pm & put aboard a train in which we spent 12 hours and eventually arrived at Groningen, a town of considerable size in the very north of Holland. We are quartered in a Military barracks.[24]

Another naval reservist, Able Seaman Jeremy Bentham of Benbow Battalion, kept a diary and recorded the circumstances of their apprehension by the Dutch:

After a train journey of more than 12 hours, we finally arrived into Groningen at noon on Sunday 11th October. Every man sported a 7-day beard, and we looked filthy and dishevelled. A huge throng of people witnessed our arrival. Afterwards,

Members of the RND interned in Holland. Second from left front row is Able Seaman W. Anderson of North Shields.

we were marched to the Rabenhauptkazerne [barracks] on the Hereweg. It did not look very hospitable, and the Dutch Landstorm kept a strict guard. This consisted of mainly older reservists from the Dutch army. We slept in large halls, with iron bunk beds where the air was incredibly stale at night. We were allowed to send a postcard home to reassure our loved ones, and to advise them that we had safely arrived at Groningen. Officers were housed in hotels, under word of honour. The men were under the direct command of a Dutch CO and our own NCOs. In order to kill the time, we were ordered to perform the weirdest of chores in the morning, like cleaning etcetera. We had nothing else to do for the rest of the day, and we were soon bored silly.

Private Phillip Gouldsmith, Chatham Battalion RMLI, who was interned at Groningen, Holland.
(Pat Gariepy)

Breakfast consisted of half a loaf of bread, which had to last the rest of the day. It tasted of nothing, and we thought it was made of potato peelings and husks. There was a small piece of margarine and coffee, without any milk or sugar. Porridge was issued not until much later. Our lunch consisted of either boiled pork with potatoes or boiled leg of pork with beans, covered in lard. Our 'tea' consisted of tea with a piece of Dutch cheese. There was no variation, and everyone was fed up with the monotonous food after a while. Extra food could fortunately be purchased from street merchants.[25]

In fact Bentham was to escape from internment in Holland in 1915, and went on to serve with the RND in the Gallipoli campaign. Most of the 1,500-strong contingent in

Private Herbert Appleton RMLI, who served at Antwerp with the Portsmouth Battalion, and escaped from the city when it fell.

Holland however were destined to see out the next four years in the camp which became known as 'Timber Town'.

Dutch captivity was however preferable to the German variety, and other members of the Royal Naval Division were to fall into enemy hands during the chaotic retreat from Antwerp. A clash occurred at Moerbeke, between the Bavarian *Landwehr Regiment Nr.1* and the rearguard formed by the Portsmouth Battalion, RMLI. Having missed the last train, the battalion marched to the next station (picking up stragglers of the 1st Naval Brigade on the way) and boarded a train. When this was de-railed by a shell, the marines attacked the enemy in the gathering gloom. In the firefight about half of the marines, under their Colonel, escaped. However some 600 naval ratings and 300 marines, together with 5 officers, fell into enemy hands here. One of these five, Lieutenant T.J. Dobson of the Collingwood Battalion, has left a good account of the incident from the perspective of the sailors and marines involved:

> I was wounded on the night of October 9th, 1914, near St Giles, while trying to reach Ostend after the retreat from Antwerp. With a mixed force of Royal Naval Division and Royal Marine Light Infantry, in all I believe about 700 to 800 of various battalions, we had intercepted a train somewhere in the vicinity of St Giles. This train had started from Antwerp, and was full of civilian refugees, men, women and children. It was about 9 p.m. when we entrained, and after proceeding for about half an hour, we were, as I heard subsequently, turned in to a siding and fire was opened on us by a force of Germans who were waiting for us.
>
> I was on top of an open truck full of boxes containing various kinds of war material, such as field telephones, etc., and was wounded by a bullet which passed through my elbow-joint, fracturing all three bones by taking away the end of the radial part of the ulna and damaging the humerus.
>
> I have not much recollection of what followed, as I soon became unconscious from loss of blood, but remember being helped to the ground by Lieutenant Carlisle, R.N.D., and a man.
>
> I was attended to almost at once by Staff-Surgeon L. Greig, R.N., attached to the marines, who was on the train. But for his help I believe I should have bled to death. Whilst lying on the ground I suffered no inconvenience or ill-treatment by the Germans, and was eventually carried to a convent near by which was being used as a hospital. Here I was immediately dressed by German doctors, and during the three days I was there I received every kindness and consideration which could be expected. The German officers whom I came across were all that could be desired, and one or two of them went out of their way to do small acts of kindness to me. For instance, one of them took off my boots whilst I was lying unconscious, because, as he afterwards told me, I looked so uncomfortable. Nothing was stolen from me, not even a little gold which I had. Doctor Greig attended to me for two or three days and performed an operation on me.
>
> Lieut.-Commander Crossman of my battalion was allowed to visit me before the unwounded prisoners were sent to Germany. Doctor Greig was sent with them.[26]

Royal Naval Division prisoners of war at Doberitz camp in Germany.

An account from one of the Germans of the Bavarian *Landwehr Regiment Nr.1* who was present describes the treatment of other British prisoners in their hands. By his own admission this was less than sympathetic, and certainly contrasts with that received by Dobson:

> We marched quickly [to Moerbeke] and at nightfall arrived. The station and the entire town were now searched with the accompaniment of the Burgo-meister. In the process we learned to our great regret, that around the middle part of the day from 10am to 6pm six English troop trains had passed through, and also Belgian troops had left from here on the highway. Thus we had arrived too

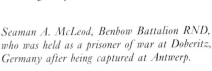

Seaman A. McLeod, Benbow Battalion RND, who was held as a prisoner of war at Doberitz, Germany after being captured at Antwerp.

late. Some beat their fists and a few grim words were muttered. Gladly would we have liked to meet up with these English gentlemen. At 11 o'clock that night, a single shot suddenly rang out, and thereafter came the news that a locomotive was coming in. Thus there was still one train left. The station was occupied by just a few men, likewise the railway embankment [but] the train was brought to a halt. The commander of No 7 company with about fifty men boarded the wagons and challenged the English to capitulate. Their answer was a heavy salvo and on the ground fatally wounded lay the commander and ten men, while about ten more were badly injured. Now however we let loose like a thunderstorm and paid them back thoroughly. About thirty English lost their lives. Our artillery now fired four shells over the train and this produced the desired effect. The 1,200 English showed themselves and were immediately disarmed. Once they saw how few in numbers we were (we were not quite 200 men) they were terribly angry. They were now sent towards E. . . . (one hour away). As the trains left an English officer led an escape attempt. After he had had several warnings he ran into our escort troops, who threw him in a roadside ditch.

The warm-hearted Bavarians did not leave the joke there. They formed up against the prisoners and gave a well-timed burst of rapid fire. A few English, who wanted to flee over garden fences, did not try any longer after they came into contact with our freshly sharpened bayonets. The mutiny was suppressed, but around twenty English paid for this escape attempt with their lives.

The English officer was later court martialled and shot. After the prisoners were accommodated in a local church, we made our way back to the station to excavate some fire trenches. We expected the enemy to arrive, perhaps from Antwerp. The whole night we lay out in the open, making it the third night without sleep, however no enemy arrived. The 10th October dawned and early on, at 6am, some Belgian cycle patrols were fired upon. We made ourselves very comfortable on the high street and awaited events. At 11am the fallen Hauptmann of No 7 company was carried through our lines – right to the last the dead hero was honoured.[27]

The British officer who was executed by the Germans was Lieutenant Commander Oswald Hesketh Hanson RNVR, of Benbow Battalion, RND. A letter in connection with this from Commodore Henderson, dated 15 February 1918, stating evidence from Lieutenant Commander F.C. Grover, Hawke Battalion, RNVR reads:

Poor Hanson was shot by the Germans on the 10th October 1914. He had struggled with a sentry who was about to fire on one of our own men trying to escape after we were taken prisoner on the night of the 9th, and under German Military Code such an act can be punished with death. I tried to get the sentence mitigated, and so did the Commandant of the troops guarding us, for it was evident that Hanson was overwrought by the fatigues of the previous days. The matter was referred to the highest authority; at that time, General von der Goltz was Military Governor of Belgium, but it was of no avail, and Hanson was shot by firing squad at midday, and is buried by the Church at Exaerde.[28]

A German sailor writing of the aftermath of the Antwerp debacle describes how, on 10 October, there was still confusion on his side as to whether the RND had left entirely, or whether some of its men were still in possession of the forts:

> On Saturday we were awoken at 3 o'clock in the morning. Twenty five volunteer sailors were sought, to take the waterway to Antwerp. Antwerp itself was in our hands, but two forts on the left bank of the Schelde were still occupied by the English. The canal and the Schelde were probably infested with mines, but if we got through, we could facilitate the crossing of the army over the Schelde. We expected the journey from Willebroeck, some 22 kilometers distance, to take about 4½ hours. In fact it was 7½. Up beyond a destroyed bridge we took the boat. The sun shone blood red

Able Seaman Cecil A. Tooke RNVR, who was captured by the Germans at Antwerp. (Andrew Marsh)

in the east, like a fireball. For miles the sunlight reflected upon the flooded countryside, and the trees cast long eerie shadows. Very cautiously, we ran slowly on. In the water, shimmering with oil, floated pieces of wood from blown up bridges and burning ships. Our rather chilly mood was warmed up by hot coffee. After one and a half hours we reached the Schelde. The officer by the mast watched ahead with binoculars. An English fort came into view. 'Full speed ahead!' 'Take cover!' 'Ready your weapons!' We lay behind the gunwale, loaded rifles in our hands. We could clearly see the position of the battery. The gaping mouths of the guns lay ahead of us. What would the next seconds bring? A single shell could mean the destruction of our steamboat. The water rippled in our wake, and the German battleflag quietly fluttered in the wind. One minute went by – we were past. It was an unguarded stretch of water. Our boat commander thought either that the English were so stunned by our temerity that they forgot to shoot, or that they took us for English sailors. Half an hour later the drama repeated itself. Again luckily we came through. The previously clear sky clouded over and became almost like night. Rain? No, it was clouds of smoke from massive fires burning in the petrol tanks of the lower Schelde. The shining tip of the spire of Antwerp cathedral made it stand out against the dark sky. Half an hour later it was knocked down, to the accompaniment of cheers, by a recently arrived field battery. 'Look out below!'

The artillery provided a half-hour shooting display; aiming their guns through the streets. However, our journey made us the first sailors to enter Antwerp. The streets were rather empty, and shops mostly closed. Now and again a few frightened figures showed themselves. Often they rushed forward to greet us, blustering greatly about the departed 'Englishman'. All were now glad that peace should return. The town is hardly damaged; at particular places however one could see the horrible effects of German shells. Two hours after our arrival, our infantry and cavalry appeared, their rifle barrels and saddlery richly decorated with flowers. To the cheers of our thrilled comrades we removed the Belgian flag from the tower of the cathedral and replaced in with the German one. Proudly it flapped in the fresh sea breeze, a reminder of German will and power. Germany, I salute you![29]

Meanwhile, the British 7th Division, which had been intended as reinforcements for the British and Belgian troops at Antwerp had landed at Zeebrugge; however the former city fell to the Germans before they could reach it. Marching east, they were in the vicinity of Ghent when they encountered the Belgian field army moving west. The military situation was at this point very fluid, and they were also just as likely to meet Germans (particularly cavalry patrols) as there were no front lines as such. The advanced guard of the 7th Division was provided by its cavalry, in particular the 1st Dragoons (the Royals). Private John Cusack was one of the regiment's scouts; he and another trooper ranged ahead, on the look out for and reporting German movements. As they made their way across country heading ultimately now to Ypres, they encountered the straggling remains of the Belgian army, and also an ubiquitous character who seemed to be everywhere. Cusack remembered that:

A remarkable man called Commander Samson, who was – or had been – with a naval reserve unit, dashed on to our scene. The Commander was a little rotund, weather-beaten man, in naval uniform with a 'Captain Kettle' beard and whiskers, driving round in a Rolls-Royce armoured lorry, the size of a taxi. He had mounted on it a three-pounder gun on a pivot, and he had a sailor with him as his driver. He told us, 'We've just come out from Antwerp. Makin' ourselves a bit useful with this naval armoured car!' Round his hat he had a white band, on which he had painted, in black, '2,000 MARKS'. He said, 'That's the price the Germans have put on my head if they capture me.'[30]

When it became evident that Antwerp would have to be abandoned, the armoured cars were given the task of harassing the Germans who were approaching the escape route to Zeebrugge. After Antwerp Samson continued to work with the British cavalry, providing reconnaissance information as to German movements, until the front line finally settled to the east of Ypres. Cusack continued:

Whenever we made contact with a German patrol within his gun range, he would thank us and then, rapping out some nautical order like 'Action on the starboard quarter', he would fire several rounds at the Germans with his three-pounder. He never stayed to receive acknowledgement when the Germans fired back, and it was we who unfortunately bore the brunt of his reprisals. He had an assistant

Commander Charles Rumney Samson RN, who waged a one-man war against the Germans in Belgium in 1914.

called Major Ed Haynes, who had got out of Antwerp with him, and was also scouting round in an armoured Rolls-Royce with a machine-gun. We liked to see them, because they were the only people who gave us any reliable information about the enemy's positions. One day Samson came bowling up in his armoured car with two Uhlan lances propped up on the front of it and trussed to the gun itself was an Uhlan prisoner. Samson was gaily wearing his prisoner's helmet.[31]

Was it all worthwhile? Churchill thought so. His strongly held view was that but for the resistance offered at Antwerp, and for the measures taken to prolong that resistance, the considerable German forces engaged would have been free to carry out an almost uninterrupted march upon the Channel ports. He believed that had the German siege army been released on 5 October and, followed by their great reinforcements already available, advanced at once, nothing could have saved Dunkirk, nor perhaps Calais and Boulogne. The loss of Dunkirk was a certainty, and that of Calais and Boulogne was probable. Apart from anything else the loss of these vital supply ports would have been a disaster for the BEF. Ten days' delay to the Germans was all that was needed to get British troops into Belgium from the Aisne, and those ten days were nobly won by the Royal Naval Division and its comrades in arms.

Chapter 5
The Glory of War

Having managed to keep its withdrawal from the Aisne front a secret from the Germans, the BEF entrained for the north, once more to take up its position on the left of the French army. It was hoped that this manoeuvre would allow them to find an open flank, around which to encircle the heavily entrenched German forces on the Aisne. The Germans however had similar plans, and a major battle was now to develop on the portion of front between Armentières in the north and La Bassée to the south. This was allotted to the British II and III Corps, which were to be strengthened by the arrival in France of the Indian Corps, consisting of the Lahore and Meerut Divisions. These divisions in turn comprised brigades of Indian soldiers – Gurkhas, Sikhs, Hindus and Muslims, each with a single British battalion thrown in. Although the Indian Corps provided vital reinforcements at a critical juncture, not all of the Indian soldiers adjusted well to the cultural shock of arriving in Europe for the first time, and fighting in unfamiliar country against previously unencountered weapons. There were

The bridge over the Lys at Estaires, 11km west of Armentières. Estaires was the assembly point for the Indian Corps upon its arrival in France in October 1914; it was selected because from here the Indian battalions could support either the II Corps or III Corps as required.

also problems within the command structure of the Indian army, and the dietary requirements of the soldiers would present logistical challenges.

The country here was low lying and flat, but as yet still not criss-crossed by trenches and barbed wire. The race was now on to secure the ground that offered the most advantage to the defender, before the enemy arrived there. In some cases, however this was given away by poor communication and co-ordination between the British and French. Lance Corporal Edward Dwyer of the East Surrey Regiment would be awarded the Victoria Cross for his exploits later in the war, but of his experiences in this sector he wrote:

> We went to relieve the French round La Bassée. The regiment we took over from was the 14th Alpine Chasseurs and I have never seen such a sight. They left their trenches at 2 o'clock in the afternoon and all the Germans did was to follow them up. The consequence was they ran right into us and we left half our Division behind wounded. That was three weeks nightmare to me.[1]

An anonymous officer of the Royal Scots recorded in his diary the sense of urgency as battalions raced to secure key features; in this landscape bisected at regular intervals by canals, bridges were of critical importance:

> October 12–16. – March to Vieille Chapelle, but cannot get there, as the Germans have got there before us; at least, they are holding the canal just north of it. The Gurkhas are sent to hold the crossing at La Fosse, the Middlesex and Royal Irish have crossed in the south. The Royal Scots receive orders to rush a footbridge over the canal between the two, which is strongly held by the enemy.
>
> The ground for several miles west of the bridge was absolutely open, and is cut up by a series of dykes which are very deep and cannot be crossed except by small bridges at intervals. It was impossible to reconnoitre the position of the bridge owing to the nature of the country, and we were told to rush it at once. We had two companies, 'A' and 'B' Companies, in the firing line under Captain Tanner and Captain Heathcote, and two, 'C' and 'D', in support under Captain Morrison and Captain Henderson. We had no sooner started the attack than we came under heavy rifle fire. The men behaved as they always do, with the greatest coolness, and extended as though they were on an ordinary parade. The leading companies were led with the greatest gallantry by Captain Tanner and Captain Heathcote, the latter being wounded, the bridge being finally taken with the loss of about a hundred men.[2]

At the northern end of this front the Cavalry Corps was ordered to secure the important high ground to the east of the Mont des Cats. Instead they met determined German resistance from the direction of Meteren; the village was well sited for defence, its church tower offering good observation to the enemy, and the cavalry, unable to turn the Germans out, asked for infantry assistance.

Among the young officers experiencing war for the first time that summer and autumn was a 26-year-old named Bernard Law Montgomery, who would go on to scale the heights of the British military establishment, and to achieve some of the greatest victories in the annals of the British army. The event that was to alter the course of

Montgomery's career was to come on 13 October 1914, here at Meteren, where he and his battalion, the 1st Royal Warwickshire Regiment, were tasked with driving out the German defenders. The Warwicks had already received a baptism of fire in the chaos and confusion of the retreat from Mons. This time, as 'Monty' recorded many years later in his *Memoirs*,

> There was a plan and there were proper orders. Two companies were forward, my company on the left being directed on a group of buildings on the outskirts of the village of Meteren. When zero hour arrived I drew my recently sharpened

Major John Kirwan Gatacre, King Edward's Own Lancers, Indian Army (attached 4th Hussars). On 13 October he was reconnoitring for the advance beyond Meteren, near Mont des Cats, when he was killed.

sword and shouted to my platoon to follow me, which it did. We charged forward towards the village; there was considerable fire directed at us and some of my men became casualties, but we continued on our way. As we neared the objective I suddenly saw in front of me a trench full of Germans, one of whom was aiming his rifle at me.

In my training as a young officer I had received much instruction in how to kill my enemy with a bayonet fixed to a rifle. I knew all about the various movements – right parry, left parry, forward lunge. I had been taught how to put the left foot on the corpse and extract the bayonet, giving at the same time a loud grunt. Indeed, I had been considered good on the bayonet-fighting course against sacks filled with straw, and had won prizes in man-to-man contests in the gymnasium. But now I had no rifle and bayonet; I had only a sharp sword, and I was confronted by a large German who was about to shoot me. In all my short career in the army no-one had taught me how to kill a German with a sword. The only sword exercise I knew was saluting drill, learnt under the sergeant major on the barrack square.

An immediate decision was clearly vital. I hurled myself through the air at the German and kicked him as hard as I could in the lower part of the stomach; the blow was well aimed at a tender spot. I had read much about the value of surprise in war. There is no doubt that the German was surprised and it must have seemed to him a new form of war; he fell to the ground in great pain and I took my first prisoner! A lot of fighting went on during the remainder of the day, our task being to clear the Germans from the village. During

Lieutenant Bernard Montgomery, the future Field Marshal. (Lord Montgomery)

these encounters amongst the houses I got wounded, being shot through the chest. But we did the job and turned the Germans out of the village. It was for this action at Meteren that I was awarded the D.S.O. I was still only a lieutenant. My life was saved that day by a soldier of my platoon. I had fallen in the open and lay still hoping to avoid further attention from the Germans. But a soldier ran to me and began to put a field dressing on my wound; he was shot through the head by a sniper and collapsed on top of me. The sniper continued to fire at us and I got a second wound in the knee; the soldier received many bullets intended for me. No further attempt was made by my platoon to rescue us; indeed, it was presumed we were both dead. When it got dark the stretcher-bearers came to carry us in; the soldier was dead and I was in a bad way. I was taken back to the Advanced Dressing Station; the doctors reckoned I could not live and, as the station was shortly to move, a grave was dug for me. But when the time came to move I was still alive, so I was put in a motor ambulance and sent back to a hospital. I survived the journey and recovered, I think because I was very fit and active after two months of active service in the field. I was evacuated to hospital in England and for some months I took no further part in the war.[3]

The Germans evacuated the village after dark, and it was occupied by British infantry. By the time Montgomery returned to France, he had had a chance to reflect on where his future lay, and opted to become a staff officer rather than remain as a platoon commander, as this would better suit his aptitudes. It was the beginning of a career that would take him to the rank of Field Marshal.

On 16 October a general advance eastwards was ordered along the whole of the British Armentières–La Bassée front, in an effort to keep up the pressure on the Germans. The Cavalry Corps in the north was ordered to attempt to force its way across the River Lys, but was largely unsuccessful. Lieutenant T.L. Horn was the machine-gun officer of the 16th Lancers and has left a dramatic account of the attempt to take

Meteren. It was in these fields that Lieutenant Bernard Montgomery was shot and wounded by a sniper firing from the church tower.

Warneton, as part of this drive. The town was still very much intact and there was severe house-to-house street fighting, with the Germans also firing from behind barricades. He wrote:

> [at 4.30pm] it was ... decided that we should attack the centre of the village, which was barricaded. One of my [machine] guns had been placed on a roof overlooking the barricade, a hole being knocked through the tiles. The plan was that one [field] gun of 'E' Battery [Royal Horse Artillery] was to be manhandled up a side street, and then pushed quickly round the corner and fired at the barricade, under cover of my M.G. firing from the roof, and then one troop of 'C' Squadron was to rush the barricade, backed up if necessary by the rest of 'C' Squadron and half of 'A' Squadron. It was quite dark by the time all this was arranged.
>
> We were all standing along the sides of the street, with a certain amount of odd sniping going on towards the village centre, when the gun went off – I've never heard such a row – a deafening crash, and then the breaking and falling of glass all over and around one, as of course every window was broken to pieces, and most of the houses were three stories high. Three shells were fired, and then 'C' squadron rushed and took the barricade ... a good deal of shooting was going on from windows and doorways: it was pitch dark and one couldn't tell where it was coming from or who was shooting, as one could see the flash from a rifle whether it was being fired towards one or from one, also wherever the bullet struck a brick or stone there was a flash. One reaching the centre square there was another barricade down a right handed street leading to the canal: one M.G. was placed at the corner so that it could fire at this, and the man could lean round and have a look occasionally, but could fire it from behind the corner, merely putting his hand out to press the button. I took the other gun across to the opposite side of the square, each of us being covered in turn as we ran across, by the gun already in position ...
>
> All this time there was odd shooting going on, and all the side roads were being barricaded and picketed. A big house was on fire on our side of the square, making any movement visible, but luckily one had also caught fire near their barricade, and they couldn't move much without being seen. Suddenly a 'Verey' flare light came over and dropped almost into the square, lighting up everything as though it was daylight: it was our first experience of them, and one could see everyone crouching as close to the walls as possible, wondering what was going to happen next, personally I thought when it touched the ground there would be an awful explosion, but of course nothing of the sort happened ... The next item was a machine-gun opening fire from their barricade onto my other gun, which promptly replied, and it was the most extraordinary though horrid sight to see these two M.G.s like a couple of angry cats spitting at each other not more than 25 yards apart, sparks flying wherever the bullets hit the cobbles or walls, and the noise of course being deafening. Thank goodness our gun had been set up and laid when not under fire, whereas their gun had been brought up under fire and consequently badly aimed ...[4]

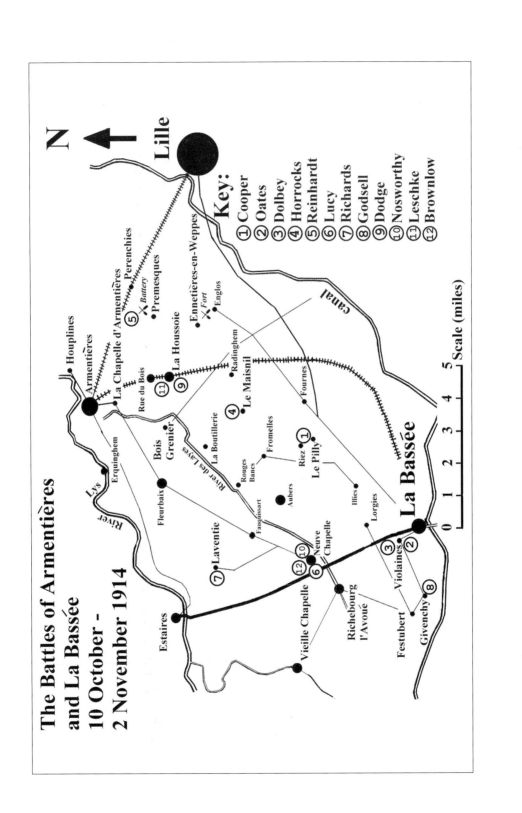

The Battles of Armentières and La Bassée – 10 October – 2 November 1914

N

Key:
1. Cooper
2. Oates
3. Dolbey
4. Horrocks
5. Reinhardt
6. Lucy
7. Richards
8. Godsell
9. Dodge
10. Nosworthy
11. Leschke
12. Brownlow

Scale (miles)
0 1 2 3 4 5

Lille

Houplines
Armentières
La Chapelle d'Armentières
Perenchies
Premesques
Battery
Ennetières-en-Weppes
Fort
Englos
La Houssoie
Rue du Bois
Radinghem
Le Maisnil
Fournes
canal
Erquinghem
Lys
River Lys
Bois Grenier
La Boutillerie
Fromelles
Riez
Le Pilly
Illies
Lorgies
La Bassée
Fleurbaix
River des Layes
Rouges Bancs
Aubers
Fauquissart
Laventie
Neuve Chapelle
Vieille Chapelle
Richebourg l'Avoué
Festubert
Givenchy
Violaines
Estaires

There was more success when the town of Armentières was captured by the British 4th and 6th Divisions, a few days after Meteren, on 17 October. The place was full of French refugees from Lille. The Germans had only recently abandoned it and there were signs of a hasty flight. Indeed some German soldiers had been left behind and fired at the British from the houses, though they were dislodged without too much difficulty. The British advanced guard then pushed on north-eastwards towards

British soldiers arrive at the front line by bus, Armentières, 1914.

Houplines. Private Frederick Woods, of the 1st Battalion Royal Irish Fusiliers was among them and remembered an incident that occurred on this day:

> Going into Armentières on the very heels of the Germans was an exciting and dangerous performance, and as we advanced along the streets we went on each side, not knowing on which side shots would come from windows, but ready for anything that happened, as the men on one side had their rifles handy for any German that appeared on the other. This was a better plan than being on the look-out for trouble from the windows just above your head. Luckily not many shots were fired upon us at this stage; but we soon came to a farm where one of the most desperate little fights that I can call to mind took place.
>
> We were wary in entering the farm, for we saw at once the sort of thing we had to tackle. There were four Germans concealed in a cellar the window of which was on a level with the ground, so they had full control of the yard and the entrance-gate.
>
> Some of our boys, with Captain Carbery, went in and tried to persuade the Germans to surrender, but their answer to the coaxing was a volley which killed the officer and wounded the men. The captain was terribly mutilated, for he had been struck full on the body, not by an ordinary honest bullet, but an explosive bullet, and the men had been badly hurt. As they lay on the ground they cried for help, and all the time the Germans were firing on them and succeeded in hitting them on the legs and shoulders. Two of our men, brave fellows, volunteered to try and save their wounded comrades, and they dashed into the yard, only to be shot and killed as soon as they entered ...
>
> It was useless to waste further life in the attempt to get the Germans out of their strong little position, from which they could fire without making themselves targets, so our officer sent for some engineers to undermine the farm and blow it up. The Germans were warned what was going to be done, and were called upon to surrender. This they refused to do.
>
> During that night the engineers were working like moles, and I didn't envy the feelings of the Germans who were trapped in the cellar, nor was there any pity for them next morning when the engineers finished their work.
>
> There was a crash and a flame and a shaking of the ground – and when, later, things having settled, we went to see what had happened we found one badly damaged German hanging over an iron girder on to which he had fallen after being blown up. We made a prisoner of him. His three companions had been killed, and we saw that they had been blown to pieces.[5]

That day the BEF also managed to get a foothold onto the gently rising ground of the Aubers Ridge, though German resistance was hardening. On 19 October the 2nd Battalion Royal Irish Regiment captured the nearby hamlet of Le Pilly. French troops alongside them failed to make headway, but the Royal Irish hung on in anticipation of another advance. Instead, a strong German counter-attack was launched which cut off the village. Some 300 survivors of the battalion, nearly all wounded, were eventually captured here, after a heroic resistance. Colour Sergeant Cooper, a native of

Clonmel, wrote to his relatives in Ireland about the action. The letter was subsequently published by the *Cork Examiner*, and part of it read:

> In the afternoon we got into it again, when we were ordered to reinforce the French in a place called Piley [Le Pilly]. My experiences here I shall never forget. The following morning I was sent out with a company to reconnoitre, and found the Germans entrenched about 800 yards away. They outnumbered us by about 10 to 1. They were entrenched in angular formation. We got orders to advance. We fixed bayonets and charged them. They were driven from their position and we got into the village (Piley). We then thought everything was all right, and we unfixed our bayonets, only to find we were in a hornet's nest. We re-fixed bayonets and charged them up the street and around the village till we chased them out altogether. In this engagement we had the heaviest casualties. When the Corps was called to muster up I found there was only 30 answered out of 210.

Corporal Harry Silvester 1st Battalion Royal Irish Regiment. Taken prisoner when the battalion was cut off and fought to the last round at Le Pilly, in October 1914.

Altogether we had only three bayonet encounters, but the work of our infantry has little chance against the 'Jack Johnsons.' When the Germans see our bayonets fixed they run like a pack of sheep. They commenced squealing like pigs when they saw them, and are running yet. We took the village, but I am sorry to say half our company was captured.

As regards the Royal Irish, there is no such thing as men scheming. They fight their best every time and never turn back. The artillery fire of the Germans is terrific and deadly, but their rifle fire was a 'wash out.' Our fellows are doing very well, but, oh, for the big guns of the Germans. You get no chance from shrapnel shot, and though I have often heard of the barbarity of the Germans I never believed it, but I do now, for I know it is a fact. I am wounded in the left thigh; the flesh is all torn away, and I think it is a wound caused by a Dum-Dum bullet.

Private William Lewry, 1st Battalion Royal Irish Regiment, who was also captured at Le Pilly. A boy soldier at the time of his enlistment, he was born in Calcutta.

But I will tell you of their methods of warfare. They are murder. On the morning of the 20th October the ambulance corps, whose bravery cannot be too highly spoken of were out with the stretcher-bearers gathering in the wounded. They found one in an out-house. Dr. Jackson was there and he did heroic work, but I fear the poor man is gone. That was the last I saw of him at any rate. When the ambulance corps were bringing the wounded across the place we had traversed the previous day, the Germans shelled them with fire from their maxim guns. They fired across the stretcher-bearers, but, fortunately, they escaped, but for that there is no thanks to the Germans but our good luck, and they are such bad marksmen. We got back safely to an improvised hospital in the village. There was six or seven hundred of us. Whether the Germans knew it was an hospital or not I do not know, but they shelled us in it, and here again the Middlesex suffered severely. The house was burned, and the bravery and sacrifice of the Royal Army Medical Corps alone got us out. I got behind a hay-stack, but the Royal Army Medical Corps got us all back to the hospital base as quickly as they could.[6]

Another member of the Royal Irish, this time an officer by the name of Lieutenant J.A. Smithwick, wrote to his brother from a German prison camp at Crefeld, describing his experiences in this battle:

I am here, wounded and a prisoner, and am being well treated. As you have seen by the casualty list, the regiment suffered very heavily. It is bad luck being here, but I am lucky to be above ground. I escaped until half an hour before the end without a scratch; then while trying to retire with some of my men to deal with a machine-gun which was enfilading us from our left rear I was grazed twice on the shoulder and on the hand. They next got me plumb on my right breast. It hit my compass, then on to a rib, and through the muscles on top of my stomach and out at my left side. Narrow squeak! It knocked me clean out at the time, and I am a bit stiff and sore, but it is going on well and there is no danger. This letter is censored at both ends, so I cannot make it too long.[7]

Captain Arthur F.H. Mills, a novelist and crime author, was serving with the 1st Battalion Duke of Cornwall's Light Infantry in the line nearby. He wrote about his experiences in action in 1914 under the pseudonym 'Platoon Commander'. His book *With My Regiment* is a detailed account of the activities of the battalion between the time when Mills joined them in late September to when he was wounded near La Bassée, though he has changed the names of many regiments and soldiers. In the book he writes of a night action which probably occurred around 18 or 19 October. It shows the reliance that even experienced officers placed upon their senior NCOs, and also the strain of remaining continuously alert through the long hours of darkness:

My section of trench had already been worked on by the company we took over from. The officer before me had scooped out a dug-out for himself at one end and lined it with straw. This I marked off for my own use, and then went along the line to see that all the men were busy. By the time I had inspected the trench and put out an advanced post it was quite dark, and I settled myself down in my own dug-out with a pious hope that the night would remain fine and we should all be able to pass it comfortably. There was no sound from the front, and it looked as though we should be undisturbed. One by one the stars came out, the night grew colder, and I pulled on my greatcoat. It was weird lying there in the darkness, hearing nothing, seeing nothing, with only the dark shapes of the men on each side and the occasional tinkle of an entrenching tool against a stone to remind one that one was taking part in a great war …

As I lay there I heard far away on the right the sound of rifle fire. Were they our troops or the French? … Hullo! The sound of firing was drawing nearer and swelling in volume. That must be the brigade on our right engaged. Ah! There were two sharp shots from the farm where the next company lay.

'Pass along the word for every man to stand to,' I called, jumping to my feet.

'Sergeant X,' I said to the N.C.O. next to me, 'go down the trench and see that every man is awake.'

Pht! pht! pht!

I ducked down into the trench. Half a dozen bullets came singing through the edge. There was sharp firing now on our right. The next company was evidently engaged. Away beyond the rifle fire had swelled into one big crash of sound. Suddenly a hot fire broke out in front of us. To the left I heard our two Maxims, like watchdogs, barking viciously. It was a night attack, then – the enemy had come up to have a go at us …

'They're getting closer, aren't they?' I said to Sergeant X, listening to the enemy's fire.

'I think they are, sir,' He refilled his magazine and bent once more over the rifle.

'By gad! Did you see that flash – they are only a hundred yards off. Here, give me that.' I took the rifle from a man next me who had been wounded, and laid it, with the bayonet fixed, on the parapet in front. At the same time I drew my revolver and put it ready for use by my other hand. It was getting exciting this – quite pleasantly so.

'What do we do if they charge – get out and meet 'em?' I asked. My sergeant had had more experience of action than I, and I felt I could well afford to ask his advice.

'Just stay where we are, sir,' he answered; 'but they won't do that; they don't like these' – he tapped his bayonet. He was a splendidly calm fellow, that sergeant, and it was good to feel him firm as a rock beside me. All men, NCOs, officers, and privates, instinctively lean towards each other when the corner is tight.[8]

By now the high-water mark of the British advance towards La Bassée had been reached, and German counter-attacks began to force the weakened battalions of the BEF back. Private Robert Oates, a reservist serving with the 1st Battalion Cheshire Regiment was wounded on 21 October as the battalion tried to hold the ground that it had won at Voilaines two days previously. He wrote to his brother:

I have been up at Lille and La Bassée. Oh it is terrible to see the houses that are destroyed … Well I have had my share of fighting for a bit. We have been taking position after position, just a little at a time, and it has been awful, I can tell you.

Private Robert Oates, 1st Battalion Cheshire Regiment. A veteran of the Boer War, he was hit in the leg by a dum-dum bullet, and his wound resulted in amputation.

Their big guns, with their shrapnel, are terrible, and if it gets anywhere near us it means at least a dozen men [dead] … One afternoon, about five o'clock, we got an order to advance. We had to take a factory in the village, which the Germans had occupied, and had a Maxim gun there, which was doing a lot of damage. We were told to take it at all costs. I was in the first company to advance, and we got about 150 yards off them, and then it was like hell – bullets flying all over us, so we had to take cover, and the Germans had men on the tops of houses and in trees, sniping at us … I got hit when taking cover. I had to run across an open space, and while crossing this space one of the German snipers got me in the leg and smashed two bones. I think it was a dum-dum bullet; it made such a terrible hole when it came out. I have a compound fracture of the leg between the knee and ankle, and it will be some time before it is all right. It was awful lying there wounded, with shells flying all around. The agony was terrible. The stretcher bearers could not get near me, the fire was too heavy.[9]

An eyewitness to this attack was the Medical Officer of the 1st Battalion King's Own Scottish Borderers, Captain Robert Dolbey, who we met last on the Aisne. He wrote:

I went up to the top attic [of the house]. And as I looked the enemy attack developed and the German infantry left their trenches. To me it was in many ways the most interesting sight I had seen; for, from this point of vantage we could watch the whole attack from the beginning. Now we were always told, and up to now it had been our experience, that German soldiers had no initiative, that they were automata; that they charged in swarms, because the individual advance was impossible to such men drilled so thoroughly by the machine that they were incapable of separate independent action. But these Germans broke all these rules as they had so often done in other ways before. They poured out of the ends of the trenches, spread out into most perfect open order and advanced at the double; nor was any officer visible. Some ran and dropped, so that I thought the whole line had been wiped out by our fire, but these men were foxing; and those who fell facedownward soon got up to run forward again. Not so with the killed or wounded, they lay on their sides or, spinning round in the air, they fell supported by their packs, in a half reclining position. They were sitting with their backs to our trenches, their heads dropped forward, and they looked as if they were asleep. We saw that that was the sleep that knows no waking; for they stayed like this, quite still, all the afternoon. Taking the cover of every natural object, they got behind trees or wagons or mounds of earth; so they advanced up to within 100 yards of our position, and our field of fire not being good, there they found shelter. The under-officer was especially gallant, for he ran to a mount of light soil, laid his glass on the top and closely examined our trenches, with elbows spread upon the top. From time to time he would turn his head to speak to two orderlies who crouched beside him like spaniels. The Cheshires fired a number of rounds, but owing to the intervening leaves and branches, they could not get him. I knew him for an under-officer by the shape of his helmet and the sword that hung by his side.[10]

The troops around him were forced to withdraw, but Dolbey's duty was to his severely wounded patients, who were too badly injured to move and who grew increasingly frightened as the German attack came closer. With no Red Cross flag to denote this was a dressing station, Dolbey and his orderlies moved them into the cellar for greater protection:

Down the steps we dragged them and blocked the foot with empty barrels. Then they burst in; still quite dark. How could they know we were a hospital? One could not have blamed them if they had bayoneted us. Again they feared an ambush and would only come to the top of the cellar steps, firing at us through the barrels. This, I thought, is the finish! But contenting themselves with placing a guard on the top of the cellar steps and over the cellar window that opened to the grass outside, they left us. Then came the dawn and they saw the blood-stained dressings, the medical equipment, the surgical panniers. It was clearly only a hospital. They quieted down and I essayed a journey up the steps to make our surrender.

As I advanced, the sentry fired; I was very quickly back and resolved to try the window. If fear of death proclaims the coward, then all men are cowards; but fearing death as they do, there are yet many men who fear more to appear afraid. Only in the imagination of the lady novelist or the war correspondent or those who fight their battles at the Base, does the man exist who knows no fear. I next tried my luck with the sentry over the cellar window, Thompson pushing me through. My friend the sentry was calm, and waved to me to come forward. I did not even have to put up my hands. But Thompson was less lucky, for another soldier came round the corner of the house and his bayonet went through Thompson's tunic. The under-officer, a tall man with a very decent face and a large goitre, spoke to me in French; told me he had got the stretcher-bearers too. He made me responsible for any attempt at escape. Beyond that, I was free to attend to the wounded and to keep the stove alight. But he must trouble me for my field glasses, my camera. No! German soldiers do not loot cigarette cases or money from prisoners.[11]

On the same day, a young lieutenant of the 1st Battalion Middlesex Regiment was also to be badly wounded and taken prisoner. The young man was Brian Horrocks, much later in another war to become the commander of XXX Corps in Europe and

Montgomery's most trusted subordinate. In his autobiography Horrocks wrote of his early experiences in war; and of the relationship between officers and men:

> My chief memory of those days, and the memory retained by all platoon com-
> manders, was of marching – endless and exhausting marches. I had never realised
> before that it was possible to go to sleep while the legs continued automatically to
> function. It was during those hard, comfortless days that I first met that priceless
> Cockney sense of humour. A small private soldier in the rank in front of me
> looked up at his neighbour, who was blessed with a long lugubrious face, and said
> 'Why don't you give your face a holiday, chum? Try a smile.'
>
> [The company commander Captain Gibbons] held me completely responsible
> for the welfare of the men in my platoon. Woe betide me if I attempted to have
> my own meal without first reporting to him, 'All ranks in number sixteen platoon
> fed, sir.' Once we arrived in pouring rain to find that a muddy field which had
> previously been rather over populated by cows had been allocated as our bivouac
> area for the night. It was a depressing thought, but my spirits rose when the
> adjutant appeared and said that officers could sleep in a house nearby where
> battalion HQ was billeted. Gibbons was furious. 'If the men sleep out, we sleep
> out.' My heart sank but I knew instinctively that he was right.[12]

Horrocks brushes over the circumstances of his capture, though it is known that on
21 October the 1st Middlesex, which was spearheading its brigade and pushing eastwards, was in action at Le Maisnil, where one company suffered severely, losing some
seventy men. That day Lieutenant Colonel B.E. Ward, the commanding officer, was
killed. Horrocks continued by stating that:

> I was taken to a German military hospital on the outskirts of Lille, where I
> was placed in a bed beside a private soldier from a Highland regiment who had
> lost a leg. As I had been shot through
> the lower stomach, neither of us was
> very mobile. At that time the Germans
> were accusing the Allies of using dum-
> dum bullets ... I had never even heard
> of dum-dum bullets but periodically,
> Germans used to collect round my bed,
> give me a British rifle and shout ...
> 'Now you British swine, show us how
> you make dum-dum bullets.'[13]

*Private Herbert Ruler, 1st Battalion East Kent
Regiment, who was aged just 18 when he was
killed in action on 21 October 1914. On this day
the Buffs had driven part of* Infanterie
Regiment Nr. 139 *from the village of
Radinghem, and were digging in, when they
were heavily counter-attacked.*

There was at least one better-disposed German soldier facing the British in this sector, an artillery officer named Leutnant Walther Reinhardt. He was later to write his memoirs of the first six months of the war, but also described some of his experiences in a letter to a newspaper at home. He, like some other German officers, writes with a curious sense of admiration for the British soldier, and more particularly his equipment:

> For ten days we remained west of Lille, not far from Armentières, fighting across open country with an English army opposite us – my battery was merely a link in a gigantic chain; regularly the enemy showered us with a hail of fire and iron, and we had long since ceased to count the days of battle.
>
> Daily we realised that we had before us an opponent of unprecedented determination and stamina, which the sharpest rifle fire and most terrible shrapnel hardly shook. Slowly, desperately slowly, we gained territory from them; each inch of earth was dearly purchased with sacrifice. In the captured fire trenches lay the English dead, mowed down by the dozen, but they had not yielded and fell only to the rifle butt and the bayonet. One must understand that from a military standpoint these enemy soldiers were deserving of the highest respect. We Germans possess the finest army in the world, and can be justifiably proud of it. However let us not forget also that in many respects we can learn from the English way of warfare. In many practical things, particularly clothing, rations and signalling apparatus, the British are probably superior. It was quite amazing to see, in particular, the masses of excellent tinned food of all types which we found in the captured English trenches. In a very effective way the English have transferred their experience in colonial wars to European circumstances ... The cut and material of their uniform, also field tested in the colonies, are extremely practical; it seems to me that especially worthy of imitation are their elasticated puttees, which we use only for sport. I myself wore them throughout several days of fighting and found them a perfect fit; comfortable, warm, and quick to dry out even after being wet through, also allowing plenty of movement. We may even see our officer corps adopting these English puttees.
>
> On the first day of the battle to the west of Lille the German army moved quickly and inexorably forwards. One of many English positions fell into our hands. The terrible scenes in this over-run position offered us just a small glimpse of the gigantic panorama of misery and horror at the centre of which we stood. Near our battery position, which we have now occupied for ten days, was an over run trench. In it lay a dead officer of 40 or 45 years of age. From his identity papers I discovered his name: Captain H.J. Maffett, 2. Leinster Regiment. Alongside the dead man, written with indelible pencil, lay a report card, which I translated:
>
> 'To Lieutenant Daly. My position lies 600 feet northwest of point 42 the fort "Batterie Sénarmont", near the margin of the Lille map. One platoon lies 300 feet forward and to the right. I cannot quite advance to the "Batterie Sénarmont", because I am under heavy machine-gun fire from the enemy fire trench, nor

Captain Henry Telford Maffett, of Fingles, County Dublin. He was killed serving with the 2nd Battalion Leinster Regiment on 20 October 1914.

remain in front of it. Please request the artillery to bombard them. It is possible that I shall order a retirement to the skirmish line. Maintain a good fire position.'

Here the message broke off in mid sentence. Perhaps he was in the instant of writing when a German shell splinter hit him? I have kept the report card and have it on my person, along with an empty envelope with the address of the wife of the dead man. Perhaps after the war I will have a chance to pass on to her the last words of this man. I shall also offer her his wrist compass, which I now wear.[14]

Maffett was killed in action on 20 October 1914, and the discovery of his body by Reinhardt probably took place the day after. In the event he did indeed contact Maffett's widow after the war, and passed on his letters and other papers, together with the information that he had buried the body, which now lies in Houplines Communal Cemetery extension.

By this point the British government had grasped the fact that the BEF alone was not strong enough to face the might of the German army. Its reserves were being depleted too rapidly, but a supply of trained men was at hand within the Empire, and the first of them were about to make an appearance on the battlefield, as Cecil Brownlow testifies:

> On the afternoon of 22nd October I happened to turn from a lane on to the straight road which connects Neuve Chapelle and Estaires. To my astonishment I saw a column of Indian infantry swinging through the flat prosaic country as unconcernedly as if they were marching down the Grand Trunk Road in the swirling dust beneath the peepal trees and brazen sun. No tribute could have been more fitting than that which India paid to the altar of the British Empire when at the hour of destiny her armed manhood arrived to hold the sagging line against the assaults of the mighty enemy. And no pathos more poignant than the fate of these soldiers from the plains of the five rivers and the hills beneath the Safed Koh, who crossed the oceans to die in the mists of a strange land.[15]

The Germans meanwhile now came to regard Neuve Chapelle as the key to the British positions in this sector, and on 23 October threw everything they had into taking the village. John Lucy's battalion, in the front line before Neuve Chapelle, stood ready to receive whoever or whatever came at it. Under terrific bombardment and anticipating an attack at any time, Lucy remembered:

> All that long day the heavy shells came slowly down with thud and crash, their concussions alone shaking landslides from the back and front of our trenches, and making the earth rock as in an earthquake. Fieldguns and smaller howitzers joined in, punctuated by the nasty stinging crash of five-nines. The slow ranging fire of all the guns speeded up to a regular bombardment, as the enemy found our position, and we crouched wretchedly, shaken by the blastings, under a lasting hail of metal and displaced earth and sods, half blinded and half choked by poisonous vapours, waiting for the enemy infantry, while our overworked stretcher-bearers busied themselves with new dead and wounded.
>
> A 'whizbang' (7.7 shell) came into our trench and stuck unexploded in the back wall; another blew in the bay on my right, and yet another scattered the sandbags from the top of the traverse on my left, under which I was crouching. I willed myself smaller and smaller, and prayed like the devil. As lulls occurred I shouted the warning, 'Stand by', to my dazed men, and then to the unfortunate sentry on look out, 'Anything doing?' and each time he answered: 'No, nothing coming.' I would confirm this with a slow and careful look over the top. I took off my cap, and tilted my head back to make it as small a target as possible, looking over the ground in front along my nose. Time seemed to stand still; an hour was a day under this torture. We smoked nervously, lighting up and passing cigarettes with trembling fingers. The battle smoke killed the taste of the nicotine. As the day grew on we felt hungry, but we had no desire to eat. Our mouths were parched by the poisonous vapours, and with the thought that we would have to stand up to the German infantry attack any moment, we had no saliva. We drank as much water as we dared, not knowing when our quart bottles would again be filled.[16]

In spite of the devastating fire they were under, Lucy notes proudly that the line held. Frank Richards' 2nd Battalion Royal Welsh Fusiliers was in the trenches south west of Armentières, near Laventie. On 24 October it likewise was heavily attacked, but Richards was confident that the line here could also be held. Like that of Lucy and his men, the training of these regulars stood them in good stead and more than made up for any inferiority in numbers:

> Shells began bursting all along our front ... Some of the enemy had now come out of the trees and no doubt intended to advance a little way under cover of their barrage. But the shelling was not severe enough to prevent us opening out rapid fire at them. I don't think any one of them ran twenty yards before he was dropped. To good, trained, pre-War soldiers who kept their nerve, ten men holding a trench could easily stop fifty who were trying to take it, advancing from a distance of four hundred yards. The enemy now put up a tremendous barrage on our trench, but fortunately for us, the shells were dropping short. More of the enemy had advanced at the run under cover of this barrage and had dropped down behind some little tumps of ground about two hundred and fifty yards away. I was watching the ground in front but it was very difficult to make

anything out through the smoke and showers of dirt being blown up by the exploding shells. [Captain Stockwell] came into the bay I was in: he had his glasses out and was peering through them but seemed unable to see more than we had done. Most of us now had our heads well below the parapet, waiting for the barrage to lift. The enemy opened out with rifle-fire, and although they could not see us their bullets were kicking up dirt all around. [Captain Stockwell] was as cool as a cucumber: he had plenty of guts, I'll say that for him. He passed down the trench warning us as soon as the barrage lifted to be prepared to stop an attack.

At last the barrage lifted: the shells were now exploding about a hundred yards behind us. We were all on the alert and stood to. The enemy rose up and started to advance. They were stopped at once: with the parapet as a rest for our rifles it was impossible to miss. The attack was over before it had really commenced. From somewhere under cover by the trees the enemy then opened out with rifle-fire on our trench and a couple of men in the next bay to me were shot through the head. We directed our fire in that direction. Stevens shouted at me to look at one of the men in our bay: he had his head well below the parapet and was firing in the air. We made him put his head well up and fire properly. The whole of the men in the bay threatened to shoot him dead if he done it again.[17]

On the extreme southern edge of this sector, at Givenchy, the British line met that of the French. Lieutenant Kenneth Godsell was a Royal Engineers officer here with 17th Field Company, charged with improving the defences in front of the village. He spent the night of 23 October out in front of the trenches and had completed 400yd of barbed wire fence by 2am – an improvement on the situation a week or so earlier when wire had been in such short supply that he had been forced to re-use strands that he found on farm fences. He and his men slumbered for most of 24 October, before going out into no-man's-land again that evening. He wrote:

It was a night of alarms & rumours of attack. Col Ballard of the Norfolks was in charge at Givenchy & in addition to his own battalion had two battalions of French under him who were very excited. He was extraordinarily calm & had his HQ quite close to the church which was always a shell trap. The French kept asking for reinforcements but he was insistent that the Bosch would not attack & they got nothing out of him. We got on very well with the work which was rather trying at one point as we were wiring in front of the French who were fresh troops and simply itched to let off their rifles. I had great difficulty in keeping them quiet while we were wiring their front but we managed it alright and joined up our fence with No 4 section. I collected the section and sent them back in the village to wait for me at a certain house & I went & had a final look to see that all was right. When I came back I passed a French sentry who challenged me. When I replied 'Genie' [engineers] he asked if the job was finished. I told him yes. He replied with an excited gesture, 'Then I may fire!' I told him for all I cared he could (in my best French). He chuckled & turned round & blazed away into the darkness & continued to do so all night probably. He had not finished by the time I was out of earshot.

I had just left the front line when a heavy bombardment was opened up on the position in general and the village in particular. My section who were waiting for me in the village had a very rough time, a house some of them were sheltering behind had the roof blown off. They eventually got into some pits in the side of a road cutting on the western fringe of the village. I found myself in the open and bolted for the first bit of cover I could see – this was a large – very large it seemed – hole into which I jumped with a sigh of relief. When I had a chance to look round I discovered I was in a grave but there were no corpses in it although by the light of a star shell I could see several on one edge all ready for burying. It did not tend to a quieter frame of mind ...[18]

Private Fred Steward, B Company 1st Battalion Norfolk Regiment, of Norwich, killed in action on 26 October 1914 near Givenchy. His was the battalion commanded by Lieutenant Colonel Ballard.

Further north, Lance Sergeant Walter Watson, a Boer War veteran, was serving with the 1st Battalion West Yorkshire Regiment. He kept a diary of his experiences in France in 1914. More terse than some later memoirs, and written probably in a snatched few moments in the bottom of a trench rather than the comfort and safety of a postwar front room, it none the less conveys the seriousness of the situation for the British in those few days. Part of it reads:

18 October: There is a great artillery duel going on all around Lille ... we go into the attack at 3.30 and we got there at 5 and I went onto outpost.

19 October: Relieved E.W. [Ennetières-en-Weppes] and had a horrible time in the trenches shells firing over us all day, never stopped until night, we had our RP [Ration Party] sent and we can not reach them.

20 October: Terrible day. Those who came out of this day's battle bore a charmed life. Shells bursting on our trenches every second. I had a very narrow escape, a piece of shell went through my equipment and it hit me at the back of the neck.[19]

On 21 October the 1st Battalion Leicestershire Regiment had come into the line near Rue du Bois, in order to relieve Watson's 1st Battalion West Yorks, and made their headquarters in the railway station at La Houssoie. The men held a series of craters and foxholes, linked by shallow trenches, in the muddy sugar-beet fields around the station. After heavy shelling on 22 and 23 October it was on the following day

The sugar factory at La Houssoie, which lay just behind the German lines and was one of the most prominent landmarks in the area.

that the situation on this part of the British front became critical. All was quiet on 24 October until about 4pm when intense shelling began. Enemy troops were also observed massing for an attack in an abandoned distillery yard opposite the Leicestershire positions. At this point half of the battalion was pulled back to the comparatively better cover of a low railway embankment. Peering through the gathering gloom for any sign of advancing enemy troops, the Leicesters waited. Eventually at dawn the next day the expected attack was launched, and 25 October was to be a day of bitter and unremitting fighting on this part of the front. Part of D Company was overwhelmed in the initial German onslaught, and a remarkable diary survives from one who was there, a 19-year-old from Leicester named George Dodge. Dodge had enlisted only in 1913, unlike many of the older, seasoned veterans in the battalion, and this young man must have found his experiences nightmarish. Part of his diary reads:

> [The] Company ... must hold out at all costs, at night [24 October] all ammunition spent and surrounded by enemy. By dawn [25 October] back to back fighting with 85 men using dead as cover. Hand to hand fighting, finally at 10am made prisoners by at least an Army Corps sweeping down on us. Night march to German headquarters, humiliated and searched. Prisoners put in a cell at Lille prison and given black bread and water.[20]

Among the Leicesters here was a former forward with Leicester Tigers Rugby Football Club named William Dalby. An army reservist, Dalby had been recalled to the Colours upon the outbreak of war. In a letter home, he described the attack:

> The sentries in the trenches ... shout 'Stand To, everybody,' and this wakens our men ... then the Maxim guns send between 600 and 700 shots per minute, the

Field Artillery fire shrapnel rockets, and search lights illuminate the sky for miles around, 'star shells' set fire to haystacks, the Garrison artillery set fire to the villages and knock down anything else that comes in the way. The whizzing and whirring of shot and shell sounds as if every man had gone whistling mad. You cannot hear yourself shout.

It is like this for an hour or two, then the German big guns stop firing. That is the signal for their infantry to charge. They come up in thousands singing 'Wacht am Rhein' and blowing penny trumpets and making as much noise as possible. They get within a few yards of our trenches and find our fire too hot for them.[21]

Another soldier who was here described the massed German infantry attacks as coming on so thickly that it was almost impossible to miss when firing at them. He added that the first wave was swept away like leaves in the wind by the fire of the Leicesters. However the day was not to go entirely their way. The fighting was heaviest along the positions held by D Company, and at the level crossing south of La Houssoie which they were defending. Some indication of the severity of the fighting at this point comes from the number of Distinguished Conduct Medals awarded to men of the Leicesters for the battle here at the crossing. The regimental history contains an

Private George Dodge, 1st Battalion Leicestershire Regiment, captured along with some ninety other men of his regiment at La Houssoie on 25 October 1914.

Hauptmann Bencke (on the horse) and Feldwebel Beer (beside him with the gold cuff lace) with men of Infanterie Regiment Nr. 106. This Saxon regiment was heavily involved in fighting near Rue du Bois in October 1914.

anonymous account of this action, which may well have been compiled by Lieutenant J.W.E. Mosse, an officer who was present and who is known to have kept a diary around this time. Part of it reads:

> The situation up to 11am [on 25 October] was critical.
>
> The Leicesters' line was intact from Rue du Bois to the barrier at the level crossing south of the station. Close hand-to-hand fighting took place throughout the day at the barrier, the Germans, being in considerable strength, making repeated assaults on the barrier, covered by rifle fire from the house at a few yards' range.
>
> The enemy throughout the day never took advantage of the initial success gained by them shortly after dawn. This inability to do so was in a measure undoubtedly due to the excellent work performed by the machine-gun section of the K.S.L.I. and the stubborn resistance of the company of the Leicestershire Regiment occupying the road barrier at the level crossing and on the railway north of this point. Another reason undoubtedly was that the German commanders could not have known the situation on this front, and the German troops who had penetrated the gap appeared lost and in many cases wandered about aimlessly until shot down.[22]

Meantime the attacks upon Neuve Chapelle continued, reaching a crescendo on 26 and 27 October. The now sadly depleted Royal Irish Rifles were shelled out of their trenches on 27 October, and the Germans advanced through the gap to occupy part of the village. Colonel McMahon of the 4th battalion Royal Fusiliers (who had so gallantly

The grave of Kurt Richter, of Infanterie Regiment Nr. 107. *He was killed in the attack on the British lines south of Rue du Bois on 27 October 1914.*

commanded his men at Mons) was the senior officer on the spot and reorganised the line with troops from his own battalion and the 1st Battalion Wiltshire Regiment. Pressing forward in a counter-attack, McMahon's troops were too weak to do more than advance into the German lines, where they were fell upon from the front and flank. The Wiltshires lost 8 officers and 300 other ranks in this debacle. Later in the

Bandsman John T. Wilkins, 1st Battalion Royal West Kent Regiment. This long-serving soldier was acting as a stretcher-bearer when he was captured at Neuve Chapelle, on 27 October 1914. (Pat Gariepy)

Second Lieutenant Walter Martin, 1st Battalion Wiltshire Regiment. Commissioned from the ranks, he was taken prisoner on 27 October 1914, when the 1st Wilts were surrounded at Neuve Chapelle.

day the Germans also tried a similar outflanking manoeuvre against the 1st Battalion Royal West Kent Regiment who were slightly further south. Although the commanding officer was killed and some men captured, the bulk of the West Kents held on until reinforcements arrived.

By this stage in the fighting, hospital trains were equipped to evacuate the wounded from hospitals just behind the line, and get them to the coast for treatment as quickly as possible. Kathleen Luard was a nurse on one of the trains, and recorded the conditions for wounded from the fighting on this part of the front. It should be remembered that in 1914 blood transfusions and antibiotics for infected wounds were some years in the future, but Luard and her nurses worked valiantly:

October 25th

Guns were cracking and splitting all night, lighting up the sky in flashes, and fires were burning on both sides. The Clearing Hospital close by, which was receiving the wounded from the field and sending them on to us, was packed and over-flowing with badly wounded, the M.O. on the station said.

We had 368; a good 200 were dangerously and seriously wounded, perhaps more; and the sitting-up cases were bad enough. The compound-fractured femurs were put up with rifles and pick-handles for splints, padded with bits of kilts and straw; nearly all the men had more than one wound – some had ten; one man with a huge compound fracture above the elbow had tied on a bit of string with a bullet in it as a tourniquet above the wound himself. When I cut off his soaked three layers of sleeve there was no dressing on it at all.

They were bleeding faster than we could cope with it; and the agony of getting them off the stretchers on to the top bunks is a thing to forget. We were full up by about 2am, and then were delayed by a collision up the line, which was blocked by dead horses as a result. All night and without a break till we got back to Boulogne at 4 p.m. next day (yesterday) we grappled with them, and some were not dressed when we got into Bailleul. The head cases were delirious, and trying to get out of the window, and we were giving strychnine and morphia all round. Two were put off dying at St Omer, but we kept the rest alive to Boulogne. The outstanding shining thing that hit you in the eye all through was the universal silent pluck of the men; they stuck it all without a whine or complaint or even a comment: it was, 'Would you mind moving my leg when you get time,' and

Inside a British hospital train, like the one in which Kathleen Luard nursed the wounded.

'Thank you very much,' or 'That's absolutely glorious,' as one boy said on having his bootlace cut, or 'That's grand,' when you struck a lucky position for a wound in the back. One badly smashed up said contentedly, 'I was lucky – I was the only man left alive in our trench'; so was another in another trench; sixteen out of twenty-five of one Company in a trench were on the train, all seriously wounded except one. One man with both legs smashed and other wounds was asked if it was all by one shell: 'Oh yes; why, the man next to me was blowed to bits.' The bleeding made them all frightfully thirsty (they had only been hit a few hours many of them), and luckily we had got in a good supply of boiled water before-hand on each carriage, so we had plenty when there was time to get it.[23]

Once at Boulogne, the wounded were transferred to a Stationary Hospital, which at this early stage in the war had been established in a disused sugar warehouse by the docks. Although it would develop into a first-class surgical hospital as the war progressed, at this point in time conditions were primitive. A Voluntary Aid Detachment (VAD) nurse, Kate Finzi, takes up the story of the treatment of the wounded here:

The worst part of the wounds is the fearful sepsis and the impossibility of getting them anything like clean. 'First time I've had my boots off for seven weeks!' is the kind of exclamation that recurs all day, as we literally cut them off. Hardly any of the boots have been off for three weeks, with the result that they seem glued on, whilst the feet are like iron, the nails like claws. Some of the men have not had their wounds dressed since the first field dressing was applied, for the simple reason that the rush on the hospital trains makes it impossible to attend to any but the worst cases, many of whom, as it is, are dying of haemorrhage, accelerated by the jolting on the journey. There is no time to do anything but the dressings, and if we did want to wash the patients there is nothing but the red handkerchiefs we hang round the lights for shades by night, for towels by day. Water, especially boiling water, is at a premium, as it all has to be fetched from outside where the veteran cook stokes hard all day in the driving rain, ladling us out a modicum into each bowl from his cauldrons. 'I never thought to see such sights,' exclaimed a nurse of thirty years' experience as a new trainload came in. But we have no time to think of our own sensations. Fingerless hands, lungs pierced, arms and legs pretty well gangrenous, others already threatening tetanus (against which they are now beginning to inoculate patients), mouths swollen beyond all recognition with bullet shots, fractured femurs, shattered jaws, sightless eyes, ugly scalp wounds; yet never a murmur, never a groan except in sleep. As the men come in they fall on their pallets and doze until roused for food.[24]

Back on the battlefield, Neuve Chapelle continued to entrance both sides. On 28 October an attack was made by British and Indian troops to try to recover the village. This involved severe fighting, in which a wing of the 47th Sikhs, the 9th Bhopals, and the 20th and 21st Companies of the Indian Sappers and Miners played a major part, suffering heavy casualties. Such was the shortage of line infantry at this point in the fighting, that as a final reserve these skilled engineer troops were thrown into the fray. The village was re-taken, but, in the face of the murderous machine-gun fire encountered in the streets, had eventually to be evacuated. In the Sapper companies, every one of the eight officers was a casualty, and nearly 50 per cent of the Indian rank and file; but they covered themselves with glory. Lieutenant F.P. Nosworthy of the 20th Company wrote afterwards:

> My section came under heavy fire from the right, and we swung right and charged a German trench with the bayonet. Meanwhile the Bhopals were heavily engaged on our right rear. After entering Neuve Chapelle there was bitter street fighting. Havildar Muhammad Khan rushed up to me, trying to speak, but he could not do so as he had been shot through the throat and was bleeding profusely. I persuaded him to go back, but his wound proved mortal and so I lost a particular friend. Then Hayes-Sadler (a Lieut. in the 20th Coy.) appeared with his section and together we worked steadily forward, clearing the main street, house by house. At the cross-roads in the centre of the village, a machine-gun opened fire on us at point-blank range, and Hayes-Sadler charged forward against it. He was killed immediately, but we soon got that machine-gun and avenged his death. Though now in complete possession of the cross-roads, we could get no further. Less than twenty men remained with Rait-Kerr (another Lieut. in the 20th Coy.) and myself in the centre of the village. Others had joined forces with the 47th Sikhs on our left. We barricaded the main street with furniture and I sent Rait-Kerr to get reinforcements. Sappers posted in windows covered the road block, and three attempts to dislodge us failed with heavy loss. Rait-Kerr never returned, nor did reinforcements arrive. It appears that Rait-Kerr made his way to the south-western edge of the village where he saw some Bhopals under Major G.A. Jamieson trying to check a German outflanking attack. With a few sappers he went to join them but was wounded in the arm and collapsed.

> We were now completely isolated and were too weak to send out patrols as only Subadar Ganpat Mahadeo and 13 Sappers remained. About 4pm, however, I decided to attempt to find out what had happened and recon- noitered alone down the main street. At the outskirts of the village I met Major Jamieson who was surprised to hear that we were in the middle of the place and advised a withdrawal. This was accomplished successfully, taking with us as many wounded as we could. On the way we came across Rait-Kerr

Musketier Michael Maier, Infanterie Regiment Nr. 16, *killed on 28 October 1914 during the battle that drove the British out of Neuve Chapelle.*

sitting in a shell-hole with a shattered arm. This ended our fight at Neuve Chapelle. On the day after the battle there was not a single British officer available for duty with either of the two Bombay sapper companies.[25]

Both Lieutenants Nosworthy and Rait-Kerr gained the Military Cross in this action. Nosworthy told fellow officers, when he returned to the front some months later (minus a thumb, but otherwise recovered from his many wounds) that he had never enjoyed a day so much, and that he had run his sword clean through a fat German officer! The 47th Sikhs lost a fine man killed in Captain Robert McCleverty; Major 'Buster' Browne of this regiment, one of the most popular officers in the Indian army, and a fine sportsman pre-war, was severely wounded. The 9th Bhopals also had heavy losses. Kathleen Luard treated some of the wounded men from the former regiment:

> Friday, October 30th, Boulogne ... After filling up at Nieppe we went back to Bailleul and took up 238 Indians, mostly with smashed left arms from a machine-gun that caught them in the act of firing over a trench. They are nearly all 47th Sikhs, perfect lambs: they hold up their wounded hands and arms like babies for you to see, and insist on having them dressed whether they've just been done or not. They behave like gentlemen, and salaam after you've dressed them. They have masses of long, fine, dark hair under their turbans done up with yellow combs, glorious teeth, and melting dark eyes. One died. The younger boys have beautiful classic Italian faces, and the rest have fierce black beards curling over their ears. We carried 387 cases this time.
>
> Later – we got unloaded much more quickly to-day, and have been able to have a good rest this afternoon, as I went to bed at 3am and was up again by 8. It was not so heavy this time, as the Indians were mostly sitting-up cases. Those of a different caste had to sleep on the floor of the corridors, as the others wouldn't have them in. One compartment of four lying-down ones got restless with the pain of their arms, and I found them all sitting up rocking their arms and wailing 'Aie, Aie, Aie', poor pets. They all had morphia, and subsided. One British Tommy said to me: 'Don't take no notice o' the dirt on me flesh, Sister; I ain't 'ad much time to wash!' quite seriously. Another bad one needed dressing. I said, 'I won't hurt you.' And he said in a hopeless sort of voice, 'I don't care if you do.' He had been through a little too much.[26]

The Germans had less success in subsequent attacks further north near Rue du Bois. In an attack on the 1st Battalion East Yorkshire Regiment in this sector the enemy got no closer than 50yd from the British front-line trenches. The *Official History* states that the Germans left a hundred of their dead behind but James Brindley, of the East Yorks, rated the scale of the German losses as much higher. In 1914 he had like many other senior NCOs been given an emergency commission, and now, as Second Lieutenant Brindley, he recorded in his diary:

> 29th October 1914: Following its move north from the Aisne sector the battalion is at Le Armee [L'armée], south of Armentières. 'C' Company is billeted in a farm house – very comfortable! During the night of 28th–29th the battalion was attacked in the trenches by the Germans who were slaughtered as they advanced

with 300–400 being left dead on the battlefield and around the British trenches. Twelve of the enemy surrendered or were taken prisoner, with these men afterwards looking quite pleased at being taken prisoner. The battalion was tired out by the fighting and deserved a good rest; it certainly earned the praise which followed from the General. Our casualties included five officers and 114 other ranks killed or wounded. However the Germans have been taught a lesson and do not appear to be anxious to repeat the experience.[27]

In successive days of heavy fighting, three Saxon regiments, namely *Kgl. Sächs. 7. Infanterie-Regiment König Georg Nr. 106*, *Kgl. Sächs. 8. Infanterie-Regiment Prinz Johann Georg Nr. 107* and *Kgl. Sächs. 14. Infanterie-Regiment Nr. 179*, which had been brought south from the Ypres area for the attack, drove the Leicesters back from La Houssoie and gained a foothold in Rue du Bois. The published history of *Infanterie Regiment Nr. 107* states under the date 28 October:

6.20am precisely began the firing of our artillery. For ten minutes all of our guns placed a heavy barrage upon Rue du Bois. The infantry in the front line, who benefited from the experienced gained in the preceding days, moved up under these shells as closely as possible to the enemy. 6.30am precisely the infantry attack began along the whole front. The III battalion with parts of the III battalion Infanterie Regiment Nr. 179 pressed forward beyond the main street of the village to a barricade in the middle. Here they came under heavy machine-gun fire, and did not succeed in capturing these defences. Heavy fire forced the attackers to halt in the gardens and houses ... slowly the advance ground to a halt, because it was not possible to withstand the crossfire of the defenders.

Through the fire, Leutnant Leschke with his machine-gun platoon rushed forward and reached a farmhouse, in which they remained immovable. Another farmhouse south of the road also fell into the hands of the III battalion. To the left of the III battalion were parts of the I and II battalions, which succeeded in reaching and crossing the position called Poplar Trench. In tough fighting, bit by bit were the English driven out of Poplar Trench with hand grenades and pressed back. The trenches were densely packed with the exhausted remnants of the attacking troops. It was not possible to continue the assault, due to the strength of the enemy garrison in the village and by the increasing exhaustion of our troops after the past three days of battle. All the commanders of the front line companies had been killed, among them Oberleutnant Mehlig, who on the first night had volunteered to participate in a night attack. Leutnant der Reserve Thilo, who had proved his courage in many dangerous situations, was badly wounded at Poplar Trench. Hauptmann Otto, a reserve officer of the III battalion, fell right at the beginning of the attack, when he took his 9 Company towards the east side of Rue du Bois. The staff officers of the III battalion led it in the attack on one of the captured farms of Rue du Bois, where a shell splintered the flagpole of the battalion standard. A large number of brave NCOs and men had met their deaths with their leaders, and lay out in parallel rows. It was clear that in this location, further attempts at attacking must cease.

Our own artillery fell once more on the village, to assist in holding the captured ground. Soon the enemy artillery also joined the struggle, and succeeded in claiming the position. In particular the house which Unteroffizier Haupt, of 5 Company, had occupied since 27 October with his faithful band, suffered heavily under the enemy fire. Despite further casualties, it was held with the greatest bravery, though the garrison had nothing to eat for two days, and though the smoke and dust were unbearable, it was no longer possible to quench one's thirst from the bullet-scarred well, which could not be reached. Also, the house where the machine-gun platoon were deployed came under heavy artillery fire. Leutnant Leschte vacated the farmhouse when it was in flames, and after one machine-gun had already been destroyed by fire. The enemy did not succeed in regaining the farmhouse. Once it was burnt down, a section of the III battalion rushed it again and positioned themselves afresh in the still-smoking ruins.[28]

The Germans launched further determined attacks on this portion of the line in the days that followed. Captain James Jack recorded in his diary for 30 October:

Last night, just after midnight, the enemy suddenly opens intense shell and machine-gun fire on the brigade front. Our battalions reply immediately in order to stop an infantry assault ... About 2am the enemy's guns lift to our support line; their machine-guns redouble their fire for a minute or two, before stopping

A patriotic postcard of Reserve Infanterie Regiment Nr. 224. *The spirit of Germany leads the men in a charge in 1914. Many would be cut down in a hail of British bullets at Rue du Bois.*

abruptly. At once the German infantry advance with consummate courage, cheering and bugles blowing, the survivors getting right up to the trenches ... I am now despatched to discover and report on the situation. An orderly with loaded rifle and fixed bayonet accompanies me as we hurry forward to La Boutillerie. There we learn that the [Argyll and Sutherland] Highlanders ... have restored the position with great promptitude, bayoneting or capturing about 50 of the enemy ... The attacks cease at dawn. They have been a total failure. Three hundred German bodies, mostly 223rd and 224th Infantry Regiments, are counted lying in front of our trenches.[29]

In fact prisoners of both of these units – *Reserve-Infanterie Regiment Nr. 223* which was raised at Oberhofen in August 1914, and *Reserve-Infanterie Regiment Nr. 224* raised at Erfurt at the same time from a cadre of reservists from three regular regiments – were also taken. The captives, with their distinctive shoulder numerals, revealed the presence of a new German division opposite this front. Like the other German reserve regiments that were raised in 1914, these formations comprised a core of seasoned officers and NCOs, with the bulk of the rank and file being recent recruits. Effectively they were the German equivalent of Kitchener's Army. The widespread observation that, if having penetrated the British line, they often had little idea of what to do next, parallels some German reports of the British New Army divisions at the Battle of Loos in 1915; having broken through the German front line, the British soldiers there in certain instances had little understanding of the need to move forward and in some cases actually sat down to await further orders.

The front line here had now settled into a pattern of trench warfare which, apart from a few minor changes, would not move radically until the major offensives of 1918. In these early days however there were few if any communication trenches, and most of what was needed in the front line, including food and ammunition, had to be carried in the open. Captain Heber Alexander, of the 9th Mule Corps, provides an illustration of the monotonous but vital work of his unit in supplying the front-line troops – work that was not without danger:

> Whilst the Division was in the Festubert-Givenchy trenches, the mule-drivers came in for their share of bad times, and a good many casualties occurred. There was a lot of shelling behind the lines, and the roads along which the transport took up rations at night were swept by stray bullets. The drivers with units had in many cases to camp in the open, and do the best they could with tarpaulins and straw to make some sort of a living-place under their carts: this entailed great suffering in wet and frosty weather. But always I received enthusiastic reports of their behaviour and of their absolute contempt of fire. Kot Duffadar Fatteh Khan and six drivers were recommended for special reward. On one occasion, when their mules carrying ammunition should have been met by a regimental party at a point behind the trenches, the party did not put in an appearance. Fatteh Khan and his men without a moment's hesitation unloaded the mules and took up the boxes themselves across the open under heavy fire.[30]

Artillery subaltern Cecil Brownlow, tasked with a turn as Forward Observation Officer for his battery, visited the trenches in this sector at the beginning of November 1914. His account of this illustrates how dangerous approaching the front line could be:

> Mounting a bicycle, I pedalled up the muddy lane which led from the battery to the trenches. The morning was muggy and a white mist lay over the ground, through which the sun showed like a large red ball. As I moved forward the whole countryside appeared deserted; here and there were shell-holes yawning in the roadway; many of the trees on either side were scored and gashed or were cut down and lay along the ground with splintered stumps bristling upwards. A solitary shell whined through the mist and burst harmlessly with a puff of smoke and a twang of bullets in an empty field on my right. The first person I met was one of our telephonists, who was mending a telephone wire which lay along a ditch by the roadside. Farther on, a turn in the road brought me upon an estaminet and a few houses all peppered with bullet marks and gaping with jagged shell-holes. I found sheltering in these houses a battalion of Gurkhas, and I met one of their officers, from whom I asked the way to the trenches.
>
> 'Straight on for about a quarter of a mile,' he said, so I continued to pedal on down the road, heavy with mud. I was brought to a halt at a cross-roads by a barricade of carts and stones, and I suddenly noticed to right and left rows of black faces looking up at me. An officer shouted, 'For God's sake, come down!' and I heard a crack that made my ears sing. My body, as if acting on its own, leaped from the bicycle and tumbled off the road into the trench at the side ... At this period the trench system consisted of the front line which generally ran along definite features of the ground, such as hedges, ditches, and roads, with a few supporting works close in rear. There were no communication trenches nor were there any sandbags, wire, or revetting material, and entrenching tools were scarce.
>
> ... The trench into which I had so hurriedly descended ran along the road to the west of Neuve Chapelle and was manned by Gurkhas. The battalion which we fired over was the Seaforths, and to reach them I had to make my way along the trench for a hundred yards or so, to where they joined the Gurkhas. The little men from the far-away hills of Nepal were mostly asleep, curled up like cats in nests which each had scooped for himself in the roadside; some, however, were working away busily with pick and spade, while at intervals sentries peered intently through loopholes at the enemy across the road.[31]

Brownlow reached the Seaforths, holding the trenches in front of his battery:

> We moved along the trench and put our heads up again. As my eyes appeared above the parapet, to my horror I found myself looking straight into the decaying and leering face of a dead German officer who lay on the far side of the parapet, not a yard off, while beyond him other dead forms, stiff and bloated, lay scattered over the field. I found out that a week previously the enemy had made a small local attack here at night and had been driven back.
>
> Suddenly there was a sharp cry to the right, the sound of a fall and of men's voices. I turned a traverse and found a man lying dead in the narrow trench.

He had been sniped, and the bullet, entering the forehead, had blown the back of his head clean off. I looked at the smashed and splintered skull, at the mess of brains and blood, and I said to myself: 'The Glory of War'.[32]

In one of the final throws of the German dice, on 2 November the 2nd Battalion 2nd Gurkha Rifles – which might well have been the formation through which Brownlow passed – were driven out of their trenches at Neuve Chapelle by a determined attack, but the lost ground was quickly retaken. The avowed intention of the German high command to break through on this front had been thwarted both by the determination of British regular soldiers such as Richards and Lucy to stand their ground, and by the timely arrival of the Indian Corps as reinforcements. Already by late October the German commanders were shifting their heavy artillery to the north, away from the La Bassée sector, in order to give all the weight that they could to their offensive at Ypres, which was also now reaching its bloody and destructive nadir.

The identity disc of a soldier of the 2nd Battalion 2nd Gurkha Rifles, who fought at Neuve Chapelle in 1914. The soldier's religion is shown as H for Hindu.

Chapter 6

At All Costs

As a result of the First World War, the Belgian town of Ypres was to become, in the words of the historian Colonel Beckles Wilson, the Holy Ground of British Arms. Winston Churchill went further, and in 1919 stated that, 'A more sacred place for the British race does not exist in the world.'[1]

Nowadays the significance attached to the town by their forefathers in the 1920s and 1930s has largely been forgotten by the British people, and the citizens of Ypres itself now seem more interested in their history as the centre of the medieval Flanders wool trade, but its defence by the British army over four years, beginning in October 1914, was of epic proportions. No wonder that for twenty years between the wars it was a place of pilgrimage for both the survivors of that defence, and those bereaved by it. Captain W.E. Duncan, arriving there in October 1914 remembered:

> We were charmed with the peacefulness and beauty of the place; it might have been Bury St Edmunds, or Lincoln. We had tea at a nice clean café, facing the Cloth Hall in the large main square. We were the first British in the neighbourhood and the women in the café asked us anxiously, 'Will the Germans bombard the city?' 'No,' we said, 'The Germans are in retreat,' and we thought that we spoke the truth. Next day, the heavy howitzers began to shell Ypres, and continued for four years, until hardly one stone stood above another.[2]

Likewise the Ypres battlefield of 1914 was almost totally obliterated (both physically and in the nation's collective memory) by the later battles that took place over the same ground. The Ypres salient in 1917 has entered the national consciousness as the image of the First World War: a shell-scarred, waterlogged moonscape in which men drowned if they left the duckboard tracks, which were the only means of crossing the battlefield. But things in 1914 were very different.

The countryside to the south-east of Ypres was dotted with woods, forming an almost continuous chain from Zonnebeke to Wytschaete. As well as mature trees they contained dense undergrowth, and provided a good deal of cover for the movement of troops and for attacking formations to assemble. A number of villages ringed the town – Langemarck was the most significant, followed by Zonnebeke, Becelaere and Wytschaete. Largest of the hamlets were Neuve Eglise, Zillebeke and Gheluvelt. All were substantially intact at this stage and again provided cover to infantry. Dotted between them were farmsteads, many of which were named by the British – names which have gained immortality. In the open fields (usually containing sugar beet or

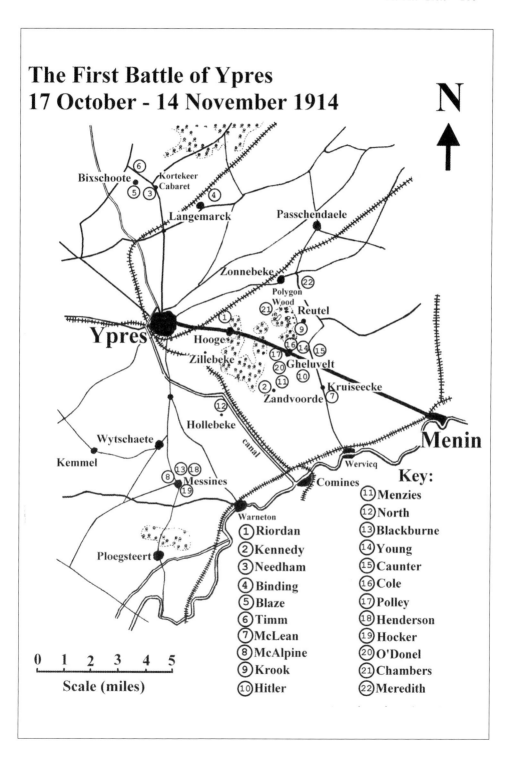

The First Battle of Ypres
17 October - 14 November 1914

N

Bixschoote
⑥ Kortekeer Cabaret
⑤ ③
④
Langemarck
Passchendaele
Zonnebeke
㉒
Polygon Wood
㉑ Reutel
① ⑨
Ypres
Hooge
⑯ ⑭ ⑮
Zillebeke
⑰
⑳ Gheluvelt
② ⑪ ⑩
Kruiseecke
Zandvoorde ⑦
⑫
Hollebeke
Wytschaete
canal
Kemmel
Wervicq
Menin
⑬⑱
⑧ Messines
⑲
Comines
Warneton
Ploegsteert

Key:

⑪ Menzies
⑫ North
⑬ Blackburne
⑭ Young
⑮ Caunter
⑯ Cole
⑰ Polley
⑱ Henderson
⑲ Hocker
⑳ O'Donel
㉑ Chambers
㉒ Meredith

① Riordan
② Kennedy
③ Needham
④ Binding
⑤ Blaze
⑥ Timm
⑦ McLean
⑧ McAlpine
⑨ Krook
⑩ Hitler

0 1 2 3 4 5
Scale (miles)

Ypres in 1914, before the city was reduced to rubble by four years of bombardment.

sometimes cereals) the only cover was afforded by drainage ditches or the occasional haystack.

In this final phase of the 'Race to the Sea', the objective of the Germans was to smash through the Allied line between the Belgians on the Yser and the French further south and to reach the Channel coast. By rolling up the Channel ports they would cut off the BEF from its supplies and neutralise it as a fighting force, while outflanking the French. The British and French forces at the outset had similar hopes of breaking through their enemy's line and outflanking him, but when faced with the German juggernaut bearing down on them were quickly thrown back on to the defensive. Their objective then became simply to hold on. The legend of Ypres as the town that saved the British Empire was thus born, for in its heroic and some would say stubborn defence the British army bought valuable time, and tied up vastly superior German forces which might have menaced Britain herself.

From the German perspective the fighting at Ypres differed from that of the previous two months, because their newly raised reserve divisions reached the front line for the first time here. These formations, known as *Jungdeutschland* divisions because they consisted of the cream of German youth, were formed mostly from volunteers under the age of 20, with little or no military experience. They were leavened with a cadre of trained men – reservists or *Landwehr*, and a small number of NCOs from the regular army. These divisions were dashed against the Franco-British defences around Ypres, and their losses were bitterly felt in Germany, much as the loss of the cream of Britain's youth on the Somme two years later would be deeply felt. The Germans coined a phrase for these battles – *kindermord* – the death of the infants.

The first British formation to reach Ypres was the 7th Division. Newly arrived via Zeebrugge, it had been destined initially for the defence of Antwerp, but arrived too late. Instead it was rushed south to Ypres, to keep it from the rapidly advancing Germans. Corporal Thomas Riordan of the 2nd Battalion Yorkshire Regiment arrived in the Ypres area on 10 October, moving up along the Menin Road through Hooge. He remembered:

We had been advancing for some time when suddenly a rifle shot came from our front. We were crossing a turnip field at the time and I don't think I have seen anyone dive for cover behind turnip tops as we all did at that moment. When I looked up I saw three strange soldiers on horses going away from us along the road as fast as the horses would go, while the Company on the right of us blazed away at them. They got away alright. We then moved forward with more alertness, but nothing happened and we arrived at the Menin Crossroads and the village of Gheluvelt. We were ordered to dig in at the north side of the village. My section was about 100 to 200 yards on the left of the Menin Road. We dug most of that day and night and by morning had got our trench to a depth of about four or five feet. We were ordered to make a parapet both front and back of the trench and our orders were that we were to hold on here at all costs for we had no reserves behind us and would not have until the British came up from the Aisne.

It was here that I saw my first German prisoners. They were five men of a Cavalry Patrol of the 19th German Hussars. I thought it strange that our first prisoners should be from the 19th German Hussars, as we were the 19th of Foot. They seemed very dejected and when I tried to talk to them they drew their fingers across their throats as though trying to say 'Are you going to cut my throat?' That rather amused me.

The next afternoon, it was a Sunday, we were ordered to fall in on the road about 50 yards to our rear and the Battalion marched off to the left of Gheluvelt. Soon we turned to the right on to a track across open country. The word trickled down the line that we were going to Menin and may bump into the Germans at any moment. We had been marching for about an hour when a staff officer rode past us towards the head of the Column. Word was passed back to halt but not to fall out. The C.O. Adjutant and R.S.M. moved to the rear of the battalion and we were turned about and made a forced march back to our trenches in front of Gheluvelt. We manned the trenches and I sent some men to a nearby farmhouse to see if they could get some wire to make trip wires in front of the trench. They came back with quite a bit and we made three or four lined with Bully tins with stones inside and attached as best we could to the wire. We had no barbed wire with the battalion nor for that matter had we any defence items at all.

We neither saw nor heard anything that evening or night to make us think that the Germans were anywhere near us. We were, therefore, very surprised when we 'Stood to' at dawn to see a line of German trenches about 100 yards in front of us. They must have dug in during the night and we had not heard a sound. I decided to put a trip wire as far as I could in front of our trench. As soon as it was dark, I went out with two men and fixed it. We were not disturbed, though we did make some noise fixing the tins on the wire.[3]

The German troops encountered by the British at this early stage of the battle were thinly spread, often little more than a cavalry screen, and there were still hopes that by pushing forward the BEF could turn the German flank. Consequently on 19 October they began to put into operation a plan to advance on Menin, in a broadly south-easterly direction. Unbeknownst to the British commanders this movement would take them diagonally across the path of strong German forces advancing westwards – including some of the newly raised reserve divisions. By 10.30am worrying reports were being received from air reconnaissances of two hostile columns, estimated to be at least a division each, which were 4–6 miles away. In fact each column comprised an army corps of two divisions. Other columns were visible behind them coming from the east.

Never the less the British advance, spearheaded by the 1st Royal Welsh Fusiliers (7th Division), continued towards Menin until at around noon they had reached

the outskirts of Dadizeele, when they came under artillery and infantry fire. Some of this fire was coming from the direction of Passchendaele to the north, and was hitting the exposed left flank of the advance. Around the same time the order reached the leading formations to break off the attack and assume a defensive position. The 1st Royal Welsh Fusiliers were already hotly engaged with the enemy and the battalion had suffered considerable casualties before it managed to extricate itself.

The following day, 20 October, the Germans launched a general attack along the whole of the British front, from Armentières in the south to Langemarck in the north. The fighting in the southern

Private Richard S. Dier, 1st Battalion Royal Welsh Fusiliers, killed in action on 19 October 1914 in the British advance on Menin.

sector has already been described in the previous chapter, but in the north the Germans launched attacks against the thinly held British lines around Ypres. Here the British 1st Cavalry Division faced attacks on its positions between Ploegsteert Wood and Messines, and all available hands were made busy digging trenches. In the centre the 7th Division was heavily attacked but the Germans were driven off. The northern flank was held by 3rd Cavalry Division which occupied positions around Passchendaele. During the day the roads around Passchendaele were thronged with refugees that passed through the British lines, though the Germans did not take advantage of this by using them as human shields. As the day wore on more British troops arrived in the Ypres area in the form of Sir Douglas Haig's 1st Division, which reinforced thinly spread French Territorial troops in the northern portion of the line.

The 21 October was to be a day of assaults of increasing ferocity along the whole British line as the Germans continued their policy of attacking everywhere simultaneously. Heavy blows fell against the 4th Dragoon Guards on the edge of Ploegsteert Wood. Some Germans had penetrated the wood and the situation appeared critical until the arrival of parties of the 9th Lancers as reinforcements. Further south the British 2nd Cavalry Division was also heavily attacked from 9.30am, being shelled out of its trenches. The Padre E.J. Kennedy, who was attached to a field ambulance in this area, recounted how he lost direction in the darkness of a night pouring with rain. The following morning, 21 October, a staff officer was able to help him rejoin his unit:

> On reaching the village of Zandvoorde, I encountered a terrible sight. The enemy was approaching from two sides, and shelling hard. The place was a slaughter-house; never have I seen so ghastly a sight. The doctors, with their coats off and shirt sleeves rolled up, looked more like butchers than medical men, and for an hour or two I found my hands full in the saddest of all work, dealing with dying men.[4]

The front-line troops withdrew to Hollebeke Château, about ½ mile east of Hollebeke village. At this point a set of orders providing for an orderly retirement if deemed necessary seem to have been misinterpreted, and the cavalry began to evacuate the château and the village behind it. General Sir Hubert Gough upon discovering the error immediately ordered the abandoned ground retaken. Although Hollebeke village was re-occupied, the château was found to be in enemy hands. That the Germans did not take

Lieutenant Colonel E.B. Cook MVO, 1st Life Guards, mortally wounded by a shell at Zandvoorde on 22 October 1914.

further advantage of this confusion is largely due to the fact that they were not fully aware of what had happened.

In the centre of the British line between Gheluvelt and Becelaere, the 2nd Battalion Yorkshire Regiment and 2nd Battalion Royal Scots Fusiliers were heavily attacked by wave after wave of German infantry from the *54th Reserve Division*. Despite their heavy losses in the face of British rifle fire they managed for a time to force their way between the two battalions, though their progress was blocked by the resolute defence of Polderhoek Château and the attack ultimately came to nothing. Every German assault was preceded by a barrage of 8in howitzer shells, though the enemy were notably unsuccessful in locating the British field batteries, so that these units carried out sterling work in breaking up the German infantry attacks throughout the course of the day. Further north, on 23 October, the Germans launched a series of violent offensives against the British near Langemarck. Hauptmann Rudolph Binding was attached to the headquarters of the *51st Reserve Division* here. Published in English as *A Fatalist At War*, his memoirs vividly describe the reality of untrained German troops thrown into battle against hardened British regulars around Langemarck, conjuring up images of enthusiastic but inexperienced young soldiers advancing along the ditches beside the road, as projectiles whistled past them; the wounded lying on stretchers in the bottoms of the culverts, unable to be moved. On one occasion a wounded man burst into Binding's temporary field headquarters, blood streaming down his face, asking for water. On 23 October he wrote evocatively of the sights that he had seen that day:

> Slow progress, if it can be called progress. Naturally the smallest success is noted with satisfaction, but a set-back is not shouted from the house-tops. Already the

A Nazi-era depiction of the German charge at Langemarck, October 1914. The sacrifice of German youth here would be exploited for propaganda value in the 1930s.

place has become a waste. Fire and death are everywhere. Empty, plundered farms; graves with a helmet stuck on them, the mounds often built up with the hands out of the solid clammy clay. The wounded often lie for days, for fighting goes on to and fro by night as well as by day.[5]

Private Frederick Bolwell of the 1st Loyal North Lancashires confirms that the German troops he encountered here between Bixschoote and Langemarck were mostly young and inexperienced, whereas the British in spite of previous losses still maintained their professional edge. His battalion was part of a counter-attack launched by General Bulfin, commanding the British 2nd Brigade, designed to throw the Germans off balance. He describes this advance which took him right up to the village of Langemarck with its distinctive windmill:

Rudolph Binding, the German author and staff officer.

We formed up well behind the front line, two companies taking the first line in extended order and two companies the second line in the same order. Thus we advanced about a mile over flat open country to the front line. We went up in short rushes, and a word of praise is due to the men who took part in it. I never even on the Barrack Square or drill-ground saw a better advance: the men went up absolutely in line, each man keeping his correct distance, and that under heavy machine-gun and rifle fire. Of course some men got knocked over; but it made absolutely no difference. One Officer, a Major Powell, carried a chair with him the whole of the way, and, on reaching a hedge, would mount this chair to get a view of the enemy. Two hundred yards off the front line, we made a combined rush into it. There we found the Camerons, with the usual one-man trench. The man I lay down behind told me that they had been out there three days and had had no rations, and also that they had had many men taken prisoners. In this front line we had a breather, the German trenches being roughly three hundred yards away, and a hedge was also running parallel between the two lines of trenches, with a big gap facing us. Through this gap we could see the enemy retiring one and two at a time from their trenches. They appeared like so many rabbits running from their holes, and, as they ran, so we took pot-shots at them.

After we had had our breather, the word was given to charge; and this we did, going through in fine style. Just behind the front line of German trenches was a house from which we took a number of prisoners. The first man of ours to reach it was a corporal. He called upon the Germans to surrender and got a bullet through the brain for his pains. The Germans then saw us, and were obliged to surrender, and were given over to men to take behind. One German Officer remarked: 'We don't mind we've got Paris, and London is in flames.' One of our Officers turned

Number 9 Company of the newly raised Reserve Infanterie Regiment Nr. 234, *in October 1914. This unit was shortly to take part in the attack at Langemarck. Note the various styles of uniform; the fly-fronted double-pocketed tunic was an obsolete pattern. The men are a mix of reservists and raw recruits.*

round and said: 'You know that's not true.' Whereon he remarked: 'I know, but the men believe it.' The troops we were fighting there were on the whole very young, and they had new clothing and equipment, and told us that they had left Germany for what they thought would be manoeuvres in Belgium, and did not expect seeing the firing line for some months. I myself really thought the war was over that day, as Germans surrendered from all directions and we overran their trenches everywhere.[6]

Not far away that day, near the Korteek Kabaret (an inn on the Langemarck–Bixschoote road) Captain E.J. Needham of the Northamptonshire Regiment lay in a roadside ditch as shells from both sides exploded around him during the too and fro fighting. He remembered:

In front of 'C' Company the ground, a field of roots, sloped away down to a little stream of the Hannebeek, the banks of which were clearly defined by pollarded willows. Behind this stream again, the ground sloped upwards gradually to a small wood stretching along a low ridge.

The stream was about three hundred and fifty yards in front of us, and the wood another four hundred yards behind that again. To our right front and about a mile away stood the church and red-roofed houses of Langemarck and beyond that again and about the same distance away from it, the church and roofs of Poelcappelle. No food had come up to us during the morning, not even our usual tea and rum, and we had to fall back on our 'iron rations' of bully beef and biscuits. About 1pm we could see large bodies of Germans collecting in the wood on the ridge opposite, and 'Jumbo' Bentley and I knelt up in our ditch so as to be able to see better what they were up to, and both scanned the wood closely through our field-glasses.

Suddenly I felt a terrific blow on my right arm just as if somebody had hit me on the funny bone as hard as he could with a sledge hammer. It spun me round like a top and I collapsed in the bottom of the trench. The man next to me rolled over and said, 'You ain't 'alf bloody well got 'it in the 'and, sir!' and on looking down I saw that my right hand was a mass of blood.

My arm still felt numb from the blow, and I could hardly realise that it was my hand that was hit, as it did not hurt at all. However, this man cut my field dressing out of my tunic, and after dousing my hand with iodine, which *did* hurt, he bound it up very well; he then made a sling out of my woollen scarf which I was wearing, insisted on giving me one of his own cigarettes and lighting it for me, and told me not to worry, I was 'for Blighty alright with that packet!' This sounded too good to be true, and I felt distinctly better.

He also said, and I then realised, it for the first time, that I had been very lucky not to be killed, as I had my field-glasses up to my eyes and the bullet which had hit my right hand would have got me in the head if it had been one inch farther to the left! He told me my right collar badge was badly dented and the bullet must have hit this after hitting my hand. About five minutes after I was hit, a man two away from me on the left was kneeling up looking out towards the Germans when he was shot straight through the head. We came to the conclusion that there must be snipers lying in one of the pollarded willows by the stream, about three hundred and fifty yards in front of us, and that they must be pretty hot shots. Anyhow, Bentley gave orders that no man was to expose himself from now onwards unless we were attacked.

All this time shells from both sides kept dropping on and around the unfortunate mill, which was now on fire in several places. I suppose it was the after-effects of the shock of being hit, but anyhow my nerve went completely. I lay in the bottom of the trench expecting the Huns to come over and wipe me out lying defenceless there. Or I began to panic that instead of going home with a nice wound, a shell would land in the trench and blow me up.[7]

Needham did make it home, but Corporal Oliver Blaze, of the 1st Battalion Scots Guards, was less lucky. He was in the front line on the left of the British 1st Division's front on the night of 23 October, opposite Bixschoote. This was at the height of the battle for Langemarck and two German divisions were committed against the British here on this day. Not long after darkness fell the Scots Guards were heavily attacked by soldiers of *Reserve Infanterie Regiment Nr. 213*. Blaze remembered:

I saw that we were being rushed, and I knew that our chance of escape was hopeless. I thought very swiftly just then, and my thought was, 'We can't get away, so we may as well stick it. If we bolt we shall be shot in the back and we might just as well be shot in the front; it looks better.' They were on us before we knew where we were, and to make matters worse, they rushed upon us from the direction of the village where we supposed the French to be. There was a scrap, short and sweet, between our outpost and the Germans, and almost in the twinkling of an eye, it seemed, two of my men were killed, one got away, and I was wounded and captured.

A bullet struck me in the right arm and I fell down, and the Germans were on me before I knew what was happening. I still had my equipment on, and to this fact and the prompt kind act of a wounded German let us be fair and say that not all Germans are brutes: there are a few exceptions I owe my life, for as soon as I fell a Prussian rushed at me and made a drive with his bayonet. Just as he did so, a wounded German who was lying on the ground near me grabbed me and gave me a tug towards him. At this instant the bayonet jabbed at me and struck between the equipment and my wounded arm, just touching my side. The equipment and the wounded German's pull had prevented the bayonet from plunging plump into me and killing me on the spot, for the steel, driven with such force, would have gone clean through my chest. That was the sort of tonic to buck you up, and I didn't need a second prick to make me spring to my feet.

I jumped up, and had no sooner done so than a second bullet struck me on the wounded arm and made a fair mess of it, and I knew that this time I was properly bowled out. I had fallen down again and was lying on the ground, bleeding badly; and the next thing I knew was that I was being stripped. Everything I had on me, my equipment and my clothing, was taken away; not for the purpose of letting a doctor examine me, as one did later, but as part of a system of battlefield plunder which the Germans have organised.[8]

Later Blaze was given morphine by a sympathetic German doctor, who amputated his arm while he lay on a stretcher on the battlefield, the German medics having constructed a tarpaulin windbreak around him. Ulrich Timm, who was before the war a student of Theology at Rostock University, might well have been among those troops facing Blaze, as he has left a gripping account of the attack made by the German *XXIII Reserve Corps* on the evening of 23 October 1914 against the British 1st Division north-west of Langemarck. Timm entirely typified the young student volunteers who might have been better used by the Germans as officers, rather than being flung half-trained as ordinary infantrymen against the experienced riflemen of the BEF. In particular, his account reveals the suffering of the wounded lying out in no-man's-land following an attack, precisely as described by Binding. With insufficient stretcher-bearers, many men were wounded a second time before help could reach them:

The bullet came from the right front, went first through my right leg, then through the left leg, and finally through my pocket, which was stuffed with filthy field-postcards, my New Testament, your last letter, my paybook, and a lot of other small books. Through all this the bullet went, so it must have been travelling with considerable velocity! The wounds only hurt badly during the first few hours; after that, and now, very little.

The whole of October 23rd we had been lying as artillery cover by the village of Merkem, not far from Dixmuide. In the evening, a little before 7, came a request from the infantry in front of us for support, as they wanted to storm the enemy position. Immediately we swarmed out of our trench, fixed bayonets and doubled to the attack, 'hurrah, hurrah!'

It was a complete failure, for in the first place, there were more of our own men in front of us, being constantly fired at not only by the enemy opposite but by their own comrades in the rear. Not a few were killed by German bullets during those days. In the second place we were still a mile or more away from the enemy position when we began storming, so that we were tired before the attack really started.

After we had stormed through a thicket and some fields of roots and crossed a broad, deep trench (not without risking our lives, for the bullets were whistling past our ears) we were supposed to capture a wide exposed hill. I was quite prepared to stick my bayonet into the body of the first Englishman I could see, when suddenly I was seized by some irresistible force and hurled to the ground. For a moment I didn't know where I was, but I soon pulled myself together. Hallo! What's happened? Aha, you've caught it, there's blood running out of your trousers! Just try and see if you can stand up. Quite alright. It can't be so bad then, but get down again quickly or you may catch it again. So, now what shall I do? Aha, there's a straw stack ten yards away! I'll crawl under there! It's not so easy. Quite a lot of men there already, wounded and unwounded Jägers. 'Hi comrade, just tie a rag around my legs! So, thank you.' But now to groan a bit for it really hurts confoundedly. 'Hallo Schliemann, are you wounded too?' 'Yes, can't see out of one eye. I'm going to the dressing station.' 'Then send help to me and my comrades, we can't walk.'

The unwounded continued the attack. It grew quieter around us. I look at the time: nearly 8 o'clock. Will help come? No – we waited in vain till the next morning. When it got light we saw stretcher bearers collecting wounded a few hundred yards away. We shouted. 'Coming to you directly.' But they did not return. We waited in vain till the evening: it was horrible. One who could still walk a little, started off. He had hardly gone a hundred yards when I saw him fall. Those damned snipers!

Another long, anxious night. At midnight I woke suddenly out of a doze. Now what's happening? We were lying in the middle of shell and rifle fire. 'Comrades, get closer to the stack! Don't anybody raise himself up!' An appalling uproar all around us – terrible! I shall never forget it as long as I live. It is gruesome when a shell bursts right over you like that. And then the fear that the stack would be set on fire. I have never prayed as I did that night. And so it passed . . . so did the next battle at 4 o'clock.

The weather next day was beautiful. But it was our second day between the English and German lines. We were in the greatest danger! The man next to me got a shell-splinter added to his body wound during the night. The others were also badly wounded. Then I thought I'd try if I could stand, and lo! I succeeded. Well then, I'll try my luck! And I got safely as far as the trench which was strewn with bodies. Opposite, a little way off, I could see Germans in their trench. 'Don't fire! I'm wounded, help!' And they came and brought me to the dressing station and then fetched the others too. I thanked God that I was saved. I had lain out there from Friday evening to Sunday morning.[9]

Binding summarises the futility of these attacks, which would enter the German folk-memory, in another diary entry:

There is no doubt that the English . . . would already have been beaten by trained troops. But these young fellows we have, only just trained, are too helpless, particularly when the officers have been killed. Our light infantry battalion, almost all Marburg students, the best troops we have as regards musketry, have suffered terribly from enemy shell-fire. In the next division, just such young souls, the intellectual flower of Germany, went singing into an attack on Langemarck, just as vain and just as costly.[10]

On 24 October French troops relieved the British in the northern part of the Ypres salient, and took over the line from Bixschoote to Zonnebeke. As far as the British were concerned the fighting now shifted to the southern portion of the salient, where the Germans continued to make determined efforts to break through their lines. Private W. McLean served with the 2nd Battalion Border Regiment, which by this point was holding the line east of the small village of Kruiseecke. Here the British front formed almost a right angle, and this was effectively the apex of the salient. Writing to a member of his family about the fighting in this part of the line he stated:

Now and again we would sing or tell tales. It was on Sunday, October 26th, just before the Germans made their final attack, much laughter was caused as we lay in the bottom of our trench by a fellow named Kirkpatrick, from Kendal, Cumberland. He kept us laughing all the afternoon telling us tales and things he had done while in civil life, but all that laughter stopped and our faces grew stern, and lips tight, our hand gripping our rifles with bayonets fixed, ready for the worst. How we longed to meet them face to face. For eight days they had kept under cover, but at last it came. It was just about 6pm, on Sunday October 26th, when it came, and we emptied our rifles into them time after time. They replied with shell, rifle and maxim gun, but we held on to our trenches.[11]

Private Thomas Cain served in the same battalion, and a letter written on 26 October 1914 complements that of McLean. Cain was the son of a joiner, but writes clearly and concisely. He stated:

Just these few lines to let you know that I am still alright, but I have had an awful time. I am sure there are grey hairs in my head. We have been up in the trenches for eight days, just a few thousand of us keeping back about 100,000 Germans . . . it was terrible; they kept on shelling us. They blew the trenches to pieces three times, but we fixed them up as soon as it got dark. Then their infantry would charge and it was slaughter. They would get to about fifty yards of us and they would lie down and would not come any further or go back. We could hear them moaning with fear, so we stopped firing. Then their officers got up and started shouting, but they would not come, so they started shooting their own men with revolvers. When we saw them doing that, we shot their officers, and then

A rare aerial photograph taken in late 1914, looking north-west towards Ypres across the southern half of the salient. The battlefield of 1914 seen here was totally destroyed in later battles.

they stopped yelling and we let them sneak away. Out of our platoon of 56 men, there are 19 left. We have about two captains and about four lieutenants left. Our colonel and adjutant are both dead. Two majors were killed and one badly wounded out of A Company, and there are about 12 men and a lieutenant left out of 250 men ... Nearly all were killed by the shells in the trenches ... My nerves are shattered with the terrible noise that has been going on. We are now in a big town trying to get the pieces sorted out. Nearly all my mates are dead. The last time we met in this house, about ten days ago, there were 12 of us, now there are only five. If I get home you will not believe me if I told you what has happened to me ...[12]

Kruiseecke was eventually lost to repeated German attacks, some of which employed subterfuge – a party of Germans, having worked their way behind the 1st Battalion South Staffordshire Regiment, then shouted 'Retire!' in English. This caused sufficient confusion amid the South Staffords that the Germans were able to break through, take the village and also cut off those men of the Border Regiment who were still in the front line.

The second phase of the battle would now centre on the village of Gheluvelt, which sits squarely astride the main road from Ypres to Menin. The Germans held much of the high ground now, holding Houlthust Forest, the ridge north of Passchendaele (and for about a mile south of it), part of the spur running eastwards from Gheluvelt, and now the knoll upon which Kruiseecke sits. The British for their part still held much of the high ground south of the Menin Road – at Hollebeke, Wytschaete, the ridge running out to Messines and Hill 63, north of Ploegsteert. The coming German offensive would hit the British positions around the Gheluvelt crossroads, 1 mile south-east of the village itself, where the Kruiseecke–Poezelhoek road crossed the Menin Road. The trenches here had originally been dug by the British as a reserve position. They were narrow, and did not form anything like a continuous line, indeed there were considerable gaps between them in places. This would inevitably cause problems for the BEF as the battle progressed.

Lieutenant D. McAlpine of the Royal Army Medical Corps was a newly arrived subaltern at Ypres in October 1914. As the junior member of his Field Ambulance he was posted on 25 October as Medical Officer to the 2nd Battalion King's Own Scottish Borderers, near Messines. He wrote to his brother of the trying time caused by German shelling in this vicinity:

> I found regimental headquarters in the cellar of a house about 300 yards behind the firing line. The officers are splendid fellows. Their losses and those of the men have been heavy. We have a major in command. The next day I found a nearby farmhouse which I made into a dressing station. Pipers and drummers, eight in all, do the work of stretcher bearers. They are all young men full of life. As I spend a good deal of time with them I have got to know them pretty well … Two days later the Germans shelled us all day with their heavy howitzers … the Germans got the range of our trenches almost exactly and about 9.30 in the morning a shell exploded in the frontline trench, burying two men. I had scarcely gone 50 yards on my way forward when I heard a shell coming. I immediately lay flat in a shallow ditch. Nearer and nearer it came and I thought it was going to do for me but it exploded about 15 yards away. Covered with mud I quickly got up and rushed on but had to lie down four or five times as shells were bursting all around. I met a man coming down from the firing line, screaming; a minute or so before a shell had exploded burying three of his comrades. He was quite off his head. I got the men onto digging and finally we unearthed one poor chap who was dying. I moved along the line towards the other casualties. I spent about an hour altogether in the front line, with those awful things bursting … When I got back to the road I found that battalion headquarters had been wrecked, but being in the cellar no officer was hit. The shelling continued for another two hours. For five successive nights the Germans attacked in our vicinity and we did not get much rest.[13]

After being relieved by an Indian army unit the 2nd King's Own Scottish Borderers went into billets in the rear. Their rest was short-lived however as the next morning (29 October) they were rushed in motor buses to the front line as reinforcements, McAlpine and another medical officer tending to the wounded in a temporary dressing station in a house at a crossroads. It was an unfortunate location, as crossroads – readily identifiable on maps – made for easy ranging points for the German gunners. A shell dropped on the house just after the last casualty had been evacuated, but the only victim was the hungry officers' dinner; as McAlpine put it, the shell causing the roof to become partially entangled with his bully beef.

This was the beginning of the Battle of Gheluvelt – the most critical phase of the First Battle of Ypres. The morning of 29 October was foggy, and the early German attacks of that day sought to take advantage of this. The first blow fell against the Black Watch holding the Menin Road east of Gheluvelt, and two under strength companies of the 1st Battalion Coldstream Guards along with it, holding ground to the north. The fog allowed the attackers to get within 50yd before the defenders saw them and opened fire, but it was not the usual withering fusillade that the Germans had come to expect from the men of the BEF. The British that day were beset with problems relating to faulty ammunition. A couple of Maxim guns on the road jammed completely due to cartridge cases that were either too large or too weak to eject fully, and all along the British line here Tommies were kicking rifle bolts or clawing at the breeches of their rifles with pocket knives to eject spent cases. Eventually the inevitable happened and a party of Germans, having broken through on the Menin Road itself, overwhelmed the Black Watch and the Coldstreamers north of the road. A further attack against the remainder of the 1st Coldstream was less successful, the Germans charging three times but on each occasion were driven off. Sergeant Thomas Riordan of the 2nd Yorkshire Regiment remembered the stragglers coming back:

> Just before dawn on the 29th October, we manned some trenches and were told that we could take off our equipment and rest. We 'stood to' at dawn with just our rifles and a cotton bandolier containing 50 rounds of ammunition. As it became lighter, I saw that our trench was on high ground just off a good wide road. I have not the faintest idea where we were, except that with the field glasses my father

Gheluvelt village in 1914. (Walter Lyneel)

had given me before I left England, I could see before me about a mile of flat open country and shells bursting as far as I could see. I assumed that this was the front line, which I later found to be correct and that we were in reserve . . . we had some biscuits and Bully for breakfast. We then settled down to try to get some sleep, but I could not sleep and got up to see what I could pick out with my glasses.

There was a large wood to our right front and another to our left front. As I looked, I saw a line of men across the front from left to right as far as I could see, coming back towards us. They must have been about a mile away, but I was able to distinguish some kilts among them, which told me that they were our troops, apparently retiring. The company was ordered forward by the company commander to the shelter of the wood to the right front, before being led out to the open ground to try to stop the rout.

Those on my side spread out and went forward and at the front edge of the wood we met what I can only call a hoard of all sorts of regiments coming back. We tried to stop them but they carried us back with them. By the time we got to the back of the wood again we had managed to get some sense into them and got them into the shallow ditch behind the wood.[14]

Captain J.E. Gibbs, commanding No. 3 Company of the Coldstream, ordered his men to open fire on the Germans now occupying positions behind them and sent others to try to form a new flank. The situation however had the potential to become critical, the Germans having now broken into the British positions. Word of the disaster reached Brigade HQ about 7am, and four companies of the 1st Battalion Gloucestershire Regiment were sent up as reinforcements; they managed to rally some of the survivors before being heavily attacked themselves.

South of the Menin Road lay the 1st Battalion Grenadier Guards who, screened by houses and the morning mist, were initially unaware of the developing disaster to the north. As the fog began to clear however they too were attacked by hordes of Germans sweeping down upon them. The fighting here became hand to hand and in spite of support from the 2nd Battalion Gordon Highlanders the Grenadiers were forced back by sheer weight of numbers. Sergeant J.F. Bell of the 2nd Gordon Highlanders has left a graphic record of the part played by his battalion here, an action in which his platoon commander would receive Britain's highest military decoration; the citation details his conspicuous bravery and great ability near Gheluvelt on 29 October, in leading two attacks on the German trenches under heavy rifle and machine-gun fire, and regaining a lost trench at a critical moment. Bell tells us:

On that night there was no sleep, as we had to dig and dig to improve the trench, and were being fired at all night. At 5am a group of us were standing in the open – everything had turned peaceful – admiring our now almost perfect trench when hell seemed let loose. All the guns in Flanders seemed to have suddenly concentrated on our particular sector of the British front. When the artillery fire subsided, Germans sprang from everywhere and attacked us. My platoon held fast; we lost some good comrades. Then we were ordered to evacuate the trench, and assist to hold a trench on the flank where the fighting was fiercest. I was a sergeant, and was told to take and hold a certain part of the trench where the occupants had just been driven out. On rushing the trench, and leaping into it, I found that the dead were lying three deep in it. After taking bearings, I told the men to keep under cover and detailed one man, Ginger Bain, as 'look out'.

After what seemed ages Ginger excitedly asked, 'How strong is the German army?' I replied, 'Seven million.' 'Well,' said Ginger, 'here is the whole bloody lot of them making for us.' We were driven from the trench, and those of us who were unscathed joined Lieutenant Brook, who had come up with cooks, transport men, and men who had been wounded but could still use a rifle. Lieutenant Brook was (outwardly) quite unperturbed, walking about the firing line issuing orders as if on the barrack square. I had served under him for nine years, and seeing him such a target for the enemy riflemen, I asked him to lie down as I felt if he was hit his loss at that particular time would be disastrous. He told me we must retake the trench I had been driven from, and to pick twenty men to do so.

All the men were alike to me – men I had known for years – so I told ten men on my right and ten on my left to get ready to rush the trench. We succeeded in this. No artist or poet can depict a trench after fighting in its stark hellishness.

If we could not be driven out of the trench, it seemed certain that we would be blown out of it. Shells kept landing near enough in front of or behind the trench to shake us almost out of it. Many got killed by rifle-fire, Ginger Bain being the first, then Big Bruce whom I boxed in a competition before going to France. I passed a message to Lieutenant Brook, informing him our numbers were so reduced that if attacked we could not hold the trench, and received back word that he had just been killed. (The VC was posthumously awarded him.)

A message was then sent to me to retire and join a platoon entrenched near us. I gave instructions to the few men (eight I think) to retire along the communication

Prisoners of war of the Gordon Highlanders receive a meal at a German camp, 1914. Scottish prisoners in kilts and glengarries were objects of fascination for the Germans.

trench, and I would join them at the head of it, and lead them to our new position. I slipped over the rear of the trench, to cut across and meet the lads as they emerged from the communication trench, but had only gone about six yards when I received what in the regiment was called the 'dull thud'. I thought I had been violently knocked on the head, but, feeling I was not running properly, I looked down and discovered that my right foot was missing.

Somehow, I stood watching men running along the communication trench. My power of speech had left me, so I could speak to none of them, then I swooned into the trench. No one had seen me being wounded, but one of the men, 'Pipe' Adams, on missing me, returned to look for me. On seeing me lying quite helpless, he prepared to lift and carry me out of the trench. I told him I was too heavy: that it was too dangerous, and that in time our regiment would retake all the ground lost, when I would be safe. When I think of the War comradeship, of unaffected and unknown bravery, I think of 'Pipe' Adams (killed later) telling me, 'Christ, Jerry [my nickname], I could not leave you here.' However, confident that our people would return, I persuaded him to go. I then put a field dressing and a shirt from my pack over my stump and lay down to wait further developments.[15]

Bell would not be collected by German stretcher bearers until the following day. He was however generally well treated by them. The fact that he was a Scot in a kilt aroused much curiousity among his captors, and this may in part account for his better treatment than most.

In an effort to restore the situation at the crossroads, an immediate counter-attack was ordered here. The 1st Battalion South Wales Borderers was sent north of the road, with the 2nd Battalion Welsh Regiment to the south of it. By 10am the Germans seemed to have grasped their unexpected advantage and began to press home their attacks on a wider frontage. Further disaster befell the 1st Coldstream Guards and their allies the Black Watch. The remaining companies of both battalions were holding positions facing Reutel, but were now attacked from the rear and surrounded by German troops who had worked their way around behind them. Around 300 Guardsmen and Highlanders were killed or captured here. Captain Campbell Krook, of the Black Watch, wrote an account of the fighting in this location for the widow of one of his men:

The attack began on the extreme right of the Coldstreams, and when it got light enough to see, Germans were visible in some of the trenches recently occupied by the Coldstream centre. These Germans fired into our backs and were evidently trying to work round the one company of the Coldstream on our immediate right. Parties were sent out to give us warning, in case the Germans got round behind us. At the same time a fairly strong attack was made on the left of my company but was held off. Things looked very serious on our right and there seemed no probability of getting any reinforcements ... I think, about a quarter past ten, I got another message saying reinforcements were coming and went myself to the left to bring them in. I was about half way ... down the trench when a noise behind me attracted my attention, and turning around I saw a party of Germans behind the right and centre of my trench and within ten yards of it. They had just come out of a thick wood which was immediately behind the trench. They fired into the trench from the back and then charged. Beyond being knocked down with the butt end of a rifle I received no injury and found myself a prisoner.[16]

The situation of the 1st Battalion Scots Guards to the north was also imperilled as a result of this disaster, and by what seems to have been an extraordinary *ruse de guerre* on the part of the Germans. A message was received at Scots Guards battalion head-quarters reading: 'On no account fire through the wood in rear I am coming to your assistance with the Black Watch [signed] Murray B.W.'[17] Major J.T.C. Murray was in command of the 1st Black Watch at this time but it seems that he issued no such message, and the Germans may well have obtained his name from prisoners taken at the crossroads earlier that morning. With the remnants of the morning mist still lingering, and bullets coming at them seemingly from all directions, it was hard to see in which direction the greatest danger lay. None the less most of the 1st Scots Guards held their ground, though isolated parties from the two right-hand companies were overrun after expending all of their ammunition. The diary of Corporal C.E. Green of 1st Scots Guards offers a personal perspective on the fate of those who were captured. The entry for 29 October reads:

At dawn Germans made heavy attack, but were repulsed, leaving behind hundreds of dead & wounded on the field. Received news the enemy had broken through on our right and were round us. About 11am they came on to us & we were made prisoners. About 200 all told. After a search they marched us of to Belulair [*sic*]. I shall never forget that search and the ensuing few hours afterwards. The ever-gallant Huns made us go on knees & proceeded to take our money, tobacco, cigarettes etc from us and make away with them. As luck would have it, the searcher gave me back my tobacco & pipes. Some fellows, who had previously obtained German money from dead Huns were very roughly handled. The soldiers in charge of us insisted on us marching with our arms over heads.[18]

Attacks continued throughout the morning but none the less this was the high-water mark of German success on 29 October, and in the afternoon a British counter-attack recovered almost all of the trenches lost earlier in the day. That evening heavy rain fell and fighting ceased. As a result of the many reinforcements of the line during the day, the troops in the front line were greatly mixed, and there was much reorganisation to be done during the hours of darkness. Thomas Riordan, having been separated from his battalion early on, had spent a difficult day moving from position to position, trying to find them. Each time he moved he was fired upon, and had numerous close shaves. At the end of the day he remembered:

It was just about dusk and I was dead beat after my hard day ... I had a look at my greatcoat which I was wearing and found some shot holes in the lower part at the back. I also saw that a bullet had ripped my puttee on the outer side of my left leg and realised how lucky I had been once again ... I got a hot meal of fried bacon, biscuits and a canteen of hot tea. We also got, later on, an issue of rum, which was the first I had had. I sat on a heap of turnips to eat my meal and then drank the rum and washed it down with the last of the tea. I was terribly tired and remember lying down on the heap of turnips and must have gone into a very deep sleep.[19]

The main attack on the morning of 29 October was made by the Bavarian *6th Reserve Division*, a war-raised unit. The leading formations that morning were Bavarian *Reserve Infanterie Regiment Nr. 16* (known as the *List Regiment* after its commander Oberst Julius List) and Bavarian *Reserve Infanterie Regiment Nr. 17*, both units that were raised in Munich in September 1914. They left the city the following month, after rudimentary training, and reached Flanders around 26 October. The recruits were enthusiastic and full of patriotic fervour but lacked skill in battle craft. They were also short of equipment and in place of spiked pickelhauben helmets had been issued

R.·R. 1.

Bayer. R.J.R.Nº **16** List

Beim Ausmarsch aus München am 10. Oktober 1914.

Nun gürt' Dir um das Schwert,
                    mein Sohn,
Freiwillig zieh'ſt in's Feld —
Gieb Gott, Du kehrſt als Sieger
                    heim,
Wenn nicht, ſo ſtirb als Held
Für's liebe teure Vaterland.
Und ich ſag' Dir zum Lohn:
„Du warſt, Du biſt und wirſt
                    es ſein
Ein braver deutſcher Sohn."

C. Naundorf.

HF.

A postcard specially produced for the departure of the Bavarian Reserve Infanterie Regiment Nr. 16 *(the* List Regiment*) from Munich on 10 October 1914. Two-and-a-half weeks later they were in action near Ypres. Note the flat-topped cap, which caused the men to be fired upon by their own side in error.*

instead with *Landwehr* caps. The flat-topped cap resembled that of the British Tommies, and on at least one occasion in 1914 the men of the *List Regiment* were fired on by their own side in error.

Contemporary reports indicate that the Bavarian *Reserve Infanterie Regiment Nr. 16* and its sister formation Bavarian *Reserve Infanterie Regiment Nr. 17* came on at a steady march in columns of four on the morning of 29 October, displaying almost fanatical and reckless bravery, and both British and German sources agree that in spite of the problems the British faced with ammunition that day they managed to inflict severe casualties on both officers and men. A German view of these events is provided by none other than Adolf Hitler, at this time serving as a private soldier with the *List Regiment*. Hitler was in fact Austrian by birth and had fled Vienna for Munich to avoid being conscripted into the

Bugler Barthel Oberwesterberger, Bavarian Reserve Infanterie Regiment Nr. 16 (List Regiment) killed in action on 29 October 1914.

Hapsburg army. The idea of fighting for the 'mongrel' Austro-Hungarian Empire with its plethora of races filled Hitler with loathing. Fighting in the German army however was a different matter and Hitler joyfully volunteered in the autumn of 1914. Ten years later in *Mein Kampf* he recorded both his eagerness for his first taste of combat, and his excitement at the 'iron salute' his regiment received in front of Gheluvelt that day:

> A single worry tormented me at that time, me, as so many others: would we reach the front too late? Time and time again this alone banished all my calm. Thus, in every cause for rejoicing at a new, heroic victory, a slight drop of bitterness was hidden, for every new victory seemed to increase the danger of our coming too late.
>
> At last the day came when we left Munich to begin the fulfilment of our duty. For the first time I saw the Rhine as we rode westward along its quiet waters to defend it, the German stream of streams, from the greed of the old enemy. When through the tender veil of the early morning mist the Niederwald Monument gleamed down upon us in the gentle first rays of the sun, the old 'Watch on the Rhine' roared out of the endless transport train into the morning sky, and I felt as though my heart would burst.
>
> And then came a damp, cold night in Flanders, through which we marched in silence, and when the day began to emerge from the mists, suddenly an iron salute came whizzing at us over our heads, and with a sharp report sent the little pellets

flying between our ranks, ripping up the wet ground, but even before the little cloud had passed, from two hundred throats the first hurrah rose to meet the first messenger of death. Then a crackling and a roaring, a singing and a howling began, and with feverish eyes each one of us was drawn forward faster and faster over turnip fields and hedges till suddenly the fight began, the fight of man against man. But from the distance the sounds of a song met our ears, coming nearer and nearer, passing from company to company, and then, while death busily plunged his hand into our rows, the song reached also us, and now we passed it on: 'Deutschland, Deutschland uber alles, uber alles in der Welt!'[20]

By an irony of history, another Munich volunteer in the ranks of the *List Regiment* that day was a young man by the name of Rudolf Hess. Hess would later be commissioned, and transferred to the air service, before later still becoming Hitler's deputy in the Nazi Party. There is no evidence however to suggest that the two knew each other in 1914.

On 30 October the Battle of Gheluvelt entered its second day. Massed German attacks were about to be made, in order to place the British and their French allies under simultaneous pressure along most of the length of the line around Ypres. The day was thus notable for the fact that the Germans now attacked on a wider front, and the battle was to spread southwards, once again to include the positions held by the Cavalry Corps. The troops of Sir Douglas Haig's I Corps however were likely to bear the brunt of the assault, and had spent the previous night reinforcing their positions as best they could. However, the reality of the situation was that much of the British front line consisted of no more than a series of isolated posts, worryingly vulnerable to a surging German attack which had the potential to force its way between them, were not the enemy kept at rifle range. The weakest portion of the line was that held by the three divisions of the Cavalry Corps, the squadrons of which by now numbered on average only eighty rifles each, on the southern flank of the salient at Zandvoorde. The dismounted cavalrymen had taken up positions in ditches, inside abandoned houses and behind haystacks as they awaited the onslaught. As one British officer put it, all they could hope to do was 'putty up the holes' by throwing in reinforcements wherever the Germans broke through.

The attack began very differently from that of the previous day. For over an hour from 6.45am the fire of over 200 German heavy guns rained down around Zandvoorde in the Cavalry Corps sector. This in itself caused much destruction but at 8am it was followed by an overwhelming infantry assault. The cavalrymen were forced back on to their reserve positions. Among those units heavily attacked here was the 2nd Life Guards. The Second World War intelligence chief and wartime head of MI6, Major General Stewart Menzies, served as a lieutenant and adjutant of the regiment. In a letter written after the war he outlined his recollections of that day:

On the 30th the Household Cavalry Regiments were in the front line ... When the German attack was launched the 7th. Division on the left were driven back, and the 2nd Life Guards on the right were also compelled to retire, I believe to

A German photograph of Zandvoorde village after capture. It was here that the Household Cavalry made their epic stand on 30 October 1914.

conform with the retirement of troops on their right. Beyond the above practically nothing is known of what occurred as the two squadrons and the machine-guns of the 'Blues' completely disappeared, and only very few survivors were taken prisoner, and on their return at the end of the war they were unable, I understand, to throw much light on the attack. My Regiment had an officer who was on the extreme left who managed to escape with slight wounds. According to his story which was somewhat confused owing to his being dazed, the attack was made by German infantry after a very heavy preliminary bombardment. I can only conclude that the squadrons were cut off owing to their somewhat forward position, and were ultimately all killed, though it is remarkable that there should have been so few wounded taken prisoner. Some of the trenches were very primitive, and I remember that one was much too deep to allow of the occupants seeing over the top, and they would hardly be in a position to offer any effective resistance. But on the other hand other trenches were quite well sighted, and the whole incident has always struck me as one of the most remarkable occurrences of the war. I fear that one must assume that the Germans behaved in an ultra-Hunlike manner and gave no quarter. According to one N.C.O. they did not trouble to remove the wounded who were left out, and he attributed his being taken to the German dressing-station to the fact that he was wearing a pair of leather gloves and may therefore have been mistaken for an officer.[21]

A German officer who was in this vicinity wrote of the battle in a letter home, making particular mention of the British use of aerial observation in order to gain the advantage:

The grave of Major Henry William Viscount Crichton, Royal Horse Guards, in Zandvoorde Cemetery. He was killed in action on 31 October 1914. (Pat Gariepy)

I'm sure that in my last letter I explained the significance which the English attributed to Ypres and the outlying villages of Zandvoorde and Hollebeke. Now, after the battle, we realise that their best troops were engaged; the guards, the Scottish and troops from colonial garrisons. Yesterday Zandvoorde and Hollebeke were attacked, so reads the official daily bulletin of 31 October. No one at home however realises the cost of defending a position, or the streams of blood which flow when it is taken. God be thanked that it is not our blood, but rather that of the English, who suffered enormous casualties.

The English efforts to hold the position, and through counter attacks to create a breathing space, were desperate. On Tuesday evening [27 October] at 5pm, we had hardly begun to rest, when the finest of the English cavalry troops, the Royal Horse Guards, attacked our fire trenches. The lie of the land meant that this endeavour was doomed to failure from the outset. The regiment was destroyed in a matter of minutes. By Wednesday our finest allies had arrived, the heavy artillery, the mortar, and the anti-aircraft gun. Now began a regular grinding of the position by artillery fire. The mortars in particular have a fearful impact. The anti-aircraft guns succeeded in shooting down five enemy fliers in two days, accompanied by frenetic cheering among our troops. The English fliers are unpleasant; they have no regard for one's peace. In less than an hour they dropped two bombs near the dragoons, unsettling their horses. Thank God they had no one hit. In the battle at Zandvoorde the fliers were eventually cleared from the skies, so that they would not report the approach of new divisions. By the Thursday evening [29 October] in complete darkness the new divisions were in position, silently occupying them, so that the English the next morning found themselves looking towards a huge mass of troops. The storming of their position was devastating for the English. It was a brutal fight, with rifle butts, bayonets, and knives all used. 2,000 English were taken prisoner there, that however is trivial, compared to the number of dead who lay in arms there ... Unfortunately phrases like, 'the great decision will soon come,' are frequently read in the newspapers in Germany, causing confusion. Everyone thinks that a new Sedan is coming for the English. However at present there is little chance. Through their many spies, through the airmen, and the wireless telegraph apparatus the enemy are able to match our movements and thus ultimately there is little potential for a breakthrough.[22]

Slightly to the north, German attacks near Hollebeke on 30 October had come to nothing – their heavy guns had inflicted little damage on the scattered cavalrymen and German infantry had made only half-hearted progress. Towards noon however the attack on Hollebeke village intensified. Some of the cavalry fell back (in good order it must be said) but the centre of the resistance in this part of the line rested on the defence of the bridge over the Ypres–Comines canal, which had not been destroyed by the Royal Engineers due to a shortage of explosives. The canal represented a significant obstacle and the Germans threw in attack after attack in an attempt to reach the bridge but all were thrown back. That the bridge was held so resolutely was in no small part due to the bravery of Lieutenant K.C. North of the 4th Hussars, who with one squadron and the Maxim detachment defended it all day. North was killed in the process by a shell, but part of the citation for his DSO read: 'The enemy were unable to reach the bridge, largely owing to Lieutenant North's handling of his machine-guns. One of these was knocked to bits and Lieutenant North was killed [but] the bridge remained in our possession until the 4th Hussars were relieved.'[23]

Three newly arrived battalions of the Indian Ferozepore Brigade, the Connaught Rangers, 57th Wilde's Rifles and 129th Duke of Connaught's Baluchis, were detached from the Indian Corps and sent in motor-buses to Hollebeke to reinforce the hard-pressed cavalry. These battalions went straight into action and all three regiments suffered heavily. Major Barwell, Captain Gordon and Lieutenant Clarke of the 57th were killed, and Captain Vincent of the 129th, Captain Forbes of the 57th and Captain Maclean of the 129th were wounded. The latter, unable to move, was left behind when the British retired, and Major Attel, Indian Medical Service, the doctor of the regiment, stayed with him; both were taken prisoners by the Germans, but shortly afterwards friendly troops retook the lost ground, and they were released. Many stories were also told of the gallantry displayed by another member of the Indian Medical Service in this episode, Captain Kanwar Indarjit Singh, the medical officer of the 57th Rifles. He was awarded one of the first Military Crosses here, but did not live to wear it, being killed in action the following month. The following day, history was to be made and even greater glory gained for the Indian Corps, when Sepoy Khudadad, a member of the machine-gun team of the 129th Baluchis, continued firing his weapon though

Shoeing Smith Herbert Sowden, 1st Royal Dragoons, killed in action on 30 October 1914 near Hollebeke.

Private Harry Edward Wood, 3rd King's Own Hussars, killed in action on 30 October 1914.

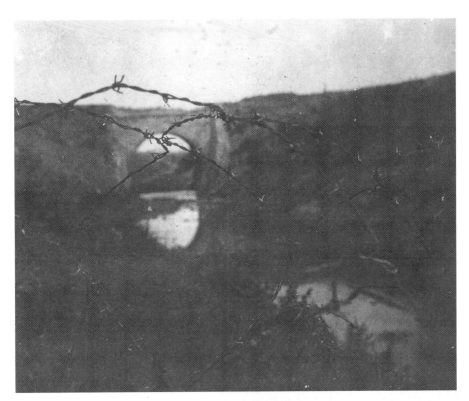

A remarkable and rare German photo, taken in the front line, of the bridge held by Lieutenant North.

Lieutenant Kenneth North, 4th Hussars, who held the railway bridge over the Ypres–Comines canal at Hollebeke with two machine-guns on 30 October 1914.

Sepoy Khudadad, 129th Duke of Connaught's Baluchis, the first Indian VC recipient. He is seen here recuperating in England after his act of bravery near Hollebeke. (Pat Gariepy)

wounded and when all the other members of his crew were dead, thus stemming the German advance. He was awarded the Victoria Cross, the first to an Indian soldier.

The 31 October was to be the most critical day of the battle for Ypres, possibly also the most critical day of the 1914 campaign, and certainly one of the most critical days of the entire war for the British. It dawned unusually warm and clear, and for the first time in Flanders the Germans were able to use a balloon to direct the fire of the heavy artillery with devastating effect. The main effort of the Germans on this day was directed towards the high ground of the Messines–Wytschaete ridge, in the southern half of the salient. The village of Messines, at the southern end of the sector, stood like a bastion in the British line. The village was defended by the remnants of three cavalry regiments, and a barricade constructed across the centre of the village was witness to bitter fighting as attack after attack was hurled at it. Captain Charles Blackburne, of the 5th Dragoon Guards, described his part in the fighting for the town in a letter to his brother:

> I had only just been back to report that we were driving [the Germans] back when I got word that we were to fall back, as on our left they had pressed our line

in. There had been a very strong attack there. It was very disappointing, as we were doing well on our side. We fell back, holding the town street by street. In the evening we re-occupied our side of the town and an attempt was made by some fresh troops to get round the flanks. But we had nothing like sufficient troops to do this as the Germans had pushed forward their whole line at this point. We held on to the side of the town we had fallen back to and there we were, Germans in one part and we in the other. We put up barricades across the street and they pushed a gun up to within a couple of hundred yards down the street and fired away at the barricade and adjoining houses, fairly bringing the place down about our ears.

My squadron was there until midnight, when we were relieved by other troops who held on until next day, but obviously it was only a question of time before we should have to evacuate it. If only we had been strong enough on the left to have held on we should have repulsed them. But once the left had to fall back we on the right were done, as they would have cut us off. Of course this is quite a small affair from the point of view of the whole show, and the falling back a kilometre at one point is of no consequence, but naturally we hated having to go when at our actual front we had driven them back. Our regiment did well and there were many brave things done that day. We had a good many casualties. Poor Captain Whitchurch was killed. He was a very good and brave officer, Wiley wounded; Collier Johnson bruised by a wall falling upon him, but he will be back, I hope, in a few days. At the moment, however, I have not a single officer in the squadron, so it is a bit of an anxious time. There is no doubt, however, that the Germans had far the worst of it. My squadron alone must have accounted for one or two hundred. I thought I would tell you about it, as you know just how I am feeling. I am very fit, and much looking forward to getting a wee bit of rest.[24]

The main focus of the attack on this day however was to be the village of Gheluvelt, astride the Menin Road. Stretched out in a line roughly 400yd east of the village lay the 2nd Battalion Welsh Regiment with one platoon actually on the Menin Road itself. To the north lay the 1st Battalion South Wales Borderers and to the south was the 1st Battalion Queen's Regiment. Just after 6am an attack began against these and the other battalions of the British 1st Division. By 9.30am the right flank of the Welsh had literally been blown out of its trenches by a concentrated artillery bombardment. Among the wounded was Second Lieutenant C.A.B. Young who recalled some sixty years later:

The Germans made their big drive against our position and they shelled it to hell. We hadn't got proper trenches. We were enfiladed because our trench left at right angles from the Menin Road and so we weren't really sheltered at all . . . we only had a little ditch. We tried to make it deeper before they started but it wasn't more than about chest more or less high and we were crouching in this and just getting plastered. Men being knocked down . . . every shell that came in knocked out about 10 or 15 men and then I thought well, this is no place to stop. I am going back to talk to the colonel (who was behind – about a hundred yards at battalion headquarters) to tell him that I didn't think I could stop there; we were losing so many men. On the way back I got hit [by a bullet]. I was wounded and had a broken pelvis. The Germans were attacking [now] and I went back and more or less collapsed, and my company commander tied me up and the Colonel, who'd been a very close friend of my father, detailed four men to carry me back, and I was carried back on a broken door as far as a horse ambulance, it was a one horse ambulance waiting about half a mile behind, and that rattled me down to Ypres, where I went into the first field dressing station. I'd had morphine but I was conscious. That night they put me on the Red Cross train to Bolougne.[25]

A good German description of this attack exists, penned by a sadly anonymous member of *Infanterie Regiment Nr. 126*. The author describes how, having driven the British from Zandvoorde the previous day, this regiment was then poised to be able to attack Gheluvelt, and the British 2nd Brigade, from the south of the Menin Road, in conjunction with other German attacks launched from the northern side of the road. The author must surely exaggerate the strength of the British defences, however what is not in doubt is the fact that this advance was met at first with unexpectedly stiff resistance, and the loss of the German commanding officer was a bitter blow:

By means of a well-executed attack we had driven the enemy cavalry from Zandvoorde, a place which had borne terrible witness to the destruction of war. Next on 31 October we advanced through woodland, which the English had heavily fortified with 10 to 20 meter deep barbed wire entanglements, up to head height. Behind this lay fire trenches reinforced with timber beams and planks. We attacked these, but with insufficient force. The attacks were failures. We then tried to break through against another position. Towards this we advanced, with several battalions bunched together. We hit the enemy with heavy artillery, field artillery, anything and everything.

These attacks succeeded, not due to artillery or technological means, but rather thanks to the great gallantry of the *Württemberg Regiment 126*, which was in the first line of the attack. I had believed previously that the wartime recruits were not very daring. That morning the colonel of the regiment was with us, and wanted nothing more than to lead the regiment into the attack, when he was hit in the head by a shell. He died that evening in our chateau.

When the men of the 126th heard, that their colonel was mortally wounded, they went bravely forwards with a marvellous bravura. Such men as Colonel von Schimpff are rarely found. He was not the only regimental commander who was killed. Naturally, among the fallen are always the best, the smartest, and the men often to be found at the most advanced point.[26]

Facing the Württembergers were the 1st Battalion Loyal North Lancashires, including Frederick Bolwell who recorded that after enduring two days under shell and rifle fire, 31 October was to be a day of disaster for his regiment. They were utterly overwhelmed by sheer weight of numbers and effectively ceased to exist:

Next morning, the thirty-first, the Germans bombarded us more violently than ever. This continued for several hours. The next thing was that we saw the Germans coming; and they did come – in their thousands. We kept them off for an hour or two when the CO of the King's Royal Rifles consulted us, or rather our CO, about retiring. I remember the two Officers having a heated argument over it, as they stood by a farmhouse immediately in rear of the line. I do not however, know what their argument was, but heard afterwards that the King's Royal Rifles had got short of ammunition. The words I did hear from our CO were: 'It's the General's orders that we hold the position at all costs, and this I'll do if I lose the whole regiment.' We continued to fire until the Germans were on our trenches and coming through the line the King's Royal Rifles had vacated on our left. I was in the third line of steps near the farm-house, where I overheard some of the conversation of the two CO's. Just in front of the King's Royal Rifles' trenches was a huge German Officer waving with one hand to the retiring Rifles to surrender and with the other waving his troops on. It did not seem of much good for us few men to attempt to fight that dense mass of Germans, but we did; and out of the thousand, or thereabouts, that we lined up with a couple of nights before very few got away, the enemy taking somewhere about four hundred of my Regiment prisoners and our casualties being about the same number.

I had a run for my life that day. A chum of mine who was with us had a cock-fowl in his valise that morning from the farm; he had wrung its neck but he had not quite succeeded in killing him; and, as we ran, this bird began to crow. As for myself, I had no equipment; I had run having left it in the bottom of the trench. It is quite funny as I come to think of it now – the old cock crowing as we ran; but it was really terrible at the time. We were absolutely overwhelmed, not only in our particular spot but all along the line, and had to concede nearly one thousand yards to the enemy.[27]

Bolwell was among the lucky few of this battalion who avoided capture – the rest were surrounded and eventually forced to surrender. Three companies of the 1st Battalion Gloucestershire Regiment – the only reserve that remained – were sent forward to try to rally the Loyals and other troops, but were themselves overwhelmed in the maelstrom. One of the officers of 1st Gloucesters was Lieutenant J.A.L. Caunter, who was taken prisoner in a sunken road immediately north of the Menin Road, 800yd east of Gheluvelt. He left the following account:

The Germans had broken through the line, and my party consisting of Major Gardner of my regiment, myself and 80 men, were detailed to go forward. We did so under cover, made a detour and came out behind the right part of the line which was still being held. We proceeded practically south to the gap made by the Germans. We rallied the men in a sunken road, only 30 men being left. We then advanced, but before we had gone 10 yards six German shells burst in the sunken road and knocked out 15 men and mortally wounded the major. I collected the remnant and brought in the Major, and looking south of the road saw that the trenches for about 300 yards were empty of British troops. The Germans then began to advance in dense masses with arms at the slope. We fired at them but they took no notice of us. Seeing that we could not stop them, I sent back half of my men to run back to the position in rear (two of them got through and reported to Lieut-Colonel Lovett CB), the rest of us started to follow them more slowly, carrying the Major. Just as we got out of the sunken road our own guns opened up and plastered us. We put the Major down and waited for our guns to stop. Meanwhile the Germans were advancing steadily. We fired at them as hard as we could, and while I was firing at one column about 100 yards off I heard a yell from one of my men, 'Here they are, sir'. It was another German column coming up a ditch. They were upon us before I knew that they were there. I dived into a hole. About a company of them came along and pricked us out of our holes with their bayonets. I counted our men afterwards by Menin church. There were about 13, four or five of them not of my company. There were no officers with the Germans at first, and the German men stood around us yelling like a crowd of pariah dogs. A private, who spoke English, prevented them from bayoneting me. They were Westphalians, an Ersatz regiment, number one hundred and something. They began tearing me to pieces. They tore off my equipment and in doing so tore my coat. One man hit me on the head with a gun. They went through my pockets but fortunately when they had looted my upper pockets our guns opened upon them and stopped them and they all lay flat on the ground.

After a little time some German officers came up and stood in the road yelling and waving their revolvers. Our guns got them nicely. After a short time, orders were given for the Germans to advance, and most of them did so. The rest went to the rear, making us run in front of them. Before being marched off I went up to a German officer and asked him in French about Major Gardner and the rest of the wounded. He said in French, 'They will be looked after all right in the evening when it gets dark.' I had bound up the Majors wounds when he was first wounded, and before we were taken away I got leave from the German officer to go round and bind up the rest of the wounded with the field dressings.

We were first halted at a field dressing station. On the way they had made us pick up a wounded German and carry him. I had to carry with the rest, though I protested that I was an officer. No dressing was done at the dressing station, but a doctor produced a long knife and made the action of drawing it across the throat saying, 'we do not take any prisoners'. I do not think he meant it, but I am sure some of the men did. Another doctor who could talk English said to me, 'You are very lucky to be alive as you were taken close to where the Bavarians were attacking and they take no prisoners'. I think, from what I heard from other officers and soldiers, that this was certainly true.[28]

In fact the Bavarian *Reserve Infanterie Regiment Nr. 16* advancing to the south had been badly weakened by the previous two days of fighting; so exhausted was it that when, on the night of 30 October, it received instructions that it was to attack and take Gheluvelt the following morning, both the regimental commander, Oberst Julius List, and the commander of the I Battalion expressed the view that it would be unwise to attack strongly entrenched British positions with tired troops, who had been without rest for three days now, and – interestingly – without adequate artillery support. (It seems that both British and German infantry at Ypres felt that they were at a disadvantage in terms of artillery.) Both officers however were overruled. Along with *Infanterie Regiment Nr. 105* and *Reserve Infanterie Regiment Nr. 247* they were ordered to take Gheluvelt the following morning. With a final handshake, resigned to their duty, the officers parted. The regimental history continues:

> At 4 o'clock in the morning in the depths of darkness the leading company advanced out of the trench; bayonets were fixed, waterbottles were inside breadbags in order to avoid unnecessary noise, and rifles as ordered were unloaded. No accidental shot would then alert the enemy. In two skirmish lines the I battalion advanced ... crossed a sunken field and ascended the slight slope of a hill. Rifle fire flew overhead. We edged forward until about 150 meters in front of the edge of the hunting park. Noiselessly lay the line on the ground, awaiting the time to attack. With clock in hand lay the commander.

Ludwig Kastlemeier, Infanterist in the Bavarian Reserve Infanterie Regiment Nr. 16 *(*List Regiment*), killed in action on 31 October 1914 near Gheluvelt. Note the flat-topped cap.* (Walter Lyneel)

At 6.30 came the signal to attack. Silently the firing line moved ahead, reaching the English fire trenches along the hedged fenceline of the hunting park almost without casualties. In the dark one saw individual shapes and little groups move and disappear – where was the enemy? The previous evening the position was strongly held. Had the enemy learned of our plans? Did an ambush await us? We occupied the trench and quickly equipped it for defence. Patrols searched the hunting park to check that it was clear. A report that the I battalion had reached the hunting park was sent to Regimental headquarters. The Regiment ordered the position to be held until progress was made on the right. It was 7am ... the day began to dawn blood red in the east. Far and wide nothing moved. Dull booms of explosions were heard from Polygon Wood.

... Finally at 8 o'clock came the advance in force. Step by step forward went the attack. Troops from three regiments worked here to drive the enemy from his strongholds and gain a vital objective. The English artillery fired furiously. The casualties grew from this heavy fire, as the enemy showed his defiance with machine-gun and rifle fire. In the hedges they lay and knelt, mowed down by gunfire, but always filling the yawning gaps with fresh soldiers. The difficulties caused by our shortage of artillery ammunition were noticeable, and they offered the attack little effective support. The morning passed in a tough, bloody struggle. The grim music of battle, a hellish concert, filled the air. The howling and whizzing of the heavy fire from the English naval guns, the steady bursts of shells, the rolling of machine-gun salvoes and the natter of infantry fire, rose into a hurricane. Rows plunged forward, only to retreat and advance again. It was madness to advance into this fire, but new waves pushed on, and all reserves were now deployed.

Finally about 3 hours later, the foremost strongpoint of the enemy, the wind-mill on the southern slope of the village, came under the encroaching fire, and was smashed by a few direct hits. That was the turning point – the way was now clear! Now the signal for a general advance was given ... in dense waves the Württemburgers and Saxons with our III battalion broke through the hedges and stormed over the windmill in a charge against the edge of the village. Momentarily the enemy fire slackened ... there at a critical moment over the whole battlefield suddenly rang out the 'charge' of the buglers! Backpacks were dropped, all rose up together to go forwards. A thousand-strong shout of 'hurrah!' echoed over the battlefield and in a wild surge our troops stormed the village. Gheluvelt was ours! The battlefield on the Ypres road was strewn with dead and wounded, an indescribable shambles, and the village was a scene of savage confusion. A short house to house struggle ensued, and then the enemy conceded the position. In these hours our regimental commander Oberst List was in the foremost battleline, amid the III battalion. With them he had gone ahead into the dense fire of the attack. When a platoon commander asked him not to expose himself to danger, he reassured him with the words: 'Have no worries about me! So long as I have such NCOs as you, there is not much danger for me!' During the assault on the hunting park of Gheluvelt, he met a hero's death.

The news of the loss of our splendid, beloved leader was a harrowing blow. However, everyone knew how little he had feared death, and how deeply he felt the responsibility of the lives of his men, and the painful loss went close to their hearts. To flinch was not in his nature! What right had we to look to our own salvation, when the commander had sacrificed himself? His body remained in Gheluvelt park until on 7 November a medical party of *Reserve Infanterie Regiment Nr. 247* ... gave him an honourable burial on the bank of a small lake near the Gheluvelt hunting lodge. His name remains forever sacred in the history of the regiment![29]

Joseph Helml, Gefreiter in Infanterie Regiment Nr. 105, *killed in action near Gheluvelt on 31 October 1914.*
(Walter Lyneel)

In the post-war clearing of the Ypres battlefields, Oberst Julius List was re-buried in the German mass grave at Langemarck. The achievement of his regiment on 31 October was however to be outshone by that of another, on the British side. The 2nd Battalion Worcestershire Regiment was almost the last available reserve of the British defence. Nearly every other unit had been drawn into the battle here and most were now wrecks; pale shadows of the proud formations that had landed in France. The Worcesters themselves could muster no more than 500 men. They were haggard, unshaven and unwashed, their uniforms caked in mud. Many had lost their puttees or their caps, but their weapons were clean and in good order, they had plenty of ammunition and three months of war had given them confidence in their fighting ability. The short period in which they had been in reserve had allowed them some sleep and a little food. They were still a fighting battalion, officers and men bound together by pride in the regiment and the discipline of Regular soldiers. Daybreak on 31 October had found the 2nd Worcesters in reserve positions west of Polygon Wood. After breakfasts were cooked and eaten, weapons were cleaned and inspected. Then for several hours the companies awaited the instruction to move.

By midday, the weight of the German attack against the British here had begun to tell. Gheluvelt was lost around 1pm and a sizeable gap had been driven into the British line. Unless that gap could be closed the BEF was in danger of being cut off from the coast. It was ordered that the 2nd Worcestershires should make a counter-attack to try to recover the lost ground. At 12.45pm A Company was detached to prevent the enemy from advancing up the Menin Road taking up position on the embankment of the light railway north-west of Gheluvelt. The company held the embankment during the following 2 hours, firing rapidly at such of the enemy as attempted to advance beyond the houses. At 1pm the remainder of the 2nd Worcestershires received orders to make a counter-attack to regain the lost positions around Gheluvelt, and at 2pm the battalion moved off in single file under cover of the trees to the south-west corner of Polygon Wood. Private John Cole was serving with the battalion, and wrote afterwards:

> We go into reserve but these days there is no rest as we are urgently needed to stop another breakthrough this time along the Ypres–Menin road. Fed up to the teeth we go forward led by our CO Major Hankey when out of the forest country come the grey hordes of Germans. At Major's command, charge! Our troops spreading out bayonets fixed and spreading out leaving it to luck how many come out alive. The German reaction was swift. A thunder of artillery burst among troops, gaps appeared but the waves of bayonets went on. More than a hundred of the battalion were killed and many wounded. These unshaven haggard men of the 2nd Worcs came face to face with the fresh faced Germans of the 244th and 245th regts tough youngsters with the swearing tommys [*sic*] in khaki with their remorseless cold steel stabbing, the heart went out of the Germans. They fled in a grey mass. Remorselessly the Worcs winkled them out. Some Saxons were able to sweep the sunken road with a withering enfilading fire from Gheluvelt, and fighting patrols went forward to clear the village itself, but Gheluvelt, apart from odd fanatics who still held out in small, ineffectual pockets was once more in British hands ... at one point along a wood in a ravine we were firing over dead

Franz Joseph Weber, a bugler in Reserve Infanterie Regiment Nr. 247. *He took part in the attack of 31 October against Gheluvelt.* (Walter Lyneel)

bodies as cover. A German badly wounded pulled out of his pocket a picture of his wife and child begging to be moved but we could do nothing our lines were not established and it was dangerous to hang around.[30]

Major Hankey was seriously wounded at the start of the attack but carried on none the less, supporting himself on the back of a chair. The advance took the Worcesters through the grounds of Gheluvelt Château, where they met the remnants of the South Wales Borderers, who had been clinging on defiantly to a position close to the ruined building, driving off all Germans who came near them. There were emotional scenes as the South Wales Borderers, who had more or less given up hope of escape, greeted their relief. The heroism of the Worcesters at Gheluvelt that day has passed into the realm of legend within the annals of the British army, and it is said that it was a former battalion commander, using the methods of Sir John Moore of Corruna a hundred years previously, who instilled in them the skills and initiative that led to success that day.

Late in the afternoon of 31 October on the 7th Division front south of the Menin Road, another remarkable counter-attack was organised. Earlier in the day the division had been forced back by hoardes of German troops advancing in thick masses. By afternoon however their advance was visibly slowing. The Germans were fatigued and their ranks had been thinned by British bullets – in particular many of their officers had fallen which caused them to waver. Now General Bulfin summoned every reserve he could find, and the shattered remains of almost every battalion in the division went forward cheering and shouting. Among them was Private H.J. Polley, one of the survivors of the 2nd Battalion Bedfordshire Regiment. He wrote later of 31 October:

> From start to finish the advance was a terrible business, far more terrible than any words of mine can make you realise. The whole Division was on the move, stretching along a big tract of country; but of course no man could see much of what was happening, except in his own immediate locality. Neither had he much chance of thinking about anything or anybody except himself, and then only in a numbed sort of way, because of the appalling din of the artillery on both sides, the crash of the guns and the explosions of the shells, with the ceaseless rattle of the rifles and the machine-guns.
>
> At the beginning, the regiments kept fairly well together, but very soon we were all mixed up, and you could not tell what regiment a man belonged to, unless he wore a kilt; then you knew that, at any rate, he wasn't a Bedford. Some of us had our packs and full equipment. Others were without packs, having been compelled to throw them away.

But there was not a man who had let his rifle go: that is the last thing of all to be parted from; it is the soldier's very life. And every man had a big supply of ammunition, with plenty in reserve. The general himself took part in the advance, and what he did was done by every other officer present. There was no difference between officer and man, and a thing to be specially noticed is the fact that the officers got hold of rifles and blazed away as hard as any man.

Never, during the whole of the war, had there been a more awful fire than that which we gave the Germans. Whenever we got the chance, we gave them what they call the 'Englishman's mad minute' that is, the dreadful fifteen rounds a minute rapid fire. We drove it into them and mowed them down. Many a soldier, when his own rifle was too hot to hold, threw it down and snatched the rifle of a dead or wounded comrade who had no further use for it, and with this fresh, cool weapon he continued the deadly work by which success could alone be won.

I do not know what the German losses were, but I do know that I saw bodies lying around in solid masses, while we passed our own dead and wounded everywhere as we advanced. Where they fell they had to stay; it was impossible to do anything for them while the fighting continued.

The whole of the advance consisted of a series of what might be called ups and downs a little rush, then a 'bob down'. At most, no one rush carried us more than fifty yards; then we dropped out of sight as best we could, to get a breather and prepare for another dash. It was pretty open country hereabouts, so that we were fully exposed to the German artillery and rifle fire, in addition to the hail from the machine-guns in the neighbouring buildings.

Here and there we found little woods and clumps of trees and bits of rising ground and ditches and hedges and you may take it from me that shelter of any sort was very welcome and freely used. A remarkable feature of this striving to hide from the enemy's fire was that it was almost impossible to escape from the shells and bullets for any appreciable time, for the simple reason that the Germans altered their range in the most wonderful manner. So surely as we got the shelter of a little wood or ditch, they seemed to have the distance almost instantly, and the range was so accurate that many a copse and ditch became a little graveyard in the course of that advance.[31]

Only at Messines, where fighting had stuttered on all day, did the situation continue to cause concern to the British commanders. As dusk was gathering, history was made again as the London Scottish, the first Territorial battalion to see action in the First World War, were rushed forward to support the hard-pressed cavalry. It was a critical juncture and the heroism of the London Scottish narrowly averted disaster. Captain T. Kidson-Allsop took part in the action, and was wounded. He stated after the event:

I was wounded in the charge of the 1st London Scottish at Messines, on the evening of October 31st, 1914, by a rifle bullet through the right lung, and when the Scottish retired I was left in one of the outbuildings of a farm that had been our dressing-station. I remained here for several days, and was hit again in the head by a bullet that pierced through the door.

The charge of the London Scottish at Messines, as depicted in a contemporary postcard.

I do not remember very well what happened the first few days. One evening [2 November 1914] a private in the London Scottish, whose name I have forgotten, and myself left the farm, with the intention of trying to gain our own lines. We had not gone more than a few hundred yards when we were held up by a German patrol. The NCO in charge of the patrol sent us back, under escort, and we were taken to a dressing-station, where our wounds were dressed.

From there we were escorted back by two soldiers, one of whom had repeatedly hit me in the back with his rifle. How long we were marching I don't know; I was very weak from loss of blood at the time, and had to rest every few yards. We passed a long file of stretcher-bearers, who refused to give us any help. Whenever I asked how much further we had to go the reply was always the same; 'Eine Stunde'. Some German cavalry passed us and I complained to the first officer I saw. He replied that he saluted me as a British officer, but would never forgive us for using black troops against them. I told him I was too exhausted to discuss the matter and he gave orders to the sentries, and within half-an-hour we arrived at another dressing-station, where our wounds were again dressed and I was given a mattress in a farm-house. The private in the London Scottish had been with me up till this time, when we were separated, and I never saw him again. He was wounded in the arm, and had been very good to me, helping me along and trying to stop the sentry hitting me.[32]

A fellow officer, Captain Ian M. Henderson, was also wounded late in the evening of 31 October, around midnight, and received similar harsh treatment from his German captors:

The party which brought me was still acting under the orders of the officer and passed me over with injunctions that I was to go in the next wagon that came. These men then left and I was in [the] charge of German Red Cross men, all armed to the teeth, most insulting and brutal. They did not carry out their instructions to remove me, but took away McCallum in the first wagon, though he could walk perfectly well, and again and again during the night passed me over though they could have perfectly well taken me. It rained very hard in the early morning, but, fortunately, I had a good coat and kept fairly dry.

In the morning masses of troops arrived and kept passing where I was lying, mostly Bavarian infantry; they deployed for attack just about this spot, and eventually a battery of field guns came up and was dug in about 50 yards behind the shed. All day these guns fired just passed us, and when spotted by an aeroplane (a Henry Farman), flying quite low, we were subject to a heavy fire from our shrapnel. It was some consolation for being under this fire to see the Germans suffer heavily. I was fortunate enough not to be touched.

No further effort was made to get the wounded away during the daytime, and we had to remain under heavy fire from our own guns. All day long I was subject to rudeness and insult from not only men, but officers who passed; they had evidently been primed by their superiors with a lot of false statements about 'dum-dum' bullets. One medical orderly spent most of the morning pointing a cocked automatic pistol in my stomach, and I think if there had been no onlookers he might have shot me; he was a brutal type of man, and used to watch me narrowly for any sign of my leg giving me extra pain: the moment he thought he saw some signs, he would shout, 'Gut! Gut! Schmertz.' This, as a matter of fact, was so comic that it made me laugh, but it shows the kind of spirit one encounters among Germans under the Red Cross. I complained of his conduct to a passing officer, who told him to stop, but seemed to regard it as a great joke.[33]

Naturally in the confusion of battle men became detached from their units and mixed up with neighbouring formations. Writing in his diary for 31 October, Private A. Moffat of the London Scottish recorded how near Wytschaete he had become confused in the darkness and advanced with the Carbineers, a dismounted cavalry unit:

> We advanced some considerable distance and line a ditch between some ploughed fields; there are only a few of us here, and great gaps on either side, and no reserves, and great masses coming on against us, things seem hopeless. Some of the Carbineers want to retire, but are ordered back. Then a man feeling fed up shouts out 'Lets charge the Beggars', so up we get, or rather some of us do, and go forward, but its useless as they run away, and we can't chase them as we should be shot down by our own men, who have not come on with us. Return to ditch again, and someone shouts, 'Reinforce on the left', so move there, as there is a big gap. Still the enemy are coming up in masses in spite of the 'rapid fire', which is going on. All around there are farms and haystacks burning. At last our officer tells us to retire, we do so, when he again shouts out 'Look there's one of our chaps can't someone go back and help him.' I say, 'Yes I will,' and turn back. I find that the poor fellow is one of 'ours', poor old Hopkins, shot in both knees, lift him up and try to help him walk, he falls and asked me to to try the other side, I do so, but he falls again, says its no use, but I try again on the other side, and again he falls, and insists its no use and I must leave him. All this time the enemy are coming up to us, and as I'm useless there for I cannot possibly carry him, I leave him hoping that they will have mercy on a wounded man, which they would certainly not have on me if I remained. I ran back to rejoin the rest who had been retiring during all this time, and as I neared them shouted out all the available English I could think of through the pitch darkness in order that they shall know that it is really one of their own men.[34]

Private Herbert Hopkins of Twickenham did not survive the battle, and given the statements of Henderson and others it seems unlikely that he would have received any mercy from the Germans that day. By nightfall an eerie calmness had descended on most of the battlefield, both sides having fought themselves to a standstill. At Bethlehem Farm, near Messines, the German writer Paul Oskar Höcker, captain in a *Landwehr* infantry battalion, was attempting to get some rest, after what must have been an exhausting day. As might be expected from a professional writer he paints a vivid picture of the situation, and the significance of the date was not lost on him:

> [it is night] but I may not sleep. Out from my breadbag I take my copy of Faust – it is no bigger than a matchbox – then my official notebook, then the latest *Deutsche Zeitung* (it is eight days old). Later I will spend a quiet night reading.

Next I take the writing paper and the indelible pencil out of the map case. I cast around; a box lies at the corner of the trench, it will serve as my writing table; an empty bottle with a candle inside it placed alongside. Thus it is that I, a modern warrior of the paper, will attempt in this strange subterranean existence, to write; at least in fleeting strokes. However paperwork is not easy. Firstly there are continual disturbances. Once, when an enemy patrol approached us, I had to douse the flame. The groundsheet offers us sanctuary only if the candle is extinguished. Gottschalt, the sergeant cook – at home he is a teacher – crawls over to me along the hedge, and as he reaches my dug-out reports to me in a whisper that the provision wagon has now appeared on the road nearby. We can now receive bread and bacon. The company is ravenous and quickly the word spreads of the presence near by of the food carriers. Canteens begin to rattle and deep voices murmur. 'Silence, silence, children!' I quietly exhort. With bread and bacon for [Leutnant] Rochlitz and myself comes Gefreiter Kern, quite a fearless man. We occupy the cellar of a shelled house, surrounded by rubble and debris. A box of sardines, a box of pineapples and six bottles of salvaged wine form the stock of our underground larder.

 . . . Nearby in a village the chimes of midnight can be heard. I hear quiet mooing of cattle, whilst chickens cackle. In the firing line an order is passed along, about the importance of keeping a close watch out, although we want to sleep. But it is unpleasantly cold. I am lucky, in that the Grenadiers have left a couple of overcoats behind in the trench. One has bullet holes in it. It is a dead man's coat. Suddenly Rochlitz draws our attention to the bank in front of us. In the moonlight there are visible six or seven figures. 'Engländer!' he whispers tersely. Yes, they are English. But they will carry out no more raids. They are dead. The brown shadows appear eerie now in the cold moonlight. . . . It is All Souls Day . . .[35]

Not all Germans were at rest however. Nearby at Wytschaete, Bavarian and other troops were preparing to launch a night attack and at at 1.30am on 1 November a heavy barrage accompanied by infantry attack developed against the remnants of the British cavalry and London Scottish on the Messines Ridge. Leutnant Karl Hofman, from Langenzenn in Bavaria, was serving with one of the attacking formations, Bavarian *Reserve Infanterie Regiment Nr. 21*. Later he wrote to his family describing the loss of Major Emil Schießl from Munich, one of the battalion commanders. Hofman, for his part, was to find himself an acting company commander in the wake of the battle:

Since Saturday 30th October we held our ground in a tremendous and violent battle against the English and French at Wytschaete. There is perhaps no other village which in this war has witnessed fighting as terrible as this. Day and night raged the battle, whilst we lay in our fire trenches. I am battalion adjutant of the 4th battalion of the 21st Regiment and as such was the faithful escort of Major Schießl both on horseback and on foot. Yesterday morning at a quarter to one – as we chatted cordially together – a heavy English shell landed near us and tore a 10 centimetre long hole across the back of Schießl's head. He died immediately without any cry of pain. My own head was about at the same level as his elbow, but through a wonder I stayed unscathed and was just overwhelmed by masses of earth. I helped with my own hands to dig his grave, I helped to carry his body and bury it, recited the Lord's Prayer and placed a bouquet of chrysanthemums upon his grave. The unremitting thunder of the guns continued through out.[36]

In spite of the loss of their senior officers, the Germans at Wytschaete found that there were simply too few of the Tommies ahead of them to form a continuous line, and they were easily able to infiltrate between their isolated posts. At first light, those British soldiers not already killed or captured saw that they were in danger of being surrounded, and withdrew.

As this campaign bogged down, the British deficiency in siege weaponry was beginning to tell. Sometimes desperate measures were called for – and taken. Artillery officer Captain W.E. Duncan wrote of an unorthodox use of a 4.5in howitzer to provide close support for the infantry:

There were trenches everywhere but no hand grenades and no trench mortars. It was decided that single field guns and howitzers must be

Franz Luger, of Bavarian Reserve Infanterie Regiment Nr. 21. *A career NCO, he fought with this unit on 1 November 1914.*

sent up to the front line for point blank or lobbing support of the infantry. In later days, the Trench mortar fraternity was known as the 'Suicide Club'. To use a field gun totally unsuited for the work was even more precarious.

On November 2nd I was sent up with a single howitzer to Veldhoeck on the Menin Road. We placed the howitzer in as sheltered position as we could find about 200 yards from the barricade on the road, and I led the gun limber, team and three drivers to the cowsheds inside a solid farmhouse with the usual fumiere in the middle. I explained to the drivers that they were safe from rifle fire and it was unlikely that the farm would be hit by a shell since it had trees in front of it. Then I returned to the howitzer where I experienced three miserable days. The only saving grace was, that the job was as exciting as it was dangerous. Our front trenches were heavily and accurately shelled whenever there was movement. At last I discovered the reason. On scanning the enemy lines I could see the top of a ladder protruding above the roof of a house and on the ladder was a man looking through glasses. He was not more than 200 yards from me, so I got a rifle and took careful aim. I was a fair rifle shot ... but I had never fired at a man before and in my excitement took up both 'pull-offs' on the trigger at the same time. I could see a puff of red dust as the bullet hit the roof; the man ducked, but five minutes later he was there again. This time I realised my fault, and he went down with a flop. The shelling ceased for two or three hours ... From a house at the barricade on the road I could see four German field guns in action, but had not got enough wire left to reach our gun. My signaller Gunner Milton volunteered to ride up and down the road 300 or 400 yards on a bicycle carrying each order. 'Add 100', 'Right 2°', and so on and we managed to inflict some losses on the guns, but the German gunners left the guns after each shell dropped and took to their trenches, they did not fire.[37]

Further north, the 1st Battalion King's Liverpool Regiment was part of a mixed force holding the line between Polygon Wood and the French troops at Broodseinde. Conditions in the line were by now fairly unpleasant to say the least, and to add to their woes, between 1 November and 4 November they were heavily attacked. Among the officers of this battalion was Second Lieutenant William Meredith. Writing to his parents on 6 November, his letter conveys something of the trying time the battalion had endured:

Between last Saturday week to Monday week we lost about a dozen officers – we had a really bad time – but thank God I managed to pull through alright. After it we stayed in the trenches another three days. I then went back for two days rest which proved no rest at all – as were [sic] still under shell fire. Then last Saturday we came up here to the trenches where we now are. It is an odd experience – we are at one point of our line only about 80 yards from the German trenches. It seems incredible. The only advantage is we don't get so badly shelled as they fear shelling their own men ... I see every prospect of the battle lasting as long as the battle of the Aisne. I am an awful sight as I have had no wash of any description for more than eight days – I did shave four days ago, but it made the rest of me look so dirty. I hope this letter will arrive – I intend to give it to my servant when he creeps up at dusk with hot tea and food tonight & he says he can

Philipp Jakob Renz, a postman from the Bavarian village of Eggenthal and a Gefreiter in Bavarian Reserve Infanterie Regiment Nr. 17. *He was killed in action near Wytschaete on 3 November 1914.*

get it off somehow. I hope he does as you must be getting anxious. I would like to move back 50 miles behind the firing line for a rest – the noise and continual strain is trying. We've been under a constant fire now for over a fortnight. I am sitting in my dug out & am writing leaning on my left elbow – at least it was my left elbow when I started but now I've lost feeling in it. Write me all the news.[38]

Conditions however were often little better for the Germans, though where possible they chose to site their trenches where they could be drained out. Unteroffizier Lothar Dietz served with *Kgl. Sächs. 6. Infanterie-Regiment König Wilhelm II. von Württemberg Nr. 105*, a Saxon regiment with its depot in Zwickau near Dresden. He describes the conditions around Hill 60 in early November in a letter to his parents:

Only 60 yards away from us are the English, and they are very much on the alert as they would be only too glad to get back our hill. We have a fairly decent trench up here, because we drain all the water into the English trenches lower down, but our neighbours on the left, the 143rd, have to keep two electric pumps going night and day, otherwise they couldn't escape the wet.

Six hundred yards behind here is our reserve position, a little wooded valley in which the most frightful hand-to-hand fighting has taken place. Trees and bushes are torn to pieces by shells and riddled with rifle bullets. All about in the shell holes are corpses, although we have already buried many. Any number of dud shells of every calibre have burrowed into the ground in the wood. There is a quantity of French equipment lying about. In the slope on one side of the valley we have constructed our dug-outs: holes in the earth, with plank floors, ceilings of tarred felt, and provided with small stoves which are certainly not enough to heat the place, but at least serve for warming up food, and even for cooking.[39]

None the less the battle had yet to run its course. The Germans were still determined to try to break through the Franco-British lines; it was a story of diminishing returns, as each attack left them weaker themselves, but that was of little consolation to those on the receiving end of a hurricane of shells. Around this time, the 4th Battalion Royal Fusiliers, veterans of the opening shots of the war, came into the line on the edge of Herenthage Wood, with French Zouaves on their left and the Northumberland Fusiliers on their right. Almost at once the battalion, now very weak, became engulfed in the crisis of Ypres. On 7 November the Zouaves were blown out of their trenches. The shelling continued all the following day, and several minor attacks were beaten off. The most serious blow fell upon Y Company, but was dealt with summarily. However, the Zouaves were forced back, and the Germans got into the wood, round the open flank of the Fusiliers. Half of Y Company delivered a violent counter-attack and penetrated to the German trenches, but few of these gallant men came back. The two officers who led it and sixty-two men were lost, but thanks to this charge and the advance of the nearby Duke of Wellington's Regiment, the line was restored.

On 11 November came the last large-scale attempt by the Germans to cut through to the coast. The attack was expected; the battalion order issued by the Adjutant, Captain

Münster-Palace
Madge.

This remarkable photograph was taken in a German POW camp. The soldier in drag is Lance Corporal Arthur Wolley 1st Battalion South Staffordshire Regiment, captured on 7 November 1914 east of Ypres.

George Thomas-O'Donel to the 4th Royal Fusiliers before it took place is notable. The order, which was to be read aloud to companies, ran as follows:

> It may be assumed that we are about to fight the decisive battle of the war. The German Emperor has arrived to command his troops in person, and Sir John French hopes that the British Army will prove to him that they are better men than the Germans. Both armies are composed of regiments more or less exhausted, and short of officers, and the result will depend very much on the prolonged energy of every soldier in the fight and the endurance shown during the next few days. Fire must be carefully controlled at night, men must assist to the

Captain George Thomas-O'Donel Frederick Thomas-O'Donel, Adjutant of the 4th Battalion Royal Fusiliers, who was with the battalion in the fire-storm of 11 November 1914.

last, be ready to cover every movement with fire, well aimed and well sustained, and there must be no straggling or straying from the platoons to which men belong. The CO hopes that every man will sustain the great reputation that the Royal Fusiliers have already made during this war.[40]

The morning dawned dull and misty, and about 6.30 a terrible shelling began, Thomas-O'Donel who was in the line, later described it as 'Much the most severe I have ever seen.'[41] It continued for 2 ½ hours. The front trenches were knocked to pieces, and many of the men were killed or buried. Then followed the infantry attack by the twelve battalions of the German *Guard Division*. The *Königin Augusta Garde-Grenadier-Regiment Nr. 4*, advancing south of the Menin Road, seem to have struck the Royal Fusiliers, and the little band of men received the first assault with the bayonet and hurled it back. Thomas-O'Donel by this time had been wounded, and only one officer of the Fusiliers was still in the front line. The *Garde-Grenadiers* delivered a second charge. Some of the Fusiliers were driven from their trenches, and their appearance in the rear created a panic among the battalion supports, who appear to have been chiefly special reservists, a draft that had arrived on the day before the battle and had not yet been organised into their platoons.

The fighting of 11 November around Ypres was probably the second most critical day of the entire battle, after 31 October (though on this occasion there was not the same sense of crisis as that day when Gheluvelt was lost). Though the Germans did not break through the British lines, they in fact did penetrate at a number of points, most notably at Nonnen Boschen, and there was certainly the potential to roll the BEF back into the sea. Any and all reserves the British army had were thrown into the front line. Much was made later by British veterans of the size and stature of the men of the Prussian guard units, but they met the same withering fire from the British as other German regiments. The German guards regiments comprised a fusilier battalion, a first and a second battalion. The history of *Kaiser Franz Garde-Grenadier-Regiment Nr. 2* (which was met by the 2nd Battalion Duke of Wellington's Regiment that day just north of the Menin Road) states that:

> The artillery preparation continued during the early hours of the morning and the assault followed at 9am. The Fusilier battalion overran the enemy's front position without difficulty and penetrated into the wood. As, however, the troops on either flank were not abreast of it, it was surrounded on all sides in the thick under-growth and suffered heavy losses. Attempts made by the I battalion to relieve it did not succeed in passing the enemy's front trench ... in the afternoon the Fusilier battalion had to be regarded as lost.[42]

Soldiers of Garde-Grenadier Regiment Nr. 4 Königin Augusta, *in Berlin before the outbreak of the First World War.*

In fact the Fusilier battalion had suffered casualties amounting to 15 officers and 500 other ranks. A letter survives from a young German guardsman who was present that day in the *3. Garde-Regiment zu Fuß* (3rd Foot Guard Regiment), the immediately adjacent regiment. The account is full of the usual Teutonic bravado, but is valuable none the less. It reads:

> On the 10th [November] our artillery bombarded the English fire trenches. That evening I received the news of [brother] Victor's heroic death, at the same time as the order to go into the attack, at 10am on the morning of the 11th. You may well imagine with what emotions and courage I proceeded. You will have read of the battle, because the English were overwhelmed by this massive attack. There were some sights to see here, like how the rifle butt was used as a weapon; we advanced too slowly using the bayonet, so we removed them. Then we could reverse our rifles, and as a result advanced much faster. We were so far forward, that we held a fire trench with the English, we were separated from them only by a breastwork; so we remained for three days, friend and foe in the same trench.[43]

Along with the *1. Garde-Regiment zu Fuß* (1st Foot Guard Regiment), they attacked the south-western face of Polygon Wood, and the account places this man directly opposite the lines held by the Black Watch, whose trenches were captured by the enemy on 11 November. The neighbouring unit, 1st Battalion King's Liverpool,

An artist's impression of the repulse of the Prussian Guard near Ypres, in 1914. The original sender of this postcard has identified the Maxim machine-gun in the centre as the most deadly thing that he and his comrades had to face.

recorded sardonically in its War Diary that it was '[now] supported on the right by the Prussian Guard [!]'[44] The King's soon received reinforcements from the 5th Field Company, Royal Engineers. There were no 'second-line' troops that day – all fought as infantry, engineers included. Corporal Arthur Chambers was a member of the 5th Field Company, waiting in reserve on the western side of Polygon Wood. His diary for 11 November records:

> The bombardment of our trenches is awful. Having breakfast in dug-outs at 7am an order to turn out at once is given, we all know that something serious has happened. We double across a field and learn from a wounded Jock they have broken through. Sapper Stone falls dead & we know by the crack of bullets that we are under heavy fire. The company is in rather a muddle & no one appears to know what to fire at. Six of us a little apart from the rest under Lieut. Collins spot the Germans right on top of us. We blaze away & many fall at such close range. Lieut Collins falls mortally wounded. The air is humming with bullets. The Germans, who are enormous men enter the wood on our right and we fear a surprise rush from there, a farm in the wood catches fire, and the smoke is blinding us. We continue to fire all day & pick off a great number of them. One big fellow got to very close quarters, but he had to give best to 303 at 20 yards' range. We hang on till 2.30pm & hold up the attack & learn that reinforcements are coming up on the right – the Black Watch, Ox & Bucks and the Irish Guards are advancing in skirmishing order on our right towards us. When they get level with us we all charge. I shall never forget the sensation, but it certainly isn't fear.

The Germans broke and ran for it, but we captured a good many. I got on ahead somehow with Lieut Renny-Tailour [*sic*] & six sappers & I fear that the company has been badly knocked about as men were going down all round when we ran on. Am lying in a turnip field with Lieut Tailour & six men & are under the German parapet isolated, as the others have been called off into the wood. We are in a warm shop. The machine-guns are sweeping the tops off the potatoes and turnips in which we are lying. Mr Tailour says we will make a bolt to the communication trench on the right but I think it risky to try. He makes the attempt but falls riddled with bullets. I crawl to him and find that he is dead, & I order the sappers to try to wriggle through the turnips back to the wood. French shells begin to burst all around and one of my sappers gets his wrist badly shattered. We all get in

Sergeant Arthur Chambers, 5th Field Company, Royal Engineers, awarded the DCM for the action at Polygon Wood on 11 November 1914. (Liddle Collection; reproduced with the permission of Leeds University Library)

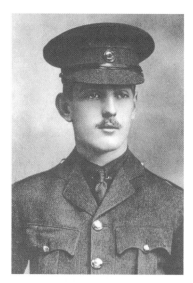

Lieutenant Henry Renny-Tailyour, 5th Field Company Royal Engineers. He was killed leading a charge at Polygon Wood on 11 November, after which Sir John French forbade RE officers from involvement in such actions, as they were too valuable.

eventually & I report that Lieut. Tailour is killed … But we have done a good days work & saved the situation. I am deeply moved at our losing 4 officers & 27 men … A staff officer has asked me my name.[45]

This last incident undoubtedly led to Chambers' award of the DCM. The history of the *1. Garde-Regiment zu Fuß* (which regarded itself as the 'most noble regiment in Christendom') confirms his account of events and further states that its two leading companies were:

Diverted by heavy flanking fire from right and left [and] turned right towards the strongly held Nonne Boschen, and left towards the white chateau in Herenthage Wood. Only a weak portion continued straight on, the companies in second line advanced over the captured trenches, received heavy fire from the right and turned against the strongly wired Verbeek Farm. Attempts to storm it failed, and the troops, like their neighbours, were forced to lie down and dig in.[46]

The Germans mounted a second attempted breakthrough on 14 November but this was a much weaker affair than that of three days previously, and met with the same result. The anonymous soldier from the German *3. Garde-Regiment zu Fuß* continued:

Our battalion commander [now] gave the order to attack. This was on the 14th and again we went forward with cheers against the hated English. On this day we took 200 prisoners and captured two machine-guns. Finally we had to come to a halt, since we were too far in front, and we were receiving flanking fire from three sides. Here we now entrenched ourselves, and had to wait until those on the left and right of us could also proceed. However, hardly anything was now possible, as this area is all swamp so that one cannot advance. Even in the fire trenches we stood ankle deep in water, so we built ourselves a foot rest, in order that we could at least stand dryly to some extent.[47]

German reinforcements continued to arrive in the Ypres area. In mid-November, *Infanterie-Regiment Herzog Friedrich Wilhelm von Braunschweig (1. Ostfriesisches) Nr. 78* reached the front here, the regiment being assigned a section of line approximately 5km south-east of Ypres at the foot of Hill 60, with the objective of continuing the offensive. The regimental history takes up the story:

16.11.14 At length, the two assaulting battalions (I and III) which had been selected by ballot, reached the sections of trench to which they had been assigned,

Guardsman Francis
Henry Sowden,
1st Battalion, Scots
Guards, killed in action
on 12 November 1914.

at around 5am. With delight, the troops of the *15th Army Corps (I.R. 126, 132, 143 and 172)* left the furrows in the mud (trenches would not be an appropriate term) in which they had lived up to that point, defying the weather and the enemy. The men settled in as much as the circumstances would permit. The dawn revealed a horrible scene to the soldiers looking over the edge of the trench. Shredded trees, houses completely smashed, the corpses of friend and enemy, still locked together in the embrace of death. In the farms, the carcasses of animals had begun to decay. Over the whole scene lingered the revolting odour of corpses, burned timber and the smoke of English lyddite shells. In this environment, the men spent the 16th November and the night of 16th/17th November. Already during this time serious losses had been sustained, because the enemy snipers, who were located in skilfully chosen positions, opened fire at every opportunity into the shallow and inadequate trenches. It was worst at the 'Totenecke' (Corner of Death) in the section of 10 company, which had to suffer eight dead and several wounded even before the main attack was launched. In this area in particular, the trench was not deep enough.

The departing troops of the *15th Army Corps* had warned the regiment of the deadly work of the English snipers and had advised them to remove the spikes from their helmets, because these would attract the attention of the snipers, lurking nearby. However the 78ers had moved into the position with the determined intention of being victorious in their attack, at what seemed to be a decisive moment of the Western Front. For them, such a measure was a sign of weakness. They answered with the ancient East Frisian freedom motto, 'Better to be dead than live as a slave'. A heavy artillery barrage fell upon the front line and reserve positions all day and for part of the night as well. Rations had to be brought some 3 km up to the front line – a difficult task because of the continuous rifle and artillery fire.[48]

At 1pm on 17 November *Infanterie-Regiment Nr. 78* made its attack. According to the regimental history the men cheered loudly as they left their trenches. For morale the men were instructed to sing the regimental song, Beethoven's *Yorksche Marsch*, however it was drowned out by the appalling din of battle. Despite the bullets and shells that sliced through their ranks, a handful made it to the English trenches, where hand to hand fighting took place. In total the attack cost the regiment 183 dead. It was one of the last German gasps as their efforts to break through at Ypres petered out. On numerous occasions their commanders had simply asked too much of their men, as physical exhaustion as much as British bullets brought many of their attacks to

a halt. One cannot however ever underplay the heroism and determination of the BEF in the battle that sounded its death knell as a Regular fighting force. So many of its men, who had spent years honing their skills as soldiers in the heat of India or South Africa, met their end in a cold, muddy field on the outskirts of Ypres. The final vale to the men of the BEF who stood their ground here must go to a German soldier, the editor of the *Berliner Tageblatt*, who was serving as a Reserve *leutnant* in Flanders at this time.

Unteroffizier Gerd Wibben, Infanterie Regiment Nr. 78, *killed in action at Hill 60, on 17 November 1914.* (Harm Dirkson)

After the battle he wrote a telling – and surprisingly candid – piece about the soldierly qualities of the British Tommy in his newspaper. In it he said:

> They soon gave us practical proof that they could shoot, for in the first few engagements our battalion was reduced to about half … we were at once struck with the great energy with which their infantry defended itself when driven back and by the determined efforts made by it at night to recover lost ground. In this it was well supported by its field artillery which … is at least as good as ours … The main strength of the British undoubtedly lies in the defence and in the utilization of ground. Their nerves undoubtedly react better than those of the Germans, and their sporting instincts render them easier than our men to train in shooting, and in the use of ground and patrolling. The hardiness of their infantry was very apparent near Ypres. The shelter trenches were so well constructed that they could not be discovered with the naked eye … my own observation shows me that the British are excellent at patrol work, which I cannot say of our men.[49]

High praise indeed, from one who had nothing to gain by such public admiration of his opponents. In the four years that followed, other British soldiers would come to Ypres, and much more fighting would take place here, as Belgium lived up to her reputation as the 'cock-pit' of Europe. However that extraordinary year of 1914, which had already witnessed so many dramatic events, had one further surprise in store.

Chapter 7

A Most Peculiar Christmas

It would not be appropriate to end this examination of the British and German armies in the battles of 1914 without discussion of the remarkable series of spontaneous – and never again repeated – truces that broke out in certain points of the line on Christmas Eve and Christmas Day. It may be tempting to think of the fighting dying away after the First Battle of Ypres and as Christmas approached, but in fact the Truce is all the more remarkable when one considers the fact that there was heavy fighting in some sectors right up to Christmas Eve.

From the Ypres salient, an anonymous Bavarian soldier wrote home to Landshut on 26 December to describe the events of the previous day. Only one Bavarian regiment participated in the truce in this area, the Bavarian *Reserve Infanterie Regiment Nr. 17* which faced the men of the BEF at Kemmel, thus allowing us to locate the events that he describes quite closely:

> I must straight away recount to you what occurred yesterday on Christmas Day in the part of the line held by our regiment. It was Christmas Eve and we sang 'Silent Night, Holy Night' in our fire trench, which in places is only 40, 50, 90, 100 and at most 150 metres distant from the English. After we had finished singing the English applauded, and afterwards sang also, at which we applauded; then an Englishman came out of the trench, waved and shouted 'Hurrah!' Others went further, and also shouted 'Hurrah!' across. One of our men, who spoke English, shouted back and then he went across without his rifle. We followed him, and we and the English reached out to shake hands. Many had a very pleasant time. We exchanged cigars, cigarettes, gloves whatever one had, with each other. Afterwards, until two in the afternoon, there was no shooting. During the day it happened that first one came out, then several; finally there stood together a group of 40 to 50. One Englishman even gave one of us a haircut. At New Year they intended to meet us again, if we were in the line. However we have now been relieved and are having three days rest ...[1]

By this stage in the war, more British Territorial formations were beginning to take their place in the line, alongside Regular battalions. Private E.R.M. Fryer served with one of the first such units to reach France, the Honourable Artillery Company, and he was also in the line in the Kemmel sector, opposite the Bavarians. He remembered a gloomy yuletide:

> We had Christmas Day in the front line, a thick fog making things even pleasanter. We dropped our plum puddings in the mud, and altogether it was

very dismal. However, the Boche was very quiet, and we had no shelling at all, so we were thankful for small mercies. This Kemmel had been the scene of a bloodsome conflict between the French and the Boche, and the dead still lay thick on the ground; there was one particularly nasty group of Frenchmen caught by some wire and mown down.[2]

Private Alfred Pollard was with the same unit, and provides a more detailed description of the events here at Kemmel:

We spent Christmas Day in the front line. At midnight on Christmas Eve we sang all the carols we could remember; the whole company in one huge chorus. After we had exhausted our repertoire there was a lull. Then the Bavarians started in their trenches. Christmas Day was uneventful. There was no shelling and both sides were unusually quiet. At noon [we] decided to let Fritz know we were on the alert and contemptuous of him. We climbed on to the fire-step and fired off five rounds rapid. There was no reply. Christmas dinner consisted of bully beef and biscuits and Christmas pudding. The pudding was supplied by

Captain E.M. Crawley-Boevey, Royal Sussex Regiment, attached 4th Battalion Royal Fusiliers, killed in action near Bailleul on 24 December 1914.

the kindness of the *Daily Express*. They were in tins, one between three men. We got a cup of hot tea to wash it down. The cold was intense; the ground was in the grip of a hard frost.[3]

Slightly further south was another Territorial battalion, the 1st/6th Cheshires. One of its members gave an account of events here, the animals present attributable to the fact that before the war came to this part of Belgium only a few weeks previously, it had been farming country:

Soon after daylight arrived someone in our lines began to play 'Christians, awake!' on a mouth organ, and the thoughts of the men in the trenches immediately turned to the folks at home, who they knew were living under better conditions than they were. It was, says one who was there, nothing but mud, mud, mud, a parapet and two strands of wire between us and the Boche, who was 200 yards away. After 'Christians, awake!' the Boche responded with the popular melody 'Come over here!' and lo! we saw the Boche coming out of his trenches and we wondered whether it was an attack. The Germans were waving their arms, and immediately our men went out to meet them in No Man's Land, where we fraternized. We ate their Sauerkaut, and they our chocolate, cakes, etc. We had killed a pig just behind our lines. There were quite a lot of creatures rambling about the lines, including an old sow with a litter and lots of cattle and poultry. We cooked the pig in No Man's Land, sharing it with the Boche. We also buried several dead French-men who were lying out there. So ended our first Christmas in the line.[4]

Private Joseph Killey of the 2nd Battalion Lancashire Fusiliers in a letter to his brother wrote of the truce near Ploegsteert Wood, not far away. Clearly the gifts from home were as important at this time of year as was the respite from warfare:

But as for fighting we have done nothing worth talking of since Xmas Eve but we might get a dam [sic] warm time yet like we had about a forenight [sic] ago . . . thank your lucky stars you are at home and not out here for on Xmas Eve and night some of our poor

Private Albert Victor Read, of the 1st/6th Battalion Cheshire Regiment. This battalion was one of the first Territorial units to arrive in France, and Read was with it when it participated in the Christmas Truce south of Kemmel.

chaps were near frozen to the ground as they were up to there [sic] knees in water & mud and on Xmas Day the [sic] was not a shot fired worth talking about for were [sic] we are I have heard them say that we have to wait a bit as we a [sic] to [sic] far ahead and we have to let the Lancs get up to make advance along the line when they get up. Well Ned the RFA has done a big share of the fighting up heare [sic] as it is all duels very near only a bit of sniping at night time when we relieve one another in the trenches which is 4 days in and 4 days out. We are out for the New Years Day but we were in all Xmas and I got Lillies card and pipe & tobacco which I was very thankful to her for sending them.[5]

No clearer contrast between the social classes of enlisted man and officer in the BEF could be provided than that demonstrated by Killey's testimony and that of Lieutenant J.C.W. Francis of the 19th Hussars. This unit provided the divisional cavalry of the 4th Division, in the southern part of the British line near Ypres. Though apparently not in the front line at Christmas, Francis never the less recorded his approval of the events of which he was aware in a diary entry:

Christmas Day: What a wonderful day no cannons going off no rifles, nothing, absolute peace. I have now quite forgotten there is a war going on at all, one goes

Private Joseph Killey of the 2nd Battalion Lancashire Fusiliers; he wrote home: 'on Xmas Day ... was not a shot fired worth talking about'.
(Courtesy of Manx National Heritage)

about wishing people happy Christmas everybody looks merry and bright and bar a wagon or two one might be in the most peaceful part of Europe. Everybody seems to have stopped doing anything as if by mutual consent too busy thinking about their plum puddings etc I suppose but it is perfectly ripping.[6]

Further south, Private H.A.Taylor of the 1st Battalion Cameronians, was in the line near Armentières. He remembered many years later the details of events and also a special memento:

The opposing lines were so close one could hear the Boche singing carols, they were Bavarians. Not a shot was fired during Xmas eve or Christmas Day and on Boxing Day only a sniper was having potshots, but no casualties were reported. On Xmas eve a corporal and I escorted the rations up the line, we made the usual distributions to companies including the rum issue and found that we still had a jar of rum left, we gave our drivers a good issue and sent them back to our lines. We sat, of all places, outside the cemetery of Houplines having a tot or two, listening to the singing of the troops. It was a beautiful night moonlit and serene. We heard someone approaching, it turned out to be our new Regimental Sergeant Major, he enquired what we were doing there, we explained that we were listening to the singing. We offered him our jar of rum, meantime I told him his batman had drawn his issue, by the time he left we were all merry, wishing us a Merry Xmas he made his way to Headquarters and we strolled back to billets, which was a large school building. Our Quarter Master was surprised when told of the singing etc. after two hours rest we were ordered to Steenwerck our rail-head to collect the Princess Mary's gift box to the British Expeditionary Force. It was an ornamented brass box, bearing the portrait of her and allied flags, containing cigarettes and tobacco. Everyone received his box, even those in hospital and next of kin of those killed of my regiment had one sent to them. I still have mine, polished and in a prominent place.

At the railhead were three trucks loaded with large bundles of gifts for Scottish troops at the front, just that, no specific regiment being mentioned. Our

The tin and its contents sent by HRH Princess Mary's fund to soldiers in France at Christmas 1914. This example belonged to Private Bernard Smith of the 1st Battalion Leicestershire Regiment, who sent it home to his mother in Leicester.

Q.M. Seargeant marked twenty of these bundles, '1st Batt. The Cameronians BEF' and ordered us to load them on our G.S. waggon. Inside them, after opening, were everything from shaving soap to socks, balaclava caps, sweets and a host of other things including cigarettes and plenty of well wishing notes from the donors, [and] many a romance commenced through these innocent notes.[7]

Possibly the freely available rum had a worse effect on some than on others. Captain R.C. Money was in the same battalion and recalled that while there was no fraternisation, one soldier decided upon his own impromptu Christmas celebration:

So far as I know the only unrecorded incident was that one of our jocks, who had seen the rum rather too frequently, paraded down No Mans land, being cheered

A Christmas card sent home to his mother in the Leeman Road area of York by Private John Knott, King's Royal Rifle Corps, at Christmas 1914.

by the Germans, and an officer in the Royal Welsh Fusiliers whose front he had got onto by this time requested him to come in, and Jock replied, in terms that Jock was wont to use, that if he was wanted he could come and fetch him! It did lead to trouble in due course for the poor man, when he was sobered up![8]

Private Frank Richards was serving with the neighbouring battalion, the 2nd Royal Welsh Fusiliers, and although he does not confirm the incident with the drunken Cameronian, he none the less has provided a detailed account of events from the point of view of his battalion. He wrote:

On Christmas morning we stuck up a board with 'A Merry Christmas' on it. The enemy had stuck up a similar one. Platoons would sometimes go out for twenty-four hours rest – it was a day at least out of the trench and relieved the monotony a bit – and my platoon had gone out in this way the night before, but a few of us stayed behind to see what would happen. Two of our men then threw their equipment off and jumped on the parapet with their hands above their heads. Two of the Germans done the same and commenced to walk up the river bank, our two men going to meet them. They met and shook hands and then we all got out of the trench. [An officer] rushed into the trench and endeavoured to prevent it, but he was too late; the whole of the company were now out, and so were the Germans. He had to accept the situation, so soon he and the other company officers climbed out too. We and the Germans met in the middle of no-man's-land. Their officers was also now out. Our officers exchanged greetings with them. . . . We mucked in all day with one another. They were Saxons and some of them could speak English. By the look of them, their trenches were in as bad a state as our own. One of their men, speaking in English, mentioned that he had worked in Brighton for some years and that he was fed up to the neck with this damned war and would be glad when it was all over. We told him that he wasn't

Bringing good cheer to the troops in France: the Royal Engineers Postal section, Christmas 1914.

the only one that was fed up with it.... . The German Company-Commander asked [our officer] if he would accept a couple of barrels of beer and assured him that they would not make his men drunk. He accepted the offer with thanks and a couple of their men rolled the barrels over and we took them into our trench ...[9]

To the south, at L'Epinette, the line was held by the 1st Battalion Royal Fusiliers. A soldier serving with this battalion wrote of the truce in a letter to his sister. Tantalisingly the soldier is identified only as Ted, but on his part of the front the beer was going in the opposite direction:

On Christmas Eve, the Germans stopped firing, and our chaps did the same. No firing was done that night, and on Xmas Day our chaps, ready for sport, went over to the Germans and shook hands with them. We exchanged beer and cigarettes for wine and cigars, and one of the Germans cut off all his buttons and gave them to one of our men in exchange for a pair of puttees. Then we took a football over, and we were just going to play them a match when along came one of their fussy officers, three parts drunk, and raised Cain. He went off shocking, and ordered them back again, so we played ourselves, and they watched us and cheered. This is the truth, but as soon as 12 o'clock came, we started to fight again.[10]

Alongside the Fusiliers in the British 6th Division, was the 1st Battalion Leicester-shire Regiment, in the Rue du Bois district of the Armentières sector. Sergeant E.B. Hayball of this unit wrote:

Christmas Eve found the Battalion trenches covered with snow, and a brilliant moon lit up No Mans Land and the enemy trenches. After dusk the sniping from the German trenches ceased and the enemy commenced to sing; their Christmas carol grew louder as their numerous troops in the reserve trenches joined in, and eventually ended with loud shouts and cheering. 'A' Company of our battalion then began a good old English carol, the regiments on right and left joining in also, and this was received by the enemy with cheers and shouts of 'Good! Good!'
    On Christmas Day snow fell heavily, and as the enemy did not snipe when the men exposed their heads, several of 'B' Company got out of their trench and stood upright in full view of the enemy; they were surprised to see the Germans do likewise, waving their hands and shouting in broken English ... At dusk the sentries manned the parapet as usual, but the enemy remained quiet ...[11]

In fact, Hayball is wrong in this last assertion as one man from this battalion was indeed sniped on Christmas Day. Lance Corporal George Sutton was shot and killed late on the afternoon of 25 December, his friend Private Bernard Smith was standing next to him at the time, and the tragic incident remained with him for the remainder of his days. At Christmas in later years he would recount to his daughter the story of how a German shouted a warning, but a shot followed all too quickly.
    On the nearby Bois Grenier front, the Signals officer of 22nd Brigade Captain Richard O'Connor (later General Sir Richard O'Connor) was in the habit of visiting

the units of his brigade in the front line each morning. He remembered his astonishment on one of his regular inspection visits to find a truce in full swing:

> My Brigade was in the line ... and I went down on Christmas morning to the various units that I always used to go to and I saw it just start. I saw the enemy come over with white flags and then various people on our side walked out, and I amongst them, and we ... eventually came and talked to the Germans, and some agreement was arrived at about burying the dead; and I remember meeting one officer who was a German who said that he had been a member of the RAC but had been taken off it at the outbreak of war. However we went on. I stayed there a good deal of the morning and then went back and told the General about it ... some of his staff officers came out without red hats and had a look around and found out all there was to be found out and eventually we returned ...[12]

Private Bernard Smith (seated) and his friend Lance Corporal George Sutton, who was killed on Christmas Day.

After O'Connor had left, explicit instructions were issued to the front-line troops that the truce was to end forthwith, which it did, with both sides returning to their lines. As O'Connor noted, often the truce had a practical motive, that of providing a proper burial for the many corpses that littered no-man's-land. Lieutenant W.B.P. Spencer of the 2nd Battalion Wiltshire Regiment wrote to his mother on 28 December of just such a task:

> Well here we are again after a very cold Xmas in the trenches. We went in on Xmas eve and saw about 9 or 10 lights along the German lines. These I said were Xmas trees and I happened to be right. There was no firing on either side during the night, which was one of very severe frost. On Xmas Day we heard the words 'Happy Christmas' being called out whereupon we wrote up on a board 'Gluchliches Weinachten' and stuck it up. There was no firing so by degrees each side began gradually showing more of themselves and then two of them came halfway over and called out for an officer. I went out and found that they were

Lieutenant W.B.P. Spencer, Wiltshire Regiment, wearing the British army's winter-issue goatskin coat. (Liddle Collection; reproduced with the permission of Leeds University Library)

willing to have an armistice for 4 hours and carry our dead men back halfway for us to bury. A few days previous we had had an attack with many losses. This I arranged and then – well you could never imagine such a thing. Both sides came out, met in the middle, shook hands, wished each other the compliments of the season and had a chat. This was a strange sight between two hostile sides, then they carried over the dead. I won't describe the sights which I saw and which I shall never forget. We buried the dead as they were, then back to the trenches with the feeling of hatred growing stronger after what we had seen. It was strange after just shaking hands and chatting with them. Well it was a very weird Xmas Day. There was very little firing during the two days.[13]

Sergeant Jim Davey of the 2nd Field Company Royal Engineers, part of the same division, wrote in his diary of the opportunity that the Truce presented for defensive work:

[Christmas eve] Went out at 8pm with a sapping party to work all night. When we got in the trenches we found our infantry and the Germans out between the two lines talking to each other and exchanging things. Went over myself and exchanged p[laying] cards and cigarettes with a German officer. Being Xmas eve both sides in this quarter ceased firing by mutual understanding. Everyone walking on top of trenches so we did our job on top. Could hear them singing all night.

Boxing Day: Went to the trenches at 7.15am. Still no firing in our quarter everyone knocking about on top. Most peculiar Christmas I've ever spent and ever likely to. One could hardly believe the happenings. Bitterly cold all day & snowing slightly. Xmas pudding for dinner. Rum issue at night.[14]

Captain R. Archer-Houblon was a Royal Horse Artillery Forward Observation Officer close by in the front-line trenches at La Boutillerie. He remembered taking the opportunity for exploration of no-man's-land:

I was still up in the trenches, but the Yorkshires had relieved the Bedfords on Christmas Eve. Christmas Eve was a clear bright frosty night, and all through the long evening hours the Germans had been very merry and singing all along the line. They had, too, a violin, a cornet, a flute and an accordion, and the strains of these, together with several men with remarkably good voices, could be heard in the still sharp air as clearly as if they had been but a few short yards away. While we were looking out over the parapet and listening to the concert, suddenly we became aware of a voice in No Man's Land calling out to us not to shoot, and proposing that someone should come out to discuss and arrange a truce to celebrate Christmas the following day. After some hesitation the company com-mander, a subaltern who knew a little German, went out to meet the emissary and, I think, finally agreed that if we could get permission we would put a flag on the parapet the next morning. Christmas morning was bitterly cold and dawned in a dense blinding fog; not twenty yards could be seen from the trenches, so, forgetting all about the proposal for a truce, I seized the opportunity to go out and explore the ruins of La Boutillerie. Then, somewhat later, I returned, when as

I approached our trench the mist began to rise, and presently to my astonishment disclosed a No Man's Land filled with numbers of unarmed Germans! They had not troubled to wait for a flag to appear on our parapet, but had flocked out of their trenches in the fog, and here was the truce in full swing, a 'fait accompli'! What was to be done? As a matter of fact, before anything could be done, everyone had climbed out into the open and had joined in the fun. It was of course not long before urgent messages began to come from in rear to put a stop to the proceedings; but though it was naturally frowned upon by the authorities, there was however no real harm in the truce. It was due simply to sheer curiosity. Many of us, even among those who had been out quite long, had never seen a hostile German at such close quarters before; and not only to see them close, but also to be able to examine every detail of their features and uniform, was a temptation no keen soldier could resist. In fact it was all most deeply interesting. They were, as far as I can remember, the 16th Prussians, and they looked very clean and bright, we thought, and like everyone else they said that they wished the war was over. One said that he had lived in Brighton, another that he had been to school in Birmingham, and a third, an officer, had lived most of his life in America – details lamentably dull now, but amazingly interesting when told us in No Man's Land by an enemy in time of war. I exchanged one of our newspapers for a German one, and the men dealt in all sorts of odds and ends.[15]

A German newspaper exchanged in no-man's-land by Major R. Archer-Houblon for a copy of the Daily Mail, *during the Christmas Truce.*

In fact, Archer-Houblon retained the copy of the *Täglichen Rundschau* which he had received in exchange for a copy of the *Daily Mail* for the rest of his life, a prized memento of one of the most extraordinary incidents in the history of warfare.

Second Lieutenant M.D. Kennedy of the 2nd Battalion Cameronians was in the line near Neuve Chapelle, where a truce was signalled by the Germans somewhat earlier than on other parts of the front:

> With us it wasn't Christmas Eve, it was 23rd December. One of my men suddenly called out to me and said to me 'There are some Germans Sir, out there, they are getting out of their trench and waving to us!' Well I was wondering what to do about it, I had a look, they were obviously friendly, but I got an order from my company commander, 'Count the Germans, but on no account go out to meet them.' So that's what happened. This went on for most of that day. That evening we were relieved in the trenches, and while that was happening the Germans started singing Christmas carols. As far as my company was concerned there was no fraternising, but in the company on my left, they allowed two Germans to come over and they met in the middle.[16]

This account seems to chime with that of Karl Aldag, a philosophy student at Marburg before the war, and now serving with one of the German reserve regiments. He was in the Fournes area, south of Armentières, and wrote to his parents:

> Christmas at the Front! We were relieved on the evening of the 23rd around 10 o'clock. The English had been singing hymns, including a fine quartet. On our side too the beautiful old songs resounded, with only now and then a shot in between. The sentry posts in the trenches were decorated with fir branches and tinsel from home, also the dug-outs ... it was the clearest, most beautiful night

German soldiers unpack Christmas boxes sent from home, December 1914.

we have had for a long time, just as still and pure as Christmas ought to be. It was freezing too, which put an end to the mud and filth. I thought much about home ...[17]

The line south of here was held by the Indian Corps, and Captain Alexander, of the Indian Mule Corps, remembered that the Sikh and Muslim soldiers under his command were also provided for with royal gifts:

> The village in which our billets lay was called Burbure, and here we spent Christmas Day which was fine and frosty – one of the nicest days we had had for some time. In the morning Rennison and I paid a visit to the refilling point to exchange the season's greetings with our friends. There was a larger crop of presents than ever. Sergeant Grainge, the quartermaster, required extra carts to carry them away. Every man had a Christmas card from the King and Queen, with photographs of their Majesties. Princess Mary's present of an artistic box, containing a pipe, tobacco and a packet of cigarettes, was distributed to all ranks. From Queen Mary also each man received a pair of socks. All these were highly appreciated, and many announced that of course they would not wear the socks: they would be treasured for all time. After the distribution on parade of the royal presents, Ressaidar Amir Khan called for three cheers for the King and Queen, and three more for the Badshahzadi (the Princess). These were given with great enthusiasm ... A turkey purchased in Bethune, and a plum-pudding from England made our Christmas dinner reminiscent of home.[18]

It was a remarkable conclusion, to an extraordinary four months. Nothing like the Truce would be seen again in the ensuing four years of war, just as nothing like the battles of those four months would ever be seen again. Europe was on the cusp of history, turning away from battles waged by glittering cavalry and combat conducted like it was a summer exercise on Salisbury Plain or the Juteborg, towards an industrialised, impersonal form of war. Henceforth, men were to be just the fodder, fed into its voracious jaws.

The first five months of the Great War had borne witness to bitter fighting, with selfless heroism and bitter savagery abundant in equal measure. If the protagonists believed that the rule book of warfare had been torn up in the campaign of August to December 1914, little were they to know that this was just the curtain raiser for the next four years. If the men of the BEF were to overcome an enemy as numerous, resourceful and powerful as the Germans had proved themselves to be in the battles from Mons to Ypres, it would require every ounce of resolve that they possessed. The final word in this goes to a British soldier writing home just before Christmas 1914. This man, Private Clement Ruscoe, had been in France since the initial landing of the Expeditionary Force in August. In his letter he told his former employer:

> I think the Germans by this time will know that the British Tommy is a terrible being once he is properly aroused. The Germans have gone the proper way about things to fairly rouse our men, by their ferocious and wanton behaviour in Belgium, and there can be no turning back until the power for a repetition of this terrible work is forever taken out of their hands.[19]

Christmas Day 1914 in the front line, but no fraternisation; men of the Black Watch in trenches near Givenchy. (Liddle Collection; reproduced with the permission of Leeds University Library)

If, as many assert, the British Regular had arrived in France in August 1914 with a professional soldier's disinterest in who or what his enemy was and what he represented, then his direct first-hand experience of that enemy, and what he was capable of, bred in him a desire to smash German militarism once and for all. It was a conviction that would stay with and sustain the BEF through four brutal and bloody years on the Western Front.

Notes

Introduction
1. Edward Packe, unpublished memoir.
2. Thomas Burke, *The German Army from Within*, London, 1914, p. 83.

Chapter 1
1. James E. Edmonds, *Military Operations France & Belgium, 1914*, Vol. I, London, 1922, p. 63.
2. E. Thomas, 'I Fired the First Shot!', in Sir John Hammerton (ed.), *The Great War . . . I was There!* , London, n.d., p. 41.
3. W. Wildgoose, unpublished manuscript recollections, Liddle Collection, University of Leeds.
4. Quoted timings of events during the Battle of Mons are often difficult to reconcile, both between British and German accounts and even between different British accounts. This is in part due to the fact that German time was an hour ahead of GMT, but also due to the fog of war.
5. Quoted in *Memorials of Rugbeians who fell in the Great War*, Vol. 1, Medici Society Ltd, 1916.
6. Quoted in Walter Wood, *Soldiers' Stories of the War*, London, 1915, p. 83.
7. *Ibid.*
8. Quoted in A. St John Adcock, *In the firing line: stories of the war by land and sea*, London, 1914, p. 43.
9. WO 161/95/100, 526, The National Archives, London.
10. Quoted in H.C. O'Neill, *The Royal Fusiliers in the Great War*, London, 1922, p. 60.
11. WO 161/99/145, 1929, The National Archives, London.
12. WO 161/99/243, 2336, The National Archives, London.
13. Sidney Godley interview, BBC Radio (recorded 15 April 1954); British Library Sound Archive reference 1CDR0001911.
14. Raimund Von Gleichen-Ruszwurm and Ernst Zurborn, *Die Schlacht Bei Mons*, Oldenburg, 1919, p. 30.
15. Quoted in Sir Reginald U.H. Buckland, 'Demolitions Carried Out at Mons and During the Retreat', *The Royal Engineers Journal* (March 1932), p. 22.
16. C.G. Martin VC, tape-recorded recollections, Liddle Collection, University of Leeds.
17. Quoted in Wood, *Soldiers' Stories of the War*, p. 6.
18. Malcolm Vivian Hay, *Wounded and a Prisoner of War, by an Exchanged Officer*, Edinburgh, 1916, p. 46.
19. Quoted in Alwin Wünsche, *Kriegslesebuch über den Krieg von 1914; die besten Kriegserzählungen aus Deutschen, österreichischen und schweizerischen Zeitungen, als Vorlesebuch für den Schulgebrauch, hrsg. von Dr. Alwin Wünsche*, Leipzig, 1915, p. 77.
20. Quoted in Gustav Manz (ed.), *Von Flandern bis Polen; Feldpostbriefe der Täglichen Rundschau aus dem Weltkriege*, Berlin, 1915, p. 108.
21. Heinrich Heubner, *Unter Emmich vor Lüttich, unter Kluck vor Paris*, Schwerin i. Mecklb., 1915, pp. 70–4.

22. Quoted in J.A. Kilpatrick, *Tommy Atkins at War, As Told In His Own Letters*, New York, 1914, p. 85.
23. Quoted in Buckland, 'Demolitions Carried Out at Mons and During the Retreat', p. 23.
24. Harry Beaumont, *Old Contemptible*, London, 1967, p. 34.
25. WO 161/98/551, 34, The National Archives, London.
26. Quoted in Kilpatrick, *Tommy Atkins at War*, p. 78.
27. Walter Bloem, *The Advance From Mons*, London, 1930, p. 69.
28. *Ibid.*, p. 73.
29. *Ibid.*, p. 75.
30. G.R.P. Roupell, tape-recorded recollections, Liddle Collection, University of Leeds.
31. J.B.W. Pennyman, *Diary of Lieut J.B.W. Pennyman*, Middlesbrough, 1915, pp. 6–7.
32. *Ibid.*, pp. 7–8.
33. *Ibid.*, pp. 8–9.
34. Ernst Zipfel, *Geschichte des Infanterie-Regiments Bremen (1. Hanseatisches) Nr. 75*, Bremen, 1934, p. 44.
35. *Ibid.*, p. 46.
36. John Lucy, *There's a Devil in the Drum*, London, 1938, p. 113.
37. Thomas Christopher O'Donnell, recollections published on www.firstworldwar.com.
38. Arthur Corbett-Smith, *The Retreat From Mons, By One Who Shared In It*, London, 1916, pp. 79–82.
39. Quoted in Joachim Von Delbrück, *Der Deutsche Krieg in Feldpostbriefen*, 8 vols, Munich, 1915, Vol. V, p. 40.
40. Gustav Schubert, *In Frankreich Kriegsgefangen, meine Erlebnisse auf dem Vormarsch der 1. Armee durch Belgien und Frankreich sowie in der Französischen Kriegsgefangenschaft*, Magdeburg, 1915, p. 37.
41. Arthur Nugent Floyer-Acland, unpublished typescript diary, Liddle Collection, University of Leeds.
42. Arthur Nugent Floyer-Acland, tape-recorded recollections, Liddle Collection, University of Leeds.
43. Arthur Nugent Floyer-Acland, unpublished typescript diary, Liddle Collection, University of Leeds.
44. Paul Oskar Höcker, *An der Spitze meiner Kompagnie*, Berlin, 1915, pp. 69–70.

Chapter 2
1. Emile Audrain, manuscript diary, Liddle Collection, University of Leeds.
2. *Yorkshire Post*, 4 January 1919.
3. Herbert Arthur Stewart, *From Mons to Loos, being the Diary of a Supply Officer*, Edinburgh, 1916, p. 25.
4. Heubner, *Unter Emmich vor Lüttich, unter Kluck vor Paris*, pp. 76–82.
5. *Times Literary Supplement*, 11 September 1919.
6. Cordt Von Brandis, *Die Stürmer von Douaumont: Kriegserlebnisse eines Kompagnieführers*, Berlin, 1917, p. 19.
7. *Ibid.*, p. 20.
8. WO 95/1571, The National Archives, London.
9. Sir Roger Chance, tape-recorded recollections, Liddle Collection, University of Leeds.
10. Harry Easton, manuscript recollections, Liddle Collection, University of Leeds.
11. Quoted in Kilpatrick, *Tommy Atkins at War*, p. 47.
12. Easton, manuscript recollections.
13. Quoted in Alfred W. Pollard, *Two Brothers; Accounts Rendered*, London, 1917, p. 35.
14. *Isle of Man Times*, 26 September 1914.
15. John Trusty, tape-recorded recollections, Liddle Collection, University of Leeds.
16. Corbett-Smith, *The Retreat From Mons*, pp. 148–50.
17. Quoted in Wood, *Soldiers' Stories of the War*, p. 237.
18. Quoted in Kilpatrick, *Tommy Atkins at War*, p. 41.

19. Benjamin O'Rorke, *In the Hands of the Enemy: Being the Experiences of a Prisoner of War*, London, 1915, p. 19.
20. *Ibid.*, p. 25.
21. Audrain, manuscript diary.
22. Frank Richards, *Old Soldiers Never Die*, London, 1933, p. 15.
23. Cecil A.L. Brownlow, *The Breaking of the Storm*, London, 1918, p. 79.
24. Karl Storch, *Vom feldgrauen Buchhändler: Stimmungsbilder, Briefe und Karten von Karl Storch*, Magdeburg, 1917, p. 38.
25. Quoted in Wood, *Soldiers' Stories of the War*, p. 56.
26. Frederick Luke VC, manuscript recollections, Liddle Collection, University of Leeds.
27. *London Gazette*, 17 December 1914.
28. Quoted in Lawrence Weaver, *The Story of the Royal Scots (Lothian Regiment)*, London, 1915, p. 208.
29. Hay, *Wounded and a Prisoner of War*, p. 67.
30. Corbett-Smith, *The Retreat From Mons*, p. 164.
31. Edward Packe, typescript diary on www.gwydir.demon.co.uk/diaries/index.htm.
32. Arthur Green, *The Story of a Prisoner of War*, London, 1916, pp. 3–9.
33. WO 161/95/63, 359, The National Archives, London.
34. *Kildare Observer*, 5 September 1914.
35. *Ibid.*, 12 September 1914.
36. Quoted in John Terraine, *General Jack's Diary*, London, 1964, p. 38.
37. H.J. Taylor, unpublished manuscript recollections, Liddle Collection, University of Leeds.
38. WO 161/100/22, 2456, The National Archives, London.
39. Storch, *Vom feldgrauen Buchhändler*, p. 39.
40. Quoted in A.F. Wedd, *German Students' War Letters Translated and Arranged from the Original Edition of Dr Philip Witkop*, London, 1929, p. 244.
41. Heubner, *Unter Emmich vor Lüttich, unter Kluck vor Paris*, pp. 86–8.
42. Quoted in Gustav Manz (ed.), *Von Flandern bis Polen*, p. 107.
43. Quoted in Jessie Louisa Moore Rickard, *The Story of the Munsters*, London, 1918, p. 60.
44. *Week*, 13 November 1914.
45. Frederick Coleman, *From Mons to Ypres with French*, London, n.d., p. 22.
46. Alfred Clifton-Shelton, *On the road from Mons with an Army Service Corps train; by its commander*, New York, 1917, p. 77.
47. *Isle of Man Times*, 26 September 1914.
48. *Ibid.*, 7 November 1914.
49. *Ibid.*, 5 December 1914.
50. A.P. Corcoran, *The Daredevil of the Army*, New York, 1918, p. 23.
51. William Henry Lowe Watson, *Adventures of a Despatch Rider*, Edinburgh and London, 1915, p. 50.
52. Quoted in anon., *Hundert Briefe aus dem Felde; was die Soldaten über den Krieg Erzählen*, Nürnberg, 1915, p. 85.
53. Richards, *Old Soldiers Never Die*, p. 18.
54. Frederick Bolwell, *With a Reservist in France*, New York, 1917, p. 27.
55. A.C. Osburn, 'Epic Story of St Quentin', in Hammerton (ed.), *The Great War ... I was There!*, pp. 95–6.
56. *Ibid.*
57. Tom Bridges, 'Toy Drum and Tin Whistle', in Hammerton (ed.), *The Great War ... I was There!*, p. 100.
58. http://www.dublin-fusiliers.com/battaliions/2-batt/campaigns/1914-retreat-mons.html.
59. *London Gazette*, 19 August 1916.
60. Original postcard, author's collection.
61. http://www.lneryoca.org.uk/page_322793.html.
62. William Clarke, unpublished typescript recollections, Liddle Collection, University of Leeds.

63. Lionel E. Blackburne, *Charles: (Lieutenant Colonel G.H. Blackburne DSO 5th Dragoon Guards): A Memoir*, London, 1919, p. 147.
64. http://www.stadt-land-oldenburg.de/i_weltkrieg.htm (author's translation).
65. H.M. Hill, unpublished papers, Liddle Collection, University of Leeds.
66. Aubrey Herbert, *Mons, Anzac and Kut*, London, 1919, p. 41.

Chapter 3
1. Bloem, *The Advance From Mons*, p. 152.
2. C.T. Baynham, unpublished typescript recollections, Liddle Collection, University of Leeds.
3. Bloem, *The Advance From Mons*, p. 167.
4. *Barrovian*, March 1916, p. 15.
5. Sir John Crabbe, unpublished typescript recollections, Liddle Collection, University of Leeds.
6. *Ibid.*
7. *Ibid.*
8. W.G. Pelling, manuscript diary, Liddle Collection, University of Leeds.
9. *Journal of the 5th Inniskilling Dragoon Guards*, 1935, p. 127.
10. *Ibid.*
11. Brownlow, *The Breaking of the Storm*, p. 127.
12. Richards, *Old Soldiers Never Die*, p. 25.
13. Quoted in C.R. Simpson, *The History of the Lincolnshire Regiment 1914–1918*, London, 1931, p. 32.
14. Bolwell, *With a Reservist in France*, p. 37.
15. Arnold Gyde, *Contemptible*, London, 1916, p. 59.
16. Crabbe, unpublished typescript recollections.
17. *Ibid.*
18. C.E. Green, manuscript diary, Liddle Collection, University of Leeds.
19. Baynham, unpublished typescript recollections.
20. Martin, tape-recorded recollections.
21. Wood, *Soldiers' Stories of the War*, p. 30.
22. C.A.B. Young, tape-recorded recollections, Liddle Collection, University of Leeds.
23. *Isle of Man Times*, 26 September 1914.
24. *Ibid.*
25. Joe Cassells, *The Black Watch A Record in Action*, New York, 1918, p. 91.
26. Quoted in Kilpatrick, *Tommy Atkins at War*, p. 59.
27. Bolwell, *With a Reservist in France*, p. 47.
28. *Isle of Man Times*, 24 October 1914.
29. Quoted in Kilpatrick, *Tommy Atkins at War*, p. 44.
30. Von Brandis, *Die Stürmer von Douaumont*, pp. 36–7.
31. Quoted in Weaver, *The Story of the Royal Scots (Lothian Regiment)*, p. 213.
32. *Ibid.*
33. Robert V. Dolbey, *A Regimental Surgeon in War and Prison*, London, 1917, p. 51.
34. WO 95/1280, The National Archives, London.
35. E.J. Needham, 'German White Flag Treachery', in Hammerton (ed.), *The Great War ... I was There!*, pp. 159–62.
36. *Ibid.*
37. *Ibid.*
38. Kenneth Hooper, tape-recorded recollections, Liddle Collection, University of Leeds.
39. *Ibid.*
40. Quoted in Wedd, *German Students' War Letters*, p. 245.
41. Francis Bickerstaffe-Drew, *John Ayscough's Letters to his Mother*, London, 1919, p. 25.
42. *Ibid.*, p. 28.
43. John Giles, *The Western Front Then and Now*, London, 1992, p. 66.
44. WO 161/96/11, 584–90, The National Archives, London.

45. Quoted in Wood, *Soldiers' Stories of the War*, p. 147.
46. *Ibid.*, p. 149.
47. Quoted in Franz Tolle, *Unser 64er – Kurzer Abriß aus der Geschichte des Inf R. General-Feldmarschall Prinz Friedrich Karl von Preußen (8.Brandenburgisches) Nr. 64*, Prenzlau, 1937, pp. 52–3.

Chapter 4

1. L.F. Robinson, *Naval Guns in Flanders 1914–1915*, New York, 1920, p. 19.
2. *Ibid.*, p. 22.
3. *Ibid.*, p. 23.
4. Geoffrey Sparrow and J.N. Macbean Ross, *On four fronts with the Royal Naval Division*, London, 1918, p. 6.
5. Unpublished Begent family papers.
6. *Worksop Guardian*, 1 October 1915.
7. Henry Clapham-Foster, *At Antwerp and The Dardanelles*, London, 1918, p. 30.
8. Sparrow and Ross, *On four fronts with the Royal Naval Division*, p. 22.
9. Quoted in Von Delbrück, *Der Deutsche Krieg in Feldpostbriefen*, Vol. VIII, p. 53.
10. *Ibid.*, Vol. VIII, p. 42.
11. Arthur Ruhl, *Antwerp to Gallipoli – a year of war on many fronts, and behind them*, Toronto, 1916, p. 47.
12. *Ibid.*, p. 49.
13. Arthur Tisdall VC, unpublished papers, Liddle Collection, University of Leeds.
14. ADM 116/1814, The National Archives, London.
15. *Ibid.*
16. Quoted in Manz, *Von Flandern bis Polen*, p. 184.
17. Begent papers.
18. Robinson, *Naval Guns in Flanders 1914–1915*, p. 30.
19. Gottfried Sender, *Leutnant Sender, Blätter der Erinnerung für Seine Freunde, aus Seinen Feldpostbriefen Zusammengestellt von dr. M. Spanier*, Hamburg, 1916, p. 35.
20. Clapham-Foster, *At Antwerp and The Dardanelles*, p. 37.
21. *Worksop Guardian*, 1 October 1915.
22. Tisdall VC, unpublished papers.
23. Sender, *Leutnant Sender*, p. 36.
24. Begent papers.
25. http://www.wereldoorlog1418.nl/englishcamp/part-03.html.
26. WO 161/95/62, 340, The National Archives, London.
27. Quoted in Von Delbrück, *Der Deutsche Krieg in Feldpostbriefen*, Vol. VIII, p. 37.
28. Dix Noonan Webb archive, www.dnw.co.uk, 25 September 2008.
29. Quoted in Von Delbrück, *Der Deutsche Krieg in Feldpostbriefen*, Vol. VIII, p. 44.
30. John Cusack, *Scarlet Fever A Lifetime with Horses*, London, 1972, p. 46.
31. *Ibid.*

Chapter 5

1. E. Dwyer VC, letter 30 May 1915, Surrey History Centre ref: ESR/25/DWYE/2.
2. Quoted in Weaver, *The Story of the Royal Scots (Lothian Regiment)*, p. 215.
3. Bernard Law Montgomery, *The Memoirs of Field Marshal Montgomery*, London, 1958, p. 33.
4. T.L. Horn, typescript recollections, Liddle Collection, University of Leeds.
5. Quoted in Walter Wood, *In the Line of Battle*, London, 1916, p. 104.
6. *Cork Examiner*, 27 October 1914.
7. *Irish Times*, 4 November 1914.
8. Arthur F.H. Mills, *With My Regiment – From the Aisne to La Bassée*, London, 1915, p. 130.
9. *Isle of Man Times*, 7 November 1914.
10. Dolbey, *A Regimental Surgeon in War and Prison*, p. 113.
11. *Ibid.*, p. 118.

12. Brian Horrocks, *A Full Life*, London, 1974, p. 16.
13. *Ibid.*, p. 17.
14. Quoted in Von Delbrück, *Der Deutsche Krieg in Feldpostbriefen*, Vol. VII, p. 148.
15. Brownlow, *The Breaking of the Storm*, p. 192.
16. Lucy, *There's a Devil in the Drum*, p. 223.
17. Richards, *Old Soldiers Never Die*, p. 35.
18. Kenneth Godsell, typescript recollections, Liddle Collection, University of Leeds.
19. John Watson, *Sergeant Watson's Diary of the World's War*, Leeds, 1990.
20. George Dodge, typescript diary, author's collection.
21. *Leicester Mail*, 12 December 1914.
22. Quoted in H.C. Wylly, *History of the 1st & 2nd battalions the Leicestershire Regiment*, Aldershot, 1928, p. 12.
23. Kathleen Luard, *Diary of a Nursing Sister on the Western Front*, London and Edinburgh, 1915, p. 89.
24. Kate Finzi, *Eighteen months in the war zone; the record of a woman's work on the western front*, London, 1916, p. 29.
25. Quoted in E.W.C. Sandes, *The Indian Sappers and Miners*, Chatham, 1948, p. 443.
26. Luard, *Diary of a Nursing Sister on the Western Front*, p. 97.
27. Giles, *The Western Front Then and Now*, p. 68.
28. Georg Hans Reinhardt, *Das Kgl. Sächs. 8. Infanterie-Regiment Prinz Johann Georg Nr. 107 während des Weltkrieges 1914–1918*, Dresden, 1928, p. 68.
29. Terraine, *General Jack's Diary*, p. 75.
30. Heber Maitland Alexander, *On two fronts; being the adventures of an Indian mule corps in France and Gallipoli*, New York, 1917, p. 97.
31. Brownlow, *The Breaking of the Storm*, p. 204.
32. *Ibid.*, p. 210.

Chapter 6

1. http://www.cwgc.org/learning-and-resources/histories.aspx.
2. W.E. Duncan, typescript recollections, Liddle Collection, University of Leeds.
3. Thomas Riordan, typescript recollections, Liddle Collection, University of Leeds.
4. E.J. Kennedy, *With the Immortal Seventh Division*, London, 1916, p. 53.
5. Rudolf Binding, *A Fatalist At War*, London, 1929, p. 18.
6. Bolwell, *With a Reservist in France*, p. 75.
7. E.J. Needham, 'Cabaret of Death!', in Hammerton (ed.), *The Great War ... I was There!*, p. 207.
8. Quoted in Wood, *In the Line of Battle*, p. 20.
9. Quoted in Wedd, *German Students' War Letters*, p. 137.
10. Binding, *A Fatalist At War*, p. 19.
11. *Isle of Man Times*, 7 November 1914.
12. *Ibid.*
13. D. McAlpine, typescript letters, Liddle Collection, University of Leeds.
14. Riordan, typescript recollections.
15. Quoted in Charles B. Purdom, *Everyman at War*, London, 1930, p. 17.
16. Quoted in Angus Macnaghten, *Missing*, n.p., n.d., p. 53.
17. James E. Edmonds, *Military Operations France and Belgium, 1914*, Vol. II, London, 1929, p. 270.
18. Green, manuscript diary.
19. Riordan, typescript recollections.
20. Adolf Hitler, *Mein Kampf*, New York, 1941, p. 213.
21. http://secondlifeguards.wordpress.com/category/191410/.
22. Quoted in Von Delbrück, *Der Deutsche Krieg in Feldpostbriefen*, Vol. VIII, p. 246.
23. *Memorials of Rugbeians*.
24. Blackburne, *Charles*, p. 153.

25. Young, tape-recorded recollections.
26. Quoted in Von Delbrück, *Der Deutsche Krieg in Feldpostbriefen*, Vol. VIII, p. 249.
27. Bolwell, *With a Reservist in France*, p. 87.
28. WO 161/96/19, 637–45, The National Archives, London.
29. Fridolin Solleder, *Vier Jahre Westfront – Geschichte des Regiments List R.I.R. 16*, Munich, 1932, p. 36.
30. John Cole, manuscript recollections, Liddle Collection, University of Leeds.
31. Quoted in Wood, *In the Line of Battle*, p. 281.
32. WO 161/96/57, 857–9, The National Archives, London.
33. WO 161/95/64, 362–75, The National Archives, London.
34. A. Moffat, manuscript letter, Liddle Collection, University of Leeds.
35. Höcker, *An der Spitze meiner Kompagnie*, p. 211.
36. Quoted in Von Delbrück, *Der Deutsche Krieg in Feldpostbriefen*, Vol. VIII, p. 272.
37. Duncan, typescript recollections.
38. William Meredith, manuscript letter, Liddle Collection, University of Leeds.
39. Quoted in Wedd, *German Students' War Letters*, p. 62.
40. O'Neill, *The Royal Fusiliers in the Great War*, p. 59.
41. *Ibid.*, p. 60.
42. Friedrich Wilhelm Von Rieben, *Kaiser Franz Garde-Grenadier-Regiment Nr. 2*, Oldenburg, 1929, p. 21.
43. Quoted in Von Delbrück, *Der Deutsche Krieg in Feldpostbriefen*, Vol. VIII, p. 306.
44. Eitel Friedrich, Prinz Von Preußen, Rudolf Von Katte, *Das Erste Garderegiment zu Fuß im Weltkrieg 1914–18*, Berlin, 1934, p. 50.
45. Arthur Chambers, typescript diary, Liddle Collection, University of Leeds.
46. Quoted in Edmonds, *Military Operations France and Belgium, 1914*, Vol. II, p. 436.
47. Quoted in Von Delbrück, *Der Deutsche Krieg in Feldpostbriefen*, Vol. VIII, p. 306.
48. http://www.forum14-18.de/index.htm.
49. Quoted in Edmonds, *Military Operations France and Belgium, 1914*, Vol. II, p. 456.

Chapter 7

1. Quoted in Von Delbrück, *Der Deutsche Krieg in Feldpostbriefen*, Vol. VIII, p. 323.
2. E.R.M. Fryer, *Reminiscences of a Grenadier*, London, 1921, p. 27.
3. Alfred Oliver Pollard, *Fire-eater: the Memoirs of a VC*, London, 1932, p. 44.
4. Quoted in Charles Smith, *War History of the 6th Battalion The Cheshire Regiment (TF)*, n.p., 1932, p. 4.
5. Joseph Killey, manuscript letter, Manx National Heritage, MS 09832.
6. J.C.W. Francis, manuscript diary, Liddle Collection, University of Leeds.
7. H.A. Taylor, manuscript recollections, Liddle Collection, University of Leeds.
8. R.C. Money, tape-recorded recollections, Liddle Collection, University of Leeds.
9. Richards, *Old Soldiers Never Die*, p. 65.
10. *Mona's Herald*, 13 January 1915.
11. Quoted in H.C. Wylly, *History of the 1st & 2nd battalions the Leicestershire Regiment*, p. 15.
12. Richard O'Connor, tape-recorded recollections, Liddle Collection, University of Leeds.
13. W.B.P. Spencer, manuscript letters, Liddle Collection, University of Leeds.
14. Jim Davey, manuscript diary, Liddle Collection, University of Leeds.
15. R. Archer-Houblon, typescript recollections, Liddle Collection, University of Leeds.
16. M.D. Kennedy, tape-recorded recollections, Liddle Collection, University of Leeds.
17. Quoted in Wedd, *German Students' War Letters*, p. 33.
18. Alexander, *On two fronts*, p. 103.
19. *Shrewsbury Chronicle*, 1 January 1915.

Bibliography and Websites

Bibliography

Adcock, A. St John, *In the firing line: stories of the war by land and sea*, London, 1914

Anon., *Hundert Briefe aus dem Felde; was die Soldaten über den Krieg Erzählen*, Nürnberg, 1915

Alexander, Heber Maitland, *On two fronts; being the adventures of an Indian mule corps in France and Gallipoli*, New York, 1917

Beaumont, Harry, *Old Contemptible*, London, 1967

Bickerstaffe-Drew, Francis, *John Ayscough's Letters to his Mother*, London, 1919

Binding, Rudolf, *A Fatalist At War*, London, 1929

Blackburne, Lionel E., *Charles: (Lieutenant Colonel G.H. Blackburne DSO 5th Dragoon Guards): A Memoir*, London, 1919

Bloem, Walter, *The Advance From Mons*, London, 1930

Bolwell, Frederick, *With a Reservist in France*, New York, 1917

Brownlow, Cecil, *The Breaking of the Storm*, London, 1918

Buckland, Sir Reginald U.H., 'Demolitions Carried Out at Mons and During the Retreat', *Royal Engineers Journal* (March 1932)

Burke, Thomas, *The German Army from Within*, London, 1914

Cassells, Joe, *The Black Watch A Record in Action*, New York, 1918

Clapham-Foster, Henry, *At Antwerp and The Dardanelles*, London, 1918

Clifton-Shelton, Alfred, *On the road from Mons with an Army Service Corps train; by its commander*, New York, 1917

Coleman, Frederick, *From Mons to Ypres with French*, London, n.d.

Corbett-Smith, Arthur, *The Retreat From Mons, By One Who Shared In It*, London, 1916

Corbett-Smith, Arthur, *The Marne and After*, London, 1917

Corcoran, A.P., *The Daredevil of the Army*, New York, 1918

Cusack, John, *Scarlet Fever A Lifetime with Horses*, London, 1972

Dolbey, Robert V., *A Regimental Surgeon in War and Prison*, London, 1917

Edmonds, Brigadier General Sir James E., *Military Operations France & Belgium, 1914*, 2 vols, London, 1922 and 1929

Finzi, Kate, *Eighteen months in the war zone; the record of a woman's work on the western front*, London, 1916

Fryer, E.R.M., *Reminiscences of a Grenadier*, London, 1921

Giffard, Sydney, *Guns, Kites and Horses: Three diaries from the Western Front*, London, 2003

Giles, John, *The Western Front then and Now*, London, 1992

Green, Arthur, *The Story of a Prisoner of War*, London, 1916

Gyde, Arnold (pseud. 'Casualty'), *Contemptible*, London, 1916

Hammerton, Sir John (ed.), *The Great War ... I was There!*, London, n.d.

Hay, Malcolm Vivian, *Wounded and a Prisoner of War, by an Exchanged Officer*, Edinburgh, 1916

Herbert, Aubrey, *Mons, Anzac and Kut*, London, 1919

Hitler, Adolf, *Mein Kampf*, New York, 1941

Höcker, Paul Oskar, *An der Spitze meiner Kompagnie*, Berlin, 1915

Horrocks, Brian, *A Full Life*, London, 1974

Heubner, Heinrich, *Unter Emmich vor Lüttich, unter Kluck vor Paris*, Schwerin i. Mecklb., 1915

Jones, J.P., *A History of the South Staffordshire Regiment 1705–1923*, Wolverhampton, 1923

Journal of the 5th Inniskilling Dragoon Guards

Kennedy, E.J., *With the Immortal Seventh Division*, London, 1916

Kilpatrick, James A., *Tommy Atkins at War, As Told In His Own Letters*, New York, 1914

Luard, Kathleen (attrib.), *Diary of a Nursing Sister on the Western Front*, London and Edinburgh, 1915

Lucy, John, *There's a Devil in the Drum*, London, 1938

Macnaghten, Angus, *Missing*, n.p., n.d.

Manz, Gustav (ed.), *Von Flandern bis Polen; Feldpostbriefe der Täglichen Rundschau aus dem Weltkriege*, Berlin, 1915

Memorials of Rugbeians who fell in the Great War, Vol. 1, Medici Society Ltd, 1916

Mills, Arthur F.H. (pseud. 'Platoon Commander'), *With My Regiment – From the Aisne to La Bassee*, London, 1915

Montgomery, Bernard Law, *The Memoirs of Field Marshal Montgomery*, London, 1958

O'Neill, H.C., *The Royal Fusiliers in the Great War*, London, 1922

O'Rorke, Benjamin, *In the Hands of the Enemy: Being the Experiences of a Prisoner of War*, London, 1915

Osman, Hans, *Mit den kriegsfreiwilligen über die Yser*, Bielefeld und Leipzig, 1915

Pennyman, J.B.W., *Diary of Lieut. J.B.W. Pennyman*, Middlesbrough, 1915

Pollard, Alfred Oliver, *Fire-eater: the Memoirs of a VC*, London, 1932

Pollard, Alfred W., *Two Brothers; Accounts Rendered*, London, 1917

PrinzVon Preußen, Eitel Friedrich and Von Katte, Rudolf, *Das Erste Garderegiment zu Fuß im Weltkrieg 1914–18*, Berlin, 1934

Purdom, Charles B., *Everyman at War*, London, 1930

Reinhardt, Georg Hans, *Das Kgl. Sächs. 8. Infanterie-Regiment Prinz Johann Georg Nr. 107 während des Weltkrieges 1914–1918*, Dresden, 1928

Richards, Frank, *Old Soldiers Never Die*, London, 1933

Rickard, Jessie Louisa Moore, *The Story of the Munsters*, London, 1918

Robinson, L.F. (pseud. 'L.F.R.'), *Naval Guns in Flanders 1914–1915*, New York, 1920

Ruhl, Arthur, *Antwerp to Gallipoli – a year of war on many fronts, and behind them*, Toronto, 1916

Sandes, E.W.C., *The Indian Sappers and Miners*, Chatham, 1948

Schubert, Gustav, *In Frankreich Kriegsgefangen, meine Erlebnisse auf dem Vormarsch der 1. Armee durch Belgien und Frankreich sowie in der Französischen Kriegsgefangenschaft*, Magdeburg, 1915

Sender, Gottfried, *Leutnant Sender, Blätter der Erinnerung für Seine Freunde, aus Seinen Feldpostbriefen Zusammengestellt von dr. M. Spanier*, Hamburg, 1916

Simpson, C.R., *The History of the Lincolnshire Regiment 1914–1918*, London, 1931

Smith, Charles, *War History of the 6th Battalion The Cheshire Regiment (TF)*, n.p., 1932

Solleder, Fridolin, *Vier Jahre Westfront – Geschichte des Regiments List R.I.R. 16*, Munich, 1932

Sparrow, Geoffrey and Ross, J.N. Macbean, *On four fronts with the Royal Naval Division*, London, 1918

Stewart, Herbert Arthur, *From Mons to Loos, being the Diary of a Supply Officer*, Edinburgh, 1916

Storch, Karl, *Vom feldgrauen Buchhändler: Stimmungsbilder, Briefe und Karten von Karl Storch*, Magdeburg, 1917

Terraine, John, *General Jack's Diary*, London, 1964

Tolle, Franz, *Unser 64er – Kurzer Abriß aus der Geschichte des Inf R. General-Feldmarschall Prinz Friedrich Karl von Preußen (8.Brandenburgisches) Nr. 64*, Prenzlau, 1937

Von Brandis, Cordt, *Die Stürmer von Douaumont: Kriegserlebnisse eines Kompagnieführers*, Berlin, 1917

Von Delbrück, Joachim, *Der Deutsche Krieg in Feldpostbriefen*, 8 vols, Munich, 1915

Von Gleichen-Ruszwurm, Raimund and Zurborn, Ernst, *Die Schlacht Bei Mons*, Oldenburg, 1919

Von Rieben, Friedrich Wilhelm, *Kaiser Franz Garde-Grenadier-Regiment Nr. 2*, Oldenburg, 1929

Watson, John, *Sergeant Watson's Diary of the World's War*, Leeds, 1990

Watson, William Henry Lowe, *Adventures of a Despatch Rider*, Edinburgh and London, 1915

Weaver, Lawrence, *The Story of the Royal Scots (Lothian Regiment)*, London, 1915

Wedd, A.F., *German Students' War Letters Translated and Arranged from the Original Edition of Dr Philip Witkop*, London, 1929

Wood, Walter, *Soldiers' Stories of the War*, London, 1915

Wood, Walter, *In the Line of Battle*, London, 1916

Wylly, H.C., *History of the 1st & 2nd battalions the Leicestershire Regiment*, Aldershot, 1928

Wünsche, Alwin, *Kriegslesebuch über den Krieg von 1914; die besten Kriegserzählungen aus Deutschen, österreichischen und schweizerischen Zeitungen, als Vorlesebuch für den Schulgebrauch, hrsg. von Dr. Alwin Wünsche*, Leipzig, 1915

Zipfel, Ernst, *Geschichte des Infanterie-Regiments Bremen (1. Hanseatisches) Nr. 75*, Bremen, 1934

Websites
www.home.arcor.de/berot/1914-1919.html
www.begent.org/james.htm
www.stadt-land-oldenburg.de/i_weltkrieg.htm
www.gwydir.demon.co.uk/diaries/index.htm
www.firstworldwar.com/diaries/index.htm
www.wereldoorlog1418.nl/englishcamp/part-03.html
www.lneryoca.org.uk/page_322793.html
www.dublin-fusiliers.com/battaliions/2-batt/campaigns/1914-retreat-mons.html
www.grandadswar.mrallsophistory.com/files/War%20Diary.pdf
www.forum14-18.de/index.htm
www.warlinks.com
www.green-tiger.co.uk
www.haithitrust.org
www.greatwardifferent.com/Great_War/Copy_index.htm

Index